Workshop Manual JAGUAR XK-E & E-Type 3.8 & 4.2 Series 1 & 2

A Floyd CLYMER Publication by:
www.VelocePress.com
Copyright 2017 Veloce Enterprises

INTRODUCTION

Welcome to the world of digital publishing ~ the book you now hold in your hand, was printed using the latest state of the art digital technology. The advent of print-on-demand has forever changed the publishing process, never has information been so accessible and it is our hope that this book serves your informational needs for years to come. If this is your first exposure to digital publishing, we hope that you are pleased with the results. Many more titles of interest to the classic automobile and motorcycle enthusiast, collector and restorer are available via our website at www.VelocePress.com. We hope that you find this title as interesting as we do.

NOTE FROM THE PUBLISHER

The information presented is true and complete to the best of our knowledge. All recommendations are made without any guarantees on the part of the author or the publisher, who also disclaim all liability incurred with the use of this information.

TRADEMARKS

We recognize that some words, model names and designations, for example, mentioned herein are the property of the trademark holder. We use them for identification purposes only. This is not an official publication.

INFORMATION ON THE USE OF THIS PUBLICATION

This manual is an invaluable resource for those interested in performing their own maintenance. However, in today's information age we are constantly subject to changes in common practice, new technology, availability of improved materials and increased awareness of chemical toxicity. As such, it is advised that the user consult with an experienced professional prior to undertaking any procedure described herein. While every care has been taken to ensure correctness of information, it is obviously not possible to guarantee complete freedom from errors or omissions or to accept liability arising from such errors or omissions. Therefore, any individual that uses the information contained within, or elects to perform or participate in do-it-yourself repairs or modifications acknowledges that there is a risk factor involved and that the publisher or its associates cannot be held responsible for personal injury or property damage resulting from the use of the information or the outcome of such procedures.

WARNING!

One final word of advice, this publication is intended to be used as a reference guide, and when in doubt the reader should consult with a qualified technician.

INDEX

ENGINE
Specifications ... 7
- Cylinder Head ... 7
- Valves, Guides and Springs ... 7
- Cylinder Block and Liners ... 7
- Pistons, Piston Rings and Gudgeon Pins ... 8
- Crankshaft and Main Bearings and Connecting Rod ... 8
- Camshafts and Camshaft Bearings ... 9
- Timing Chains and Sprockets ... 9
- Tappets and Tappet Guides ... 9
- Lubrication ... 9
- Torque Wrench Settings ... 9

Description ... 10
Engine Assembly ... 10
- To Remove — 3.8 Litre Cars ... 10
- To Remove — 4.2 Litre Cars ... 12
- To Install — All Models ... 12

Cylinder Head ... 13
- To Remove ... 13
- To Install ... 14
- To Dismantle ... 14
- To Inspect ... 15
- To Reface Valves and Valve Seats ... 15
- To Check Valve Springs ... 15
- To Renew Valve Guides (3.8 Engines and Early 4.2 Engines) ... 16
- To Renew Valve Guides (Later 4.2 Engines) ... 16
- To Renew Tappet Guides ... 16
- To Renew Valve Seat Inserts ... 16
- To Assemble ... 17
- To Adjust Valve Clearance ... 17

Engine Sump ... 18
- To Remove and Install (3.8 Engines) ... 18
- To Remove and Install (4.2 Engines) ... 18

Oil Pump ... 18
- To Remove and Install ... 18
- To Dismantle ... 20
- To Check Pump Components ... 20
- To Assemble ... 20

Pistons and Connecting Rods ... 20
- To Remove and Dismantle ... 20
- To Inspect Cylinder Bores (Dry Liners) ... 20
- To Fit New Piston Rings ... 22
- To Assemble and Install ... 22

Flywheel and Converter Drive Plate ... 23
- To Remove and Install ... 23

Crankshaft and Main Bearings ... 23
- To Remove and Install ... 23

Timing Cover and Timing Gear Assembly ... 25
- To Remove ... 25
- To Dismantle ... 25
- To Check and Inspect ... 25
- To Assemble and Install ... 26
- To Adjust Valve Timing ... 26

Distributor ... 29
- To Remove ... 29
- To Instal Distributor and Set Timing ... 29

Camshaft and Tappets ... 30
- To Remove ... 30
- To Check and Inspect ... 31
- To Install ... 31

Manifolds
- To Remove and Install Inlet Manifold ... 32
- To Remove and Install Exhaust Manifold ... 32

Engine Mountings ... 32
- To Remove and Install Front Mountings ... 32
- To Remove and Install Rear Mountings ... 32
- To Assemble Engine Stabiliser ... 32

Engine Fault Diagnosis ... 33

FUEL SYSTEM
Specifications ... 37
- Carburettors ... 37
- Fuel Pump ... 37

Description ... 37
Routine Maintenance ... 38
- 2500 Miles Stage ... 38
- 5000 Miles Stage ... 38
- 10,000 Miles Stage ... 38

Carburettors ... 39
- To Remove and Install (3.8) ... 39
- To Remove and Install (4.2 and 2+2) ... 39
- Piston and Suction Chamber — To Clean ... 39
- To Tune-up Carburettor ... 40
- To Adjust Fast Idle Speed ... 41
- To Check and Adjust Float Level ... 41
- To Centre The Jet ... 43

Fuel Pump ... 43
- Description ... 43
- To Remove (Early Type Pump) ... 44
- To Remove (Later Type Pump) ... 44
- To Check and Adjust (Early Type Pump) ... 44
- To Dismantle (Later Type Pump) ... 44
- To Check and Inspect ... 45
- To Reassemble ... 46
- Contact Gap Setting ... 49

Fuel Tank ... 49
- To Remove ... 49

Fuel System Fault Diagnosis ... 50

COOLING SYSTEM
Specifications ... 53
Description ... 53
Radiator ... 53
- To Remove (3.8) ... 53
- To Check and Test ... 54
- To Remove (4.2 and 2+2 Cars) ... 54

Radiator Cowl ... 54
- To Remove ... 54

Radiator Header Tank ... 54
- To Remove ... 54

Fan Motor ... 54
- To Remove ... 54

Fan Motor Relay (Early 3.8 Models Only) ... 55
- To Remove ... 55

Water Pump Belt	55
Adjustment (Early Models)	55
To Remove (3.8 Models)	56
To Remove (4.2 and 2+2 Cars)	56
Thermostat	56
To Remove and Install	56
To Test	56
Fan Thermostatic Switch	56
To Remove	56
Water Pump	58
To Remove and Install	58
To Dismantle	58
To Check	59
To Reassemble	59
Cooling System Fault Diagnosis	59
CLUTCH	
Specifications	61
3.8 Models	61
4.2 and 2+2 Models (Where Different From 3.8 Model)	61
Description	61
Clutch Unit	62
To Remove and Install	62
To Check and Inspect	63
Clutch Throw-out Bearing	64
To Remove and Install	64
Master Cylinder	65
To Remove and Install	65
To Dismantle	65
To Clean and Inspect	65
To Assemble	65
Slave Cylinder	67
To Remove and Install	67
To Dismantle	67
To Clean and Inspect	67
To Assemble	67
Hydraulic System	67
To Bleed	67
Adjustment	67
To Adjust Throw-out Lever Free Travel	67
To Adjust Hydrostatic Slave Cylinders	68
Clutch Fault Diagnosis	68
MANUAL TRANSMISSION	
Specifications	69
3.8 Model	69
4.2 and 2+2 Models	69
Propeller Shaft	69
Gearbox — 3.8 Model	69
Description	69
To Remove and Install	70
To Dismantle	70
To Clean and Inspect	72
To Assemble	72
Gearbox — 4.2 and 2+2 Models	75
Description	75
To Remove and Install	75
To Dismantle	75
To Clean and Inspect	79
To Assemble	79
Propeller Shaft	84
Description	84
To Remove and Install	84
To Dismantle and Assemble	84
Manual Transmission Fault Diagnosis	85
Gearbox	85
Propeller Shaft	86
AUTOMATIC TRANSMISSION — FITTED TO 2+2 MODELS ONLY	
Specifications	87
Description	88
Hydraulic Fluid	88
To Check and Top Up	88
To Drain and Refill	89
Forward Speed Band	89
To Adjust	89
Reverse Band	89
To Adjust	89
Transmission Shift Linkage	90
To Adjust	90
Carburettor and Downshift Valve Linkage	90
To Adjust	90
To Remove and Install Cable	90
Transmission Assembly	91
To Remove and Install	91
Automatic Transmission Fault Diagnosis	91
REAR AXLE	
Specifications	93
Torque Wrench Settings	93
Description	93
Rear Axle Assembly	93
To Remove and Install	93
Differential Assembly	96
To Remove from Carrier	96
To Dismantle Differential	96
To Assemble Differential	96
To Instal and Adjust	96
To Dismantle Output Shafts	97
To Assemble Output Shafts	98
Drive Opinion	98
To Remove	98
To Assemble and Adjust	99
Fault Diagnosis	100
STEERING	
Specifications	101
Description	101
Steering Wheel	102
To Remove	102
To Install	102
Steering Column	102
To Remove	102
To Dismantle	102
To Assemble	102
To Install	103
Rack and Pinion Assembly	104
To Remove	104
To Dismantle	104

To Clean and Inspect	105
To Assemble	105
To Install	106
Lower Steering Column Shaft	107
To Remove and Install	107
Steering Fault Diagnosis	108

FRONT SUSPENSION

Specifications	109
Description	109
Front Hub	109
To Remove and Dismantle	109
To Clean and Inspect	109
To Assemble and Install	110
Suspension Unit	110
To Remove	110
To Dismantle and Assemble	111
To Clean and Inspect	112
To Install	113
To Check and Adjust Torsion Bar	113
Stabiliser Bar	114
To Remove	114
To Install	114
Suspension and Steering Angles	114
To Check Castor and Camber Angles	114
To Check and Adjust Toe-in	115
To Check and Adjust Castor Angles	116
To Check and Adjust Camber Angle	116
Suspension Fault Diagnosis	117

REAR SUSPENSION

Specifications	119
Description	119
Shock Absorbers	119
To Remove and Install	119
To Test and Bleed	119
Suspension Unit	120
To Remove	120
Radius Arm	121
To Remove	121
Suspension Arm	121
To Remove	121
To Install	121
Suspension Arm Outer Pivot	123
To Remove	123
To Dismantle	123
Clean and Inspect	123
To Install	123
Bearing Adjustment	123
Inner Fulcrum Suspension Mounting Bracket	125
To Remove	125
To Install	125
Rear Wheel Camber Angle — Adjustment	126
Rear Suspension Fault Diagnosis	127

BRAKES

Specifications	129
3.8 Model	129
4.2 Model	129
Description — 3.8 Model	129
Master Cylinder — 3.8 Model	130
To Remove and Install	130
To Dismantle	131
To Clean and Inspect	131
To Assemble	131
Front Wheel Disc Brakes — 3.8 Model	132
To Remove Brake Calliper	132
To Instal Brake Calliper	132
To Remove and Install Brake Discs	132
To Remove and Install Disc Pads	133
To Dismantle Calliper Piston Assembly— (Early Models)	133
To Assemble Calliper Piston Assembly	133
To Dismantle Calliper Piston Assembly (Later Models)	134
To Assemble Calliper Piston Assembly	134
Rear Wheel Disc Brakes — 3.8 Model	135
To Remove Brake Calliper	135
To Instal Brake Calliper	135
To Remove and Install Brake Discs	136
To Remove and Install Disc Pads	136
To Dismantle Calliper Piston Assembly	136
To Assemble Calliper Piston Assembly	136
Handbrake Assembly — 3.8 Model	136
To Remove and Install Handbrake Pad Carriers	136
To Dismantle and Assemble Pad Carriers (Early Model)	138
To Dismantle and Assemble Pad Carriers (Later Model)	138
To Remove and Install Handbrake Pads	138
To Remove and Install Handbrake Cable	138
To Adjust Handbrake Cable and Pads (Early Model)	139
To Adjust Handbrake Cable and Pads (Later Model)	140
Brake Pedal Assembly — 3.8 Model	140
To Remove and Install	140
To Dismantle and Assemble	141
Vacuum Servo Assembly and Vacuum Reservoir — 3.8 Model	142
Description (Vacuum Reservoir)	142
To Remove and Install Vacuum Reservoir	142
Description (Servo Assembly)	142
Check Valve	143
Air Valve Adjustment	143
Air Filter	143
Rubber Hoses and Connections	143
Hydraulic System	143
To Bleed	143
Description — 4.2 and 2+2 Models	144
Slave Cylinder and Vacuum Servo Assembly	145
To Remove and Install	145
To Dismantle	145
To Inspect	145
To Assemble	146
Master Cylinder and Booster Reaction Valve Assembly	147
To Remove and Install	147
To Dismantle	147
To Assemble	149

Brake Pedal Assembly 150
  To Remove and Install 150
Brake Fault Diagnosis 151
ELECTRICAL SYSTEM
  Specifications 153
    Battery 153
    Generator — Early Models 153
    Generator — Late Models 153
    Lucas A.C. System (4.2 and 2+2 Cars) 153
    Generator Regulator 153
    Lucas A.C. System (4.2 and 2+2 Cars) 153
    Distributor — 3.8 Model 153
    Distributor — 4.2 and 2+2,
      Also fitted to Later 3.8 153
    Spark Plugs 153
    Starter Motor 154
  Battery 154
    Maintenance 154
  Generator and Regulator 154
    Description 154
    To Remove and Install 154
    To Dismantle and Reassemble (Lucas) ... 155
    To Test in Position 156
    To Test Field Coils 156
    Open Circuit Test 157
    To Test Armature 157
    To Check Brushes 157
    To Recondition Commutator 158
    To Renew Bearings 158
    To Check and Adjust Voltage Regulator... 158
    To Check and Adjust Current Regulator ... 159
    To Check and Adjust Cut-Out
      Electrical Settings 159
    To Check and Adjust Mechanical Settings 160
    To Clean Unit Contacts 160
  Alternator and Regulator 161
    Description 161
    Operation 161
    Remove and Install 161
    To Test in Position 162
    No Load Test 162
    Full Load Test 163
    Diode Test 163
    Dismantle and Assemble 163
    To Assemble 164
    Inspection of Brushgear 164
    Inspection of Slip-rings 164
    Bearings 165
    Slip-ring End Bracket Bearing Replacement 165
    Drive-End Bracket Bearing Replacement ... 165
    Check and Adjust 166
  Warning Light Control Unit 167
    Description 167
  Starter Motor 167
    Description 167
    To Test in Position 167
    To Remove and Install 167
    Dismantle and Reassemble 168
    To Test Field Coils 169
    To Check Armature 170
    To Test Armature 170
    Open Circuit Test 170

    To Test Brush Gear and Commutator 171
    To Renew Brushes 171
    To Renew Bearings 171
    To Check and Adjust Pinion Movement
      (Pre-Engagement) 172
    To Check Operation of Starter Switch 172
  Distributor and Ignition Circuit 172
    To Remove and Install 172
    To Dismantle 172
    To Reassemble 173
    To Install 173
    To Adjust Ignition Timing 173
    Using a Stroboscope 174
    To Check Operation of Vacuum
      Advance Using Stroboscope 174
    To Adjust Contact Breaker Points 175
    To Time Ignition 175
  Spark Plugs 176
    To Service 176
  High Tension Cables 176
    To Check 176
  Fluid and Handbrake Warning Light 176
    Description and Operation 176
  Traffic Hazard Warning Device 177
    Description 177
  Windscreen Wiper 177
    Description 177
    To Test 177
    Remove and Install 177
  Lights 178
    Description 178
    Remove and Install Headlamp 178
    Adjustment of Headlights 179
  Instruments and Miscellaneous Units 179
    Removal of Instrument Panel 179
    Fuse Unit 180
    Flasher Unit 180
    Horns, To Remove, Adjust and Install 180
    Carburettor Mixture Control Warning Light 184
    Tachometer and Clock 184
    To Adjust Clock 184
    Instrument Voltage Regulator 184
  Electrical Fault Diagnosis 184
    Battery and Generator System 184
    Battery and Starting System 186
    Headlamp System 186
    Direction Indicator Light System 186
    Ignition System 187
HEATING AND WINDSCREEN WASHING EQUIPMENT
  Heater and Ventilation
    Description 189
    Temperature Control 189
    Air Distribution 189
    To Remove and Install 189
  Windscreen Washing Equipment 189
    Description 189
    Operation 189
    Replenishment of Container 190
    Adjustment of Jets 190
    Lubrication 190

Test in Position	190
Dismantle	190
Bench Check	190

BODY

Windscreen and Rear Window	191
To Remove — Open Cars	191
To Install	191
To Remove — Fixed Head Coupe	191
To Install	191
Remove Rear Window — Fixed Head Coupe	192
Refit Rear Window	192
Door Glass	192
Remove and Install Door Glass	192
Door Glass Regulator	192
To Remove and Install	192
Door Locks and Handles	192
Remove and Install Interior Handles	192
Exterior Door Handles	192
Door Lock Mechanism	192
Striker Plate Assembly	193
Door Trim	193
Remove and Install	193
Bonnet and Luggage Compartment Lid	193
Remove, Adjust and Install Bonnet	193
Adjust (Early Cars)	194
Adjust (Later Cars)	194
To Remove and Install Luggage Compartment Lid	194
Seats and Runners	194
Removal	194

WHEELS AND TYRES

Specifications	197
Description	197
Wheel and Tyre Assembly	197
To Remove — Wheel	197
To Maintain	197
To Remove — Tyre and Tube	197
To Install	198
Tyre Wear Diagnosis	199

LUBRICATION AND MAINTENANCE

Engine, Cooling System, Fuel System, Gearbox, Rear Axle, Propeller Shaft, Steering Gear, Rear Suspension, Front Wheel Bearings, Rear Wheel Bearings, Tyres, Battery, Body, Brake and Clutch Reservoirs, Clutch, Brakes, Generator or Alternator, Starter Motor, Distributor 201

NOTES

ENGINE

SPECIFICATIONS

Bore diameter – standard:
   3.8 litre .... 3.2427" + .00075"
                                   – .00000"
   4.2 litre .... 3.6247" + .00075"
                                     – .00000"
RAC rating:
   3.8 litre 25.2
   4.2 litre 33.5
Capacity .... 3.8 litre or 4.2 litre
Compression ratio .... 8:1 or 9:1

CYLINDER HEAD

Type .... Aluminium alloy
Valve seat angle:
   Inlet .... 45°
   Exhaust .... 45°
Valve seat inserts:
   Inside diameter, Inlet ...... 1.500" + .003"
                                        – .001"
   Inside diameter, Exhaust ... 1.379" + .004"
                                        – .000"
   Fit in head .... .003" interference
Valve throat diameter:
   Inlet .... 1.500"
   Exhaust .... 1.375"
Valve guides:
   Bore diameter, Inlet .... .3110" + .0010"
                                        – .0000"
   Bore diameter, Exhaust .... .3110" ± .0005"
   Overall length, Inlet .... 1.8111"
   Overall length, Exhaust ..... 1.9375"
   Fit in head .... .0005" + .0017"
                                       – .0000"
                                       Interference

VALVES, GUIDES AND SPRINGS

Valve head diameter:
   Inlet .... 1.750" ± .002"
   Exhaust .... 1.625" ± .002"
Valve stem diameter:
   Inlet .... .3110" + .0000"
   Exhaust ....   – .0010"
Valve stem to guide clearance:
   Inlet .... .001" + .003"
                                  – .000"
   Exhaust .... .001" + .003"
                                  – .000"

Valve face angle:
   Inlet .... 45°
   Exhaust .... 45°
Valve timing (with valve clearance at .010"):
   Inlet opens .... 15° btdc
   Inlet closes .... 57° abdc
   Exhaust opens .... 57° bbdc
   Exhaust closes .... 15° atdc
Valve lift .... .375"
Valve clearance:
   Inlet .... .004" (touring) .006"
                                  (racing).
   Exhaust .... .006" (touring) .010"
                                    (racing).
Valve spring free length:
   Inner .... 1.6562"
   Outer .... 1.9375"
Valve spring fitted length:
   Inner .... 1.2187"
   Outer .... 1.3125"
Valve spring load at fitted length:
   Inner .... 30.330 lb
   Outer .... 48.375 lb

CYLINDER BLOCK AND LINERS

Type .... Dry liners
Cylinder bore diameter – standard:
   3.8 litre .... 3.2427" + .00075"
                                     – .00000"
   4.2 litre .... 3.6247" + .00075"
                                     – .00000"
Maximum rebore size .... .030"
Block bore for liners:
   3.8 litre .... 3.5610" + .0020"
                                     – .0000"
   4.2 litre .... 3.7610" + .0020"
                                     – .0000"
Length of liners:
   3.8 litre .... 6.9687"
   4.2 litre .... 6.9590" + .0200"
                                     – .0000"
Outside diameter of liners:
   3.8 litre .... 3.566" + .000"
                                     – .003"
   4.2 litre .... 3.766" + .000"
                                     – .001"

Fit of liner in block bore:
    3.8 litre .... .0010" + .0040"
                                             − .0000"
                                             Interference
    4.2 litre .... .0030" + .0020"
                                               − .0000"
                                              Interference
Outside diameter of liner lead-in:
    3.8 litre .... 3.5580" + .0020"
                                              − .0000"
    4.2 litre .... 3.7580" + .0020"
                                              − .0000"
Main bearing in line bore ...... 2.9165" + .0005"
                                              − .0000"

PISTONS, PISTON RINGS AND GUDGEON PINS

Piston type .... Semi-split skirt
Compression height:
    8:1 ratio .... 2.0690" + .0000"
                                              − .0050"
    9:1 ratio .... 2.2470" + .0000"
                                              − .0050"
Oversize pistons available ...... .010", .020", .030"
Piston skirt clearance in
    cylinder bore .... .0011" + .0006"
                                              − .0000"
Number of compression rings .. 2
Number of oil control rings 1
Ring width:
Compression (upper and lower):
    3.8 litre .... .0787" + .0000"
                                              − .0010"
    4.2 litre .... .0780" + .0000"
                                              − .0010"
Oil control:
    3.8 litre .... .1560" + .0000"
                                              − .0010"
    4.2 litre .... Self-expanding
                                              (Magniflex)
Ring thickness:
Compression (upper and lower):
    3.8 litre .... .1300" + .0000"
                                              − .0060"
    4.2 litre .... .1580" + .0000"
                                              − .0070"
Oil control:
    3.8 litre .... .1270" + .0000"
                                              − .0080"
    4.2 litre .... Self-expanding
                                              (Magniflex)

Ring clearance in groove − all rings
except self-expanding (Magniflex) .0010" + .0020"
                                                − .0000"
Ring gap, fitted:
Compression (upper and lower):
    3.8 litre and 4.2 litre .... .0150" + .0050"
                                                − .0000"
Oil control:
    3.8 litre .... .0010" + .0050"
                                              − .0000"
    4.2 litre .... .0150" + .0180"
                                              − .0000"
Gudgeon pin:
Type .... Fully floating
Diameter:
    Inside .... .6250"
    Outside .... .8750" + .0002"
                                              − .0000"
Length:
    3.8 litre .... 2.8400" + .0050"
                                              − .0000"
    4.2 litre .... 3.0000"
Bore in piston boss:
    3.8 litre .... .8749" + .0002"
                                              − .0000"
    4.2 litre .... .8753" + .0018"
                                              − .0000"

CRANKSHAFT AND MAIN BEARINGS AND CONNECTING ROD

Number of main bearing journals 7
Main bearing journal diameter:
    3.8 litre − Front, centre and rear .. 2.7505" + .0000"
                                              − .0005"
          − Intermediate .... 2.7500" + .0000"
                                              − .0005"
    4.2 litre − Front .... 1.5625"
          − Centre .... 1.3745" + .0015"
                                              − .0000"
          − Rear .... 1.6875"
          − Intermediate .... 1.2136" + .0040"
                                              − .0000"
Main bearing journal length:
    Front .... 1.4495" + .0100"
                                              − .0000"
    Centre .... 1.7500" + .0010"
                                              − .0000"
    Rear .... 1.8750"
    Intermediate .... 1.2167" + .0040"
                                              − .0000"

Main bearing length:
    Front, centre and rear .... 1.5000" ± .0050"
    Intermediate .... 1.0000" ± .0050"
Crankpin:
    Diameter .... 2.0866" + .0000"
                                      − .0006"
    Length .... 1.1872" + .0009"
                                      − .0000"
Undersizes for regrinding .... .010", .020",
                                      .030", .040"
Main bearing working clearance ..... .0025" + .0017"
                                      − .0000"
Crankshaft end float .... .004" + .002"
                                      − .000"
End thrust taken at .... Centre bearing
                                      thrust washers
Thrust washers serviced .... .0920" ± .0010" &
                                      .0960" ± .0010"
Connecting rod length between
    centres .... 7.750"
Big end bearing working
    clearance .... .0015" + .0018"
                                      − .0000"
Big end width .... 1.1795" + .0020"
                                      − .0000"
Big end float on crankpin .... .0058" + .0029"
                                      − .0000"
Big end bearing bore .... 2.3300" + .0005"
                                      − .0000"
Undersize bearings for service .... .010", .020",
                                      .030", .040"
Small end bush width .... 1.0781"
Bore for small end bush .... 1.0000" ± .0005"
Small end bush bore diameter .... .8750" + .0002"
                                      − .0000"

CAMSHAFTS AND CAMSHAFT BEARINGS

Number of journals per shaft 4
Journal diameter .... .9995" + .0000"
                                      − .0005"
Camshaft end float:
    3.8 litre .... .0045" + .0035"
                                      − .0000"
    4.2 litre .... .0040" + .0020"
                                      − .0000"
End float taken at .... Front end
Number of bearings .... Four per shaft
                                      comprising eight
                                      half bearings
Journal to bearing clearance .... .0005" + .0015"
                                      − .0000"

TIMING CHAINS AND SPROCKETS

Type .... Duplex
Pitch .... .375"
Number of link pairs:
    Top chain 100
    Bottom chain 82
Number of sprocket teeth:
    Crankshaft sprocket 21
    Intermediate sprocket − outer 28
    Intermediate sprocket − inner 20
    Camshaft sprocket 30
    Idler sprocket 21

TAPPETS AND TAPPET GUIDES

Tappet outside diameter .... 1.3742" + .0000"
                                      − .0006"
Tappet fit in guide .... .0008" + .0011"
                                      − .0000"
Tappet guides services inside
    diameter .... 1.3530" + 0040"
                                      − .0000"
Tappet guide, fitted − inside
    diameter reaming size .... 1.3750" + .0007"
                                      − .0000"
Tappet guide fit in head .... .003" Interference,
                                      shrink fit
Tappet adjustment pads serviced .. .085" to .110" by
                                      increments of .001"

LUBRICATION

Type of oil pump .... Eccentric rotor
Pump gear clearances (maximum):
    At end of lobes .... .0060"
    End clearance .... .0025"
    Between outer rotor and body .0100"
Oil pressure (hot) .... 40 psi (maximum) at
                                      3,000 rpm
Oil filter type .... Full flow, replaceable
                                      element
Engine sump capacity .... 15 Imp pt

TORQUE WRENCH SETTINGS

Bearing cap nuts .... 15 ft/lb
Connecting rod bolts .... 37 ft/lb
Main bearing bolts .... 83 ft/lb
Cylinder head nuts:
    Prior to engine No. 7E9210 .... 54 ft/lb
    From engine No. 7E9210 .... 58 ft/lb
                                      (thicker gasket)

1. DESCRIPTION

The six cylinder in-line ohv engine incorporates chain and sprocket driven twin overhead camshafts with 3/8" lift cams.

Compression ratios of 8 to 1 or 9 to 1 are obtained by varying the crown design of the piston.

A chrome-iron cylinder block integral with the crankcase employs pressed in dry liners.

An aluminium-alloy cylinder head has machined hemispherical combustion chambers and straight ports. Valve seat inserts, tappet guides and valve guides are a shrink fit in the cylinder head casting.

Inlet valves are of silicon-chrome steel and exhaust valves are Austenitic steel and both have dual valve springs.

A steel pad for adjusting valve clearance is interposed between the underside of the tappet and the valve stem.

A manganese-molybdenum steel counter-balanced crankshaft is supported in seven lead-bronze steel backed shell bearings. End thrust is taken at the centre main bearing by two semi-circular white metal faced steel thrust washers fitted in recesses in the centre main bearing cap.

A balanced vibration damper and pulley assembly is installed at the front end of the crankshaft. A flywheel with integral starter gear teeth is secured to the flange on the rear of the crankshaft by setscrews retained by a locking plate.

The crankshaft with vibration damper and pulley assembly, clutch and flywheel are balanced as a complete assembly.

Stamped steel connecting rods have lead-bronze steel-backed shells in the big end bearings.

A fully floating gudgeon pin is located by circlips in the piston boss and operates in bushes in the connecting rod small end and in the piston boss. The small end is lubricated by an oil drilling from the big end through the connecting rod.

Pistons are of low expansion aluminium alloy, are semi-split skirt type and incorporate two compression rings and one oil control ring. The compression rings are taper faced with the upper ring chromium plated. The 4.2 litre has a self-expanding oil control ring.

NOTE: Later 4.2 engines with compression ratios of 8:1 have solid skirt pistons with a modified oil control ring (see text).

Twin camshafts are supported in four white metal steel backed pairs of bearing shells. End float is taken on the flanges provided on the camshaft at each side of the front bearing.

An external pipe delivers oil from the oil gallery to the camshaft rear bearing and thence via a longitudinal drilling in the shaft and cross drillings to the other three bearings.

Inlet manifolds consist of three separate castings each feeding two cylinders. They are water heated from the cylinder head by passages cast in the manifolds.

Two exhaust manifolds are each connected to three cylinder head exhaust ports.

An eccentric rotor oil pump feeds oil to the working parts via a full flow oil filter with replaceable element. A pressure relief valve is located at and retained by the oil outlet adaptor. The filter incorporates a balance valve to provide unfiltered oil direct in case the filter is blocked.

The aluminium sump has a connection for the oil return hose from the oil filter head. A gauze type bowl oil filter is attached to the sump baffle plate.

The camshaft sprockets are driven by the rear intermediate sprocket and top chain. This chain also runs over an idler sprocket, mounted on an eccentric shaft, providing for top chain adjustment.

The front intermediate sprocket (on the same shaft as the rear intermediate sprocket) is driven by the lower chain from the crankshaft sprocket. The bottom chain is tensioned by a hydraulic tensioner.

Rubber or nylon pads bear against the chains to damp out vibrations.

A breather connection from the front of the cylinder head communicates by flexible hose with the top of the air cleaner. Engine fumes and blow by gases are thus recirculated in the engine providing positive crankcase ventilation.

2. ENGINE ASSEMBLY

TO REMOVE – 3.8 LITRE CARS

(1) Remove the bonnet. See *ENGINE BONNET – TO REMOVE AND INSTALL.*

(2) Drain the cooling system at the cocks at the bottom of the radiator and on the side of the cylinder block.

(3) Disconnect the battery leads.

(4) Release the clip on the breather pipe, undo the two wing nuts and remove the top of the air cleaner.

(5) Disconnect the tank to carburettor petrol feed pipe at the union below the centre carburettor.

(6) Slacken the clips on the hoses connecting the cylinder head and header tank, the radiator and header tank.

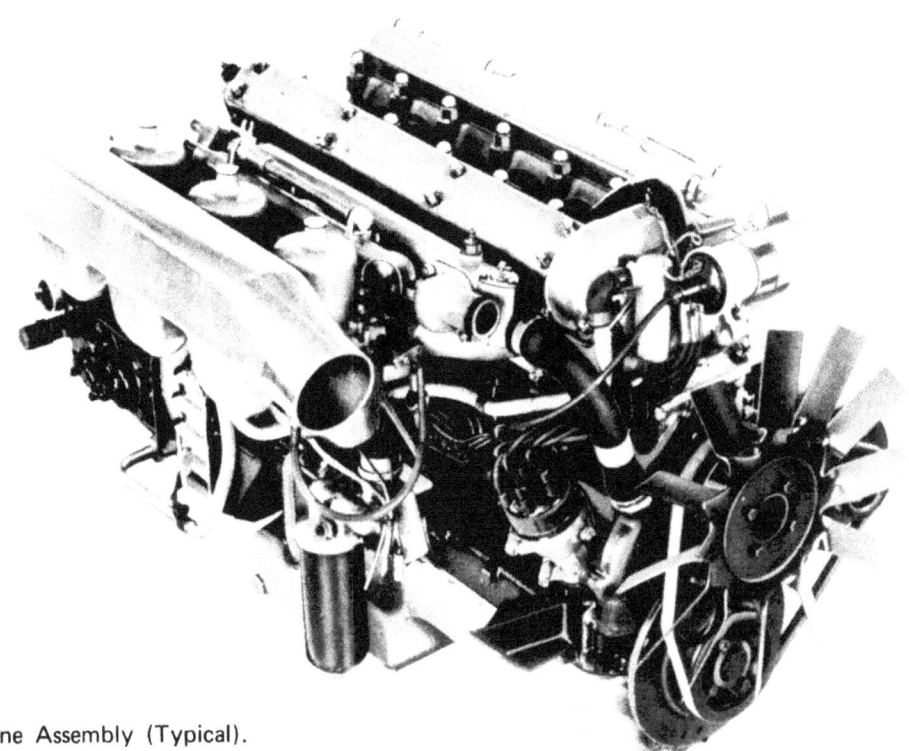

View of Engine Assembly (Typical).

(7) Slacken the clips securing the heater hoses to the manifold.

(8) Disconnect the vacuum-servo pipe from the inlet manifold.

(9) Disconnect the leads from the fan control thermostat in the header tank together with the anchoring clip.

(10) Remove the two nuts and bolts fastening the header tank mounting bracket to the front crossmember.

(11) Disconnect the radiator header tank overflow pipe.

(12) Remove the header tank together with its mounting bracket.

(13) Disconnect the throttle linkage at the rear carburettor.

(14) Disconnect and remove the cable from the water temperature sending unit and the LT cables from the distributor and coil.

(15) Disconnect the solenoid switch cable and the battery cable from the starter motor.

(16) Remove the bolt from the oil filter body and withdraw the body and filter from below the vehicle.

(17) Remove the crankshaft pulley and damper assembly and the fanbelt.

NOTE: Mark the pulley and damper to ensure reassembly in original position.

(18) Remove ignition timing pointer from sump.

(19) Remove the upper clip from the water pump hose.

(20) Remove the rpm generator complete with cables.

(21) Remove the cable from the oil pressure sending unit.

(22) Disconnect the cables from the 'D' and 'F' terminals on the generator (3.8 litre) or the alternator electrical connections (4.2 litre) and Lucar connector for warning light, if fitted.

(23) Undo and remove the four nuts and washers fastening each downpipe to the exhaust manifold. Unclip the down pipes at the silencer assembly and withdraw the pipes. Collect the sealing rings between the downpipes and the exhaust manifold.

(24) Remove the earth strap from the left hand side member.

(25) Remove the seats, ash tray and radio, if fitted.

(26) Remove the three screws securing the propeller shaft cover to the body. Apply the handbrake and remove the gear change lever knob.

(27) Slide the propeller shaft tunnel cover over the handbrake and gear change levers and withdraw the tunnel cover.

(28) Turn back the carpet, remove the six drive screws and withdraw the plastic gearbox bellows.

(29) Remove trim and screws securing the gearbox cover and remove the gearbox cover and gear change lever.

(30) Remove the engine rear mounting plate.

(31) Remove the four bolts and self-locking nuts and disconnect the propeller shaft from the gearbox flange.

(32) Remove the two leads from the reverse light switch on the gearbox top cover.

(33) Disconnect the clutch slave cylinder.

(34) Remove the lower nut securing one of the torsion

bar reaction tie plates and drift the bolt back so that it is flush with the face of the tie plate.

With the aid of a second person, lever between the head of the bolt and the torsion bar to relieve the stress on the upper bolt.

Remove the nut on the upper bolt and drift the bolt back so that it is flush with the face of the tie plate.

Repeat the above procedure on the other side of the vehicle and tap the tie plates off the bolts.

NOTE: It is important that the stress on the upper bolts is relieved before they are tapped back to obviate stripping of threads.

(35) Attach suitable lifting equipment to the engine; support under the gearbox with a trolley jack from the front of the vehicle.

(36) Remove the self-locking nut and stepped washer from the engine stabiliser.

(37) Remove the bolts from the front engine mountings and remove the speedometer cable.

(38) Raise the engine at an angle with the front higher than the rear and manoeuvre it clear through the bonnet opening.

NOTE: Ensure that the water pump pulley clears the sub frame top cross-member and that the bellhousing clears the anchor brackets at the rear of the torsion bars. Also ensure that the rear ends of the camshaft covers clear the bonnet drain channel and that the brake pipe is not damaged.

TO REMOVE – 4.2 LITRE CARS

Standard transmission

(1) Carry out procedures (1) to (24) as for *TO REMOVE – 3.8 LITRE CARS*.

(2) Remove the seats and the knob and locknut from the gear change lever.

(3) Remove setscrews and nuts and detach radio/ash tray console panel from the gearbox tunnel.

(4) If a radio is installed, disconnect electrical leads from control head in order to completely remove panel.

(5) On 2 + 2 cars – Raise the central arm rest and lift out the bottom panel. Withdraw the self-tapping screws and remove the arm rest. Lift off the cover panel from the gearbox tunnel.

(6) Other cars – Withdraw the two pan headed screws and two seat belt attachments before lifting off the trimmed cover. Withdraw the self-tapping screws and remove the gearbox cover.

(7) Remove the two leads from the reverse light switch on the gearbox top cover and disconnect the speedometer drive cable from the gearbox.

(8) Disconnect the clutch slave cylinder.

(9) Remove the four bolts and self-locking nuts and disconnect the propeller shaft from the gearbox flange.

Automatic transmission

(10) Withdraw the transmission dipstick and screw the dipstick tube out from the transmission oil pan.

(11) Move the selector lever to L position and, working underneath the vehicle, unscrew the nut securing the selector cable adjustable ball joint to the transmission lever. Release the nut securing the outer cable clamp to the abutment bracket.

(12) Remove the speedometer cable from the transmission extension housing.

(13) Disconnect the transmission oil cooler pipes from the right hand side of the radiator block and from the transmission unit. Withdraw the clips and remove the pipes.

(14) Disconnect the kickdown cable at the rear of the cylinder head.

(15) Remove the central arm rest and lift off the cover panel from the gearbox tunnel. Withdraw the self-tapping screws securing the cover plate on the transmission tunnel.

(16) Remove the four bolts and self-locking nuts and disconnect the propeller shaft from the gearbox flange.

All 4.2 Litre Models

(17) Carry out procedures (32) to (38) as described under *TO REMOVE – 3.8 LITRE CARS*.

TO INSTALL – ALL MODELS

Installation is a reversal of the removal procedure with special attention to the following:

Ensure that the brake pipes are not damaged at the front sub-frame crossmembers.

Ensure that the engine does not foul the torsion bar anchor brackets or displace the silver steel locating bars.

Replace the exhaust manifold sealing rings.

If the cylinder head has been removed torque the head nuts to 54 ft/lb.

When replacing the oil filter body and element use a new rubber sealing ring.

The reverse light switch cables can be fitted to either terminal.

Bleed the clutch hydraulic system (manual transmission).

Reset the manual mixture control and adjust the engine stabiliser. See *TO ADJUST ENGINE STABILISER*.

On automatic transmission models, the kickdown cable must be adjusted and the manual linkage connected as described under *AUTOMATIC TRANSMISSION*.

3. CYLINDER HEAD

TO REMOVE

(1) Remove the bonnet. See *ENGINE BONNET – TO REMOVE AND INSTALL*.

(2) Drain the cooling system at the cocks at the bottom of the radiator and on the side of the cylinder block.

(3) Disconnect the battery leads.

(4) Undo the wing nuts and remove the air cleaner elbow from the top of the air cleaner.

(5) Disconnect the accelerator shaft from the ball joint on the throttle spindle and remove the setscrews from the backing plate and from the bush carrying plate.

NOTE: Ensure that the push-in cage nuts do not fall out of the bulkhead.

(6) Turn the throttle spindle to the fully open position and remove the short spindle from the ball joint socket.

(7) Disconnect the distributor vacuum control pipe from the front carburettor and the vacuum-servo pipe from the connection at the rear of the inlet manifold.

(8) Disconnect the fuel feed pipe at the float chamber unions.

(9) Unclip the float chamber overflow pipes at the oil filter mounting bolt.

(10) Disconnect the mixture control inner and outer bowden cables.

(11) Disconnect the leads from the rpm generator at the rear of the cylinder head.

(12) Disconnect the top header tank water hose and the by-pass hose from the front of the inlet manifold water jacket.

(13) Disconnect the wires from the ignition coil and remove the coil.

(14) Remove the high tension leads from the sparking plugs and the high tension lead carrier from the cylinder head studs. Remove the spark plugs.

(15) Disconnect the exhaust manifolds from the engine.

(16) Disconnect the two camshaft oil feed pipe unions from the rear of the cylinder head.

(17) Disconnect the heater box from the rear of the inlet manifold water jacket.

(18) Disconnect the heater pipe clips from the inlet manifold lower securing nuts.

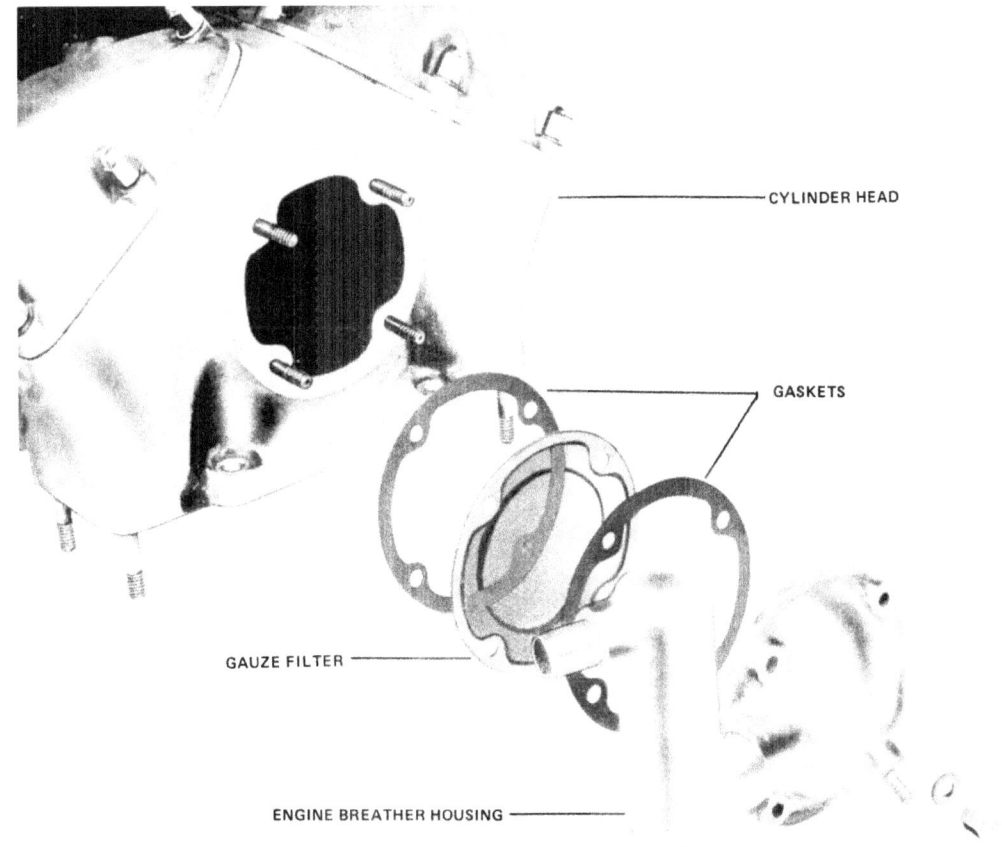

Engine Breather Components (Typical).

(19) Disconnect the lead from the water temperature sending unit in the inlet manifold jacket.

(20) Remove the dome nuts from each camshaft cover and lift off the covers.

(21) Remove the four nuts securing the breather housing to the front of the cylinder head. Withdraw the housing and breather pipe.

NOTE: Observe the position of the baffle plate with the two holes vertical.

(22) Slacken the nut on the eccentric idler sprocket shaft, depress the spring loaded stop peg and rotate the serrated adjuster plate clockwise in order to release the tension on the top timing chain.

(23) Break the locking wires on the setscrews securing the camshaft sprockets to their camshafts.

(24) Remove one set screw only from each of the camshaft sprockets. Rotate the engine until the two remaining setscrews are accessible and remove these two screws.

NOTE: Do NOT rotate the engine or the camshafts after the sprockets have been disconnected in order to obviate fouling of the inlet and exhaust valves or the valves and the pistons.

(25) Slide the camshaft sprockets up along the slots on the support brackets.

(26) Slacken the fourteen cylinder head dome nuts progressively in the reverse order of tightening as shown in the illustration.

(27) Remove the six nuts securing the front of the cylinder head.

(28) Lift off the cylinder head complete with inlet manifold and carburettors.

(29) Support the cylinder head on wooden blocks at each end.

NOTE: The valves which are in the fully open position protrude below the cylinder head joint face. The cylinder head must therefore not be placed joint face downwards on a flat surface.

TO INSTALL

Before replacing the cylinder head it is very important that the two camshafts are correctly positioned in relation to each other and to the piston positions in order to obviate fouling between valves and between valves and piston crowns.

Use the special gauge to ensure that the keyways in the front flanges of the camshafts are vertical to the camshaft housing face. Having positioned one camshaft, do not rotate the other camshaft to obtain correct positioning without slackening the camshaft bearing cap nuts in the second camshaft to their fullest extent to allow the valves to be released.

Crank engine to position No. 6 (front) piston at tdc on compression stroke, i.e. with distributor rotor pointing to segment wired to spark plug on No. 6 (front) cylinder.

The relative positions of the engine and the camshafts as obtained above should not be disturbed till the camshaft sprockets have been connected to the camshafts.

Install the cylinder head gasket with side marked TOP uppermost and install the cylinder head with manifolds and carburettors to the cylinder block.

NOTE: The second cylinder head stud from the front on the left hand side is a dowel stud.

Fit the sparking plug lead carrier to the third and sixth studs from the front on the right hand side. Fit plain washers to these and the two front stud positions. Fit 'D' washers to the remaining studs.

Torque the fourteen large cylinder head dome nuts progressively in the order illustrated to 54 ft/lb. Also tighten the six nuts securing the front end of the cylinder head.

NOTE: A thicker cylinder head gasket is installed from engine 7E9210. These gaskets are double varnished and do not require use of a jointing compound. The cylinder head bolts must be torqued to 58 ft/lb when this gasket is installed.

TO DISMANTLE

(1) With the cylinder head removed from the engine as described in the preceding section, remove the inlet manifold with carburettors and the rpm generator.

(2) Remove the four bearing caps from each camshaft and lift out the camshafts.

NOTE: Observe the mating marks on each bearing cap to ensure assembly in original positions.

(3) Remove the twelve tappets and adjusting pads interposed between the tappets and the valve stems.

NOTE: The tappets and pads should be kept in a numbered rack or in suitable receptacles to ensure that they are reassembled in their original guides.

(4) Place a suitable block of wood in the combustion chamber of No. 1 cylinder to bear on the inlet and exhaust valve heads and to rest on the work bench. Press down on the valve collars and remove the split cotters. Remove the collars, valve springs and spring seats.

(5) Remove any burrs from the valve stem cotter guides to prevent damage to the valve guides when the valves are removed.

(6) Repeat this procedure on the other cylinders and

Sequence for Slackening and Tightening Cylinder Head Nuts.

keep the valves on a suitable rack to ensure replacement in original locations.

TO INSPECT

(1) Clean the valves thoroughly and discard burned, warped and cracked valves.

(2) Measure the valve stems for wear. If wear exceeds .003" replace the valve.

(3) If valve stem to guide clearance is excessive replace valve guides and install new valves. See *TO RENEW VALVE GUIDES*.

(4) Remove carbon and any deposits from the inside of valve guides.

(5) Remove all traces of carbon and deposits from the combustion chambers and from the induction and exhaust ports.

NOTE: Avoid scrapers and sharp pointed tools to prevent damage to the aluminium alloy cylinder head. Use worn emery cloth and paraffin.

(6) Clean carbon deposit from the piston crowns and clean the top face of the cylinder block particularly round the cylinder head studs.

(7) Flush and clean out the water passages in the cylinder head.

(8) Reface valves and valve seats and renew valve seat inserts as necessary. See following sections.

TO REFACE VALVES AND VALVE SEATS

(1) Check that the valve seat angle is 45°.

(2) Inspect the remaining margin after the valves are refaced. Valves with less than 3/64" margin should be discarded.

(3) When refacing the valve seats, it is important that the correct size valve guide pilot be used for reseating stone. A true and complete surface must be obtained.

(4) The total run out should not exceed .003". When the seats are correctly finished, the width of the seats should be .050" ± .010" for inlet valves and .075" ± .010" for exhaust valves.

TO CHECK VALVE SPRINGS

(1) Check the valve spring free length and length at fitted load (see Specifications).

(2) Check that the springs are not bent or distorted from heat.

If a spring tester is not available, check the springs by comparison with new springs. This can be done by using a surface plate and straight edge for checking the free length and by using a new spring and a used spring in a vice end on end, with a plate in between. Measure from the plate to the vice jaw adjacent to both the new and used springs. A used spring is serviceable if it does not show collapse in excess of five percent when subjected to this comparison test.

TO RENEW VALVE GUIDES (3.8 ENGINES AND EARLY 4.2 ENGINES)

(1) Remove and dismantle the cylinder head as previously described and clean thoroughly in solvent.

(2) Press out the worn valve guides from the top of the cylinder head towards the combustion chambers using a suitable piloted drift.

NOTE: The drift should have a spigotted end the same diameter as the valve stems and the outer diameter slightly less than the diameter of the valve guide, so that it will pass through the valve guide bore in the cylinder head.

(3) Ream the valve guide bore in the cylinder head to a diameter of $.5048"\ ^{+\ .0007"}_{-\ .0000"}$ to suit the replacement guides serviced.

(4) Heat the cylinder head by immersing in boiling water for 30 minutes.

(5) Lubricate the outer diameter of the new valve guide with graphite grease and, using the spigotted drift, start the new guide into the cylinder head from the combustion chamber end.

NOTE: The end of the guide with a chamfer and a lead-in should enter the head first. The exhaust valve guide is longer than the inlet valve guide.

(6) The installed position of the guides will be correct when the top of the guide which is chamfered protrudes 5/16" above the facing for the valve spring seat.

TO RENEW VALVE GUIDES (LATER 4.2 ENGINES)

The procedures are similar to those described for the 3.8 engines and early 4.2 engines except for the following important differences.

The installed position of the valve guide is determined by a circlip fitted to the valve guide. This circlip should register in the groove machined in the guide bore of the cylinder head.

The old guide must be driven out from the combustion chamber end to emerge from the top of the cylinder head.

The new valve guide should be driven in from the top of the head towards the combustion chamber.

NOTE: These guides are chamfered at the upper ends and the outside diameter reduced at the lower ends to provide a 'lead-in'.

4.2 engines after No. 7E11668 have oil seals fitted to the inlet valve guides in a second groove in the guide above the circlip groove.

TO RENEW TAPPET GUIDES

(1) With the cylinder head removed from the engine and dismantled, bore out the old tappet guide until it collapses. Do not damage the guide bore in the cylinder head.

(2) Gauge the diameter of the tappet guide bore at an ambient temperature of 68°F.

(3) Grind down the replacement tappet (1.643" diameter) to a diameter .003" greater than the gauged bore diameter.

(4) Grind off the same amount from the lead-in at the bottom of the tappet guide. The difference in diameter between the adjacent diameters should be $.0032"\ ^{+\ .0025"}_{-\ .0000"}$.

(5) Heat the cylinder head in an oven for half an hour at 300°F.

(6) Fit the tappet guide to the head and ensure that the lip at the top of the guide beds evenly in the recess.

(7) Ream the guide, concentric with the valve guide to a diameter of $.3750"\ ^{+\ .0007"}_{-\ .0000"}$.

TO RENEW VALVE SEAT INSERTS

(1) With the cylinder head removed and dismantled as previously described bore out the old valve seat insert until it collapses. Remove the insert.

NOTE: The recess for the insert should not be damaged in the process of removing the old insert.

(2) Gauge the diameter of the insert recess at an ambient temperature of 68°F.

(3) Grind down a service insert to obtain an outside diameter of .003" larger than the recess diameter as gauged.

(4) Heat the cylinder head in an oven for one hour at a temperature of 300°F.

(5) Fit the inserts and ensure that it bottoms evenly in the recess. Allow the head to cool down to room temperature.

(6) Assemble the camshafts to the cylinder head.

(7) Insert the valve into its guide and hold it down in its valve seat. Check the dimension between the valve stem and the back of the cam. The dimension should be .320" plus the valve clearance in accordance with the specifications for an inlet or exhaust valve as applicable.

NOTE: This will provide the necessary allowance for fitting of adjusting pads available for service when making the final valve clearance adjustment.

(8) If the dimension is greater than .320" plus the appropriate valve clearance, grind the valve seat down until the correct dimension is obtained.

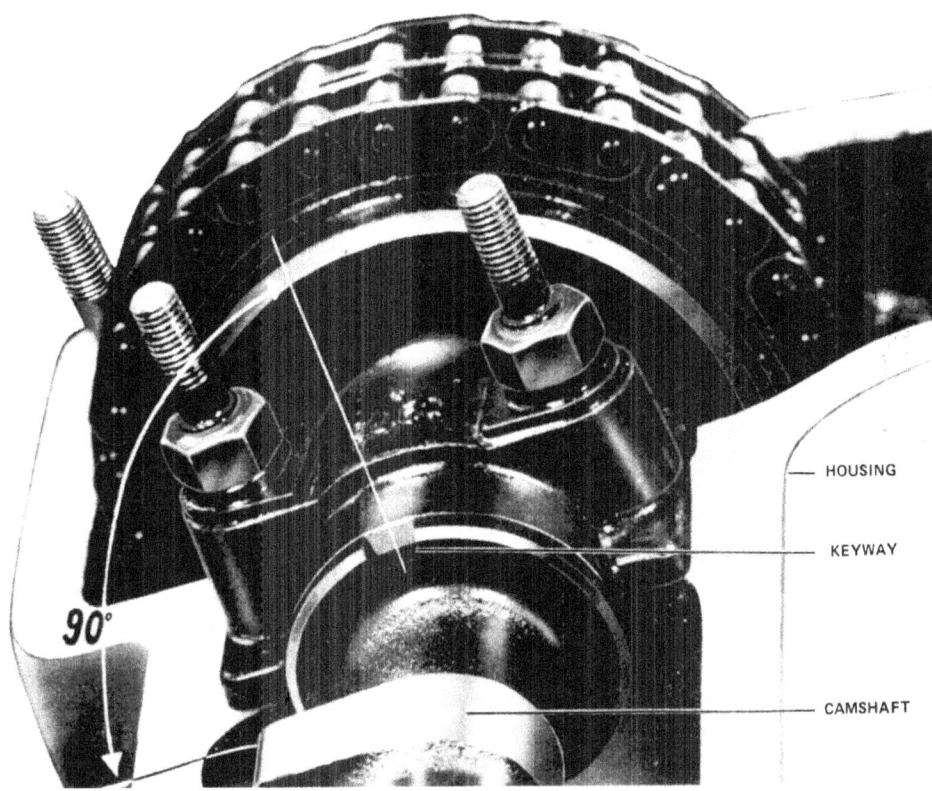

When Installing Camshaft Ensure Keyway is 90 deg. to Camshaft Housing Face.

(9) After assembling the cylinder head, check and adjust valve clearances as described in a following section.

TO ASSEMBLE

(1) Use a suitable block of wood in the combustion chamber of one cylinder to bear on the inlet and exhaust valve heads and to rest on the work bench.

(2) Assemble the spring seat, valve spring and collar on to the valve stem, depress the collar with a suitable spring compressing tool and insert the split cotters.

(3) Repeat the procedure on the other valves.

NOTE: The valves should be assembled in their original locations.

(4) Adjust the valve clearances and install the cylinder head and camshaft assemblies to the engine paying special attention to the sequence of operations in order to obviate fouling between valves, and between valves and piston crowns. See *CYLINDER HEAD – TO INSTALL* and the following section.

TO ADJUST VALVE CLEARANCE

(1) With the cylinder head removed from the engine and the valves assembled to their respective guides, replace the tappets and adjusting pads on the valves operated by one camshaft (exhaust or inlet as the case may be).

(2) Fit the camshaft to the set of valves receiving attention.

(3) Measure and record the valve clearances, using a feeler gauge between the back of each cam and the appropriate valve tappet.

(4) Any excess of valve clearance above that given in the specifications for that particular valve (inlet or exhaust – normal use or touring) should be made up by selecting an adjusting pad which will make up such excess.

Adjusting pads bearing etched lettering from A to Z are available in sizes from .085" to .110" in increments of .001".

(5) Remove the camshaft fitted, install the other camshaft and carry out the same procedures outlined above to determine the appropriate adjusting pads to be used on the valves operated by this camshaft.

(6) Fit the camshafts to the cylinder heads having installed the replacement pads (as determined above) to their respective tappets.

NOTE: The keyway in the front bearing flange of each camshaft should be at 90° to the camshaft cover face before tightening down the camshaft bearing cap nuts.

(7) Replace the cylinder head as described in *CYLINDER HEAD – TO INSTALL.*

4. ENGINE SUMP

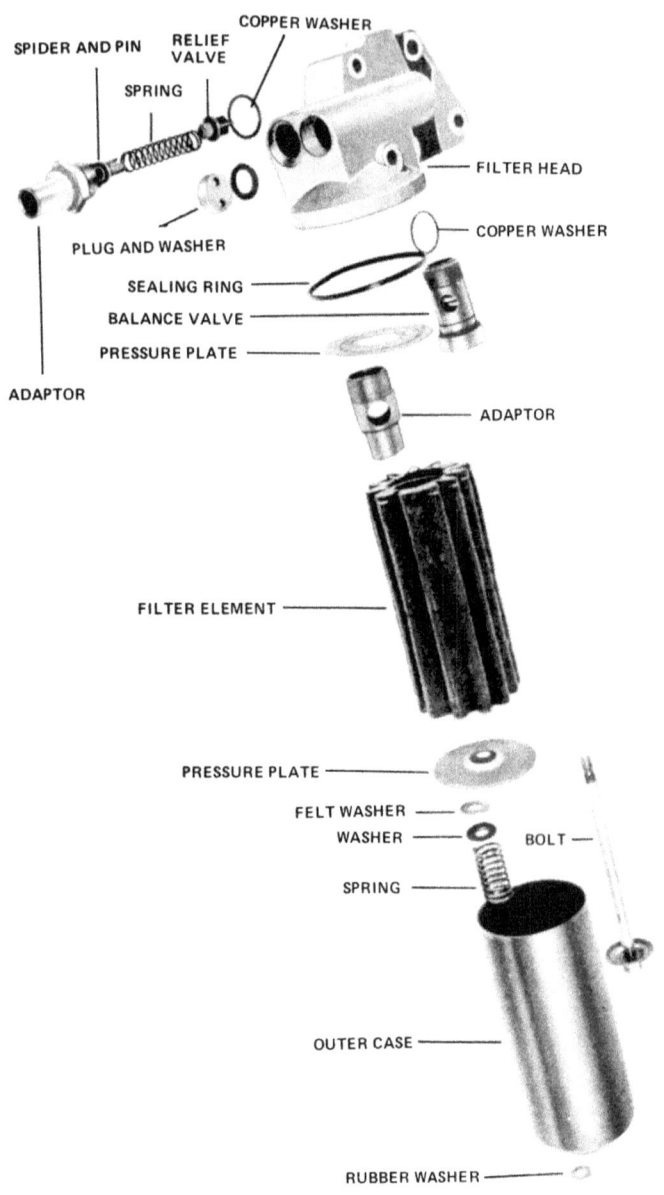

Exploded View of Oil Filter (Typical).

TO REMOVE AND INSTALL (3.8 ENGINE)

(1) Remove the engine drain plug and drain the oil from the sump.

(2) Remove the crankshaft damper. See *CRANKSHAFT AND MAIN BEARINGS*.

(3) Slacken the clips and disconnect the oil return hose at the oil filter head and at the elbow to the sump.

(4) Remove the twenty-six setscrews and four nuts retaining the sump to the cylinder block.

(5) Remove the sump from the cylinder block.

NOTE: Make a note of the short setscrew located at the right hand front corner of the sump.

It may be necessary to slacken the engine stabiliser washers in order to raise the rear of the engine before removing the sump.

Installation is a reversal of the removal procedure.

Always use new gaskets and rear oil seal. Ensure that the short setscrew is installed in its original position.

Refill the sump, start the engine and check for oil leakage.

TO REMOVE AND INSTALL (4.2 ENGINES)

(1) Carry out procedures (1) to (3) as for 3.8 engines.

(2) Remove the self-locking nut and washer from the top of the engine stabiliser.

(3) Screw down the lower flanged washer to the limit of the stud thread.

(4) Attach lifting tackle to the rear lifting loop and raise the engine approximately 1".

(5) Remove the sump securing screws, lower the front end of the sump and withdraw it forwards.

Installation is a reversal of the removal procedure.

Always use new gaskets and rear oil seal.

Adjust the engine stabiliser after fitting.

Refill the sump, start the engine and check for oil leakage.

5. OIL PUMP

TO REMOVE AND INSTALL

(1) Remove the sump as previously described.

(2) Detach the suction and delivery pipe brackets and withdraw the pipes from the oil pump.

(3) Bend back the tab washers and remove the three bolts securing the pump to the front main bearing cap.

(4) Withdraw the oil pump and collect the coupling sleeve at the top of the rotor drive shaft.

Installation is a reversal of the removal procedure with attention to the following points:

Ensure that the coupling sleeve is positioned on the top of the rotor drive shaft before offering up the oil pump into the installed position.

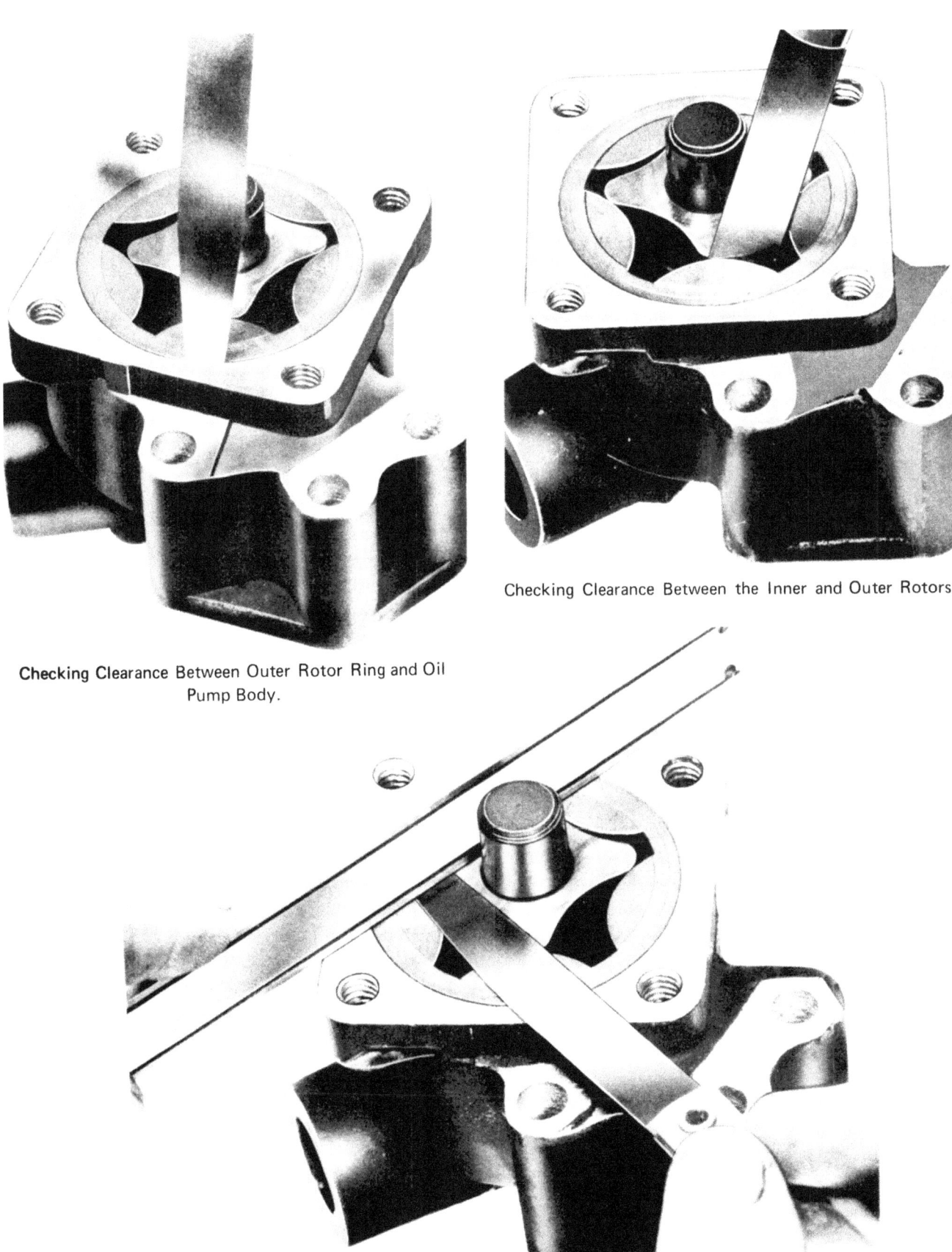

Checking Clearance Between the Inner and Outer Rotors.

Checking Clearance Between Outer Rotor Ring and Oil Pump Body.

Checking End Float of Oil Pump Rotors.

After installing the pump check that there is appreciable end float of the coupling sleeve.

TO DISMANTLE

(1) Remove the four securing bolts and separate the bottom cover from the pump body.

(2) Withdraw the inner and outer rotors from the pump body.

NOTE: The inner rotor is secured to the drive shaft by a pin which should not be removed.

TO CHECK PUMP COMPONENTS

(1) Check the clearance between the lobes of the inner and outer rotors. This clearance should not exceed .006".

(2) Check the clearance between the outer rotor and the pump body. This clearance should not exceed .010".

(3) Place a straight edge across the joint face of the pump body and measure the clearance between the rotors and straight edge. This clearance should be .0025". In an emergency it is possible to restore this clearance by lapping the pump body and outer rotor on a surface plate to suit the inner rotor.

(4) Examine the pump body and bottom cover for scoring and the drive shaft bore for signs of wear. Replace parts as necessary.

NOTE: The drive shaft, inner and outer rotors are only serviced as an assembly.

(5) Hold the drive shaft in a soft jawed vice and check that the inner rotor is tight on the securing pin.

TO ASSEMBLE

Reassembly is a reversal of the dismantling procedure with attention to the following points:

Install the outer rotor to the pump body with the chamfered end towards the drive shaft side.

Fit new 'O' rings to the suction and delivery pipe bores.

6. PISTONS AND CONNECTING RODS

TO REMOVE AND DISMANTLE

(1) With the engine removed from the vehicle, remove the cylinder head and sump as described earlier.

(2) Remove the split pins and remove the big end bearing castellated nuts and withdraw the big end bearing cap and half shell.

NOTE: The cylinder numbers should appear on the connecting rod and cap to facilitate replacement in original position. Note the side of the engine to which the numbered caps and connecting rods face.

(3) Push the connecting rod and piston assembly out through the top of the cylinder bore.

NOTE: If new pistons are to be installed, remove the ridge at the top of the cylinder bore with a suitable ridge removing tool before the piston assemblies are withdrawn from the cylinder block.

(4) Replace the big end bearing cap and shell on each respective assembly as it is removed from the engine.

(5) Remove the gudgeon pin retaining circlips from the piston bosses. Discard the circlips.

(6) Immerse the piston, gudgeon pin and connecting rod little end in a bath of oil heated to 230°F. Push out the gudgeon pin and remove the piston from the connecting rod.

NOTE: Gudgeon pins are a selective fit in the piston bosses. Pistons and gudgeon pins are available only as assemblies.

(7) If the piston rings are to be renewed, remove the piston rings over the top of the piston and discard.

(8) Remove all carbon deposits from the bottom of the ring grooves.

TO INSPECT CYLINDER BORES (DRY LINERS)

The cylinder walls should be checked for out-of-round and taper. Bores in excess of .005" out-of-round or tapered in excess of .010", or bores that are badly scuffed or scored, should be re-bored and honed, and new pistons and rings fitted. Reboring and honing is not recommended beyond .030".

After removal of the cylinder head studs check the area round the stud holes for flatness and skim flush with surrounding face prior to mounting the reboring equipment.

The worn liners must be pressed out from below using a suitable stepped block.

Before fitting a new liner lightly smear the bore in the cylinder block with a jointing compound half way down the bore and also smear the top half of the outer surface of the cylinder liner.

The new liners should be pressed in from the top, and the top of the liners lightly skimmed flush with the top face of the cylinder block.

New liners should be bored out and honed to suit the grade of piston to be fitted.

Letter on Piston Crown Indicates Selective Grade.

Standard size pistons are available in five selective grades to suit cylinder bores as follows:

	3.8 ENGINES	4.2 ENGINES
F	3.4248" + .0003" − .0000"	3.6250" + .0003" − .0000"
G	3.4252" + .0003" − .0000"	3.6254" + .0003" − .0000"
H	3.4256" + .0003" − .0000"	3.6258" + .0003" − .0000"
J	3.4260" + .0003" − .0000"	3.6262" + .0003" − .0000"
K	3.4264" + .0003" − .0000"	3.6266" + .0003" − .0000"

Pistons are stamped on the crown with the letter identification and the cylinder block is also stamped on the top face adjacent to the bores.

Oversize pistons serviced are +.010", +.020" and +.030" with no selective grades.

On completion of reboring the blanking plugs in the main oil gallery should be removed and the cylinder block oilways and the crankcase interior thoroughly cleaned.

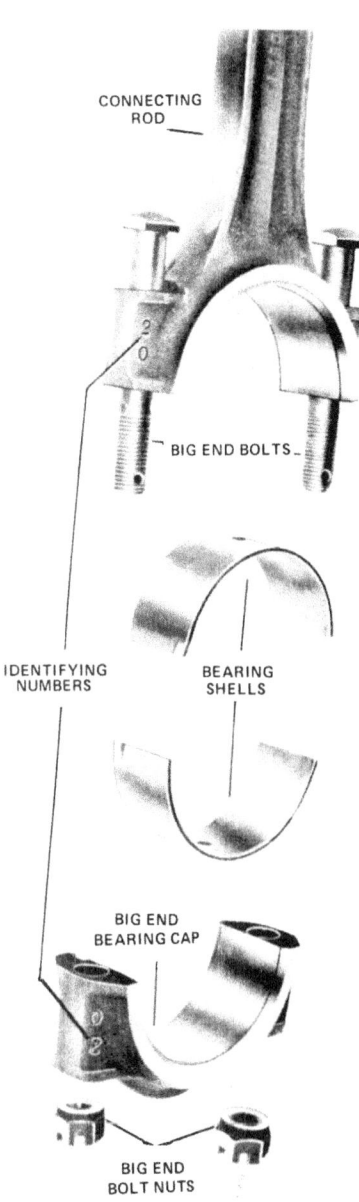

Numbers Identifying Cylinder and Matching Connecting Rod and Big End Cap.

Paint the interior of the crankcase with heat and oil resisting paint.

Liners which are fit for further service, with original pistons, but that require re-ringing, should be deglazed with a hone. Before honing, place plenty of clean rags over the crankshaft to keep the abrasive materials from entering the crankcase area.

(1) Used carefully, a cylinder bore re-sizing hone equipped with 220 grit stone is the best tool for this job. In addition to deglazing, it will reduce taper and out-of-round as well as removing light scuffing, scoring or scratches. Usually a few strokes will clean up a bore and maintain the required limit.

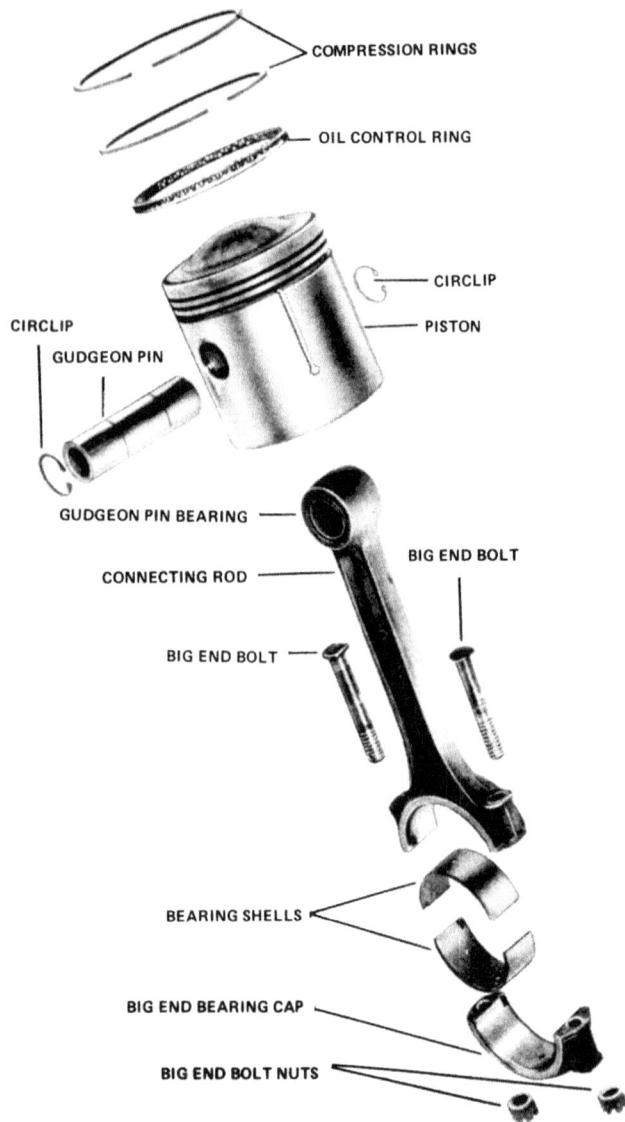

Exploded View of Piston and Connecting Rod Components.

(2) Deglazing of the cylinder walls may be done using a cylinder surfacing hone equipped with 280 grit stones; 20 to 60 strokes, depending on the bore condition will be sufficient to provide a satisfactory surface. Inspect cylinder walls after each 20 strokes. Use honing oil available from major oil distributors. Do not use engine oil, mineral spirits or kerosene.

(3) Honing should be carried out by moving the hone up and down fast enough to get a cross hatch pattern. When the hone marks intersect at 60 degrees, the cross hatch angle is most satisfactory for correct seating of rings.

(4) After honing it is necessary that the block be cleaned again to remove all traces of abrasives.

CAUTION: Be sure all abrasives are removed from engine parts after honing. It is recommended that a solution of soap and water be used with a brush, and the parts then thoroughly dried. Bore can be considered clean when it can be wiped with a white cloth and the cloth remains clean. Oil the bores after cleaning to prevent rusting.

TO FIT NEW PISTON RINGS

(1) Place each piston ring in the relatively unworn portion of the cylinder bore to which it is to be fitted, and align it squarely with the cylinder wall. This can be done by inserting an inverted piston from above and pushing the ring down the bore to approximately 2" of the bottom of the cylinder.

(2) Withdraw the piston and measure the gap in the ring with feeler gauges. If necessary, adjust the gap by filing to the dimension given in the Specifications.

Treat each ring and cylinder bore individually and ensure that the rings are assembled to the respective piston for the cylinder bore in which they were fitted for gap check.

TO ASSEMBLE AND INSTALL

The top compression ring is hard chrome plated.

On 3.8 engines at least one compression ring has tapered periphery. These rings will be marked **TOP** to ensure that they are fitted the correct way up.

On 4.2 engines both compression rings have a tapered periphery and are similarly marked for correct assembly.

On 3.8 engines the oil control ring may be fitted either way up.

4.2 engines of 9:1 compression ratio and early 4.2 engines of 8:1 compression ratio with split skirt pistons have the same type of Maxiflex self-expanding oil control ring. They consist of 2 steel rails with a spacer between. The rails are held together on assembly with an adhesive. The expander, which is fitted inside the oil control ring, should be assembled with the two lugs positioned in the hole directly above the gudgeon pin bore.

Later 4.2 engines of 8:1 compression ratio have solid skirt pistons. The oil control ring on these pistons is similar to the Maxiflex rings but the ends of the expander ring are butted together. Ensure that ends of the (internal) ring do not overlap.

The gudgeon pin should be a firm thumb push fit in the piston bosses at room temperature, and a firm sliding fit in the small end bush of the connecting rod.

Steel-backed phosphor bronze small end bushes are available for service. They are a press fit in the connecting rod. After fitting, ream or hone the bush to a diameter of $.8750" \begin{smallmatrix}+ .0002"\\ - .0000"\end{smallmatrix}$.

(1) Assemble the piston to the connecting rod so that the split skirt (except late 4.2 engines with 8:1 compression ratio) is towards the left or non-thrust side of the engine.

Pistons are marked F (front) on their crowns to assist in correct assembly. The stamping on the connecting rod (which will correspond with the stamping on the cap) should be on the same side of the engine as observed when dismantling.

NOTE: Insert the piston and connecting rod little end in a bath of oil heated to approximately 230°F to facilitate installation of gudgeon pin.

(2) Install new retaining circlips in the piston bosses and ensure that they are properly seated.

(3) Check the piston ring groove clearance according to specifications and, using a ring expanding tool, fit the rings to the piston in the following manner.

(4) Assemble the oil control ring and follow with the lower compression ring and then the upper compression ring.

(5) Position the ring gaps 120° apart, with the gap in the top ring away from the exhaust valve. Also ensure that in the case of expander type oil ring the gap in the rails and the expander gap are staggered with respect to each other.

(6) Using a ring compressor, assemble the piston and connecting rod assembly to the cylinder bore so that the mark F on the crown is to the front of the cylinder block.

NOTE: The connecting rod and piston assemblies must be replaced in the cylinders from which they were removed on dismantling and new rings must be assembled to the pistons for the cylinders to which the rings were fitted for gap check.

(7) Push the piston assembly down the cylinder bore and align the connecting rod and upper half of the big end on to the crankshaft crankpin.

(8) Install the big end bearing cap and lower bearing half, fit the retaining nuts and tighten to the specified torque. Fit new split pins to the retaining nuts.

(9) Install the other piston and connecting rod assemblies using the same procedure.

NOTE: All components must be lubricated with clean engine oil before installation.

When fitting new big end bearing shells, ensure that the small tang on each half of the bearing fits into the machined groove in the connecting rod or cap.

New standard bearings must not be scraped or filed. Undersize bearings are available for reground crankshafts.

Further assembly and installation is a reversal of the removal and dismantling procedure.

7. FLYWHEEL AND CONVERTER DRIVE PLATE

TO REMOVE AND INSTALL

(1) With the engine removed from the vehicle and the transmission bellhousing separated from the engine, mark the clutch and flywheel to facilitate reassembly or check for corresponding balance marks B on clutch and flywheel.

(2) Remove the bolts and nuts securing the clutch pressure plate assembly to the flywheel and withdraw the pressure plate assembly and the clutch driven plate from the flywheel.

Engines with automatic transmission (2+2 cars) employ a converter drive plate, instead of the flywheel, to which the starter ring gear is welded.

The flywheel on manual transmission cars and the converter drive plate on automatic transmission cars are secured by the setscrews retained by a circular locking plate and located by two mushroom headed dowels.

Both flywheel and converter drive plates have integral starter gear teeth.

(3) Knock back the tabs on the locking plate, unscrew the securing screws and remove the locking plate. Remove the flywheel or converter drive plate by tapping gently with a rawhide mallet.

Installation is a reversal of the removal procedure with particular attention to the following points:

Ensure that the marks made on dismantling or the B marks are correctly aligned when installing the flywheel and clutch pressure plate.

Use a clutch plate aligning tool or a discarded gearbox input shaft to align the clutch driven plate with the spigot bearing in the end of the crankshaft. See *CLUTCH UNIT – TO REMOVE AND INSTALL.*

8. CRANKSHAFT AND MAIN BEARINGS

TO REMOVE AND INSTALL

(1) With the engine removed from the vehicle, undo the two nuts securing the starter motor to the clutch housing and remove the starter.

(2) Remove the distributor. See *DISTRIBUTOR – TO REMOVE.*

(3) Remove cylinder head. See *CYLINDER HEAD – TO REMOVE.*

(4) Remove gearbox, clutch and flywheel. See preceding section *FLYWHEEL AND REAR ENGINE PLATE.*

(5) Unscrew the large nut on the crankshaft damper and remove the plain washer.

(6) Use two levers behind the damper and ease it off the split cone.

(7) Remove water pump. See *COOLING SYSTEM.*

(8) Remove the flexible hose connecting the oil filter head to the sump.

(9) Undo the bolts securing the oil filter head to the cylinder block and remove the filter head.

(10) Remove the sump as described in *ENGINE SUMP – TO REMOVE AND INSTALL.*

(11) Remove the oil pump and pipes. See *OIL PUMP – TO REMOVE AND INSTALL.*

(12) Remove the pistons and connecting rods as described in the appropriate section.

(13) Remove timing cover and timing gear assembly as described in the appropriate section.

(14) Tap back the tab washer securing the distributor drive gear nut. Remove the nut and washer.

(15) Tap the squared end of the distributor drive shaft through the gear. Note that the gear is keyed to the shaft.

(16) Remove the gear and thrust washer and withdraw the drive shaft.

(17) Attach a dial indicator to the rear of the cylinder block with its plunger bearing on the crankshaft flange. Prise the crankshaft forward and zero the gauge pointer. Prise the crankshaft rearwards and check the dial reading, which should be $.004'' {}^{+ .002''}_{- .000''}$.

(18) Knock back the tab washers and undo the main bearing cap retaining bolts. Remove the bearing caps and lower half bearings.

NOTE: Corresponding numbers are stamped on the caps and bottom face of the crankcase to ensure replacement in original positions.

Thrust washers are fitted to recesses in the centre main bearing caps.

(19) Detach the bottom half of the oil return thread cover from the top half (which is bolted to the cylinder block behind the rear main bearing) by unscrewing the two Allen screws.

NOTE: The two halves are located by hollow dowels.

(20) Carefully lift the crankshaft from the crankcase using care not to dislodge or damage the upper halves of the main bearings.

(21) If the main bearing shells are to be renewed, remove the upper halves of the bearings from the cylinder block.

Installation of the crankshaft is a direct reversal of the removal procedure with particular attention to the following points:

Crankshaft journals and bearing shells should be checked for excessive wear, taper or scoring. Journals that are worn or tapered in excess of .003" should be reground and appropriate undersize bearing shells should be fitted.

Undersize bearings are available in the following sizes: –.010", –.020", –.030" and –.040". Crankshafts should not be ground beyond .040".

The clearance between the oil return thread cover and the oil return thread on the crankshaft should be within the limits $.0025'' {}^{+ .0030''}_{- .0000''}$. The two halves of this cover are

Location of Matching Numbers on Crankcase and Main Bearing Cap.

serviced as an assembly together with the dowels and screws.

The thrust washers at the centre main bearing cap should be located in the recesses in the main bearing cap with the white metal side outwards.

If the end float of the crankshaft is not within specifications replace with suitable thrust washers which are serviced in standard and .004" oversize. It is permissible to fit a standard size thrust washer to one side and an oversize washer to the other.

Main bearing caps should be fitted so that the numbers stamped on the cap correspond with the numbers stamped on the bottom face of the crankcase.

Torque main bearing cap bolts to 83 ft/lb.

If the original crankshaft is being refitted remove the Allen headed plugs in the crankshaft webs and clean out oil ways with a high pressure jet followed with compressed air. Refit the plugs and stake in place with a blunt chisel.

NOTE: The tab washers for the rear main bearing bolts are longer than the others. The plain ends of these washers should be tapped down around the bolt hole bosses.

If the distributor shaft bush needs renewal press a replacement bush into the bore of the lug at the front of the cylinder block and ream the bush to a diameter of $1.750'' {}^{+ .0005''}_{- .0000''}$.

When replacing the distributor and oil pump drive gear, position the distributor drive shaft so that the mid point of the offset on the shaft is at 3 o'clock. The engine should at the same time be turned so that No. 1 and No. 6 piston are at tdc.

The end float of the distributor drive shaft should be $.004'' {}^{+ .002''}_{- .000''}$. Replace the drive gear to obtain the specified clearance.

9. TIMING COVER AND TIMING GEAR ASSEMBLY

TO REMOVE

(1) Remove the cylinder head as described previously.

(2) Remove the radiator, cowl, header tank and fan as described in *COOLING SYSTEM*.

(3) Remove the locking washer securing the damper bolt by knocking back the tabs and unscrewing the two setscrews.

(4) Remove the other two setscrews fastening the crankshaft pulley to the damper. Remove the pulley.

(5) Undo the large damper securing bolt and remove the flat washer.

(6) Use two levers behind the damper and ease it off the split cone. Withdraw the split cone.

(7) Remove the engine sump as described previously.

(8) Undo the bolts and nuts and remove the water pump from the timing cover. Note the gasket between the water pump and the timing cover.

(9) Remove the bolts securing the timing cover to the front face of the cylinder block. Remove the timing cover.

NOTE: The cover is located on the cylinder block by two dowels.

(10) Remove the bottom plug on the timing chain tensioner. Insert an 1/8" hexagonal Allen key in the end of the restraint cylinder and turn clockwise until the slipper head remains in the retracted position.

(11) Remove the two securing bolts and tab washers and remove the adjuster. Note the conical filter in the oil hole in the cylinder block.

(12) Undo the four screws securing the front mounting bracket to the cylinder block.

(13) Remove the two screwdriver slotted screws securing the intermediate damper bracket and the rear mounting bracket.

(14) Remove the timing gear assembly.

TO DISMANTLE

(1) Remove the nut and serrated washer from the front end of the idler shaft. Withdraw the plunger and spring.

(2) Remove the four nuts securing the front mounting bracket to the rear mounting bracket and withdraw the front bracket from the studs.

(3) Remove the bottom timing chain from the large intermediate sprocket.

(4) Remove the circlip from the end of the shaft in the mounting bracket, press the shaft out of the bracket and withdraw the intermediate sprockets from the shaft.

(5) Press the boss of the small sprocket from the bore of the large sprocket. Note that they are keyed together. Later models have a one piece intermediate sprocket.

TO CHECK AND INSPECT

Examine the chain for stretching and wear.
Check the sprockets and dampers for wear.
Replace chain, sprockets and dampers as necessary.

TO ASSEMBLE AND INSTALL

Assembly and installation is a reversal of the dismantling and removal procedures.

When refitting the bottom timing chain tensioner fit shims as necessary between the backing plate of the tensioner and cylinder block so that the timing chain rides centrally on the rubber slipper. Clean the conical filter in petrol before replacing it in the oil feed hole.

Do not release the locking mechanism in the chain tensioner until the tensioner has been finally mounted in the engine with the timing chain installed.

TO ADJUST VALVE TIMING

(1) Remove the camshaft covers and the engine breather at the front of the cylinder head.

(2) Tension the top timing chain as follows:

   (a) Slacken the locknut securing the serrated plate.
   (b) Press the locking plunger inwards and using a suitable pegged tube rotate by the two holes on the plate in an anti-clockwise direction.
   (c) Turn the engine both ways and ensure that there is slight flexibility on both outer sides of the chain below the camshaft sprockets.

NOTE: The chain must not be dead tight.

   (d) Release the locking plunger and tighten the locknut securely.

(3) Turn the engine to tdc on compression stroke on No. 6 (front) cylinder. The distributor rotor will be opposite the segment wired to No. 6 cylinder.

(4) Remove the locking wire from the camshaft sprocket securing setscrews.

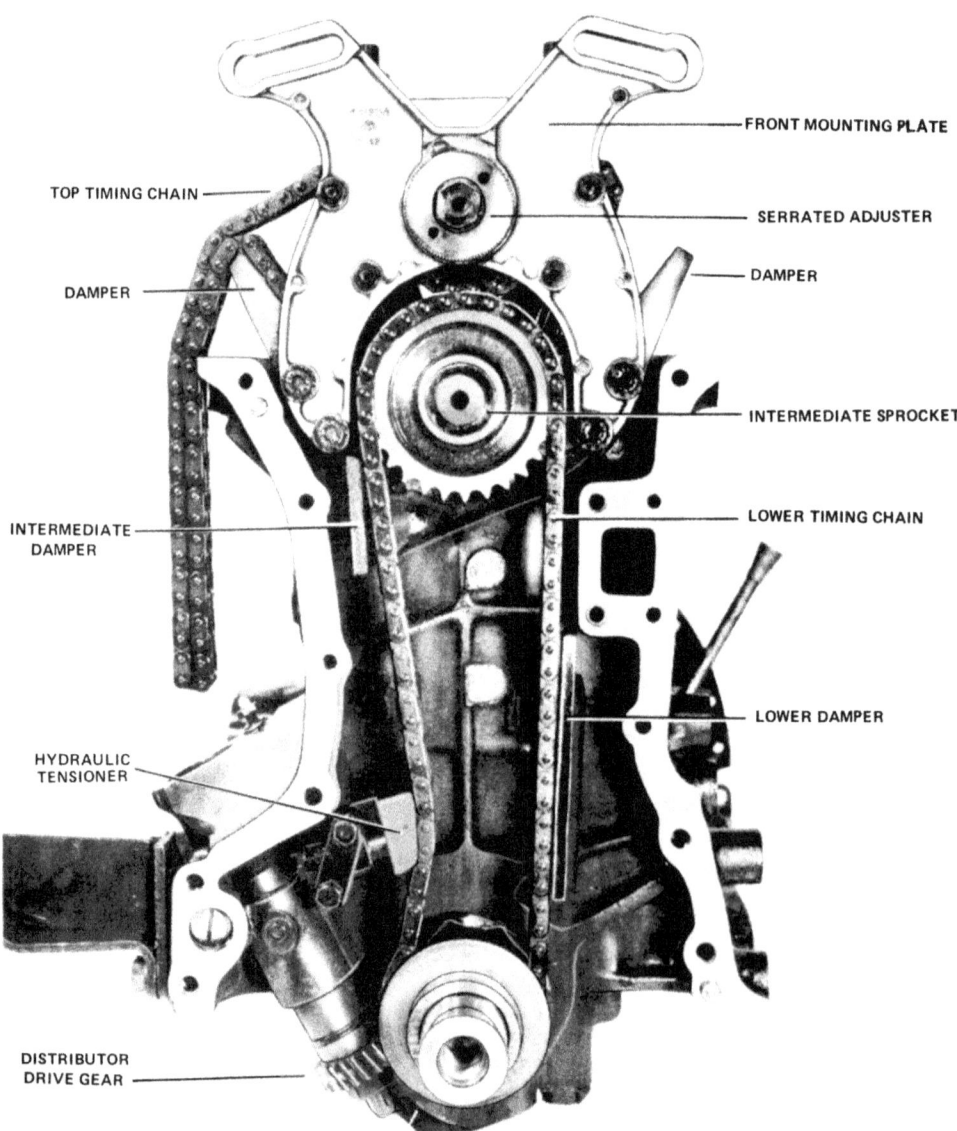

Lower Timing Chain Arrangement.

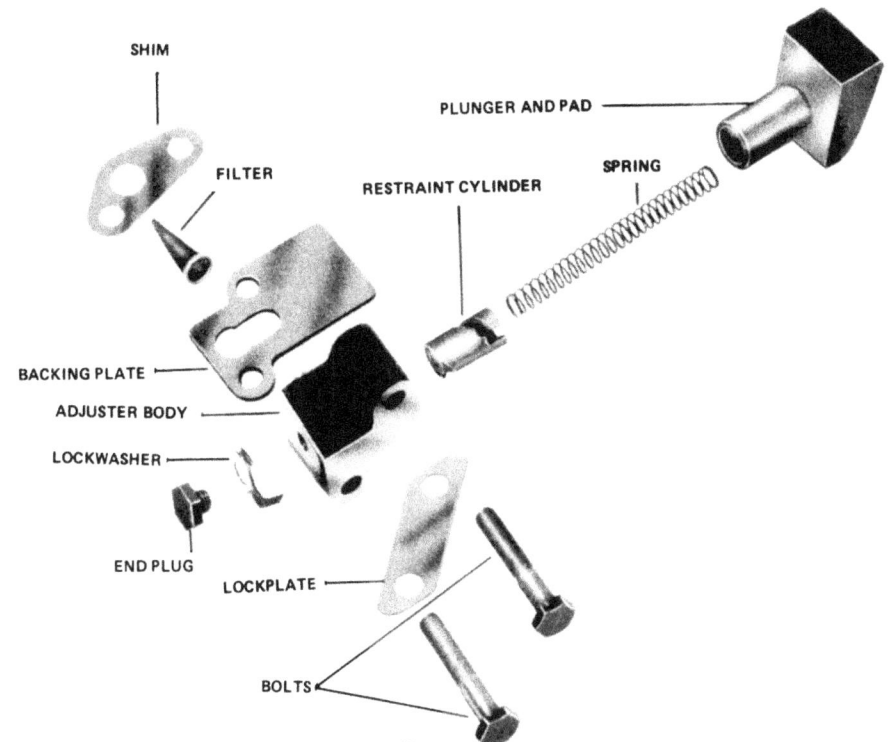

Exploded View of the Lower Timing Chain Hydraulic Tensioner.

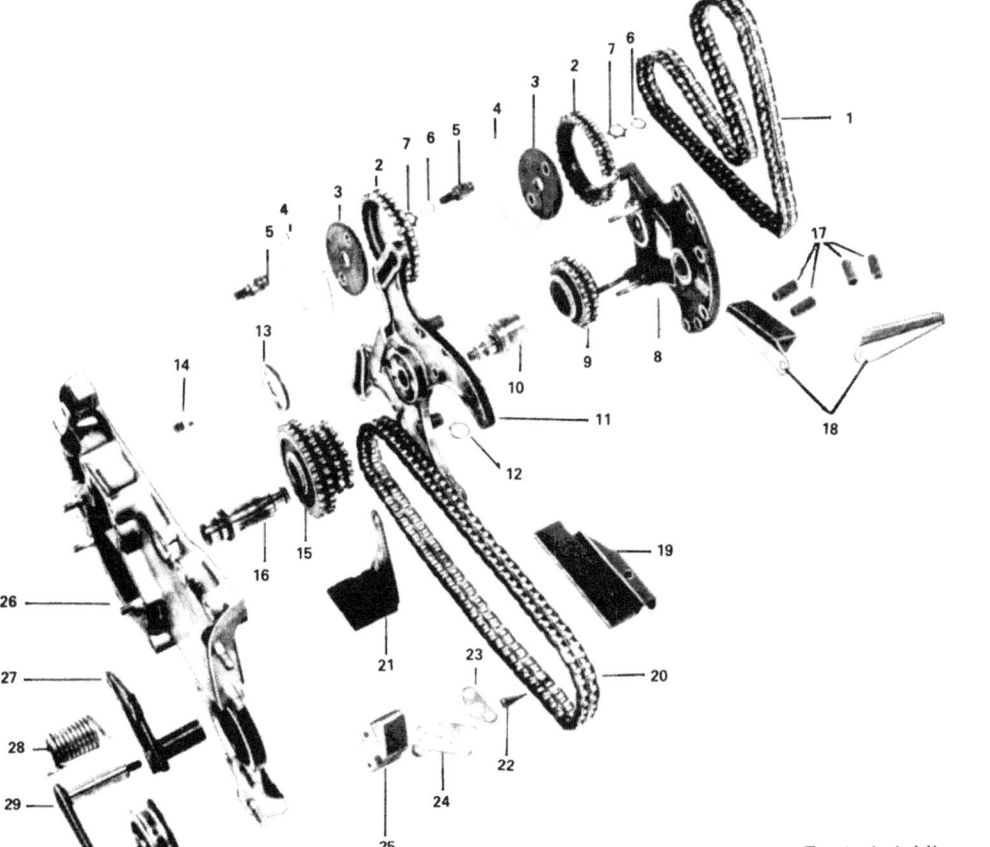

1. Top timing chain.
2. Camshaft sprockets.
3. Adjuster plates.
4. Circlips.
5. Guide pins.
6. Circlips.
7. Star washers.
8. Rear mounting plate.
9. Idler sprocket.
10. Eccentric shaft.
11. Front mounting plate.
12. Circlip.
13. Adjuster plate.
14. Locking plunger and spring.
15. Intermediate sprockets.
16. Shaft.
17. Spacers.
18. Dampers.
19. Lower damper.
20. Lower timing chain.
21. Intermediate damper.
22. Filter.
23. Shim.
24. Backing plate.
25. Hydraulic tensioner.
26. Timing cover.
27. Fanbelt adjustment bracket.
28. Spring.
29. Jockey pulley mounting.
30. Jockey pulley.
31. Pulley retaining nut.

Exploded View of Timing Gear Components.

Valve Timing Gauge Shown in Position. Gauge Must be Seated Where Arrows Indicate.

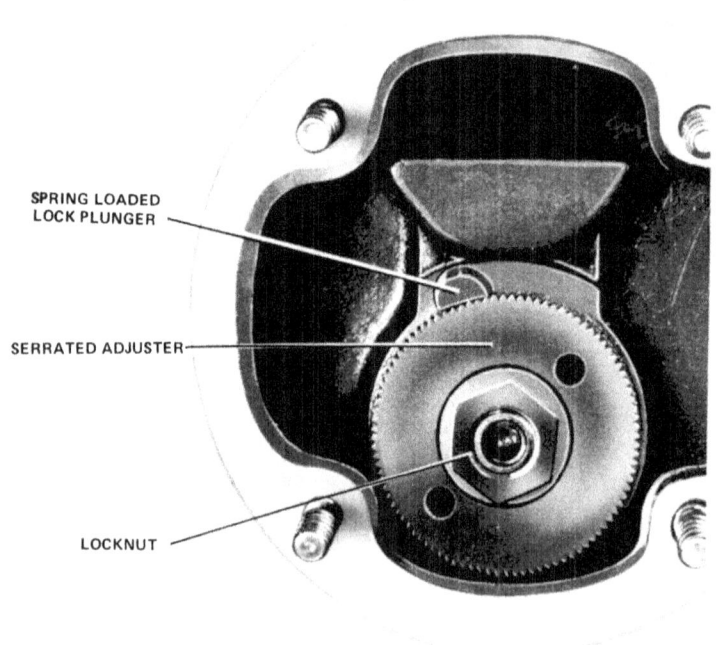

Top Timing Chain Adjuster Plate.

Top Dead Centre Marks for Numbers 1 to 6 Pistons.

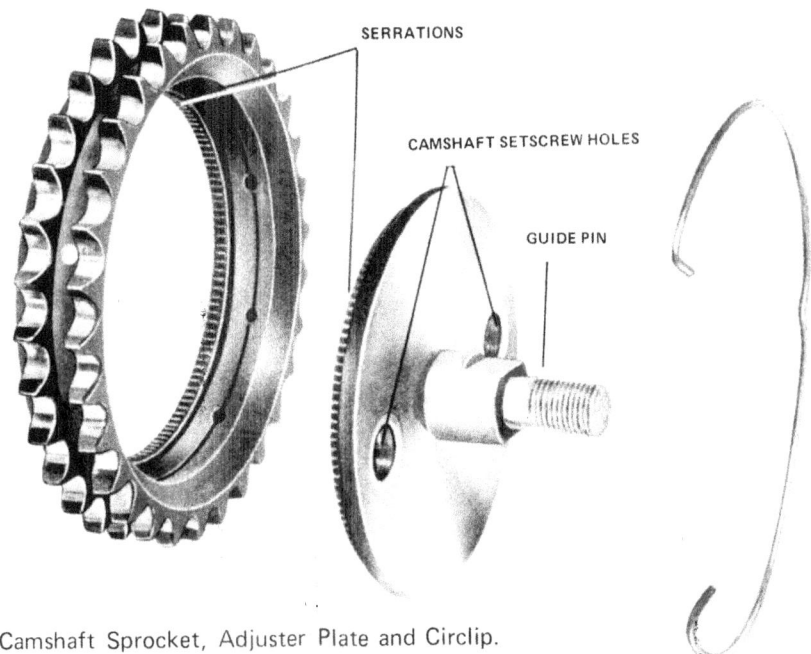

Camshaft Sprocket, Adjuster Plate and Circlip.

(5) Note the position of each inaccessible setscrew on each camshaft sprocket, rotate the engine until they are accessible and remove them.

(6) Turn the engine again to tdc on compression stroke of No. 6 cylinder. Check the tdc position at the pointer on the sump and the scale on the crankshaft damper, or the arrow marks on the flywheel and transmission housing.

(7) Tap the camshaft sprockets off the flanges of the camshafts.

(8) Position the keyways on the camshaft front bearing flanges using the valve timing gauge. Re-check that the tdc marks are in alignment.

(9) Withdraw the circlips retaining the adjusting plates to the camshaft sprockets. Press the adjusting plates forward until the serrations disengage.

(10) Replace the sprockets on the camshaft flanges and align the two holes in the adjuster plate with the two tapped holes in each camshaft flange.

(11) Press the adjustment plate rearwards to engage the serrations on the plates with the serrations in the sprockets.

NOTE: Ensure that holes in the plates are in exact alignment with the holes in the camshaft flanges. Turning the plates through 180° will facilitate alignment if they do not align exactly at first attempt.

(12) Fit the circlips to the sprockets and one setscrew to each accessible hole in each plate.

(13) Turn the engine until the other two holes are accessible and install the two remaining screws.

(14) Secure the four camshaft sprocket setscrews with new locking wire.

Further reassembly is a reversal of the dismantling procedures.

10. DISTRIBUTOR

TO REMOVE

(1) Disconnect the high tension leads from the spark plugs and the coil, and remove the distributor cap and leads from the engine.

(2) Disconnect the low tension lead and the vacuum advance control pipe at the distributor.

(3) Slacken the clamp plate pinch bolt and withdraw the distributor.

(4) Remove the setscrew and remove the clamp plate. Note the cork seal in the recess in the distributor drive bore in the crankcase.

TO INSTAL DISTRIBUTOR AND SET TIMING

(1) Fit the cork seal to the recess at the top of the bore for the distributor.

(2) Secure the distributor clamping plate on the cylinder block by the setscrew and slacken the pinch bolt.

(3) Set the micrometer adjustment on the distributor to the centre of the scale.

(4) Insert the distributor into the cylinder block bore with the vacuum control unit connection facing the cylinder block and rotate the rotor until the driving dog engages with the distributor drive shaft.

Ignition Timing Marks on Crankshaft Damper.

(5) Crank the engine until the rotor approaches the segment on the distributor cap which is wired to the front (No. 6) cylinder, and the ignition timing scale is the appropriate number of degrees before the pointer on the sump.

(6) With the rotor pointing to the segment for No. 6 cylinder, rotate the distributor gradually until the contact breaker points just commence to open. Tighten the distributor plate pinch bolt.

(7) Connect up the pipe from the vacuum control unit to the union on the front carburettor.

(8) Replace the distributor cover.

(9) Connect up the high tension leads from the distributor to the coil and to the plugs, bearing in mind the firing order and the anti-clockwise direction of rotation of the rotor. Connect the low tension lead from the distributor to the coil.

(10) Road test the vehicle and make fine adjustment on the micrometer adjuster which provides for six clicks in the advanced or retarded direction as necessary.

Also see *ELECTRICAL SYSTEM* for setting ignition using stroboscope.

11. CAMSHAFT AND TAPPETS

TO REMOVE

(1) Remove the dome nuts and copper washers securing the camshaft covers and remove the covers and gaskets. Check and record clearance between each tappet and non lift part of respective cam.

(2) Undo the Allen setscrews and remove the rpm generator and rubber sealing ring from the rear right side of the cylinder head.

(3) Similarly remove the sealing plug and rubber sealing ring from the left side of the cylinder head.

NOTE: Copper washers are fitted under the heads of the setscrews.

(4) Remove the locking wire from the camshaft adjuster plate setscrews.

(5) Rotate the engine until the keyway in the front bearing flange of each camshaft is at 90° to the adjacent cover face. No. 6 piston will be at tdc on compression stroke.

(6) Note the position of the inaccessible adjuster plate setscrews and rotate the engine till they become accessible. Remove these setscrews.

(7) Now turn the engine again to position as at (5) above and remove the two remaining setscrews.

(8) Tap the sprockets up and off their flanges.

(9) Progressively release the camshaft bearing cap nuts. Remove the nuts, spring washers and 'D' washers from the bearing studs.

(10) Remove the bearing caps.

NOTE: The bearing caps and cylinder head are numbered and the caps are located on the lower bearing housings by hollow dowels. This ensures correct reassembly and positive location.

(11) Lift the camshaft out from the cylinder head.

(12) Use a suction type valve grinding tool and lift off each tappet. Remove the adjusting pads.

NOTE: The tappets and adjusting pads must be kept in identifiable order to ensure correct reassembly and/or to carry out valve clearance, if necessary.

TO CHECK AND INSPECT

Check camshafts for wear and lift according to specifications.

Check camshaft bearings for wear. Bearings are serviced only in standard sizes.

Examine tappets and tappet guides for wear.

Clearance between tappet and tappet guide should be .0008" + .0011" / − .0000".

If tappet guides require replacement see *CYLINDER HEAD – TO RENEW TAPPET GUIDES*.

If the valve clearances determined prior to dismantling are not according to specifications select replacement adjusting pads in order to obtain the specified clearance.

NOTE: Pads are available in twenty six sizes (A to Z) from .085" to .110" by increments of .001".

Examine the pads for indentation and replace with appropriate sizes for correct valve clearances.

TO INSTALL

(1) If the crankshaft has been rotated since dismantling, turn the engine to bring No. 6 piston to tdc on compression stroke. Distributor rotor should be opposite segment for No. 6 cylinder.

(2) Fit bearing shells in their original positions and replace camshafts with the keyways in the front bearing flange at 90° to the adjacent cover face. Use the valve timing gauge.

(3) Install the bearing caps to their original positions and instal the 'D' washers, spring washers and nuts.

(4) Tighten down the bearing caps progressively and torque to 15 ft/lb.

(5) Install the sprockets to their respective camshaft flanges as described in *CYLINDER HEAD - TO INSTALL*.

Location of Matching Numbers on Cylinder Head and Camshaft Bearing Cap.

12. MANIFOLDS

TO REMOVE AND INSTALL INLET MANIFOLD

(1) Drain the radiator and remove the carburettors.

(2) Disconnect the top water hose and the by-pass hose from the inlet manifold water outlet pipe.

(3) Disconnect the lead to the temperature gauge sender unit.

(4) Disconnect the heater hose and the servo pipe from their respective connections at the rear of the manifold.

(5) Disconnect the accelerator shaft from the throttle spindle ball joint.

(6) Remove the screws from the backing plate and bush carrying plate.

NOTE: Ensure that the push-in cage nuts do not fall out of the bulkhead.

(7) With the throttles in the fully open position, remove the short spindle from the ball joint socket.

(8) Remove the eighteen nuts and spring washers, detach the heater pipe clips from the lower studs and withdraw the inlet manifolds.

(9) Remove six nuts and spring washers and remove the water manifold.

(10) Remove six nuts and spring washers and remove the air balance pipe.

Installation is a reversal of the removal procedure with attention to the following:

When fitting the throttle linkage, ensure that the backing plate is fitted with the cage nuts for the bush carrying plate offset towards the engine.

Ensure that the backing plate assembly is aligned before tightening up.

TO REMOVE AND INSTALL EXHAUST MANIFOLD

(1) Remove the eight brass nuts and spring washers fastening the exhaust pipe flanges to the exhaust manifolds.

(2) Remove the sixteen brass nuts and spring washers fastening the exhaust manifolds to the cylinder head.

(3) Remove the manifolds.

Installation is a reversal of the removal procedure.

Use new gaskets between the cylinder head and the manifolds.

Install new sealing rings between the manifold flanges and the exhaust pipe.

13. ENGINE MOUNTINGS

TO REMOVE AND INSTALL FRONT MOUNTINGS

(1) Use suitable sling and lifting tackle to hold the engine assembly at the front end.

(2) Undo the large set bolt and remove the spring washer, flat washer and bolt securing the front engine mounting bracket to the mounting rubber. Repeat this on the other side.

(3) Take the weight of the engine on the lifting tackle and raise the engine so that the front mounting brackets are just clear of the mounting rubbers.

(4) Undo the two bolts and self-locking nuts securing the front engine mounting to the support bracket on the front sub-frame. Remove the mounting. Repeat this on the other side.

Installation is a reversal of the removal procedure.

TO REMOVE AND INSTALL REAR MOUNTINGS

(1) Remove the eight brass nuts and spring washers fastening the exhaust pipe flanges to the exhaust manifolds.

(2) Remove the bolts from the five body mountings and withdraw the exhaust system from below.

(3) Remove the asbestos heat shield attached to the rear engine mounting plate.

(4) Use suitable sling and lifting tackle to take up the weight of the engine.

(5) Remove the self-locking nuts securing the lower ends of the rear engine mountings to the mounting plate through the holes in the plate.

(6) Remove the five bolts securing the mounting plate to the body and remove the plate.

(7) Remove propeller shaft tunnel cover and gearbox cowl as described in *ENGINE – TO REMOVE*.

(8) Remove the self-locking nuts securing the top ends of the engine mountings to the gearbox rear cover and withdraw the mountings from below.

Installation is a reversal of the removal procedure.

Ensure that new exhaust manifold sealing rings are installed.

TO ASSEMBLE ENGINE STABILISER

(1) With the link pin in its installed position on the clutch housing brackets screw the lower flanged washer upwards until the flange contacts the stabiliser rubber mounting.

NOTE: The lower washer is slotted on its upper face. Use a suitable screw driver through the centre hole of the stabiliser rubber mounting to raise the washer up on the pin.

(2) Fit the upper flanged washer and tighten it down on the stabiliser rubber mounting with the self-locking nut.

Holding Engine Rear Mounting Plate in Position with
Pin Punch (4.2 Model).

14. ENGINE FAULT DIAGNOSIS

(1) Engine will not start by normal cranking.

	Possible cause	*Remedy*
(a)	Dirty or corroded distributor points.	— Clean or renew and adjust points.
(b)	Carburettor flooding.	— Check needle valve and float, clean out fuel system.
(c)	Moisture on high tension wires and/or inside distributor cap.	— Dry out high tension wires and cap.
(d)	Dirt or water in carburettor and fuel system.	— Clean out carburettor and fuel system.
(e)	Incorrectly set spark plug gaps.	— Reset spark plug gaps to specification.
(f)	Faulty coil or capacitor.	— Test and renew faulty component.
(g)	Faulty low or high tension wires.	— Test and renew faulty wires.
(h)	Fuel vapour lock.	— Check source of vapour lock and insulate against heat.
(i)	Faulty fuel pump.	— Test and overhaul fuel pump.
(j)	Incorrectly set ignition timing.	— Check and retime ignition.
(k)	Broken or short-circuited low tension lead to distributor points.	— Test and renew leads.

(2) Engine will not start — weak or erratic cranking.

	Possible cause	*Remedy*
(a)	Weak or faulty battery.	— Recharge or renew battery.
(b)	Fault in starter lead or solenoid.	— Test and renew faulty component.
(c)	Faulty starter.	— Test and overhaul starter.

(3) Engine stalls.

Possible cause — *Remedy*

(a) Idling speed set too slow. — Readjust idling speed stop screw.
(b) Idling mixture too lean or rich. — Readjust idling mixture screw and idling speed screw.
(c) Carburettor flooding or float level incorrectly set. — Check needle valve or reset float level.
(d) Fault in coil or capacitor. — Test and renew faulty component.
(e) Valve clearance out of adjustment. — Adjust valve clearance.
(f) Air leak at inlet manifold or carburettor flange. — Tighten securing bolts or renew gaskets.

(4) Engine misses at idling speed.

Possible cause — *Remedy*

(a) Dirty, defective or incorrectly set spark plugs. — Clean or renew spark plugs.
(b) Burned or pitted distributor contact points. — Clean or renew and adjust contacts.
(c) Loose or broken low or high tension wires in ignition system. — Tighten or renew faulty component.
(d) Carburettor idling mixture out of adjustment. — Adjust mixture by jet screw.
(e) Burned or cracked distributor rotor. — Renew faulty component.
(f) Moisture on high tension wires, spark plug or distributor cap. — Dry out high tension system and cap.
(g) Carbon tracking or cracked distributor cap. — Clean or renew cap.
(h) Weak or faulty battery and/or corroded terminals. — Recharge or renew battery and/or clean or renew terminals.
(i) Carburettor flooding or incorrect float level setting. — Check needle valve or reset float level.
(j) Faulty coil or capacitor. — Test and renew faulty component.
(k) Excessive wear in distributor shaft and bushes or contact breaker cam. — Renew worn components.
(l) Burned, warped or pitted valves. — Carry out top overhaul on engine.

(5) Engine misses on acceleration.

Possible cause — *Remedy*

(a) Distributor points dirty or incorrectly adjusted. — Clean and readjust points.
(b) Spark plug/s dirty, faulty or gap set too wide. — Clean or renew and reset faulty plug/s.
(c) Dirt or water in carburettor. — Clean and blow out carburettor and fuel pump filter.
(d) Coil or capacitor faulty. — Renew defective component.
(e) Incorrect ignition timing. — Check and reset ignition timing.
(f) Burned, warped or pitted valves. — Carry out top overhaul on engine.

(6) Engine misses at high speed.

Possible cause — *Remedy*

(a) Distributor points dirty or incorrectly adjusted. — Clean and readjust points.
(b) Spark plug/s dirty, faulty or gap set too wide. — Clean or renew and reset faulty plug/s.
(c) Dirt or water in carburettor. — Clean out carburettor and fuel pump filter.
(d) Burned or cracked distributor rotor. — Renew faulty component.
(e) Faulty coil or capacitor. — Renew faulty component.
(f) Dirt in carburettor jet. — Lift air valve to clear jet.
(g) Incorrect ignition timing. — Check and re-set ignition timing.
(h) Excessive wear in distributor, shaft or cam. — Renew faulty components.

(7) Engine lacks power.

	Possible cause	*Remedy*
(a)	Dirty or incorrectly set spark plugs.	— Clean and reset gap to specification.
(b)	Dirt or water in carburettor and fuel system.	— Drain and clean out fuel system and carburettor.
(c)	Incorrect ignition timing.	— Check and re-set ignition timing.
(d)	Incorrect carburettor float level.	— Check and re-set float level.
(e)	Faulty fuel pump.	— Check and overhaul fuel pump.
(f)	Incorrect valve clearance.	— Check and readjust valve clearance.
(g)	Faulty distributor automatic advance.	— Check and rectify or renew.
(h)	Restricted muffler or tail pipe.	— Check and clean as necessary.
(i)	Faulty coil or capacitor.	— Renew faulty component.
(j)	Burned or cracked distributor rotor.	— Renew faulty component.
(k)	Excessive wear in distributor shaft or cam.	— Renew faulty component/s.
(l)	Incorrect valve timing.	— Check and re-set as necessary.
(m)	Burned, warped or pitted valves.	— Carry out top overhaul on engine.
(n)	Blown cylinder head gasket.	— Renew gasket.
(o)	Loss of compression.	— Carry out compression test and rectify.

(8) Noisy valve operation.

	Possible cause	*Remedy*
(a)	Incorrectly adjusted clearance.	— Check and adjust to specification.
(b)	Weak or broken valve springs.	— Check and renew faulty component.
(c)	Worn valve guides.	— Renew or ream and fit oversize valve/s.
(d)	Worn tappets.	— Renew tappets.

(9) Big end bearing noise.

	Possible cause	*Remedy*
(a)	Lack of adequate oil supply.	— Check oil level in sump, condition of oil pump and relief valve. Renew oil filter element.
(b)	Excessive bearing clearance.	— Renew bearing shells check and regrind journals if oval.
(c)	Thin oil or crankcase dilution.	— Change to correct oil grade. Check operating conditions and cooling system thermostat.
(d)	Low oil pressure.	— Check pressure relief valve and spring, oil filter by-pass valve.
(e)	Misaligned big end bearings.	— Align connecting rods and renew bearings if necessary.

(10) Main bearing noise (apparent).

	Possible cause	*Remedy*
(a)	Loose flywheel.	— Tighten securing bolts to specified torque.
(b)	Loose vibration damper.	— Renew pulley and vibration damper assembly.
(c)	Low oil pressure.	— Check bearing to journal clearance, check condition of oil pump and pressure relief valve. Recondition as necessary.
(d)	Excessive crankshaft end play.	— Renew main bearing shells.
(e)	Crankshaft journals out of round and excessive bearing to journal clearance.	— Regrind journals and renew bearings (undersize).
(f)	Insufficient oil supply.	— Replenish oil in sump to correct level.

(11) Excessive oil consumption.

Possible cause	Remedy
(a) Oil leaks.	– Check and renew gaskets as necessary.
(b) Damaged or worn valve stem oil seals (late 4.2).	– Renew damaged or worn components.
(c) Excessive clearance, valve stem to valve guide.	– Renew valve guides and valves, or fit oversize valves.
(d) Worn or broken rings.	– Renew rings.
(e) Rings too tight or stuck in grooves.	– Renew rings and clean out ring grooves.
(f) Excessive wear in cylinders, pistons and rings.	– Recondition cylinders and renew pistons and rings.
(g) Compression rings incorrectly installed. Oil rings clogged or broken.	– Renew rings.

(12) Drop in oil pressure.

Possible cause	Remedy
(a) Oil level low in sump.	– Check and replenish to full mark.
(b) Thin or diluted oil.	– Change to correct oil grade and rectify source of dilution.
(c) Oil pressure relief valve stuck or spring broken.	– Free valve or renew broken spring.
(d) Excessive bearing clearance.	– Renew bearing shells or recondition journals as necessary.
(e) Excessive wear of oil pump components.	– Renew or recondition oil pump.
(f) Air leak in oiling system.	– Rectify as necessary.

FUEL SYSTEM

SPECIFICATIONS

CARBURETTORS

Make	S.U.
Type	H.D.8
Size	2"
Number Fitted	3
Jet needle:	
Compression ratio 8 to 1	UM) with standard
Compression ratio 9 to 1	UM) air cleaner
Size of jet	0.125"
Needle valve assembly	
(From Eng.No.RA.2464)	Delrin (spring loaded pin type)
Type of air cleaner	Dry, with paper element

FUEL PUMP

Early type:
- Make .... Lucas
- Type .... Electric (2FP)
- Delivery pressure .... 2 psi

*Later type:
- Introduced – open 2 seater . Chassis No. 850786 (RHD) 880619 (LHD)
- Fixed head Coupe .... Chassis No. 861386 (RHD) 889510 (LHD)
- Delivery pressure .... 3 to 3½ psi

*Delrin float chamber needles and seats must be fitted with the later type fuel pump.

1. DESCRIPTION

Three S.U. HD.8 type carburettors with manual choke control are fitted.

The manually operated mixture control works simultaneously on all three carburettors in two stages. The first stage slightly increases the throttle opening and the second stage withdraws the jet from the jet needle thereby richening the mixture. A red indicator light is installed on the dash and remains illuminated as long as the mixture control is in operation, when the control is returned to the RUN position the light automatically switches off.

The size of the main air passage over the jet and effective area of the jet, is automatically variable according to the amount of throttle opening required. A single jet is incorporated and covers the complete throttle range. Fuel

Typical Carburettor Assembly Arrangement.

from the carburettor bowl is fed to the jet and tube assembly, a tapered metering needle attached to the piston works within the jet and governs the amount of fuel fed to the engine.

A needle valve and seating in the float chamber is operated by a float and lever which controls the level of fuel in the float chamber. From Engine No. RA2464 a modified type of float chamber cover assembly is fitted which includes a plastic needle fitted with a spring loaded pin together with a seat and float level fork. This modified assembly can be interchanged with the previous type as a complete assembly, or alternatively the new type needle and seat can be fitted to the previous type cover. However the old type needle and seat cannot be fitted to the modified covers, nor can the new type float lever fork be fitted to the previous type cover. The modified cover has on the inside of the cover AUD2283 or 2284 for further identification.

2. ROUTINE MAINTENANCE

2500 MILES STAGE

(1) Remove the cap on top of each piston housing complete with the valve, use SAE20 engine oil and fill the bore of the piston spindle.

(2) Check the idling of the engine and reset if necessary.

(3) Apply a few drops of light oil to all accelerator linkage moving parts.

5000 MILES STAGE

(1) Disconnect the fuel feed line from each carburettor and remove and clean each filter gauze. Exercise care while fitting to avoid damaging the threads of the banjo bolt and also ensure that washers are correctly seated.

(2) Remove the fuel filter glass bowl together with the filter and gasket. Wash clean the bowl and filter gauze in petrol and install with a new gasket.

10,000 MILES STAGE

(1) Remove the fuel tank drain plug and filter assembly and drain off the fuel into a clean suitable container.

(2) Wash the filter clean in petrol and check for damage.

(3) If necessary replace the gasket on the drain plug, lubricate the filter O ring and insert the filter over the fuel inlet pipe, screw up the drain plug.

(4) Filter the fuel drained from the tank to avoid returning any sediment to the tank when refilling.

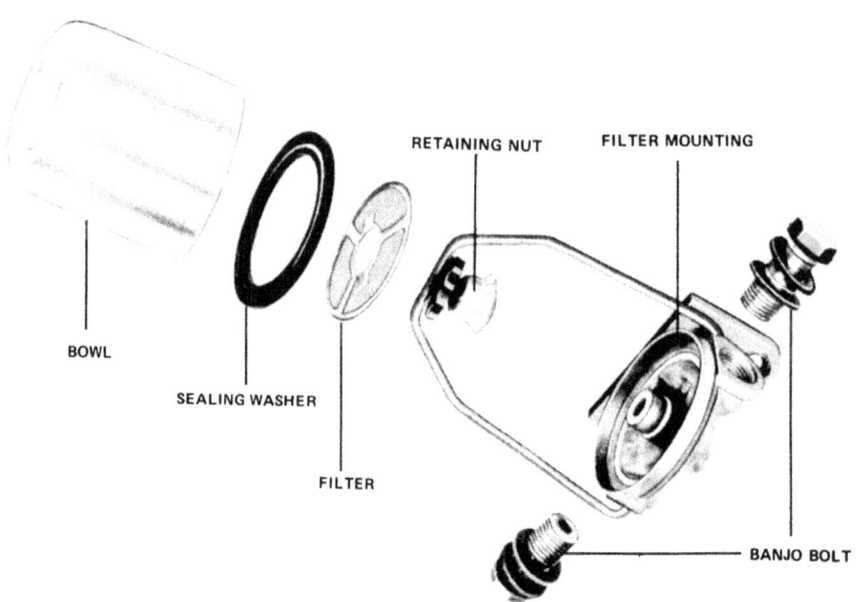

Exploded View of Fuel Supply Line Filter Components.

3. CARBURETTORS

TO REMOVE AND INSTALL (3.8)

(1) Loosen and remove the two butterfly nuts retaining the air cleaner elbow to the carburettor trumpets and detach the elbow.

(2) Remove the six nuts and washers retaining the trumpet plate to the carburettors and remove together with the three gaskets.

(3) Take out the banjo union bolt from each float chamber and remove the fibre washers and filters.

(4) Disconnect the clip retaining the float chamber overflow pipes to the oil filter.

(5) Unhook the three butterfly return springs and release each throttle link from the clip retaining it to the throttle spindle lever.

(6) Release the choke cable outer conduit and inner cable from the mixture control linkage.

(7) Disconnect the vacuum advance pipe at the front carburettor.

(8) Loosen off and remove the four nuts, washers and return spring bracket attaching each carburettor to each of the three inlet manifolds.

(9) Withdraw all three carburettors as an assembly from the inlet manifolds, and if necessary, release the mixture control linkage from each carburettor by taking out the split pins and clevis pins.

Installation is a reversal of the removal procedure.

NOTE: Ensure new gaskets are fitted at the time of installation.

TO REMOVE AND INSTALL (4.2 and 2+2)

(1) Disconnect the battery and drain off the cooling system.

(2) Disconnect and remove the water hose between the header tank and inlet manifold.

(3) Loosen and remove the two butterfly nuts retaining the air cleaner elbow to the carburettor trumpets and detach the elbow.

(4) Unhook and remove the throttle return springs.

(5) Disconnect the two wire connections from the thermostat fan control located in the header tank.

(6) Release the clip at the breather pipe hose connection.

(7) Remove the six nuts and washers retaining the trumpet plate to the carburettors and remove together with the three gaskets.

(8) Take out the banjo union bolt from each float chamber and remove the fibre washers and filters.

(9) Disconnect the clip retaining the float chamber overflow pipes to the oil filter.

(10) Release the choke cable outer conduit and inner cable from the mixture control linkage.

(11) Disconnect the vacuum advance pipe at the front carburettor.

(12) Free the retaining clip and release the throttle linkage at the rear carburettor.

NOTE: On 2+2 cars with automatic transmission it will be necessary to disconnect the kickdown cable at the back of the cylinder head.

(13) Disconnect the wire connection from the oil pressure switch.

(14) Disconnect the heater pipes at the water manifold and below the inlet manifold.

(15) Loosen off and remove as an assembly the inlet manifold and carburettors.

(16) Loosen off and remove the four nuts, washers and return spring bracket attaching each carburettor to the inlet manifold.

(17) Withdraw all three carburettors as assembly from the inlet manifold, and if necessary, release the mixture control linkage from each carburettor by taking out the split pins and clevis pins.

Installation is a reversal of the removal procedure.

NOTE: Ensure new gaskets are fitted at the time of installation. On 2+2 cars with automatic transmission, adjust the kickdown cable as described in AUTOMATIC TRANSMISSION.

PISTON AND SUCTION CHAMBER – TO CLEAN

(1) Whenever the carburettors are removed for attention or at least after about six to nine months, depending on operating conditions, both the piston and the suction chamber bore should be thoroughly cleaned.

(2) Take out the piston damper by unscrewing the cap located at the top of the suction chamber.

(3) Remove the four mounting screws from the suction chamber and detach the suction chamber and piston.

(4) Extract the piston from the chamber.

(5) With a soft clean cloth and some clean petrol, thoroughly clean the piston and bore of the chamber and allow to dry.

NOTE: Do not use any abrasive material or metal polish for cleaning as this will cause damage.

(6) Assemble the piston in the chamber and apply thin oil to the piston rod.

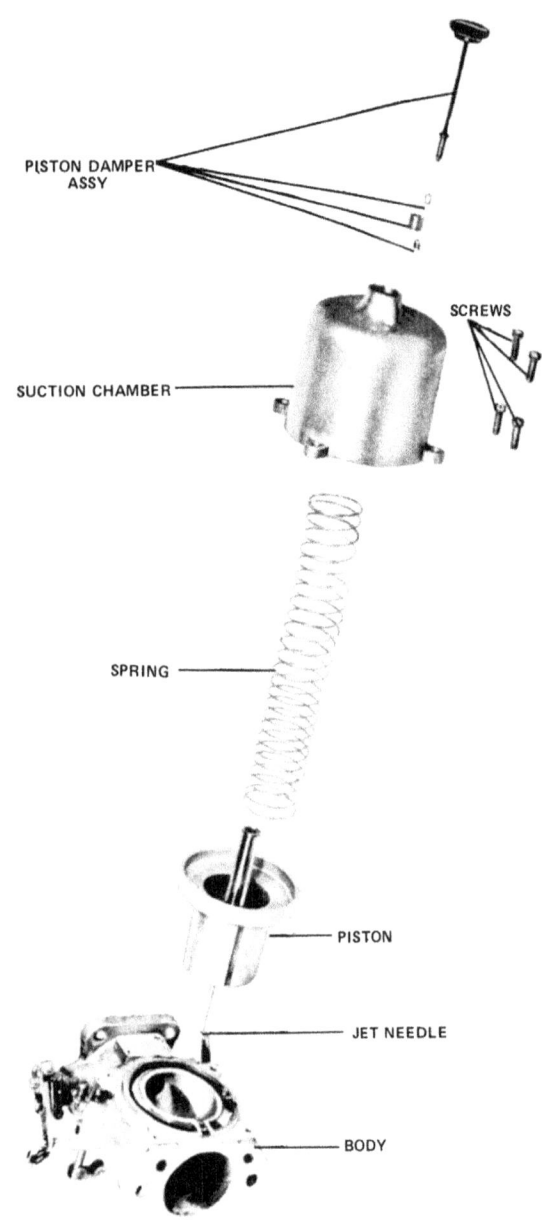

Dismantled View of Suction Chamber and Piston Components.

TO TUNE-UP CARBURETTOR

(1) Remove spark plugs and contact breaker points, clean thoroughly and reset point gaps in accordance with the manufacturers specifications. Refer to *ENGINE* section.

(2) The distributor should be inspected to ensure that it is in good order and that the vacuum advance is in good working condition without any leaks at the connections.

(3) The ignition timing should be set according to specification. Refer to appropriate section.

NOTE: As the ignition timing affects the tuning of carburettors, it is very important that it is set correctly. It may also be advisable to ascertain the engine conditon in relation to the compression also clearances of the valves.

(4) Disconnect and remove the air cleaner elbow from the trumpet plate.

(5) Disconnect the trumpet plate from the carburettor flanges by undoing the six securing nuts and washers.

NOTE: Run the engine to achieve the normal operating temperature before proceeding further.

(6) Slacken the pinch bolts which secure the throttle levers to the throttle spindle.

(7) On each carburettor fully close the butterfly valve and in this position tighten the pinch bolt with the throttle lever in the midway position. This operation should be carried out on the other two carburettors.

(8) To see if all the throttles are working together, notice the movement of the throttle stops located at the left-hand side of the spindles.

(9) The slow running volume screws should be fully screwed down and then unscrewed two complete turns.

(10) Undo the four securing screws and remove the piston and suction chamber.

(11) Disconnect the mixture control rod from below the front and rear carburettors.

(12) Each mixture adjusting screw should be unscrewed until each jet is level with the bridge of each carburettor.

(13) Install the pistons and suction chambers and check that the piston moves freely down to the bridge. This can be tested by operating the piston lifting pin located below the flange on which the suction chamber is mounted. Screw in each mixture adjusting screw two and a half turns.

(14) Start the engine and set all the three carburettors by turning the slow running adjustment screws an equal amount each until an idle speed of 500 rpm is obtained. To obtain a uniform setting on all three carburettors, compare the air intake hiss at each carburettor and adjust the slow running screws until it is similar on all three carburettors.

NOTE: On 4.2 cars with manual transmission set the idle speed to 700 rpm.

(15) With a uniform intake at all three carburettors, turn each mixture adjusting screw an equal amount either up or down until the engine is running evenly and the idle speed is at its fastest point.

NOTE: The mixture is weakened by unscrewing the mixture adjusting screws and made richer by screwing down.

(16) If the engine idle speed has increased with the mixture adjustment return it to the correct speed by adjusting the slow running volume screws.

(17) Check the mixture at each carburettor, one at a time, commencing from the front, by raising the piston with the piston lifting pin approximately .03125". The mixture strength will be indicated as follows:

Mixture correct – engine speed will increase momentarily and then steady.

Mixture rich – engine speed increases and remains faster.

Mixture weak – engine speed decreases.

(18) Carry out the necessary adjustment at each carburettor until the correct mixture is obtained. It is adviseable to recheck the front carburettor after adjustment of the others.

(19) A further check can be made at the exhaust where the mixture strength will be indicated as follows:

Mixture correct – A regular and even exhaust note.

Mixture rich – A regular misfire with black coloured exhaust.

Mixture weak – An irregular misfire with colourless exhaust.

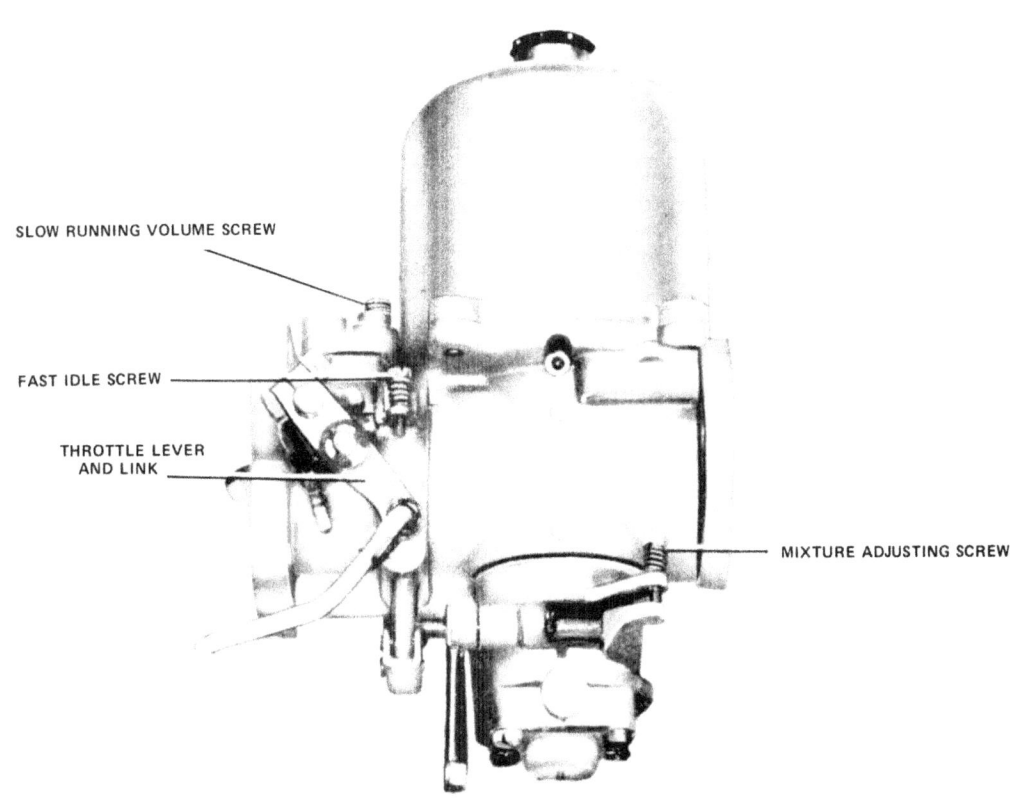

Side View of Carburettor.

(20) Connect the mixture control cable so that there is .0625" free movement at the dashboard control lever before the linkage begins to operate the jet levers.

TO ADJUST FAST IDLE SPEED

(1) Position the mixture control lever on the dashboard to a midway point but just prior to where the mixture adjusting screw levers commence movement.

(2) By adjusting the fast idle screws in the throttle stops, set the engine speed to 1,000 rpm at normal operating temperature.

TO CHECK AND ADJUST FLOAT LEVEL

(1) Remove the float chamber top covers.

(2) For checking the float level, it will be necessary to obtain a .4275" diameter metal rod.

(3) By holding the top cover in an inverted position, insert the metal rod between the cover face and the curve of the float lever fork. The needle valve should be in the shut-off position but the spring loaded plunger, in the needle valve, should not be compressed.

(4) The straight portion of the float lever fork should be parallel with the face of the top cover which checks the

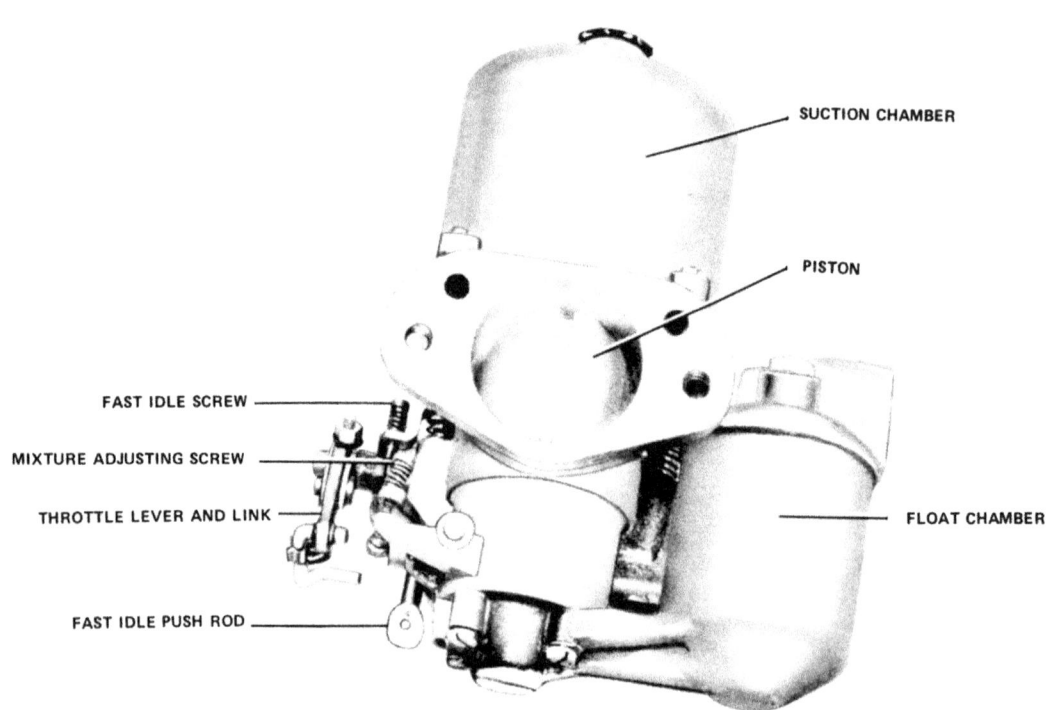

Front View of Carburettor.

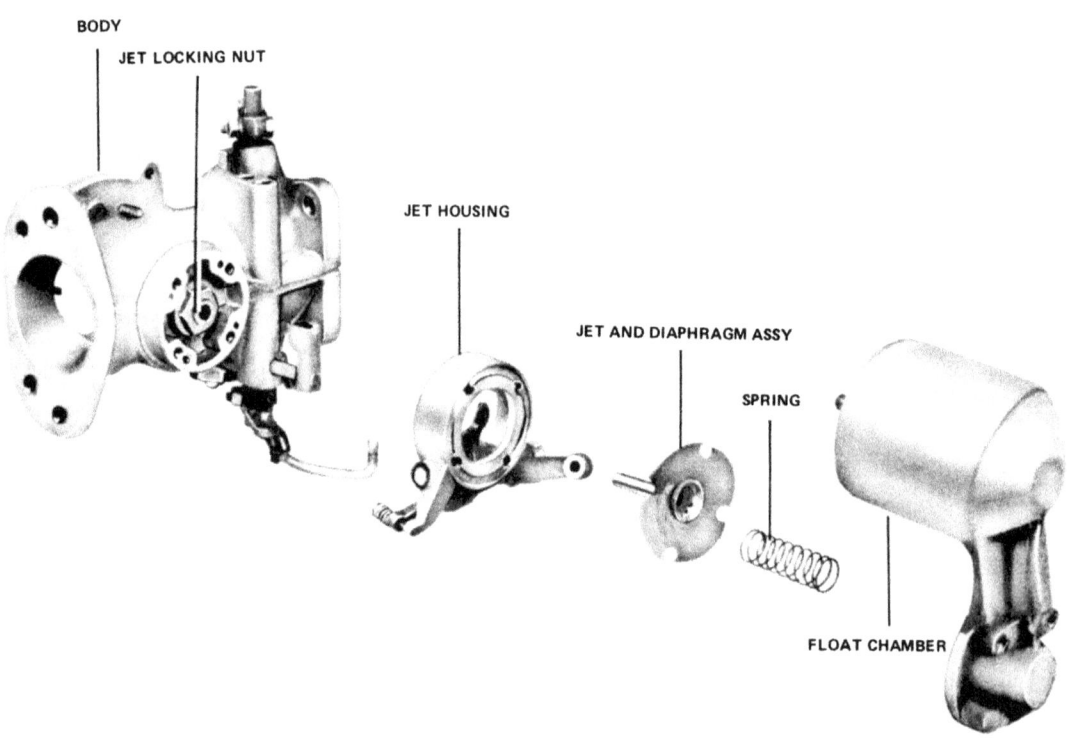

Dismantled View of Jet Housing Components.

lever setting. Adjustment if necessary should be effected at the neck of the curve by bending in the required direction. Both prongs of the fork must be level.

NOTE: With a carburettor that is functioning properly and free from flooding, where the setting only slightly differs from the specified setting, it is not advisable to alter the existing setting.

TO CENTRE THE JET

(1) The procedure previously described should be followed for removing the carburettor.

NOTE: During this operation care should be exercised to avoid bending the carburettor needle.

(2) The float chamber should be removed from the main carburettor body by unscrewing the four securing screws.

(3) Withdraw the jet housing and jet.

(4) Remove the hydraulic damper by removing the cap on top of the piston suction chamber.

(5) Slacken the jet lock nut about half a turn and replace the jet and diaphragm.

NOTE: The jet can be considered correctly set when the piston drops and comes in contact with the jet bridge with a smart click.

(6) Push up the jet diaphragm to the limit and with some suitable object, gently press down the piston to contact the jet bridge. At the same time gently tap the side of the carburettor body and secure the jet lock nut.

NOTE: The holes in the jet diaphragm should have been lined up with the screw holes in the carburettor body during the above operation.

(7) By way of testing the correctness of the centering operation, allow the piston to come into contact with the jet bridge and note if the sound is the same as was noticed previously. In case of a difference in sound, the procedure will have to be repeated till the correct setting is obtained.

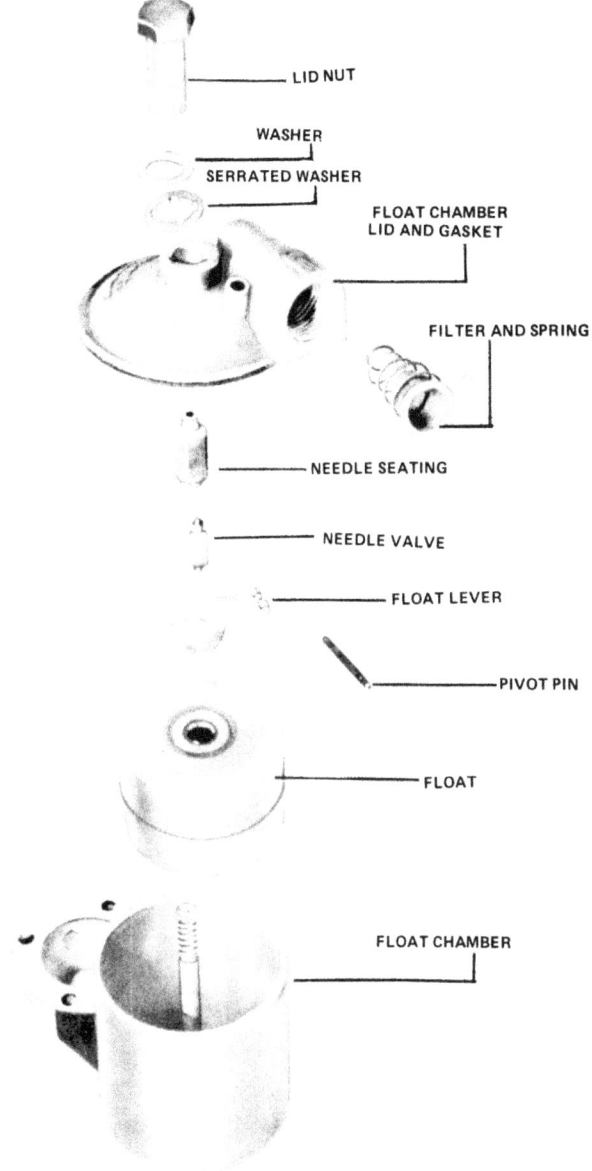

Dismantled View of Float Chamber Components.

4. FUEL PUMP

DESCRIPTION

3.8 models are fitted with the Lucas 2FP electric fuel pump which is located within the petrol tank.

The pump delivers fuel at 2psi, is connected through the ignition switch and therefore cannot operate until the ignition is switched on.

As a means of safety a 5 amp fuse has been incorporated in the electrical circuit and is located behind the instrument panel. If any fault should develop in the pump or at any of the connections, the fuse will blow. If replacement becomes necessary, ensure that a fuse of the same value is fitted.

An improved fuel pump is fitted to 4.2 and 2+2 models and from certain chassis Nos. (see specifications) on 3.8 models.

The improved fuel pump is mounted externally to the petrol tank but as in the previous pump connected electrically through the ignition switch.

Fuel is delivered at a pressure of 3 to 3½ psi. The improved pump can only be interchanged with the previous type where the carburettors are fitted with Delrin float chamber needles and seats.

TO REMOVE (EARLY TYPE PUMP)

(1) Disconnect the battery.

(2) From the luggage boot, remove the floor mat.

(3) Remove the boot floor panels after taking out the retaining screws.

(4) From the spare wheel compartment remove the cover from the cable junction box and disconnect the cables. Note the cable colours to ensure correct connection when installing.

(5) Release the delivery pipe connection from the fuel pump.

(6) Drain the petrol tank into a suitable container.

(7) Undo the securing screws from the pump carrier plate and take out the carrier plate and fuel pump complete from the tank.

NOTE: Avoid damaging the sealing joint between the carrier plate and the petrol tank.

(8) Remove the nut securing the cable conduit to the carrier plate. Disconnect the delivery pipe union from the pump.

(9) Remove the two mounting bolts and separate the carrier plate from the fuel pump.

Installation is a reversal of the removal procedure.

NOTE: While installing pump, ensure that the sealing joint between the carrier and tank is in good condition and that the star washer is in position to serve as an earth between the pump and mounting bracket.

(10) With the fuel pump in position, install the drain plug assembly.

NOTE: The drain plug cork gasket should be in good condition.

TO REMOVE (LATER TYPE PUMP)

(1) Disconnect the electric connection from the end bakelite cover terminal.

(2) Disconnect both inlet and outlet petrol connections.

(3) Remove the pump by undoing the two self-locking nuts from the mounting studs in the luggage boot.

(4) Remove and inspect the two mounting rubbers and if worn or deteriorated they should be renewed.

Installation is a reversal of the removal procedure.

TO CHECK AND ADJUST (EARLY TYPE PUMP)

If the pump fails to operate correctly after following the procedure given below it should be exchanged for a replacement unit.

It is essential that during testing of the pump on the bench, that no sparking at electrical contacts is allowed to occur and that there are no naked lights or flames present.

Lack of fuel

(1) Ensure that there is fuel in the tank and no obstructions in the petrol line between the tank and carburettors.

(2) Check all electrical connections in the anti-flash bracket located in the spare wheel compartment.

(3) Ensure that the fuse located behind the instrument panel is not blown, if a replacement fuse of the same value is fitted and blows, suspect a short circuit in either the supply cable or pump unit.

(4) Provided the fuse is not blown, check the current and voltage at the terminals in the anti-flash bracket with a voltmeter and ammeter.

NOTE: With the ignition switched on, a reading of 12 volts is required, the current should not be in excess of 1.8 amperes. No current or excessive current indicates a faulty pump. No voltage indicates broken or faulty connection in the feed, earth or switch.

Excess of fuel

(1) Check that the needle valves and seats in the carburettors are free of obstruction and are still serviceable.

(2) Connect a pressure gauge to the fuel delivery line at the carburettor end, switch on the ignition and check the gauge reading which should be 2 to 2½ psi.

(3) If the pressure is in excess of 2½ psi it will be necessary to remove the pump unit from the tank as described previously.

(4) With the pump removed from the tank, release the locknut at the pump valve and turn the adjusting screw in an anti-clockwise direction to reduce the pressure.

(5) Check the pressure prior to installing the unit in the tank by submerging in a suitable container filled with clean kerosene. Connect the pump cables to a fully charged battery, the black cable on the pump to the positive battery terminal, and check the delivery pressure.

(6) When installing the pump unit in the fuel tank ensure that the seal is in sound condition, if necessary renew.

TO DISMANTLE (LATER TYPE PUMP)

(1) Remove the end bakelite cover by taking out the insulating sleeve, nut, Lucas connector and special washer.

(2) Undo the contact blade screw from the pedestal and take out the condenser from its clip and the washer and terminal from the blade screw. Also take out the contact blade.

(3) With a broad blade screwdriver undo the screws securing the coil housing. Remove the earth screw and connector.

(4) Separate the coil housing from the pump body.

(5) Remove the diaphragm and spindle assembly by unscrewing the assembly in an anti-clockwise direction.

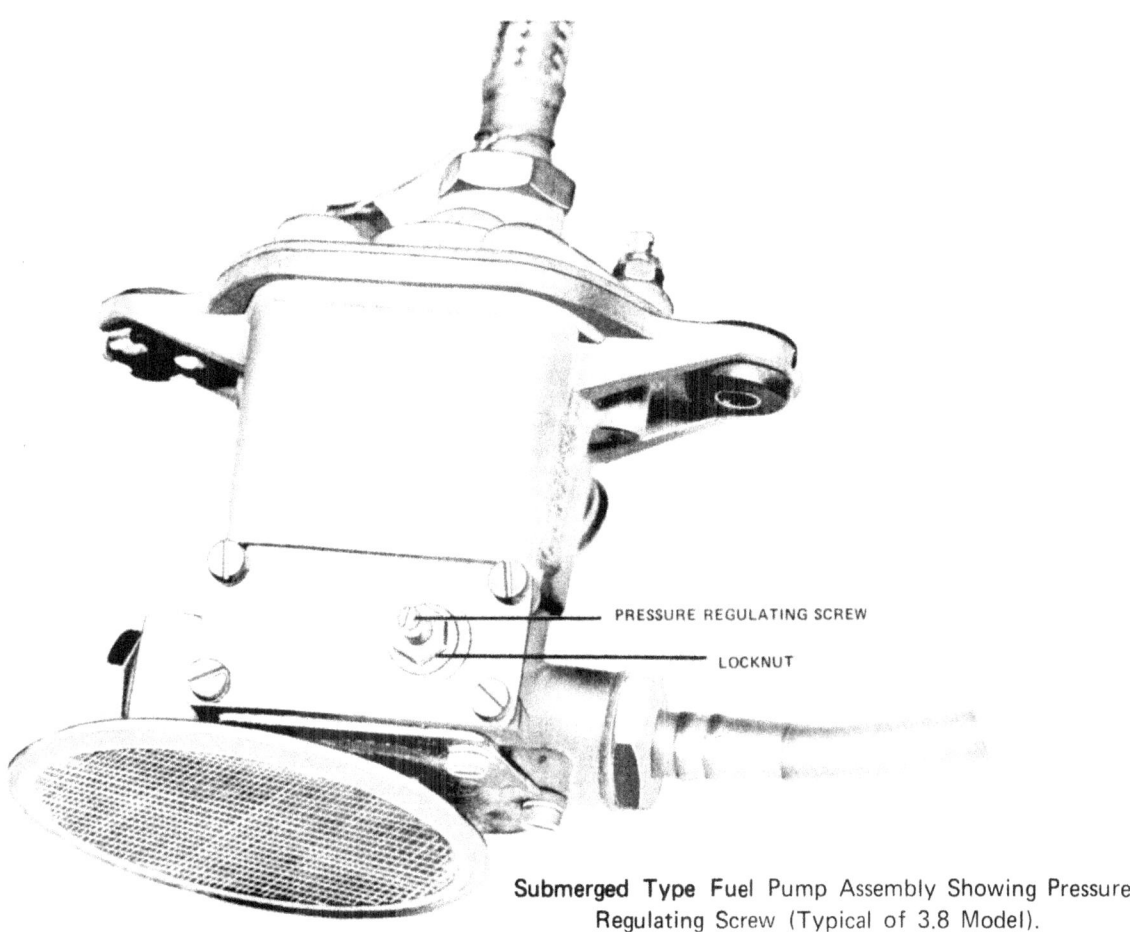

Submerged Type Fuel Pump Assembly Showing Pressure Regulating Screw (Typical of 3.8 Model).

NOTE: Care should be exercised in retrieving the eleven brass rollers fitted in the diaphragm and spindle assembly. The diaphragm and its spindle should always be renewed together and not separately.

(6) Take out the end cover sealing washer and unscrew the nut, remove the special lead washer by cutting it with some suitable tool.

(7) The terminal tag spring washer should be taken out.

(8) Take out the two 2BA screws securing the pedestal to the coil housing and dislodge the earth terminal tag and condenser support clip.

(9) Slant the pedestal and take out the terminal stud.

(10) Remove the pedestal with the rocker mechanism attached.

(11) After pressing out the steel fixing pin, separate the pedestal from the rocker mechanism.

(12) Take out the two valve clamp plate securing screws and retrieve the valve covers, valves, seal washers and filter.

NOTE: Unless it is absolutely necessary and pressure testing equipment is available, it is advisable not to dismantle the delivery flow smoothing device. With this in mind proceed as follows:

(13) Remove the four 4BA screws and dismantle the delivery flow smoothing device comprising the vented cover, diaphragm spring, rubber 'O' sealing ring, spring cap, diaphragm, barrier, diaphragm plate and sealing washer.

(14) Remove the cover and gasket from the inlet air bottle by unscrewing the 2BA screw.

(15) Remove inlet and outlet connections.

TO CHECK AND INSPECT

(1) It will be noticed that a gummy substance has accumulated on certain components. The fuel pump diaphragm should be carefully inspected to see that it is not affected and thereby rendered unserviceable, in case of any doubt it should be replaced.

(2) Steel and brass components can be reclaimed, if not damaged, by first boiling in a 20% solution of caustic soda after which dip in a strong nitric acid solution. Lastly, thoroughly wash in boiling water and then dry.

(3) Any other light alloy components should be cleaned in methylated spirits.

(4) Throughly clean the pump body and carefully inspect for cracks or any other damage.

(5) Check all the plastic valves.

(6) With a suitable brush clean the filter and check for any damage.

(7) Check the coil leads and tags for any damage.

(8) Check the condition of the contact breaker points and if they are badly pitted, the rockers and spring blade should be renewed.

(9) Check the pedestal for cracks or any other damage, the most likely part being the narrow ridge on the edge of the rectangular hole where the contact blade rests.

(10) Very carefully check condition of the diaphragm and in case of any doubt it should be renewed.

(11) Check the end cover non-return valve to ensure that the small valve is free.

(12) Check the narrow tongue on the valve cage for any distortion. .0625" is approximately the valve lift.

(13) Check the delivery flow smoothing unit and replace any damaged component. If there is any doubt as to the condition of the diaphragm, replace with new.

(14) Check the cover of the inlet air bottle for damage and the body for corrosion. In case the corrosion is excessive or the recess badly pitted, discard the body and fit new.

(15) Discard all fibre and cork washers, gaskets and 'O' sealing rings. Rollers should be carefully inspected and replaced if necessary.

TO REASSEMBLE

(1) Place the pedestal in the inverted position and by pushing the hardened steel pin through the holes in the rockers and pedestal supports fit the rocker assembly to the pedestal.

NOTE: If it becomes necessary to replace the hardened steel pin which secures the rocker mechanism to the pedestal, this should only be done with a genuine component.

(2) To obtain the correct throw-over action, position the centre lever so that with the inner rocker spindle in tension against the back of the contact point, the centre lever spring is above the spindle on which the white rollers run. Check that the rockers can freely swing on the pivot pin and that the arms do not bind on the legs of the pedestal.

NOTE: It may be necessary to square up the rockers with a long nose pair of pliers.

(3) The back of the pedestal is recessed to fit the square head of the 2BA terminal stud. Install and correctly position the stud.

(4) After assembling the 2BA spring washer, pass the terminal stud through the 2BA terminal tag then fit the special lead washer and also, to make a better contact, fit the cone nut with the coned side towards the lead washer.

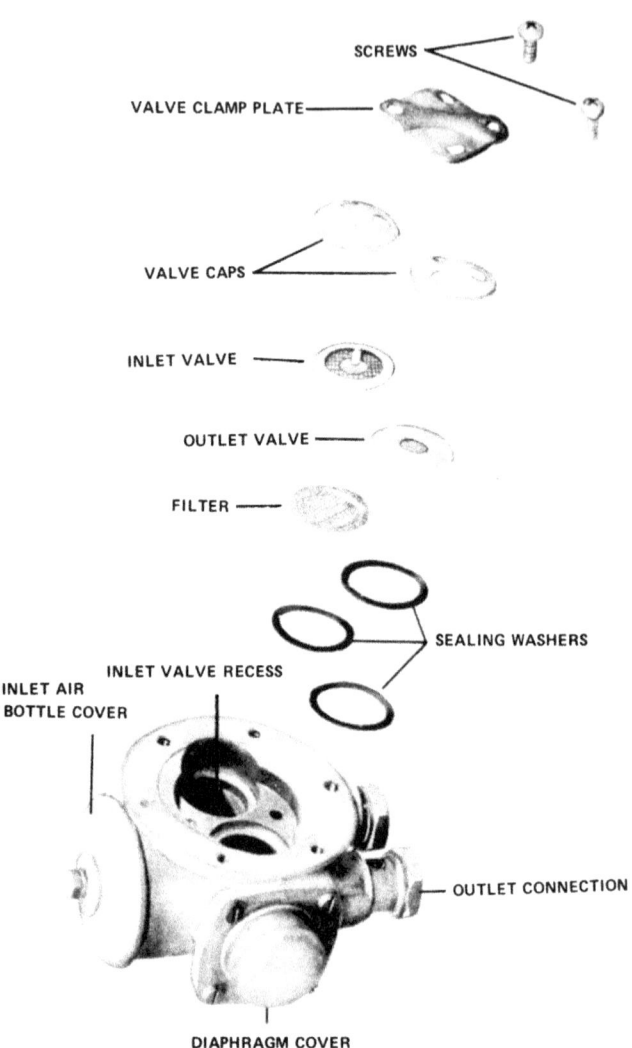

Exploded View of Valve Arrangement for Pump Body (4.2 Model Shown).

(5) Finally add the end cover seal washer after tightening the 2BA nut.

(6) Fit the 2BA pedestal screws and position the condenser wire clip in the 9 o'clock position on the left hand screw in between the pedestal and earth tag, assemble the pedestal to the coil housing and secure with the two 2BA pedestal screws.

NOTE: When a condenser is installed, the spring wire clip serves the purpose of a spring washer.

(7) Exercise care while tightening the screws and ensure that the earth tag does not turn, otherwise this is likely to break the flex wires. The screws should also be tightening sufficiently but not to damage the pedestal.

NOTE: The contact blade should not be fitted at this stage.

(8) With the large diameter facing the coil, position the armature spring within the coil housing.

(9) Position the small neoprene impact washer in the armature recess without using any jointing compound. Install the diaphragm by passing the spindle through the hole in the coil and securing the threaded end into the trunnion in the centre of the rocker assembly.

(10) The diaphragm spindle should be screwed into the rocker assembly sufficiently so that the rocker will not throw-over.

NOTE: This operation must not be confused with jamming the armature on the coil housing steps.

(11) Turn back the edge of the diaphragm to facilitate dropping the eleven brass centralising rollers in the recess in the coil.

(12) The contact blade should now be fitted and adjust the finger settings as described under contact gap setting and then remove the blade very carefully.

(13) Hold the coil housing assembly horizontally in the left hand and with the right hand thumb, firmly and steadily push the diaphragm needle.

(14) Unscrew the diaphragm and with the right hand thumb, press and release until the rocker just throws over. The diaphragm should now be unscrewed to the nearest hole and then a further four holes and with this operation completed, the diaphragm is correctly set.

(15) To secure the rollers in position, press the centre of the armature and install the retaining fork in the rear of the rocker assembly.

NOTE: It should be noted that the inlet valve recess in the body is deeper than the outlet, as the filter and an extra washer will have to be fitted in this recess.

(16) Screw into position the inlet and outlet connections with seal ring.

(17) Into the outlet recess install a joint washer, valve with tongue side facing down, and the valve cover.

(18) Into the inlet recess install a joint washer, filter with the convex side down, another joint washer, valve with tongue side up and the valve cover.

(19) After ensuring that both valve assemblies have been correctly installed, position the clamp plate on the valve covers and firmly secure with the two screws to the pump body.

(20) Position the inlet air bottle joint washer and cover and secure with the centre screw.

(21) Position in the bottom of the delivery flow smoothing device, a sealing washer, perforated diaphragm plate with the convex side below, plastic barrier and the rubber diaphragm. Into the recess insert the 'O' sealing ring which must seal evenly all round. With the larger end facing the cover, position the diaphragm spring in the cover and also the spring end cap on to the other end of the spring. Through the cover, spring and end cap, pass the assembly tool and turn it sufficiently to tension the spring. After fitting the cap and spring assembly on the diaphragm,

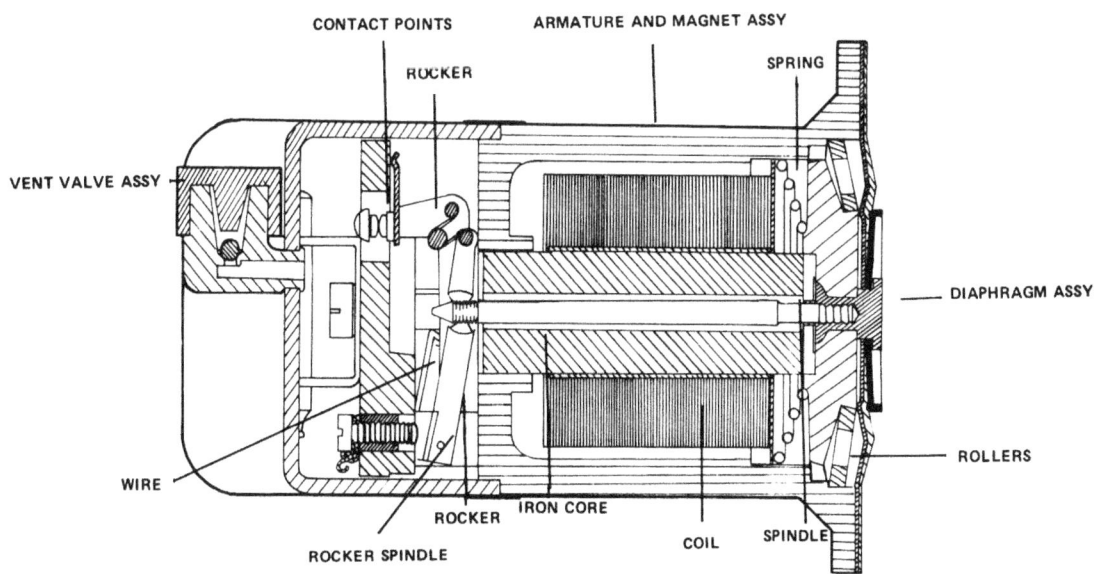

Cross Section of Coil Housing and Diaphragm, Main Components (4.2 Model).

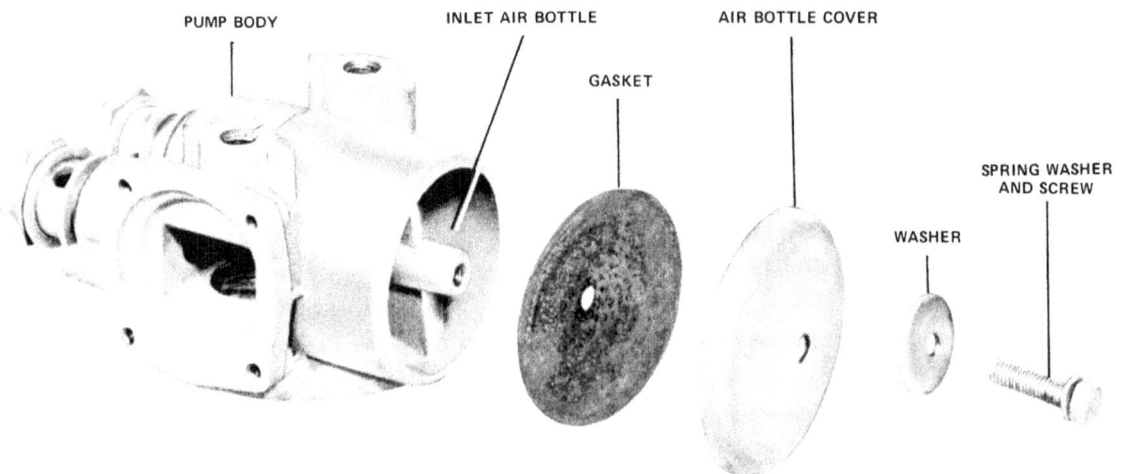

Components of Inlet Air Bottle (4.2 Model Shown).

secure the four retaining screws and remove the assembly tool.

NOTE: It will be necessary to pressure test the pump after disturbing the flow smoothing device.

(22) After aligning the screw holes, fit the joint washer to the body of the pump.

(23) Connect the coil housing to the pump body ensuring that they are mating properly.

(24) Position all the screw holes with the cast lugs on the coil housing placed below. Insert the six 2BA screws but only tighten them with the thumb and finger.

(25) Install the earthing screw with the special Lucas connector.

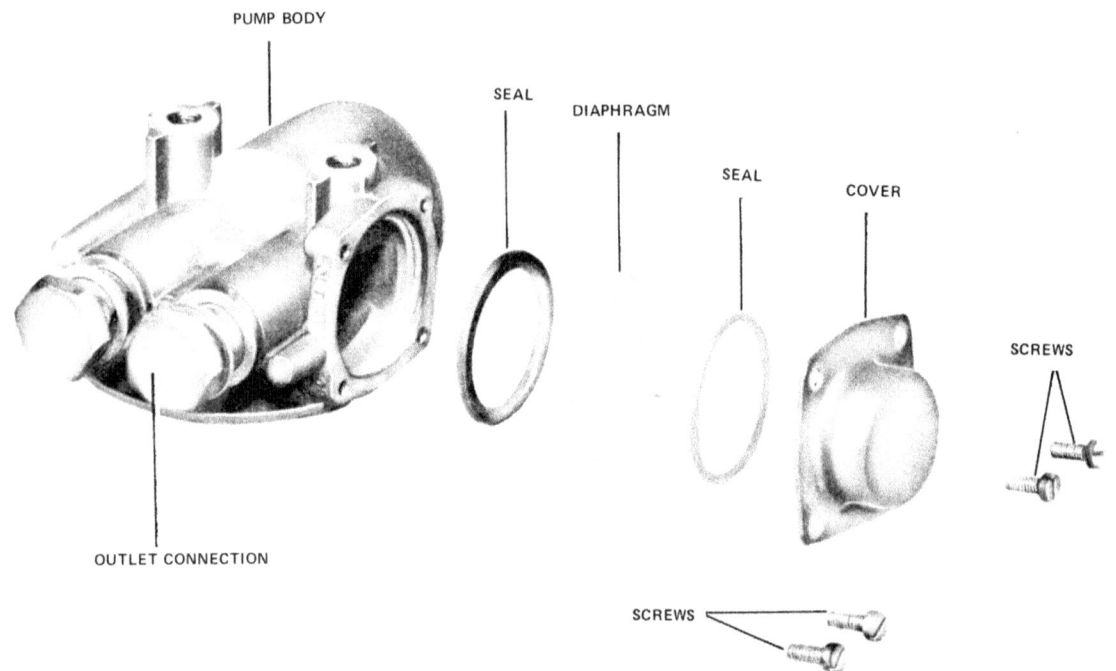

Components of Delivery Flow Smoothing Device (4.2 Model Shown).

(26) Before fulling tightening the body securing screws, remove the roller retaining fork ensuring that all rollers are in position as a dislodged roller can damage the diaphragm.

(27) Tighten the body securing screws.

NOTE: The screws should be cross-tightened, i.e. as they appear diametrically across from each other.

(28) Using the 5BA screw and washer, secure the contact blade and coil lead to the pedestal.

(29) Install the condenser with the tag located under the coil lead tag.

(30) While adjusting the contact blade, ensure that the points are a little above the points on the rocker when closed, and when contact points make and break one pair of points completely covers the other. Some degree of adjustment is possible since the contact blade incorporates a slot for the attachment screw.

(31) When the correct setting is obtained secure the contact blade attachment screws.

CONTACT GAP SETTING

(1) The contact blade should rest on the narrow ridge which projects slightly above the main face of the pedestal when the outer rocker is pressed on to the coil housing. In case this does not happened, then slacken the contact blade attachment screw, swing the blade away from the pedestal and bend it down slightly so that, when placed in position, it will just rest against the ridge.

NOTE: Do not over-tension the blade otherwise the travel of the rocker mechanism will be restricted.

The correct gap between the pedestal and tip of the spring blade should be .035" ± .005".

(2) The gap between the rocker finger and the coil housing should be .070" ± .005" and if adjustment to this

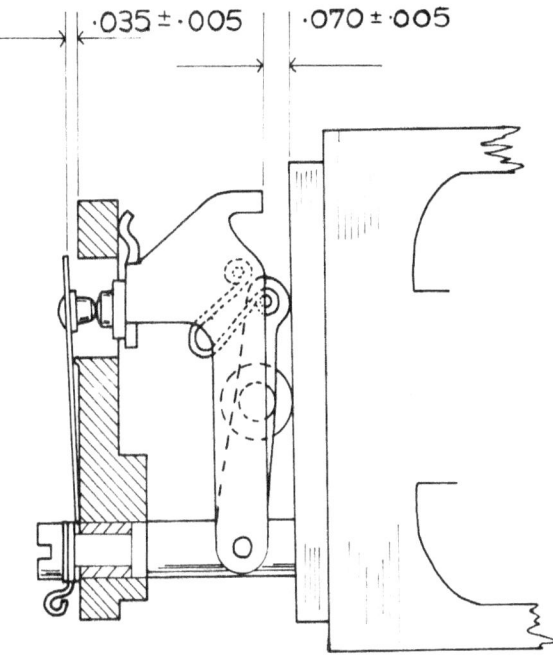

Fuel Pump Contact and Rocker Gap Settings.

figure is necessary, it can be done by bending the stop finger.

(3) All wiring within the end cover should be carefully positioned to avoid fouling the rocker mechanism.

(4) Ensure that the seal washer of the end cover has been correctly placed on the terminal stud and if so, install the bakelite end cover and lock washer and secure with the brass nut.

(5) Fit the terminal tag and insulating sleeve and test the pump, if working satisfactorily, replace the rubber band over the end cover gap and seal.

5. FUEL TANK

TO REMOVE

(1) Disconnect the battery.

(2) Remove the luggage boot floor mat and floor panels.

(3) Drain off the fuel tank into a suitable container and withdraw the filter sump.

(4) Remove the pump electrical wire connection from the terminal block, taking note of the colour of the connecting wires, and then remove the block.

(5) Disconnect the petrol pipe connection from the top of the mounting bracket, comprising the banjo bolt and fibre washers.

(6) Disconnect and remove fuel gauge wires.

(7) Slacken hose clips on the filler pipe and push the rubber hose up the filler pipe.

(8) Remove the breather pipe from the filler neck.

(9) Remove the boot lock.

(10) Remove the luggage boot water channel drain pipe.

(11) From the rear of the tank mounting bracket remove the body strengthening plate.

(12) Remove the three special mounting bolts with washers from the front and rear of the tank.

(13) Remove the tank mounting bracket.

(14) Remove the petrol tank.

(15) If necessary, the gauge unit can be removed by

taking out the six mounting screws and twelve copper washers.

(16) Slide the gauge unit out of the tank and discard the gasket. Check the operation if necessary.

Installation is a reversal of the removal procedure with particular attention to the following points:

Ensure that the rubber seal is positioned at the top of the filter sump.

Connect the fuel gauge cables with the green and black to the terminal marked T, and the white and green to the terminal W. Connect the black earth wire to the earth terminal on the housing.

Install the tank unit with a new gasket coated with sealing compound and with the float towards the back of the car.

Fuel Gauge Tank Unit with Gasket.

6. FUEL SYSTEM FAULT DIAGNOSIS

1. **Engine will not start.**

    Possible cause — *Remedy*

    (a) Lack of fuel in float bowl. — Check fuel pump delivery, sticking or clogged needle valve.

    (b) Engine flooded with fuel when cold by excessive use of choke or accelerator. — Hold accelerator flat until engine starts and revise starting procedure.

    (c) Engine flooded when hot, as in (b) above. — Hold accelerator pedal flat until engine starts.

2. **Engine stalls at idling speed.**

    Possible cause — *Remedy*

    (a) Incorrect adjustment of idling stop and/or mixture control screws. — Check and adjust control screws.

    (b) Carburettor float bowl flooding. — Check float level and for sticking needle valve or punctured float.

    (c) Carburettor starving for fuel. — Check fuel delivery at needle valve. Check fuel pump.

    (d) Carburettor to manifold attachment bolts loose. — Check and tighten bolts.

    (e) Leaking carburettor flange or intake manifold gaskets. — Check and renew faulty gaskets.

    (f) Faulty gasket or loose attachment screws, carburettor main body to top cover assemblies. — Renew faulty gaskets and tighten securing screws.

3. **Engine misfires or cuts out at high speed.**

    Possible cause — *Remedy*

    (a) Obstruction in main jets. — Dismantle and blow out jets.

    (b) Low fuel level in float chamber or float chamber starving for fuel. — Check float level setting, check fuel pump and fuel supply lines.

(c)	Failure of fuel pump to deliver sufficient fuel.	– Overhaul fuel pump.
(d)	Restriction in fuel pump filter bowl.	– Clean or renew filter.
(e)	Air leak between fuel pump and tank.	– Rectify air leak.
(f)	Air leak between carburettor and manifold.	– Check and renew gasket and tighten securing screws.
(g)	Water in carburettor.	– Drain and clean fuel system.

4. **Excessive fuel consumption.**

Possible cause — *Remedy*

(a) Float level too high. — Check and readjust float level.
(b) Air cleaner element dirty or requires renewal. — Clean element or renew.
(c) Fuel pump delivery pressure too high. — Adjust fuel pump relief valve.

NOTES

COOLING SYSTEM

SPECIFICATIONS

Water pump:
    Type .... Centrifugal impeller
    Bearing type .... Double row ball bearing and shaft assembly
    Drive .... 'V' Belt
    Pump belt – angle .... 36°
Thermostat:
    Starts to open .... 165°
    Fully open .... 187°
Fan assembly:
    3.8 Models .... Separate, motor driven with relay fitted.
    Open 2 Seater R.H. Drive Chassis No. 850274 and L.H. Drive Chassis No. 878021 also Fixed Head Coupe R.H. Drive Chassis No. 861187 and L.H. Drive Chassis No. 886749. ...... Separate, motor driven. The Fan Motor Relay has been replaced by a modified wiring harness serving the purpose of relay and harness.

Cooling system capacity:
    Including heater .... 32 Imp pt.
    Type of radiator .... Cross-flow with separate header tank.

Radiator cap:
    Type .... Relief valve
    Release pressure:
        3.8 Models .... 4 psi
        Fixed Head Coupe R.H. Drive from Chassis No. 861091 and L.H. Drive from Chassis No. 888241. Open 2 Seater R.H. Drive Chassis No. 850657 and L.H. Drive Chassis No. 879044 and onwards. .... 9 psi and heavy duty header tank with a straight hose pipe from the engine to header tank.
        4.2 and 2 + 2 Models ...... 7 psi with a heavy duty header tank.

1. DESCRIPTION

The cooling system is the thermo-siphon type with a fan and water pump assistance.

The radiator is the cross-flow type fitted with ten fins to the inch and manufactured with aluminium.

All models are fitted with a separate header tank on top of which is located the radiator pressure cap.

The radiator cap incorporates a pressure relief valve which is the controlling factor in the pressurised system. When the pressure within the system overcomes the spring loading of the relief valve excess pressure is passed out through the overflow. It is essential that a cap of the correct release pressure is fitted. (See Specifications).

The system is pressurised in order to raise the engine temperature in the quickest possible time and thereby increase the efficiency of the engine.

The pump is driven by a 'V'-belt from the crankshaft. It is fitted with a shaft and ball bearing assembly which is pre-lubricated and sealed and requires no further lubrication in service. The seal is a spring loaded carbon thrust washer and rubber bellows assembly.

A cooling fan is fitted and is operated by a separate motor which has the switch located within the header tank. This switch is thermostatically controlled by the varying water temperature. When the temperature rises above 176°F the switch cuts in and the fan operates and it will continue to do so until the temperature drops to 160°F and below. On the 3.8 model a fan relay is installed, but this has been replaced by a new wiring harness on the 4.2 and 2 + 2 cars.

Temperature in the cooling system is controlled by a thermostat which is located in the inlet manifold water jacket. A by-pass is incorporated in the system to allow restricted circulation of the coolant when the thermostat is closed.

2. RADIATOR

TO REMOVE (3.8)

(1) Drain the cooling system from a tap at the bottom of the radiator and another on the side of the cylinder block, after removing the pressure cap.

(2) Disconnect and remove the upper water hose connecting the top of the radiator to the header tank.

(3) Disconnect and remove the hose connecting the water pump and the bottom of the radiator.

(4) From the header tank mounting brackets, undo the two self-locking nuts and bolts.

(5) From the radiator mounting brackets, undo the two self-locking nuts and bolts.

(6) Carefully lift out the radiator to avoid damage to the fan or radiator in the process of removal. Note the positioning of the rubber mountings with spacers and remove.

TO CHECK AND TEST

(1) With the radiator removed from the vehicle, apply a water hose and flush out.

(2) Stand the radiator upright and, using a jet of water or air pressure to the rear of the core, remove any dirt or foreign matter that may have collected on the front of the core.

Installation is a reversal of the removal procedure.

TO REMOVE (4.2 AND 2 + 2 CARS)

(1) Drain the cooling system from a tap at the bottom of the radiator and another on the side of the cylinder block, after removing the pressure cap.

(2) Disconnect and remove the three water hoses from the top of the radiator and one from the bottom.

NOTE: On 2 + 2 cars with automatic transmission, there are pipes fitted for oil cooling on the right of the radiator which should also be disconnected and removed during this operation.

(3) From the header tank mounting brackets, undo the two self-locking nuts and bolts.

(4) From the radiator mounting brackets, undo and remove the two self-locking nuts and bolts.

(5) Carefully lift out the radiator to avoid damage to the fan or radiator in the process of removal. Note the positioning of the rubber mountings with spacers and remove.

NOTE: In case it is necessary to remove the cowl from the radiator, undo the top nuts and bolts from the upper mounting bracket and two bolts from the bottom securing the cowl to the radiator. (Refer to RADIATOR COWL – REMOVAL for details).

Installation is a reversal of the removal procedure.

3. RADIATOR COWL

TO REMOVE

(1) Remove the radiator as described under *RADIATOR – TO REMOVE*.

(2) Undo the cowl from the bottom of the radiator by removing the two self-locking nuts and also the washers.

(3) At the top of the radiator, remove the two self-locking nuts from the radiator top support bracket.

(4) Retrieve all spacers.

(5) Take out the cowl and rubber beading.

(6) Detach the radiator top securing brackets from the cowl by removing the bolts, nuts and washers and retrieve the spacers.

Installation is a reversal of the removal procedure.

4. RADIATOR HEADER TANK

TO REMOVE

(1) Remove the pressure cap from the top of the header tank.

(2) Drain the cooling system at the tap on the bottom of the radiator and the other on the side of the cylinder block.

(3) Disconnect and remove the upper hose from the cylinder head to the header tank.

(4) Disconnect and remove the upper hose from the header tank to the radiator.

(5) From the header tank disconnect the fan control thermostat electrical connections.

(6) Undo the two nuts and bolts from the header tank mounting bracket.

(7) Remove the header tank after disconnecting the overflow pipe.

NOTE: At the time of installing the fan thermostatic switch on the header tank, ensure that the black wire is fitted to the earth connection.

Installation of the radiator header tank is a reversal of the removal procedure.

5. FAN MOTOR

TO REMOVE

(1) The positive terminal should be disconnected from the battery.

(2) Remove the fan motor by releasing the four self-locking nuts and flat washer securing the motor to the front sub frame.

(3) Disconnect the wiring from the thermostatic switch and dislodge the motor from its mounting and, with the fan blades, withdraw it between the frame and the radiator from the right side.

Installation is a reversal of the removal procedure.

Location and Attachment of Fan Motor (4.2 Model Shown).

6. FAN MOTOR RELAY (EARLY 3.8 MODELS ONLY)

TO REMOVE

(1) The positive terminal should be disconnected from the battery.

(2) Disconnect the three leads from the fan relay mounted on the header tank bracket noting their locations.

(3) From the relay support plate, remove the two securing nuts and bolts and remove the relay.

NOTE: At the time of installation, great care must be taken while fitting the leads to the relay. It may be noted that the leads should be connected up as follows:

(a) Black/red ..... fix to connector on left (W.1.)
(b) Green .... fix to connector in centre (C.2.)
(c) Black/green .... fix to connector on right (C.1.)
Installation is a reversal of the removal procedure.

7. WATER PUMP BELT

ADJUSTMENT (EARLY MODELS).

(1) Loosen the two generator to mounting bracket bolts slightly.

(2) Loosen the generator adjusting bracket bolts and pull the generator away from the cylinder block sufficiently to give the belt enough tension to prevent it slipping on the pulleys.

(3) Hold the generator in this position and tighten the adjusting bracket and generator mounting bolts securely.

NOTE: Do not over tension the water pump belt as this could cause rapid wear in the water pump and generator bearings. The belt will have sufficient tension when it can be flexed approximately .5" with finger and thumb pressure applied between the generator and water pump pulleys.

The 4.2 and 2 + 2 cars have a spring tension jockey pulley hence adjustment is not necessary.

TO REMOVE (3.8 MODELS)

(1) Loosen the two generator to mounting bracket bolts and nuts.

(2) Loosen the generator adjusting bracket bolts and push the generator towards the cylinder block as far as it will go.

(3) Slip the belt off the generator pulley and then manoeuvre it off the water pump and crankshaft pulleys and remove it from the engine.

NOTE: The water pump belt must not be over stretched when installing otherwise it will be damaged.

Installation is a reversal of the removal procedure and for adjustment refer to *ADJUSTMENT* in this section.

TO REMOVE (4.2 and 2 + 2 Cars)

(1) Loosen the top adjustment bracket bolt.
(2) Below the alternator, loosen the mounting nut.
(3) Push the alternator towards the cylinder block and remove the belt.

Installation is a reversal of the removal procedure but do not unnecessarily over-stretch the belt.

8. THERMOSTAT

TO REMOVE AND INSTALL

(1) Drain the cooling system by the taps at the bottom of the radiator and the side of the cylinder block, after removing the pressure cap.

NOTE: Exercise great care to avoid the risk of scalding when removing the pressure cap, if the engine is hot.

(2) Disconnect and remove the top hose by releasing the hose clamp.

(3) Unscrew the two nuts and spring washers and remove the housing cover and gasket.

(4) Withdraw the thermostat from the housing.

NOTE: A visual inspection of the thermostat will often determine its serviceability and obviate the necessity for further testing. For instance, a thermostat with its valve open when removed from a cold engine or one in which the valve is closed when first removed from an engine at normal operating temperature, can be discarded as faulty.

Installation is a reversal of the removal procedure.
Fill the system with clean water to within half an inch below the pressure cap. Check for water leaks.

TO TEST

(1) Clean the thermostat and check that the small hole in the valve is not clogged.

(2) Check that the thermostat valve is closed when the thermostat is cold.

(3) Suspend and immerse the thermostat, together with a reliable thermometer, in a vessel of cold water ensuring that neither the thermostat nor thermometer is touching the sides or bottom of the vessel and progressively heat the water.

(4) As the water heats, note the temperature readings on the thermometer when the thermostat valve commences to open and also when the valve is fully open. A thermostat in serviceable condition should commence to open at approximately 165° and be fully open at a minimum temperature of 187°. A thermostat showing a variation of more than 5° above or below these temperatures should be renewed.

NOTE: While installing the thermostat ensure that a new gasket is fitted between the housing and cover.

9. FAN THERMOSTATIC SWITCH

TO REMOVE

(1) Disconnect the two wires from the centre connection and the earth connection on the thermostatic switch.

(2) Take out the screws and washers from the mounting plate of the switch.

(3) Lift out the switch unit, remove the gasket and clean both faces before fitting a new gasket.

Installation is a reversal of the removal procedure, but special attention is to be given while connecting the two wires to the centre connector and the earth terminal on the thermostatic switch.

On the centre connector fit the red/black wire, and the black wire to the earth terminal.

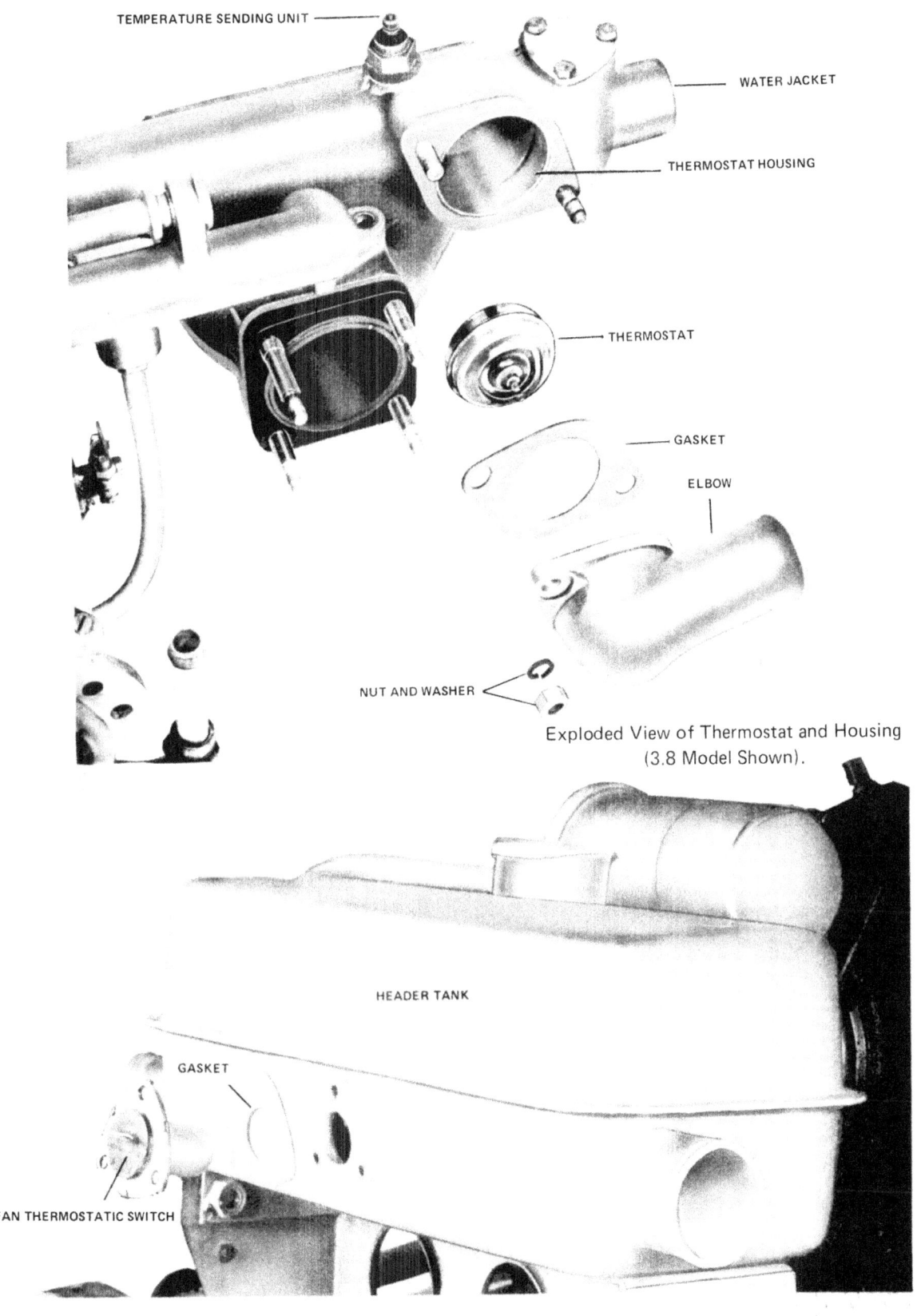

Exploded View of Thermostat and Housing (3.8 Model Shown).

Location of Fan Thermostatic Switch in Radiator Header Tank (4.2 Model Shown).

10. WATER PUMP

TO REMOVE AND INSTALL

(1) Drain the cooling system by means of the two taps located at the bottom of the radiator and in the side of the cylinder block.

(2) Loosen the hose clips and disconnect the two hose pipes to the header tank.

(3) From the thermostat fan switch, remove the two electrical wires.

(4) From the header tank mounting on the right side radiator steady bracket take out the two nuts and bolts.

(5) From the other radiator steady bracket remove the nut and bolt.

(6) From the fan relay, disconnect the three electrical leads (not for 4.2 and 2 + 2 cars).

(7) The header tank should be removed from its mounting on the sub frame by taking out the two bolts with large flat washers and rubber mounting pads.

(8) Remove the header tank support bracket and retrieve the other rubber mounting pads.

(9) Loosen the clips and disconnect the three hose pipes from the water pump body.

(10) Loosen the generator mounting bolts and push the generator towards the cylinder block and take off the water pump belt (for early models).

NOTE: For the 4.2 and 2 + 2 models, slacken the top adjusting bracket bolt, and below the alternator slacken the mounting nut. Push the alternator towards the cylinder block and remove the belt.

(11) Remove the water pump pulley from the carrier by taking out the four small bolts and washers.

(12) Remove the water pump from its mounting on the engine by taking out the six bolts, three nuts and washers.

NOTE: The gasket between the water pump and timing chain cover must be renewed and both faces thoroughly cleaned when installing the pump.

TO DISMANTLE

(1) Using a suitable puller, withdraw the pump pulley flange from the forward end of the shaft and bearing assembly.

(2) To remove the shaft and bearing assembly, first undo the locknut and unscrew the Allen headed locking screw sufficiently to clear the recess in the bearing outer race.

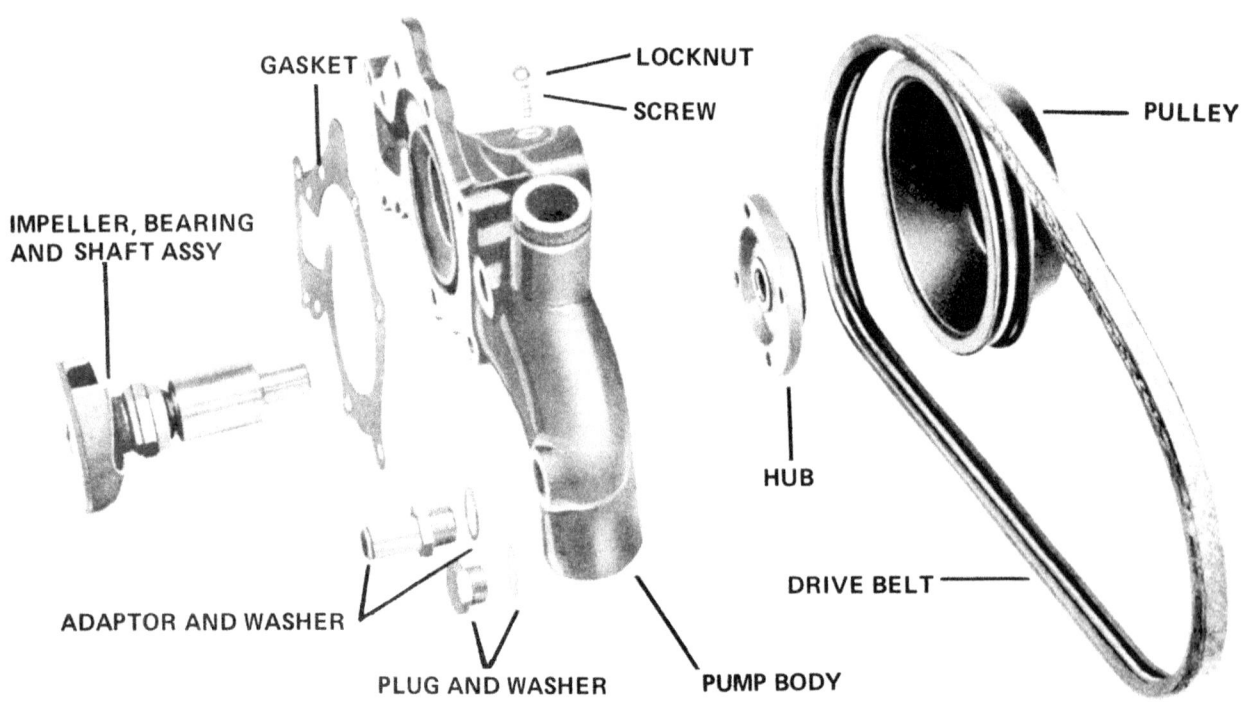

Exploded View of Water Pump Components (3.8 Model Shown).

NOTE: To press the bearing and shaft assembly out of the body and to avoid damage to the bearing, a small piece of metal pipe will be required with the outer diameter 1.093" and inner diameter .968".

(3) With the aid of a piece of metal pipe as described in the note above, correctly position the metal pipe and press out the bearing and shaft assembly from the front of the pump body.

(4) Press the impeller off the end of the shaft and bearing assembly. Remove the water slinger bush from the impeller end of the shaft.

TO CHECK

(1) Check the pump body for cracks or damage.
(2) Check the bearing for looseness in the pump body bore and for roughness in rotation.
(3) Check that the water drain hole in the body is clear.

NOTE: When cleaning the pump components, do not immerse the shaft and bearing assembly in cleaning solvent, if the assembly is to be used again.

TO REASSEMBLE

(1) Using a small quantity of waterproof sealing compound applied to the large end of the new seal assembly, press the new assembly into position in the pump body so that the carbon face of the seal will be facing the pump impeller and the recess in the bearing outer race is lined up with the hole in the pump body.

(2) Fit the Allen head screw through the hole and into the recess in the bearing outer race and tighten the locking nut.

(3) Install the water slinger in the groove on the shaft in front of the pump seal.

(4) Support the pump on the front end of the shaft assembly, install a new impeller with the blades facing the pump body and press it onto the shaft.

Installation is a reversal of the removal procedure.

11. COOLING SYSTEM FAULT DIAGNOSIS

(1) Coolant Leakage – External.

	Possible cause	Remedy
(a)	Loose hose clips or faulty hoses.	– Tighten hose clips or renew faulty hoses.
(b)	Leaking radiator core or tanks.	– Repair or renew radiator.
(c)	Worn or damaged water pump seal assembly.	– Renew seal assembly.
(d)	Worn or damaged water pump bearing assembly.	– Renew water pump bearing and shaft assembly.
(e)	Loose or rusted expansion plugs.	– Renew faulty components.
(f)	External crack in cylinder block or head.	– Renew faulty components.
(g)	Faulty cylinder head gasket or loose holding down bolts.	– Renew gasket and correctly tighten cylinder head bolts.
(h)	Leaks at thermostat cover and/or water pump joint.	– Rectify leaks.

(2) Coolant Leakage – Internal.

	Possible cause	Remedy
(a)	Crack in cylinder bore wall.	– Renew cylinder block.
(b)	Crack in cylinder head combustion chambers or valve ports.	– Renew cylinder head.
(c)	Cylinder head cracked and leaking into valve rocker compartment.	– Renew cylinder head.
(d)	Cracked cylinder block water jacket, leaking into engine tappet compartment.	– Renew cylinder block.
(e)	Cylinder head gasket leak due to warped head.	– Reface cylinder head and renew gasket.

(3) Coolant Loss by Overflow.

	Possible cause	*Remedy*
(a)	Over full system.	– Drain and refill to .5" filler neck.
(b)	Faulty pressure cap.	– Renew faulty cap.
(c)	Blocked radiator.	– Clean or renew radiator core.
(d)	Coolant foaming due to poor quality anti-freeze or corrosion inhibitor	– Drain system and renew coolant and additive.

(4) Engine Overheating.

	Possible cause	*Remedy*
(a)	Obstructed air passage through radiator core from front to rear.	– Blow out obstruction from rear to front of radiator with compressed air or water pressure.
(b)	Incorrect ignition timing.	– Check and reset ignition timing.

CLUTCH

SPECIFICATIONS

3.8 MODELS

Type	Single dry plate
Operation	Hydraulic
Driven plate:	
Outside diameter	10"
Type for normal use	Borglite
Type for competition and racing use	Arcuate
Facings for normal use	Wound yarn
Facings for competition and racing use	Wound yarn cemented
Number of cushion springs	6
Color of cushion springs:	
Normal use	Brown/Cream
Competition and racing use	Buff
Throw-out bearing	Graphite ring
Pressure plate:	
Type on early model	Borg and Beck, thrust spring
Type on later model	Laycock, diaphragm spring
Number and color of thrust springs early model	12, violet
Throw-out bearing free travel measured at the slave cylinder:	
For normal use	.0625"
Competition and racing use	Maximum possible without causing gear grate.
Clutch hydraulic fluid	Castrol/Girling Crimson.

4.2 AND 2 + 2 MODELS (WHERE DIFFERENT FROM 3.8 MODEL)

Pressure plate:	
Type on early models	Laycock, diaphragm spring
Type on later models	Borg and Beck, diaphragm spring
Clutch slave cylinder adjustment:	
Early models	.0625"
Later models	Self compensating, adjustment required only when replacing cylinder or clutch assembly.
Commencing at Engine No. 7E.4607	

1. DESCRIPTION

On all models (except automatic transmission model) the single dry plate clutch comprises a pressure plate and cover assembly and a driven plate assembly.

The driven plate has a spring cushion hub and is fitted with woven yarn facings, there are two types of driven plates specified, one for normal car usage and the alternative for competition and racing purposes.

On early model 3.8 cars the pressure plate assembly comprises a cast iron pressure plate and pressed steel cover with twelve thrust springs interposed between the plate and cover. The release levers in the pressure plate are adjustable, but they should not require adjustment in service. Release lever adjustment is carried out during initial assembly of the pressure plate and cover and is only necessary when the assembly is dismantled for reconditioning.

The assembly is balanced on manufacture and if the assembly is dismantled for overhaul the components must be fitted in their original positions to retain balance, or alternatively the assembly must be rebalanced. Special tools are required for the overhaul of all pressure plate assemblies and overhaul should not be attempted unless available.

On late model 3.8 and early model 4.2 cars the pressure plate assembly comprises a cast iron pressure plate and pressed steel cover with a diaphragm spring, retaining ring and driving plate interposed between the pressure plate and cover. If the pressure plate assembly is defective or worn a replacement assembly should be fitted. The assembly is balanced on manufacture and if the assembly is dismantled for overhaul the components must be fitted in their original position to retain balance, or alternatively the assembly must be rebalanced.

On late model 4.2 cars the pressure plate assembly comprises a cast iron pressure plate and pressed steel cover, with a diaphragm spring and two fulcrum rings interposed between the plate and cover, which are joined by three equally spaced retractor clips.

The diaphragm spring is secured inside the steel cover with rivets, and the two fulcrum rings are fitted between the cover and the shoulders of the rivets. This assembly should not be dismantled but replaced if defective or worn. Any attempt to overhaul the assembly would affect the balance and therefore the efficiency of the clutch.

The clutch throw-out bearing on all models is a **graphite ring** mounted in a steel support cup.

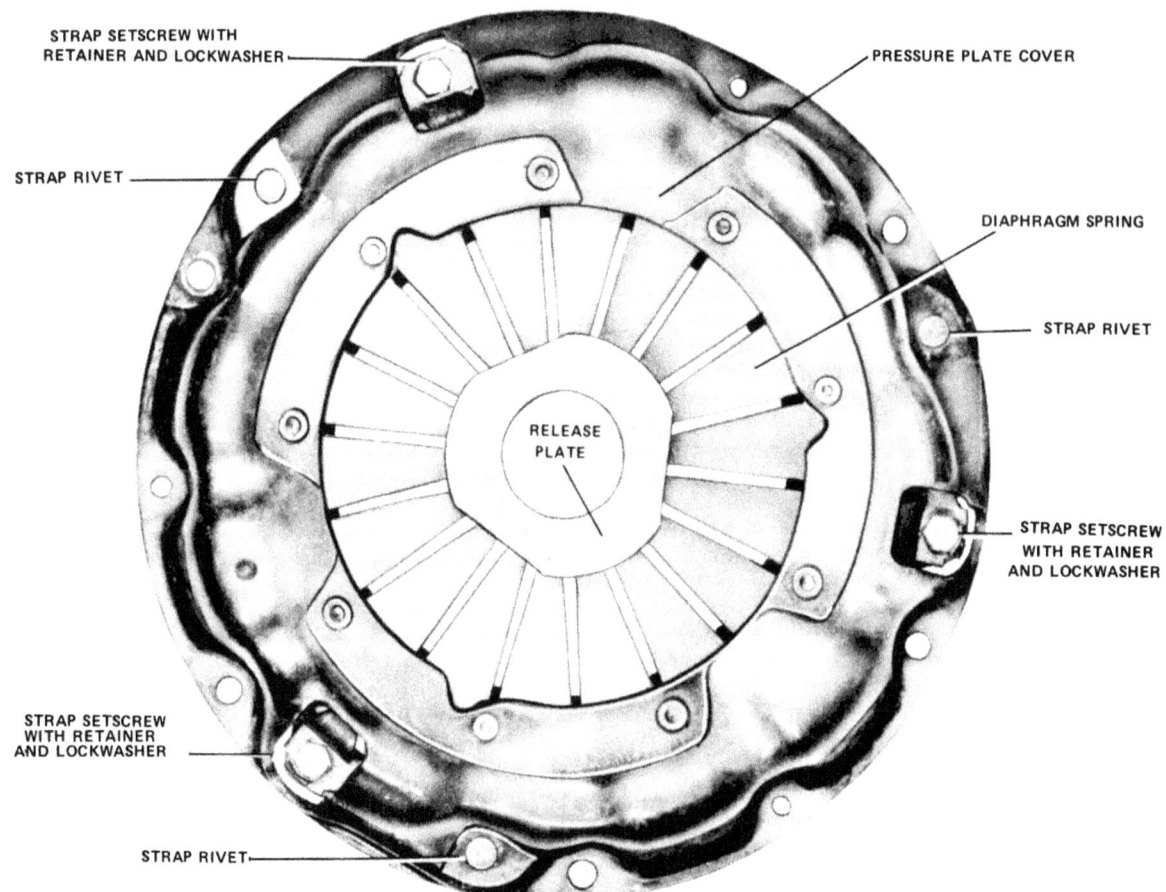

Clutch Pressure Plate and Cover Assembly (Diaphragm Spring Type).

On early models, clutch throw-out bearing free travel is adjusted at the operating rod of the slave cylinder.

On later models a self compensating slave cylinder is fitted and adjustment is only required when the clutch assembly or slave cylinder are replaced.

The slave cylinders are fitted with a bleed valve for bleeding the clutch hydraulic system, and the fluid reservoir is located on the bulkhead adjacent to the brake fluid reservoirs.

2. CLUTCH UNIT

TO REMOVE AND INSTALL

(1) Remove the engine and gearbox assembly as described under *ENGINE – TO REMOVE AND INSTALL*.

(2) Take out the securing bolts and separate the gearbox and clutch housing from the engine to expose the clutch assembly.

(3) Loosen evenly and progressively the six securing bolts and spring washers attaching the pressure plate assembly to the flywheel, remove the clutch pressure plate and cover assembly and clutch driven plate.

NOTE: Where cars are fitted with diaphragm spring pressure plate assemblies retain the balancers fitted under the securing bolt heads.

Installation is a reversal of the removal procedure with attention to the following points:

Use a special aligning tool or a used gearbox input shaft to align the centre of the driven plate hub with the spigot bearing in the rear end of the crankshaft.

NOTE: The raised boss side of the driven plate must face the pressure plate.

Align the 'B' stamped on the pressure plate cover with the 'B' stamped on the flywheel.

Instal the balancers beneath the securing bolt heads in their original positions, note that the balancers are marked

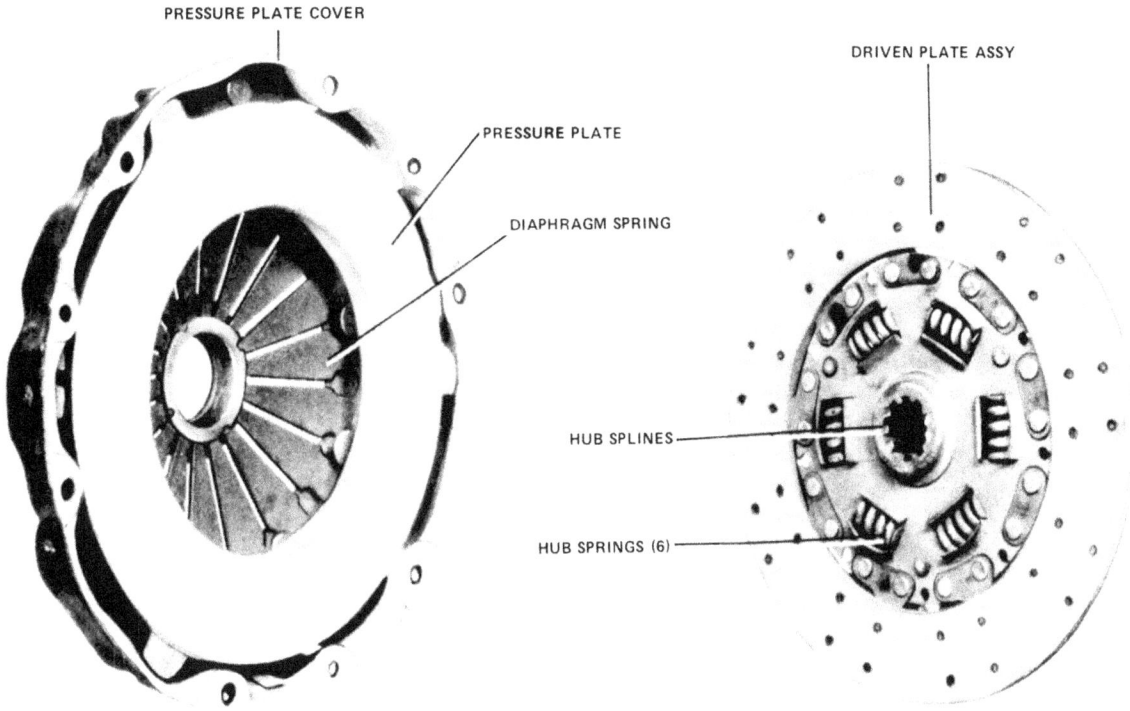

Clutch Pressure Plate and Driven Plate Assemblies (Fitted to Later Models).

1 to 3 and they should be fitted with the corresponding number marked on the flywheel.

Tighten the securing bolts evenly and progressively and do not remove the aligning tool/shaft until fully tightened.

If the clutch hydraulic system has been disconnected, it will be necessary to bleed the system.

Adjust the free play at the slave cylinder operating rod.

TO CHECK AND INSPECT

(1) Check that the driven plate facings are not gummy with burnt oil or highly glazed from oil deposits.

(2) If the driven plate facings are worn down to the rivets, check the flywheel and pressure plate faces for wear and scoring.

Clutch Pressure Plate and Driven Plate Assemblies (Fitted to Early Models).

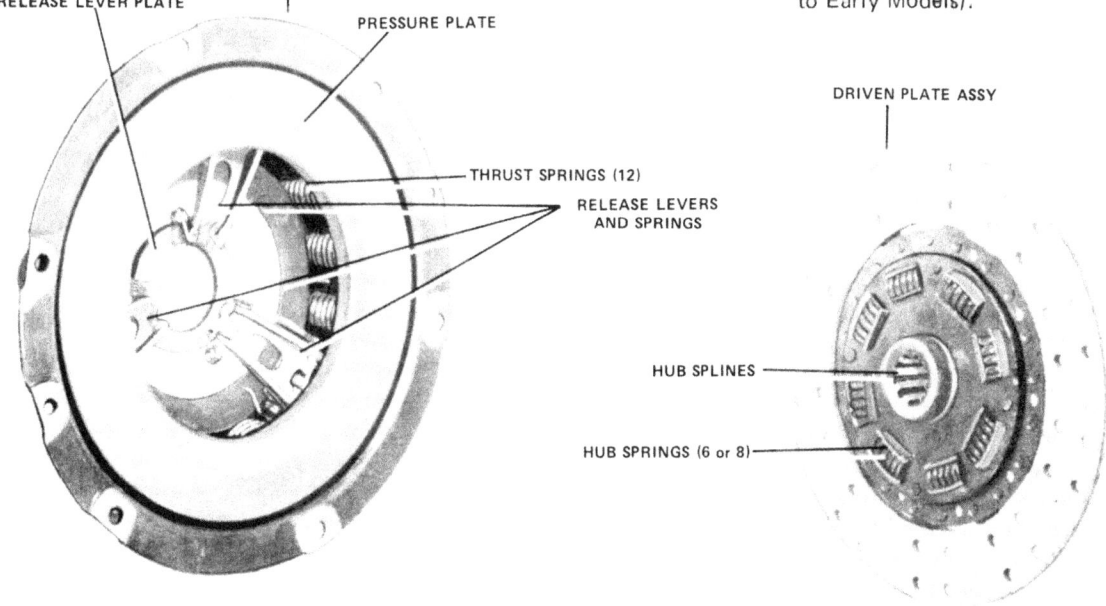

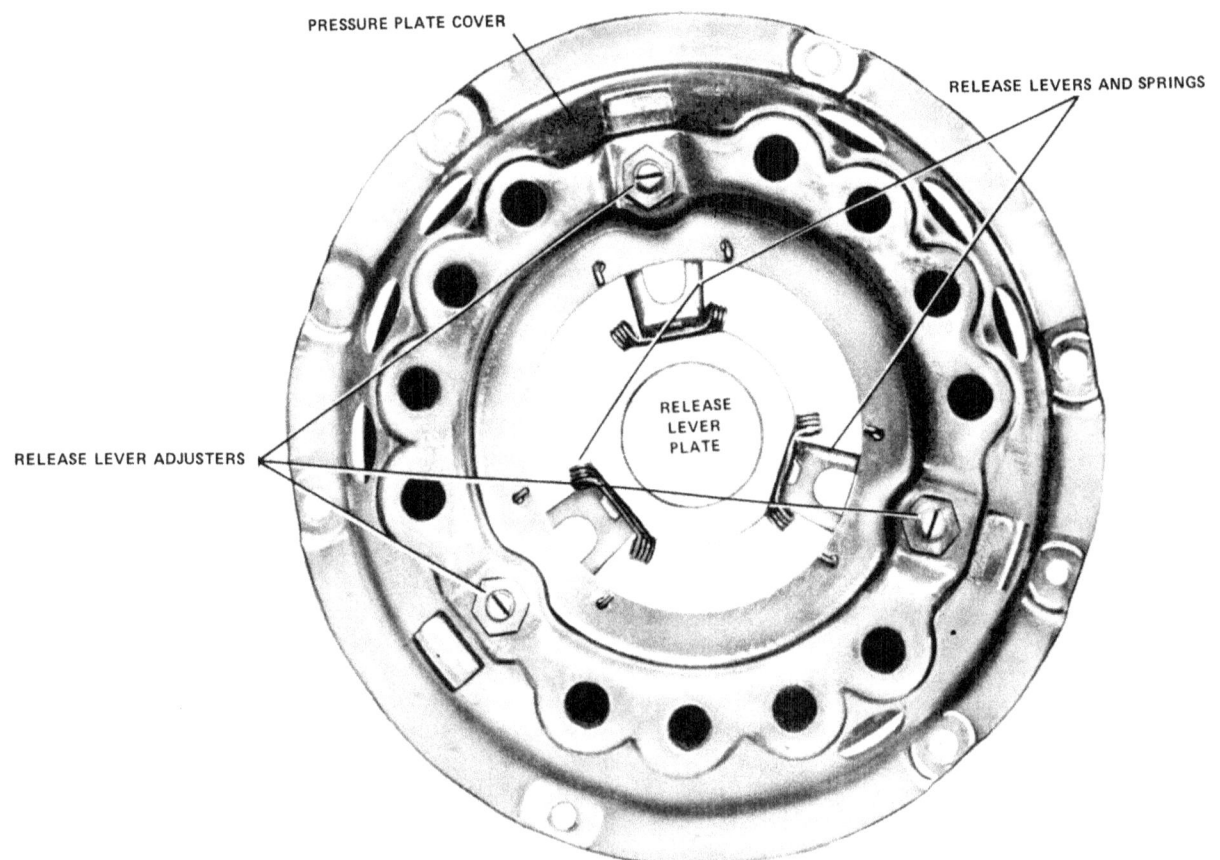

Clutch Pressure Plate and Cover Assembly (Coil Spring Type).

(3) Check the hub of the driven plate for looseness or wear in the hub splines. Check effective action of the driven plate hub cushion springs and ensure none are broken or cracked.

(4) Ensure that the main drive (gearbox input shaft) bearing in the rear flange of the crankshaft is in serviceable condition.

(5) Check the throw-out bearing graphite ring and ensure that it is not excessively worn or cracked, if so renew.

(6) Check the pressure plate assemblies for broken thrust springs, or diaphragm spring, check also on diaphragm spring assemblies that excessive wear is not present between the driving lugs of the pressure plate and the driving plate.

A worn or defective pressure plate assembly should be replaced by a complete assembly.

(7) It is very important that no oil, grease or cleaning fluid is permitted on the driven plate facings, or the flywheel or pressure plate faces. When assembled all faces should be perfectly clean and dry.

3. CLUTCH THROW-OUT BEARING

TO REMOVE AND INSTALL

(1) Remove the engine and gearbox assembly as described under *ENGINE–TO REMOVE AND INSTALL*.

(2) Take out the securing bolts and separate the gearbox and clutch housing from the engine.

(3) Working inside the gearbox bellhousing, prise out the two retaining springs one at either end of the throw-out bearing which attach the bearing assembly to the clutch fork.

(4) Withdraw the clutch throw-out bearing from the clutch fork and remove by sliding off gearbox input shaft.

Installation is a reversal of the removal procedure with attention to the following points:

Lightly smear the pivots on the clutch throw-out bearing with high melting point grease.

Ensure that the two retaining springs positioned at the pivot ends of the throw-out bearing are securely located in position.

If the clutch hydraulic system has been disconnected, it will be necessary to bleed the system.

Adjustment for free travel will be required at the slave cylinder operating rod.

4. MASTER CYLINDER

TO REMOVE AND INSTALL

(1) Drain off the fluid from the clutch reservoir into a clean container.

(2) Disconnect the fluid supply pipe and the fluid outlet pipe at the master cylinder body. Plug the holes to prevent the entry of dirt.

(3) Working inside the car, remove the split pin and clevis pin attaching the master cylinder push rod to the clutch pedal.

(4) Loosen and remove the two securing nuts attaching the master cylinder assembly to the housing on the engine side of the bulkhead.

(5) Withdraw the assembly from the vehicle.

Installation is a reversal of the removal procedure. It will be necessary to bleed the clutch hydraulic system.

Ensure that the hydraulic fluid is not spilled onto any lacquered surface.

TO DISMANTLE

(1) Pull the rubber boot off the open end of the master cylinder, remove the retaining circlip and withdraw the push rod with dished retaining washer.

(2) Remove the piston complete with seals from the cylinder body, pull out the valve assembly complete with return spring and spring retainers.

TO CLEAN AND INSPECT

(1) Thoroughly clean the master cylinder components and the inside of the bore with methylated spirits. Do not use petrol or other mineral spirits.

(2) Check the inside of the bore for wear/pitting. If necessary, hone the cylinder bore.

(3) Check the piston for wear and renew the piston sealing ring and cup.

(4) Check the valve assembly and fit new seal.

(5) Check the rubber boot for deterioration or perishing and renew if necessary.

TO ASSEMBLE

(1) Dip the master cylinder components in clean hydraulic fluid and install a new cup seal on the piston with the lip of the seal facing towards the spigot end of the piston.

(2) Install a new seal ring on the piston body ensuring that it seats correctly in the groove.

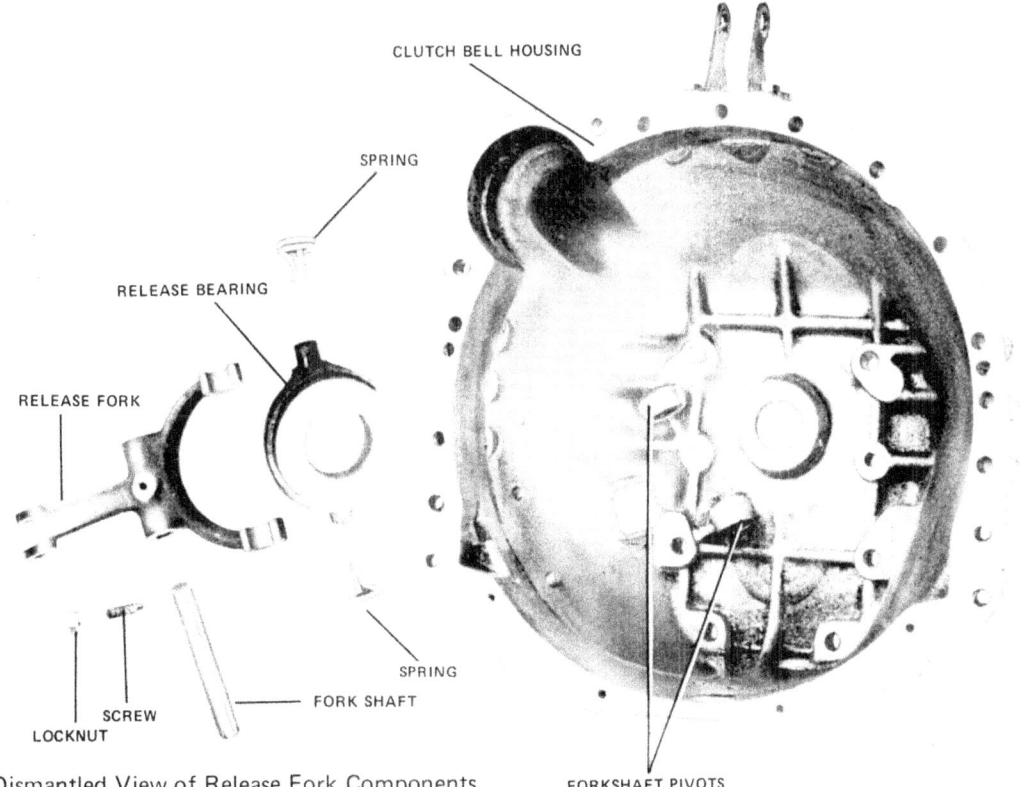

Dismantled View of Release Fork Components.

(3) Install the new valve seal on the head of the valve stem and ensure that it locates correctly in the groove.

(4) Position the valve head into the slotted aperture of the front spring retainer, ensure that the valve spring is positioned between the retainer and valve head.

(5) Install the piston into the rear return spring retainer and ensure that the valve stem fits into the bore in the piston centre.

(6) Install the complete assembly in the cylinder bore and ensure that the lips of the seals are not turned back or damaged on entry.

(7) Press in the piston assembly clear of the end of the cylinder bore and install the push rod and dished retaining washer. Fit the circlip and ensure that it locates properly in its groove.

(8) Fill the rubber boot with Castrol Rubber grease and fit over the master cylinder end, locating it in the groove.

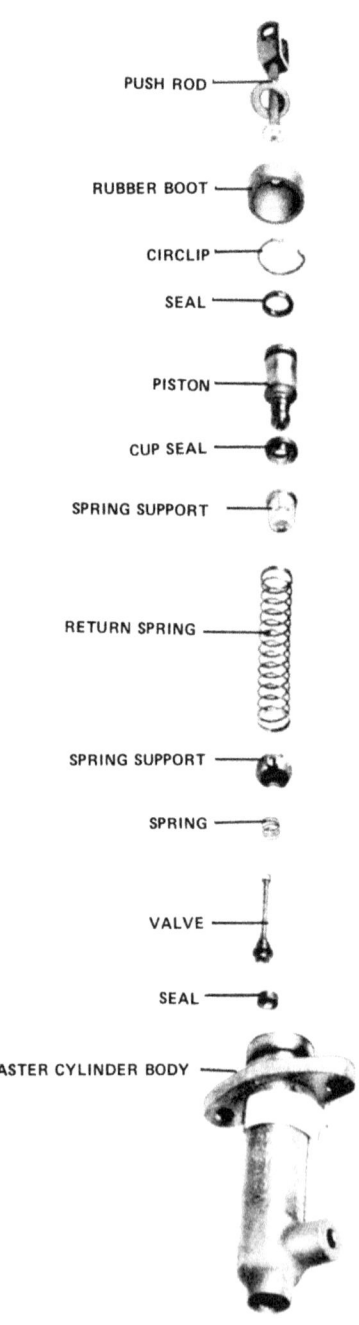

Exploded View of Clutch Slave Cylinder Components.

Exploded View of Clutch Master Cylinder Components.

5. SLAVE CYLINDER

TO REMOVE AND INSTALL

(1) Unhook and remove the clutch throw-out lever return spring between the throw-out lever and the clip on the bellhousing.

(2) Disconnect the hydraulic supply pipe at the slave cylinder and plug the pipe to prevent loss of fluid and entry of dirt.

(3) Loosen and remove the two securing nuts attaching the slave cylinder to the bellhousing, take out the push rod clevis pin if the push rod is to be removed, or if the push rod removal is not required pull the rubber boot from the open end of the slave cylinder.

(4) Remove the slave cylinder from the vehicle.

Installation is a reversal of the removal procedure with attention to the following points:

It will be necessary to bleed the clutch hydraulic system and adjust the clutch throw-out lever free travel as detailed under the appropriate headings in this section.

Ensure that the rubber boot is correctly fitted over the open end of the cylinder.

TO DISMANTLE

(1) With the slave cylinder removed from the vehicle, take out the circlip at the end of the cylinder bore.

(2) Apply a low air pressure to the hydraulic pipe hole in the cylinder to remove the piston, cup seal, cup seal support and return spring.

(3) If necessary, unscrew and remove the bleeder valve.

TO CLEAN AND INSPECT

(1) Clean and wash all parts in methylated spirits. Do not use petrol or any mineral solvent for this purpose.

(2) Check the bore of the cylinder for wear or pitting, and hone if necessary.

(3) Check the piston for wear or pitting and renew if necessary.

(4) Check the piston seal and rubber boot for wear or deterioration and renew if necessary.

TO ASSEMBLE

(1) Lubricate the bore of the cylinder with clean hydraulic fluid.

(2) Engage the end of the spring in the seating at the rear of the cup seal support, and install into the cylinder bore.

(3) Dip the new piston cup seal in clean hydraulic fluid and install in the bore lip first, take care not to turn back or damage the lip on entry.

(4) Install the piston, flat face first into the bore and secure with the circlip.

(5) If the bleeder valve had been removed, install in position. If the push rod was removed with the assembly, fill the new rubber boot with rubber grease and install on the end of the slave cylinder.

6. HYDRAULIC SYSTEM

TO BLEED

(1) Remove the cap and fill the clutch fluid reservoir with clean hydraulic fluid to within approximately half an inch of the reservoir top.

(2) Attach a bleeder tube to the bleeder valve located on the slave cylinder and immerse the other end of the tube in a glass container partly filled with hydraulic fluid.

(3) Open the bleeder valve one complete turn, press the clutch pedal down slowly but tighten the bleeder valve just before it completes a full stroke.

(4) Allow the clutch pedal to return unaided.

(5) Continue operations (3) and (4) until all air is expelled from the system, i.e. until only fluid free of air bubbles emerges from the immersed end of the tube.

NOTE: During the operation ensure that the fluid level is maintained in the reservoir, and do not use the fluid being bled from the system for topping up.

(6) Close the bleeder valve, remove the bleeder tube, top up the master cylinder to the correct level.

7. ADJUSTMENT

TO ADJUST THROW-OUT LEVER FREE TRAVEL
(On slave cylinders prior to hydrostatic type)

(1) Raise the vehicle on a hoist or place over a pit. Work the clutch and ensure that the pedal returns to the fully off position.

(2) Disconnect the clutch throw-out lever return spring between the throw-out lever and the clip on the bellhousing.

(3) Check the adjustment by feeling the free travel of the lever from the full off position, and the position when

the thrust bearing contacts the clutch release levers or sleeve. The free travel is measured at the eye of the clutch throw-out lever which should move through .0625" to be correct.

(4) If adjustment is required, slacken the locknut on the slave cylinder push rod and screw the rod into the threaded yoke to increase the free travel, or screw the rod out to decrease the free travel.

(5) Tighten the locknut and replace the return spring.

NOTE: On cars used for competition or racing purposes, adjust the push rod to give maximum free play without causing grating of the gears when the clutch is operated and first gear is engaged.

(To Adjust Hydrostatic Slave Cylinders)

Adjustment is only required on a hydrostatic slave cylinder when a clutch unit or slave cylinder has been replaced, otherwise in service the hydrostatic slave cylinder automatically compensates for clutch wear.

(1) Take out the clevis pin attaching the push rod to the clutch throw-out lever.

(2) Slacken back the locknut at the threaded fork shoulder.

(3) Push the clutch throw-out lever until the throw-out bearing contacts the clutch release ring on the pressure plate assembly. Hold in this position.

(4) Press the push rod as far as it will go into the slave cylinder and hold in that position.

(5) Measure the distance between the centre of the clutch throw-out lever eye and the centre of the push rod eye, this should be .75".

(6) If adjustment is required, screw the threaded fork in the direction required to obtain the correct measurement.

(7) Tighten the locknut and replace and secure the clevis pin.

8. CLUTCH FAULT DIAGNOSIS

(1) Clutch slipping.

Possible cause — *Remedy*

(a) Throw-out lever free travel adjustment. — Check throw-out lever free travel and adjust as described.

(b) Frozen piston in master and/or slave cylinder. — Check, free up or renew as necessary.

(c) Worn or contaminated drive plate facings. — Check and renew driven plate or facings.

(d) Weak or defective pressure plate assembly. — Check and replace assembly if necessary.

(2) Clutch shudder.

Possible cause — *Remedy*

(a) Oil or grease on driven plate facings. — Check and renew driven plate or facings.

(b) Scored pressure plate or flywheel faces. — Renew as necessary.

(c) Loose, damaged or bent driven plate hub. — Renew driven plate.

(d) Cracked or misaligned pressure plate assembly. — Fit new assembly.

(3) Clutch Grab.

Possible cause — *Remedy*

(a) Gummy or worn driven plate facings. — Renew driven plate or facings.

(b) Cracked pressure plate face. — Check and replace assembly.

(c) Loose or broken engine mountings. — Check, tighten or renew mountings.

(d) Sluggish or deteriorated slave or master cylinder rubbers. — Check and overhaul as necessary.

(4) Throw-out Bearing Noise

Possible cause — *Remedy*

(a) Graphite ring worn or damaged. — Check and renew bearing.

(b) Worn or bent driven plate facings. — Renew driven plate.

(c) Throw-out bearing loose on fork. — Check retaining springs.

(d) Driven plate hub damaged or worn. — Renew driven plate.

(e) Worn or damaged pressure plate assembly. — Check and renew assembly.

MANUAL TRANSMISSION

SPECIFICATIONS

3.8 MODEL

Type	4 forward speeds and reverse
Synchromesh	On 2nd, 3rd and top gears
Ratios:	
Top	1.00:1
Third	1.283:1
Second	1.860:1
First	3.337:1
Reverse	3.337:1
Second and third gear end-float on mainshaft	.003" ± .001"
Laygear:	
End-float	.003" ± .001"
Thrust washer thickness	5 thicknesses available from .152" to .164"
Lubrication:	
Unit capacity	2½ Imp pt
Lubricant grade	SAE 30

4.2 and 2+2 MODELS

Type	4 forward speeds and reverse
Synchromesh	All forward gears
Ratios:	
Top	1.00:1
Third	1.27:1
Second	1.74:1
First	2.68:1
Reverse	3.08:1
Laygear:	
End-float	.005" ± .001"
Thrust washer thickness	5 thicknesses available from .152" to .164".
Gear end-float on mainshaft:	
First gear	.006" ± .001"
Second gear	.007" ± .001"
Third gear	.007" ± .001"
Lubricant grade	SAE 90EP

PROPELLER SHAFT

Type	Open – tubular
Number of universal joints	2
Type of universal joint	Needle roller bearing and trunnion.

1. GEARBOX — 3.8 MODEL

DESCRIPTION

The four speed gearbox has synchromesh on second, third and top gears which are in constant mesh and are helical cut. Spur gears are employed for first and reverse, and these gears are of the sliding mesh type.

The gearbox input shaft and gear main shaft are mounted in ball type bearings located at either end of the gear casing. A roller bearing is mounted on the spigot end of the main shaft and runs inside a bore centre of the gearbox input shaft. Second and third gears are mounted with needle roller bearings to the main shaft, thrust washers are fitted to control the thrust and the second and third gear end float. Oil seals are fitted to both clutch bellhousing and gear case end cover.

The front end of the gearbox input shaft is splined to engage the splines of the clutch driven plate hub, the spigot of the input shaft enters a bearing located in the rear flange of the crankshaft, for support of the input shaft. The rear end of the gear main shaft is splined to transfer the gearbox drive to the splined driving flange which connects to the propeller shaft. The speedometer driven gear assembly is located in the gear case rear cover with the driving gear positioned on the gear main shaft.

The laygear operates on needle roller bearings positioned at either end of the layshaft. Laygear end float is controlled by a thrust washer at each end of the laygear assembly.

The gear change mechanism is of the remote control type attached to the top of the gear case by ten securing bolts and spring washers. Gear selector forks and operating shafts are fitted in the gear change top cover and hold the gear selected by means of plungers and springs which engage in the indents machined in the operating shafts.

The gear case and clutch bellhousing are separate units and are attached to each other by eight securing bolts. The gear case end cover is also detachable and is secured to the gear case by seven securing bolts.

TO REMOVE AND INSTALL

The gearbox can only be removed from the vehicle by taking out the engine and gearbox assembly. This operation is described under ENGINE – TO REMOVE AND INSTALL. Follow the procedure described and separate the gearbox from the engine when the removal operation is complete. Installation is a reversal of the removal procedure.

TO DISMANTLE

(1) With the gearbox removed from the vehicle, take out the drain plug and drain off the oil, if not already done.

(2) With the gearshift lever in the neutral position, take out the ten securing bolts and washers and detach the gear change top cover assembly from the gear casing.

(3) Prise out the retaining springs attaching the clutch throw-out bearing to the clutch fork and slide the throw-out bearing off the gearbox input shaft.

(4) If the clutch cylinder has not been removed from the clutch bellhousing, remove the return spring and two securing nuts, take out the clevis pin and detach the slave cylinder.

(5) Slacken back the locknut and take out the Allen screw attaching the throw-out fork to the pivot shaft. Remove the pivot shaft and withdraw the throw-out bearing fork.

(6) Knock back the locking plate tabs and remove the locking wire from the securing bolts inside the clutch bellhousing, take out the eight securing bolts and separate the housing from the gear case.

(7) Unscrew the knurled nut attaching the speedo cable drive attachment to the driven gear assembly and remove, take out the locating screw holding the driven gear assembly in the gear case end cover and withdraw the assembly. Note the 'O' sealing ring.

(8) Slide the gears into position to lock them, by engaging top and first gears. Take out the split pin and remove the castellated nut and washer attaching the propeller shaft drive flange to the end of the main shaft, and draw off the drive flange from the main shaft splines.

(9) Take out the seven securing bolts and washers attaching the gear case end cover to the gear case.

NOTE: Before proceeding any further, a used or new layshaft will be required, or a false shaft made up of the same dimensions.

(10) Take out the fibre insert from the layshaft locating hole at the front of the gear casing.

(11) Insert the false shaft against the end of the layshaft, and as the rear cover is withdrawn complete with layshaft and reverse idler shaft, press the false shaft through the laygear to take up the position of the withdrawn layshaft.

(12) Take out the false shaft and gently lower the laygear assembly to the base of the gear casing.

(13) Slide the speedometer driving gear off the end of the gear main shaft, followed by the spacer.

(14) Turn the gearbox input shaft so that the two cutaway sections of the driving gear are parallel with the top and bottom of the gear casing.

(15) Using a soft faced or padded hammer, gently knock the rear end of the mainshaft to remove the gearbox input shaft complete with bearing from the front of the gear casing. Withdraw the input shaft and roller bearing from the mainshaft spigot.

NOTE: Great care must be taken throughout the operation of removing the mainshaft and gear assemblies that the gears do not become wedged with any part of the laygear assembly.

(16) With the gearbox input shaft free of the casing, knock the mainshaft through until it is clear of the bearing housed in the rear of the gear casing. Knock the rear bearing backwards to remove complete with circlip from the casing.

(17) Position the reverse gear forward to disengage and clear the first speed gear on the mainshaft. By lifting the front end of the mainshaft, the mainshaft and gear

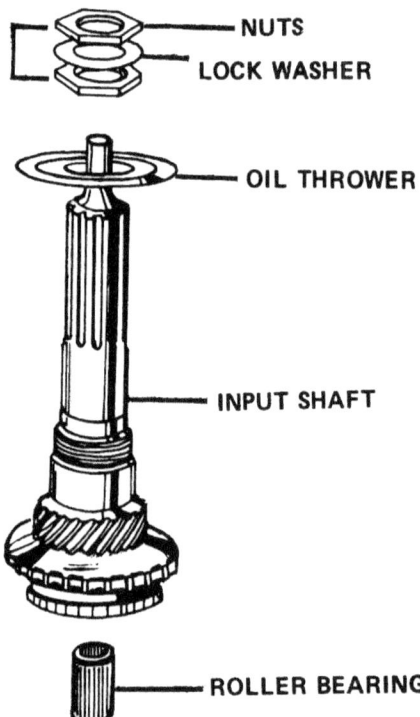

Exploded View of Gearbox Input Shaft Components (3.8 Model Shown).

assembly can now be pulled forward and out of the top of the casing.

(18) Position the reverse gear backward until it is free of the laygear first speed gear. The laygear assembly can now be lifted up and out of the gear casing.

NOTE: Two thrust washers are fitted at each end of the laygear, their position should be noted on removal. The needle rollers located at each end of the laygear will be free to fall out so ensure that none are lost.

(19) Remove the reverse gear by pushing it back into the casing and withdrawing from the top.

(20) Remove the third and top gear synchro hub and sleeve assembly from the front of the mainshaft, push the synchro hub out of the synchro sleeve and take out the six balls, springs and shims if any from the holes in the outside face of the synchro hub. Take out the plungers and balls from the holes in the centre bore of the synchro hub.

(21) Remove the second gear synchro hub complete with the first speed gear from the rear of the mainshaft, push the first speed gear off the synchro hub and take out the six balls, springs and shims if any from the holes in the outside face of the synchro hub. Take out the plunger and ball from the hole in the centre bore of the synchro hub.

(22) Remove the third speed gear at the front of the mainshaft by pressing in the plunger located between the shaft splines and locking the thrust washer in position. With the plunger fully pressed in, turn the thrust washer until the washer cutaways align with the splines of the mainshaft. Withdraw the thrust washer and third speed gear from the front of the mainshaft and take out the plunger and spring from the mainshaft.

NOTE: Second and third speed gears are mounted in needle bearings which will be free to fall out as the gears are removed from the mainshaft, ensure that none are lost.

(23) Repeat operation (22) to remove the second speed gear from the rear of the gear mainshaft.

(24) If it is necessary to replace the gearbox input shaft or bearing, separate by prising back the tab of the lock washer and loosen and remove the locknuts. Draw the bearing from the input shaft and remove the oil baffle.

(25) Remove the thrust washers at the ends of the laygear and take out the needle bearings and retaining clips.

NOTE: It should not be necessary to dismantle the remote control gear change mechanism in the top cover, but if defective proceed as follows:

(26) Remove the self locking nut, double spring washer, flat and fibre washers attaching the gearshift lever to the top cover assembly, withdraw the lever and rear fibre washer.

(27) Remove the four securing nuts attaching the selector lever cover to the top cover, remove the cover and

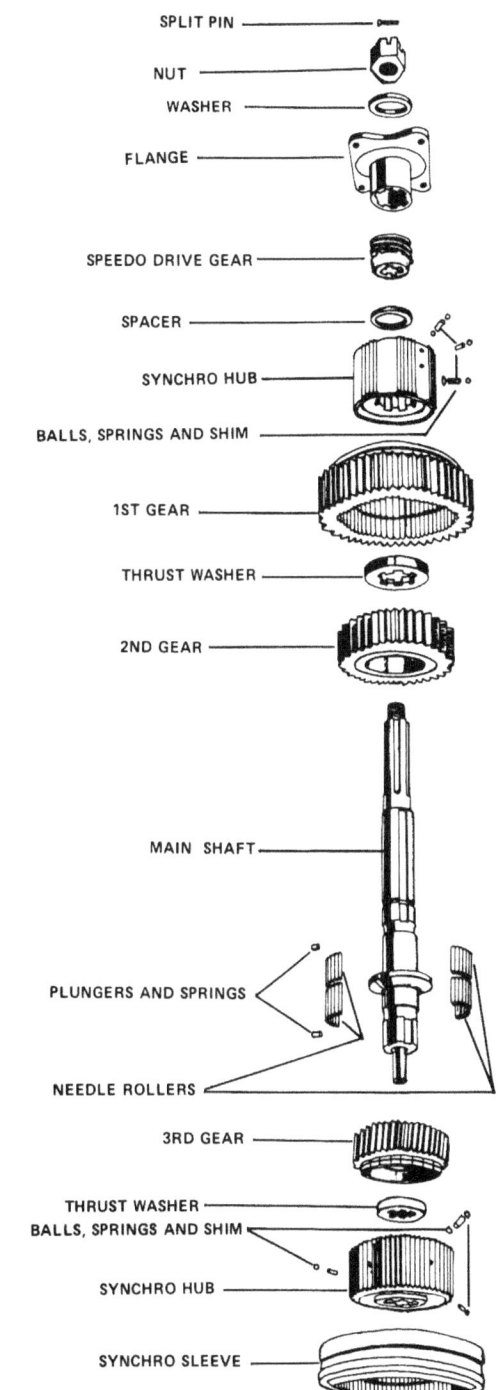

Exploded View of Mainshaft Components (3.8 Model Shown).

gasket and three balls, plungers, springs, and shims if any from the holes in the top cover.

(28) Take out the expansion plugs at the selector shaft holes at both ends of the top cover.

(29) Remove the locking wire in the heads of the retaining bolts securing the selectors and selector forks to

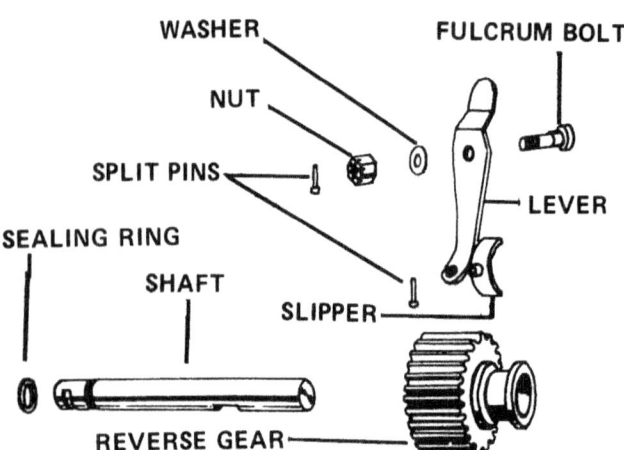

Exploded View of Reverse Gear Components (3.8 Model Shown).

the selector shafts, and loosen and remove the retaining bolts.

(30) Unscrew the reversing switch from the top cover and remove the plugs and fibre washers.

NOTE: Before removing the selector assemblies, mark the position, or draw a diagram of the selectors, selector forks and selector shafts in relation to the top cover to facilitate reassembly.

(31) With the top cover upside down, press the selector shafts through the top cover and collect the spacer, selectors and forks as they are disengaged.

NOTE: Two balls are fitted between the selector shafts at the front end of the top cover, the reverse selector is fitted with a ball and spring and a plunger and spring, note their positions.

TO CLEAN AND INSPECT

(1) Clean all the components of the gearbox and ensure that no metallic particles are left in the bottom of the gear case.

(2) Inspect all gears for wear or pitting of the teeth or wear on the synchronising teeth.

(3) Check the mainshaft and gearbox input shaft bearings for wear or roughness in operation.

(4) Check the bush pressed into the reverse gear for wear.

(5) Examine the layshaft and reverse idler shaft and the needle bearings and thrust washers for wear or pitting.

(6) Check the selectors and selector forks for wear, and detent balls and springs, for wear in the balls and loss of tension in the springs.

(7) Check the gearbox breather in the top cover and ensure that it is serviceable.

(8) Renew all worn or damaged components as necessary.

TO ASSEMBLE

(1) Install the selector shafts one at a time into position in the top cover engaging the selectors and forks, and ensure that they are fitted in their original positions as marked on dismantling.

NOTE: Ensure that the two balls are fitted between the selector shafts at the front end of the top cover. Check that the plunger and spring and ball and spring are located in the reverse selector.

(2) Install the retaining bolts and secure the selectors, selector forks and spacer to the selector shafts and lock in position with locking wire.

(3) Install new expansion plugs in the holes in the top cover using a sealing compound on the edges of the plugs prior to expanding in position.

(4) Install the reversing switch, and the plugs and fibre washers.

(5) Using a new gasket, install the selector lever cover to the top cover, positioning first the three balls, plungers, springs and shims if any. Fit and tighten the four securing nuts and washers.

(6) Install the gear lever assembly engaging the ball end of the lever in the ball socket of the main selector shaft, ensure that the washers are installed in correct sequence, with one fibre washer to the rear, and a fibre washer, flat washer and double spring washer to the front, securing the assembly with the self locking nut.

NOTE: Working the gearshift lever, ensure that all positions for gear changing including neutral, can be selected.

(7) Assemble the laygear, installing a needle roller ring into the bore at each end of the laygear, using a thick grease, coat the needle rollers and insert into position at each end of the laygear. A further needle roller ring is fitted to the front end of the laygear. Install the thrust washers in their original positions at the ends of the laygear.

(8) Install the reverse gear into the gear casing, engage the fork secured to the side of the gear casing and move the gear backwards as far as possible.

(9) Install the laygear assembly aligning the thrust washers and centre bore with the shaft holes in the casing, insert the false shaft ensuring that the needle rollers are not dislodged.

(10) Check the end-float clearance between the thrust washer and the rear casing face on which it runs, this should be .003" ± .001". If adjustment is required a thrust washer of the appropriate thickness must be fitted, thrust washers of varying degrees of thickness can be obtained for this purpose.

(11) When the adjustment is complete, position a piece of strong string around the laygear near each end and with the ends of the string up and over the sides of the gear casing, push out the false shaft allowing the laygear to drop down in the gear casing to facilitate installation of the mainshaft gear assembly. Great care must be taken throughout the operation not to dislodge the needle rollers from their positions.

(12) To assemble the gears on the mainshaft, coat 41 needle rollers with thick grease and install in position on the mainshaft at the rear of the mainshaft lip. Slide the second gear over the mainshaft and position on the needle rollers, the synchro cone end of the gear should be facing to the rear of the mainshaft.

(13) Install the thrust washer locking plunger and spring in the mainshaft, slide the thrust washer over the shaft until it abuts the plunger, line up the hole in the outer surface of the synchro cone with the top of the plunger and press in the plunger by inserting a metal pin, push in and turn the thrust washer until the splines lock behind the splines of the mainshaft and release the plunger into a recess in the thrust washer to lock it in position.

(14) Check the end-float clearance of the second gear by feeler gauge, the clearance between the face of the thrust washer and the shoulder on the mainshaft should be .003" ± .001". If adjustment is required, thrust washers of varying degrees of thickness can be obtained for this purpose.

(15) Following the procedure as described in operations (12), (13) and (14), install the third gear on the front of the mainshaft with the synchro cone facing towards the front of the shaft.

(16) Install the six balls, springs and shims if any to the holes in the outside face of the second gear synchro hub and retain them in the depressed position by fitting and tightening a hose clip over the hub and balls and springs. Engage the first gear on the second gear synchro hub mating the stop button on the outside face of the synchro hub with the machined tooth on the inside face of the first gear sleeve. Gently squeeze together the assembly in a padded vice until the spring loaded balls are within the inside face of the first gear sleeve. Remove the hose clip and press in the hub until a click is heard when the spring loaded balls will have engaged in the groove on the inside centre of the first gear sleeve.

NOTE: On both second and third gear synchro hub assemblies it should require firm pressure, i.e. 65 lbs. on second gear and 55 lbs. on third gear, to move the selector sleeves from the neutral location in the synchro hubs. Shims can be installed beneath the ball springs in the synchro hub if additional pressure is required.

(17) Install the first gear and second gear synchro assembly on the mainshaft splines and ensure that the hub moves freely on the splines, if necessary try engaging the hub on different splines until a free action is obtained. Mark the position of the hub in relation to one of the mainshaft splines when the best position has been obtained.

(18) Remove the first gear and second gear synchro assembly from the mainshaft and install the ball and plunger in the synchro hub, refit the hub to the mainshaft and ensure that the marked splines are aligned.

NOTE: The raised boss on the centre bore of the synchro hub and the selector fork recess on the operating sleeve should be facing to the rear of the mainshaft.

(19) With the front end of the mainshaft held in a padded vice, move the first gear upwards into its operating position on the hub, exert slight pressure downwards on the synchro hub assembly and check that the second speed gear rotates without drag between the synchro cones of second gear and the synchro hub. If adjustment is required, a longer plunger should be fitted to the synchro hub, plungers of varying lengths are available for this purpose.

(20) Install the six balls, springs and shims if any to the holes in the outside face of the third and top gear synchro hub and retain them in the depressed position by fitting and tightening a hose clip over the hub and balls and

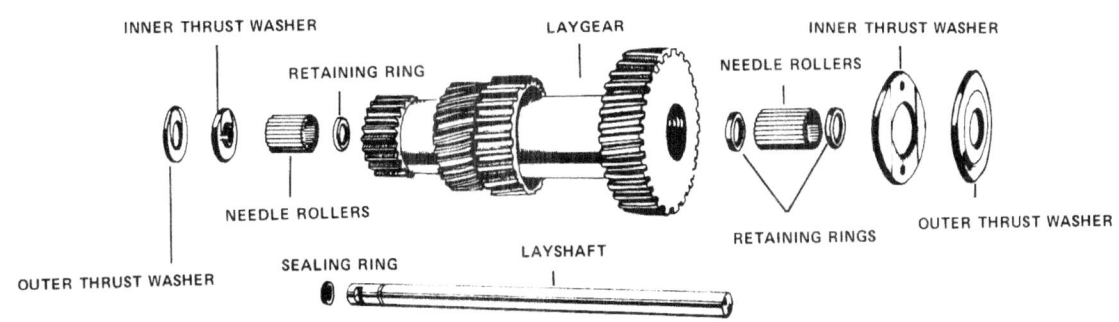

Exploded View of the Laygear Components (3.8 Model Shown).

springs. Engage the operating sleeve on the synchro hub aligning the two ball and plunger holes in the hub with the two machined teeth on the inner face of the sleeve and with the wide chamfered end of the sleeve in the same direction as the raised boss on the centre bore of the synchro hub. Gently squeeze together the assembly until the spring loaded balls are within the inside face of the sleeve. Remove the hose clip and press in the hub until a click is heard when the spring loaded balls will have engaged in the groove on the inside of the operating sleeve.

NOTE: Check the tension between the synchro hub and sleeve, adding shims below the springs if necessary.

(21) Install the third and top synchro assembly on the mainshaft splines and line the machined tooth on the inner face of the selector sleeve with the first groove, i.e. the groove nearest to the spigot end of the mainshaft, in the mainshaft splines. The wide chamfered edge of the selector sleeve should be facing also towards the spigot end of the mainshaft.

(22) Ensure that the hub moves freely on the splines, if not check the splines on the mainshaft and the centre bore of the hub and remove any burrs or obstructions until a free movement is obtained.

(23) Remove the synchro hub assembly and install the two balls followed by the plungers to the holes in the centre of the hub, install the hub assembly on the mainshaft as in operation (21).

(24) With the rear end of the mainshaft held in a padded vice, move the selector sleeve down and engage the third speed gear, by lifting and lowering the synchro hub assembly, no resistance should be felt through .094" of movement. If resistance is felt a shorter third gear plunger will be required, plungers are available in varying lengths for this purpose.

(25) Move the selector sleeve up towards the spigot end of the mainshaft and into the top gear position, by lifting and lowering the synchro hub assembly no resistance should be felt through .190" of movement. With slight pressure exerted downwards on the synchro hub assembly check that the third speed gear rotates without drag between the synchro cones. If the synchro cones drag a longer top gear plunger will be necessary, if resistance is felt on the hub assembly movement a shorter top gear plunger will be necessary. Plungers are available of varying lengths for this purpose.

NOTE: The top gear plunger is the plunger which is in line with the machined tooth in the selector sleeve when viewed from the wide chamfered end of the sleeve. The remaining plunger controls the third speed interlock.

(26) Install the oil baffle on the gearbox input shaft, slide the bearing, complete with collar and circlip located in the groove on the outside of the bearing into position on the input shaft and secure with the securing nut, fit the lock washer and locknut and after tightening bend over the lock washer tabs to secure. Lubricate the roller bearing and position in the centre bore of the input shaft.

(27) Pass the rear end of the mainshaft assembly through the top of the gear casing and out through the bearing aperture at the rear.

(28) With a new gasket positioned on the front face of the gear casing enter the gearbox input shaft with the two cutaway sections of the gear parallel with the top and bottom of the gear case, engage the spigot end of the mainshaft in the roller bearing of the gearbox input shaft. Gently knock in the gearbox input shaft until the bearing is fitted in its location with the collar and circlip against the face of the gear case.

(29) Slide the rear bearing complete with circlip over the rear of the mainshaft and into its aperture at the rear of the gear case. Supporting the gearbox input shaft, gently and evenly knock in the rear bearing until the circlip is against the face at the rear of the gear case.

(30) Bring the laygear up into position engaging the laygear and mainshaft gears by lifting the laygear with the two pieces of string, align the thrust washers and the centre bore of the laygear with the layshaft holes in the case, insert the false shaft at the front of the case and press through the assembly ensuring that none of the needle rollers are dislodged. Remove the pieces of string.

(31) Install the spacer followed by the speedo driving gear on the rear of the mainshaft, ensure that the plain end of the speedo driving gear abuts the spacer.

(32) Fit a new oil seal in the gear case rear end cover, replace the 'O' sealing ring on the layshaft and reverse idler shaft, position a new gasket on the rear face of the gear case.

(33) With the layshaft and reverse idler shaft still located in position in the end cover, engage the shafts in their respective apertures in the rear face of the gear case. Keep the false shaft in contact with the end of the layshaft and press both shafts into position forcing the false shaft out of the gear case front. Ensure that the reverse idler shaft engages the bore of the reverse gear. Install and tighten the seven securing bolts and spring washers pulling up the end cover evenly.

(34) Engage top and first gears to lock the gearbox, install the propeller drive shaft flange on the end of the mainshaft and fit the washer and castellated nut, securely tighten the nut and fit a new split pin to lock in position. Move the gears back to the neutral position.

(35) Fit a new 'O' sealing ring to the speedo driven gear and insert in position in the case rear end cover securing with the retaining bolt and spring washer. Install the speedo

drive attachment entering the square drive of the attachment in the drive of the driven gear, secure in position with the knurled nut.

(36) Install a new fibre insert in the layshaft locating hole at the front of the gear case. Fit a new oil seal to the clutch bellhousing.

(37) Position the bellhousing on the front of the gear case passing the gearbox input shaft through the centre of the oil seal. Install and tighten evenly the eight securing bolts fitting new lock washers and locking wire.

(38) Install the gearbox drain plug and fibre washer, install the clutch throw-out fork and pivot shaft, fit and tighten the Allen screw and lock in position with the locknut. Install the throw-out bearing in the fork and secure with the two retaining springs.

(39) Install the slave cylinder in position on the bellhousing engaging the push rod, fit the return spring and clip, the clevis pin and split pin and secure the assembly with the two securing nuts.

(40) With a new gasket fitted to the top of the gear case, position the top cover assembly engaging the selector forks in the selector sleeves and the locating dowels in their respective holes. Install the ten securing bolts and spring washers ensuring that the correct length bolts are fitted in the appropriate positions.

(41) Check that all gears can be engaged by selection with the gearshift lever, fill the gearbox to the correct level with the recommended oil and install the assembly in the vehicle as described previously.

2. GEARBOX — 4.2 and 2+2 MODELS

DESCRIPTION

The four speed gearbox has synchromesh on all forward gears which are helical cut. Reverse gear is operated through a reverse idler gear meshing with the laygear and reverse gear on the mainshaft. Oil is pressure fed to the gears by a gear type oil pump located and driven from the rear of the gear mainshaft.

The gearbox input shaft and gear mainshaft are mounted in ball type bearings located at either end of the gear casing. A roller bearing is located within the centre bore of the gearbox input shaft to accommodate the spigot on the forward end of the mainshaft. Needle rollers are used to mount the gears to the mainshaft and as the rollers are fitted in sets they must be kept in sets when dismantling. Oil seals are fitted to both clutch bellhousing and gear case end cover assembly.

The front end of the gearbox input shaft is splined to engage the splines of the clutch driven plate hub, the spigot of the input shaft engages a bearing located in the rear flange of the crankshaft for support of the input shaft. The rear end of the gear mainshaft is splined to transfer the gearbox drive to the splined driving flange which connects to the propeller shaft. The speedometer driven gear assembly and the oil pump assembly are located in the gear case rear cover assembly, the driving gear for the speedo is positioned on the mainshaft.

The laygear is mounted on needle rollers located at each end of the layshaft, with the laygear end-float controlled by thrust washers also located at each end of the assembly.

The gearchange mechanism is of the remote control type attached to the top cover of the gear casing, selector shafts and selector forks are mounted within the top cover and removed as an assembly with the top cover. Two balls and a pin positioned at the front and between the selector shafts ensure that two gear selectors cannot be operated together.

The gear casing, clutch bellhousing and gear case rear cover assembly are detachable, eight securing bolts attaching the clutch housing to the gear case and seven securing bolts attaching the rear cover assembly to the gear case.

TO REMOVE AND INSTALL

Follow the procedure described for the 3.8 model as under the appropriate heading.

TO DISMANTLE

(1) With the gearbox removed from the vehicle, take out the drain plug and drain off the oil, if not already done.

(2) With the gearshift lever in the neutral position, take out the eight securing bolts and two nuts and detach the gear change top cover assembly from the gear casing.

(3) Prise out the retaining springs attaching the clutch throw-out bearing to the clutch fork and slide the throw-out bearing off the gearbox input shaft.

(4) If the clutch slave cylinder has not been removed unscrew the two securing nuts and detach from the clutch bellhousing.

(5) Slacken back the locknut and take out the Allen screw attaching the clutch throw-out fork to the pivot shaft. Remove the pivot shaft and fork from the housing.

(6) Knock back the locking plate tabs and remove the locking wire from the securing bolts inside the clutch bellhousing, take out the eight securing bolts and separate the housing from the gear case.

(7) Slide the gears into first and reverse to lock the mainshaft, take out the split pin and remove the castellated nut from the rear end of the mainshaft. Draw the propeller shaft driving flange off the mainshaft splines.

(8) Take out the four setscrews and remove the rear cover at the end of the assembly.

(9) Take out the speedo driven gear assembly retaining bolt and withdraw the assembly. Remove the speedo driving gear from the rear of the mainshaft.

(10) Remove the seven securing bolts and spring washers attaching the rear cover assembly to the gear case, detach the assembly and remove the spacer and oil pump driving pin.

(11) Take out the fibre insert from the layshaft locating hole at the front of the gear casing.

(12) Knock out the layshaft from the front of the gear case with a drift of smaller diameter, ensure that the washer fitted with a locating peg at the rear of the laygear falls down in a clockwise direction (viewed from the rear of the gear case), to avoid obstructing the reverse gear during removal of the mainshaft. If necessary use a piece of wire to push the washer down.

(13) Turn the gearbox input shaft so that the two cutaway sections of the driving gear are parallel with the top and bottom of the gear casing.

(14) Insert two levers behind the driving gear and gently ease the gearbox input shaft and bearing out and clear of the gear case. If the roller bearing and spacer (if any) is left on the mainshaft spigot, withdraw from the mainshaft.

(15) Ensure that the laygear is as far down in the gear casing as possible, turn the mainshaft until a cutaway section of the third and top synchro hub is above the laygear teeth, to avoid obstruction on removal of the mainshaft assembly.

(16) With the reverse gear hard against the first gear, use a soft faced or padded hammer to gently knock the rear end of the mainshaft through the rear bearing until it is clear of the bearing shoulder on the mainshaft.

NOTE: Great care must be taken throughout the operation of removing the mainshaft and gear assemblies that the gears do not become wedged with any part of the laygear assembly.

(17) Knock the rear bearing backwards to remove complete with circlip from the casing, secure the reverse gear to the mainshaft to avoid its falling off by tying a piece of string or fastening a hose clip on the mainshaft immediately behind it.

(18) Knock back the locking tab and slacken the retaining bolt for the reverse relay lever on the side of the gear case until the lever can be moved to the rear of the case.

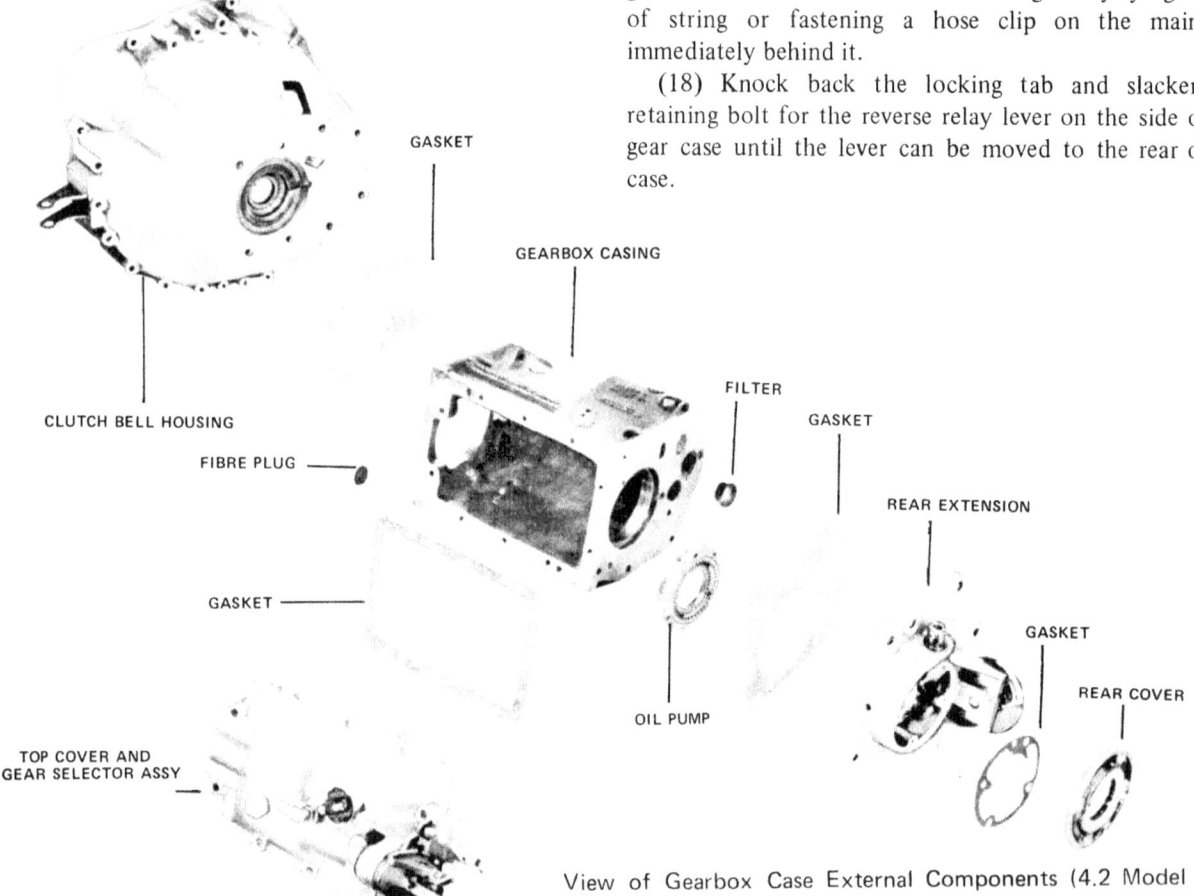

View of Gearbox Case External Components (4.2 Model Shown).

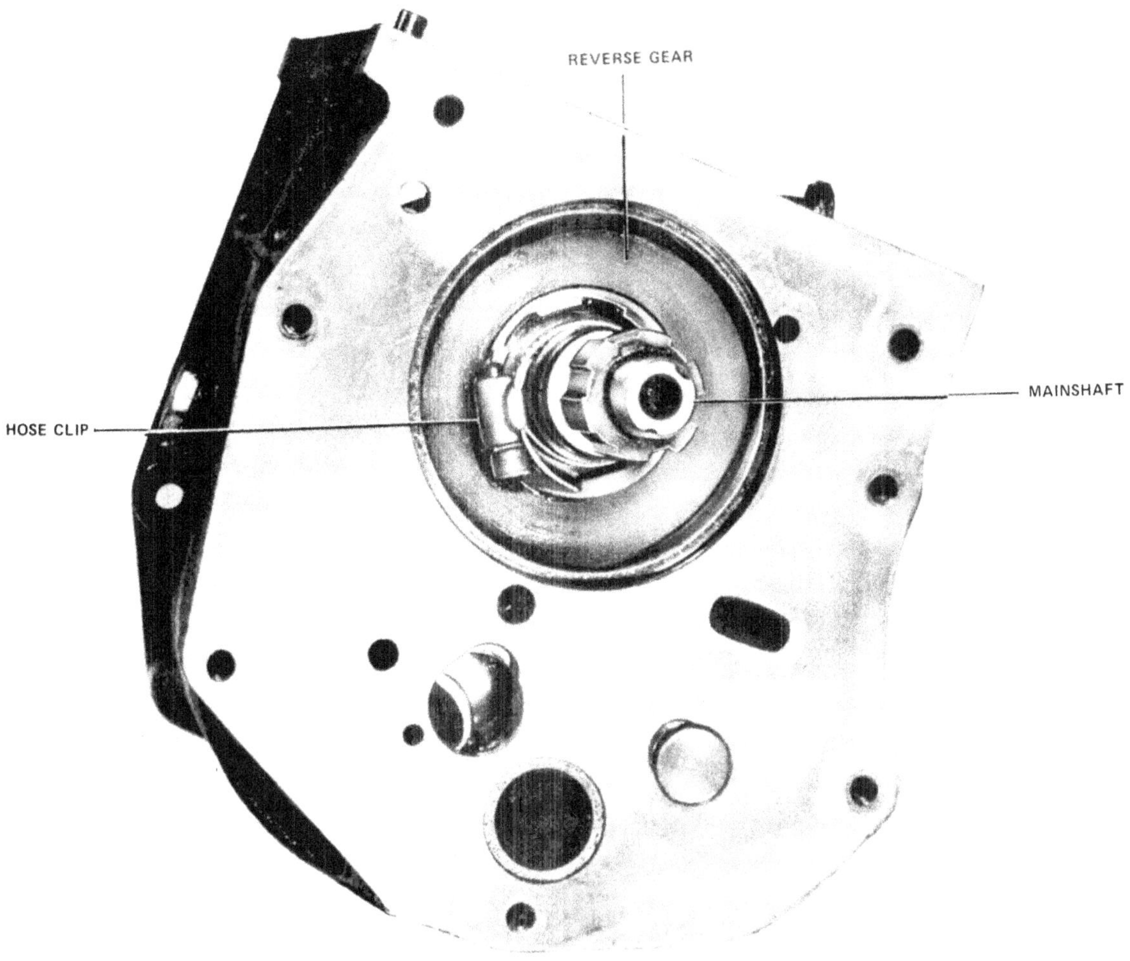

Method of Holding Reverse Gear to Mainshaft, when Removing Mainshaft from Gear Case (4.2 Model Shown).

Exploded View of Mainshaft Components (4.2 Model Shown).

1. Mainshaft.
2. Lockwasher.
3. Nut.
4. 3rd/Top synchro assembly.
5. Synchro ring.
6. 3rd gear.
7. 2nd gear.
8. Synchro ring.
9. 1st/2nd synchro assembly.
10. Synchro ring.
11. 1st gear.
12. Reverse gear.
13. Mainshaft rear bearing.
14. Circlip.
15. Bearing sleeve.
16. Speedo drive gear.
17. Drive flange.
18. Washer.
19. Nut.
20. Needle bearings for 11 (120).
21. Needle bearings for 7 (106).
22. Needle bearings for 6 (106).

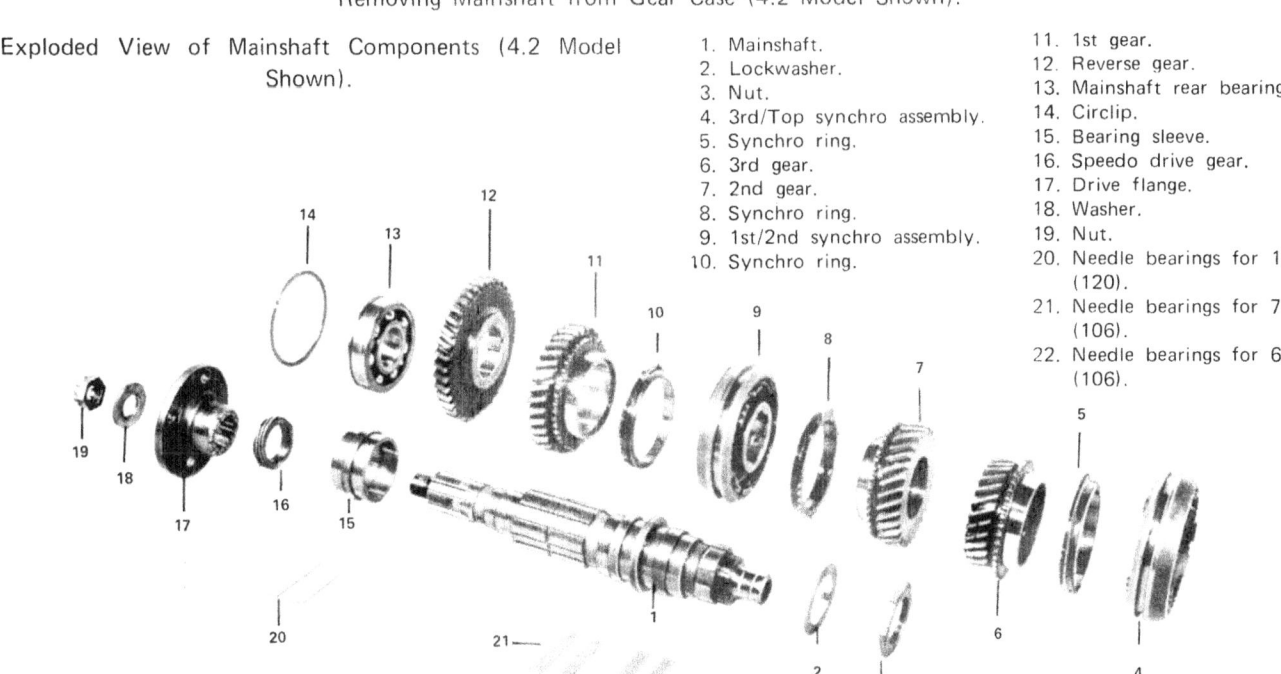

(19) By lifting the front end of the mainshaft the assembly can now be withdrawn forward and out of the casing top. Lift out the laygear assembly, pull out the reverse idler shaft and remove the reverse idler gear.

NOTE: Thrust washers are fitted at each end of the laygear, their position should be noted on removal. The needle rollers and retainers fitted at each end of the laygear will be free to fall out, so ensure that none are lost.

(20) Remove the hose clip or string holding the reverse gear to the mainshaft and slide off the gear.

NOTE: Before dismantling the gear assemblies, note that the needle rollers used to mount the gears to the mainshaft are fitted in sets and must be kept in sets throughout the operation.

(21) Draw the first gear from the rear end of the mainshaft complete with needle rollers (120), spacer and sleeve.

(22) Withdraw the first and second gear synchro hub assembly complete with synchro cones at each side, from the mainshaft.

(23) Remove the second gear from the rear end of the mainshaft complete with needle rollers (106) and spacer.

(24) Knock or prise back the tab of the locking washer and loosen and remove the nut securing the third and top gear synchro assembly to the front of the mainshaft.

(25) Withdraw the third and top gear synchro hub assembly complete with synchro cones, one at each side, from the front of the mainshaft.

(26) Remove the third gear from the mainshaft complete with needle rollers (106) and spacer.

(27) With the synchro hubs positioned over a clean container to collect the components, push the synchro hubs out of the selector sleeves and allow the balls, plungers, thrust plates and springs to fall in the container.

(28) Knock or prise back the tab on the locking washer and remove the nut securing the front bearing to the gearbox input shaft, remove the lockwasher, bearing and oil baffle.

(29) Remove the washers, retaining rings and needle rollers (29 each end) from the laygear centre bore.

(30) If necessary, remove the three countersunk screws attaching the oil pump housing to the inside face of the rear cover assembly, remove the housing by entering two of the countersunk screws into the threaded holes in the housing and screwing them up evenly until the housing is detached.

NOTE: Mark the oil pump gears in relation to the housing so that they can be fitted in their original position on reassembly.

It should not be necessary to dismantle the remote control gear change mechanism in the top cover, but if defective proceed as follows:

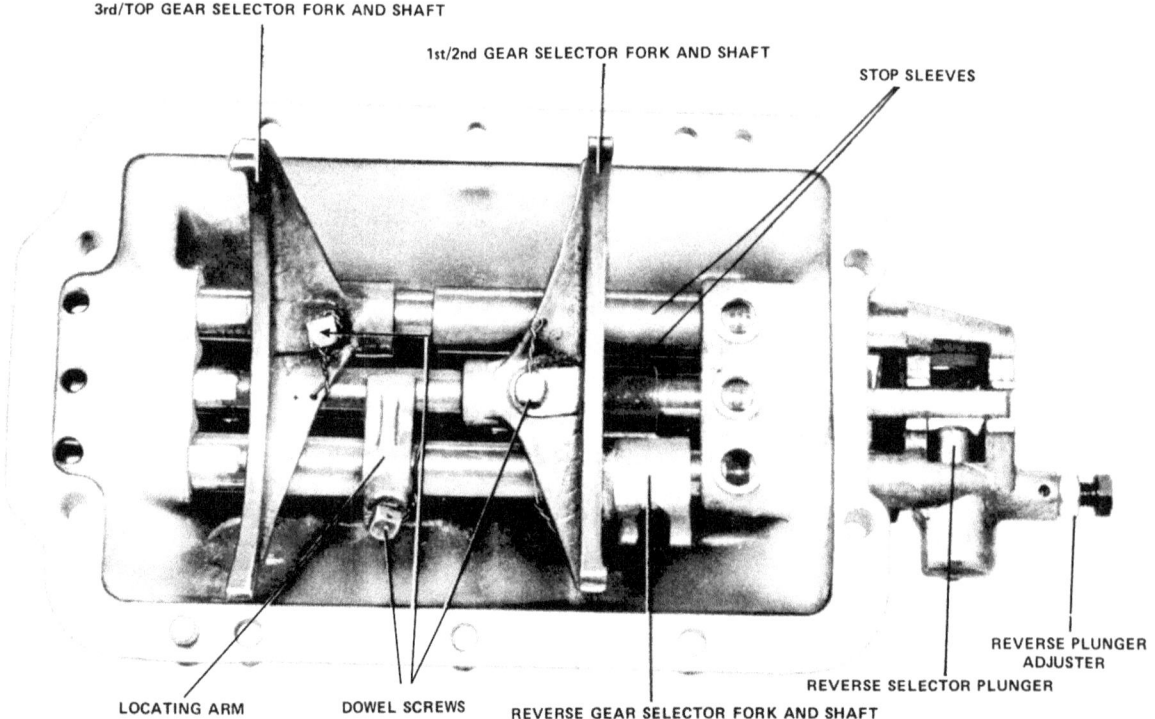

View of the Underside of the Top Cover Showing Selector Arrangement (4.2 Model Shown).

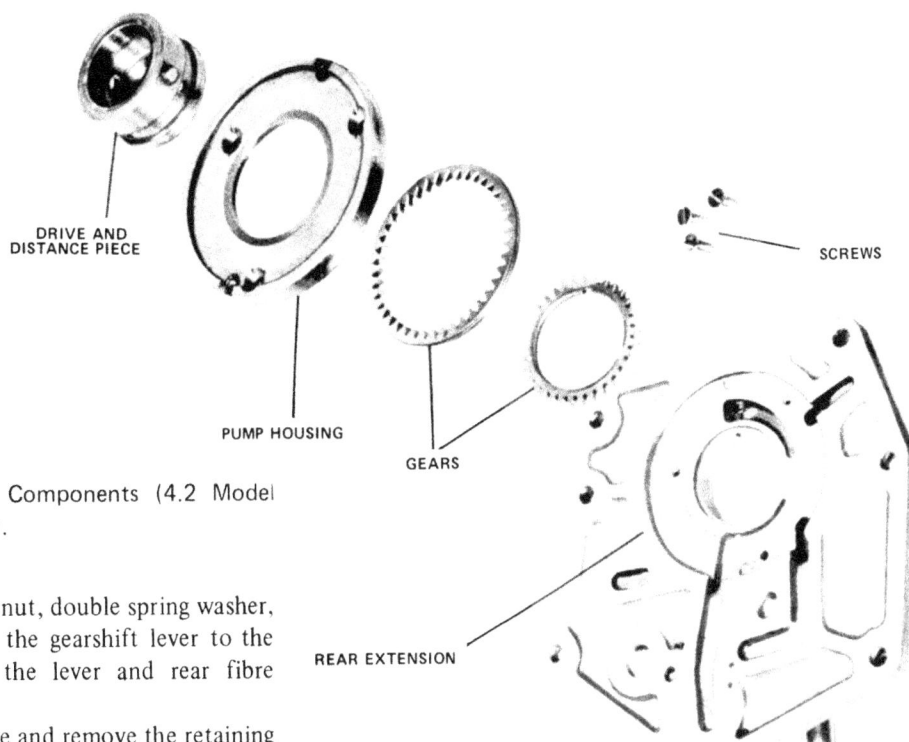

Exploded View of Oil Pump Components (4.2 Model Shown).

(31) Remove the self locking nut, double spring washer, flat and fibre washers attaching the gearshift lever to the top cover assembly, withdraw the lever and rear fibre washer.

(32) Take out the locking wire and remove the retaining bolts securing the selector forks in position on the selector shafts.

NOTE: *Before removing the selector shafts and forks, mark the position or draw a diagram of the selector shafts and forks in relation to the top cover, this will assist in reassembly.*

(33) Pull out the third and top gear selector shaft and collect the selector fork, spacer and ball located in the front of the selector shaft.

(34) Pull out the reverse gear selector shaft and collect the reverse fork, detent plunger and stop spring.

(35) Pull out the first and second gear selector shaft and collect the selector fork, spacer and remaining ball and pin located at the front of the selector shafts.

TO CLEAN AND INSPECT

Follow the procedure as described for the 3.8 model as under the appropriate heading.

TO ASSEMBLE

(1) With new 'O' sealing rings fitted to the selector shafts install the selector shafts, forks and spacers in their original positions in the top cover, ensure that the two balls with the pin between are located in position in the holes at the front of the selector shafts.

(2) If the reverse selector plunger and spring have been disturbed, adjust by slackening back the adjusting bolt and locknut at the end of the selector shaft, press in the plunger as far as possible, tighten the adjusting bolt to retain the plunger, gently slacken back the adjusting bolt until the plunger is free but retained by the ball locating in the groove in the body of the plunger. With the adjusting bolt held in this position tighten the locknut.

(3) Ensure that the selector forks are correctly positioned on the selector shafts with the bolt locating holes in line with the bolt holes in the selectors, install the retaining bolts, tighten and wire in position.

(4) Install the gear lever to the top cover, with one fibre washer at the rear, and a fibre washer, flat washer and double spring washer to the front, secure the assembly with the self locking nut.

(5) Position a retaining ring inside the centre bore at the front of the laygear, coat 29 needle rollers with thick grease and insert them in position at the front of the centre bore, coat the inner thrust washer with thick grease and position it on the front face of the laygear engaging the locating peg in the laygear face groove.

(6) Position a retaining ring inside the centre bore at the rear of the laygear, coat 29 needle rollers with thick grease and insert them in position in the centre bore of the laygear followed by another retaining ring.

(7) Install the reverse idler gear, relay lever and idler shaft in the gear casing but do not tighten the retaining bolt.

(8) Coat the rear laygear washer with thick grease and position on the boss face engaging the locating peg, coat the

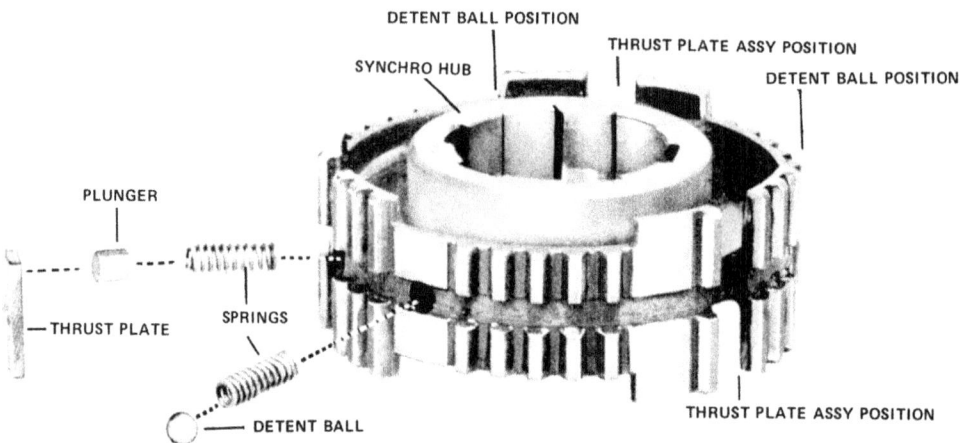

Synchro Hub Positions for Thrust Plate Assemblies and Detent Balls and Springs (4.2 Model Shown).

outer front thrust washer with thick grease and position on the front of laygear against the inner thrust washer.

(9) Very carefully install the laygear in the gear casing and insert the layshaft without dislodging the thrust washers or needle rollers.

(10) Check the end-float clearance between the rear thrust washer and the rear face of the laygear, this should be .005" ± .001". If adjustment is required, an outer thrust washer of the appropriate thickness must be fitted, thrust washers of varying degrees of thickness can be obtained for this purpose.

(11) When the adjustment is complete, position a piece of strong string around the laygear near each end and with the ends of the string up and over the sides of the gear case, push out the layshaft and lower the laygear to the bottom of the gear case.

(12) To assemble the third and top gear synchro hub, (identified by a groove machined on the edge of the hub), engage the selector sleeve on the synchro hub with the narrow chamfered edge of the sleeve in the same direction as the large raised boss of the hub centre, and with the ball and spring holes in line with the three detent grooves in the teeth in the inner face of the sleeve.

NOTE: To establish the ball and spring holes, note that the synchro hub has slots across the toothed outer face, these slots accommodate the thrust plates, with the plungers and springs located in the holes in the centre of the slots. The remaining three holes in the synchro hub outer face are the location for the balls and springs.

(13) Place the synchro hub and sleeve flat on a clean part of the workbench, by packing up the hub centre and allowing the sleeve to remain on the bench expose the ball and spring holes at a point level with the edge of the selector sleeve.

(14) Coat the synchro hub balls, plungers, thrust plates and springs with grease, install the three springs, plungers

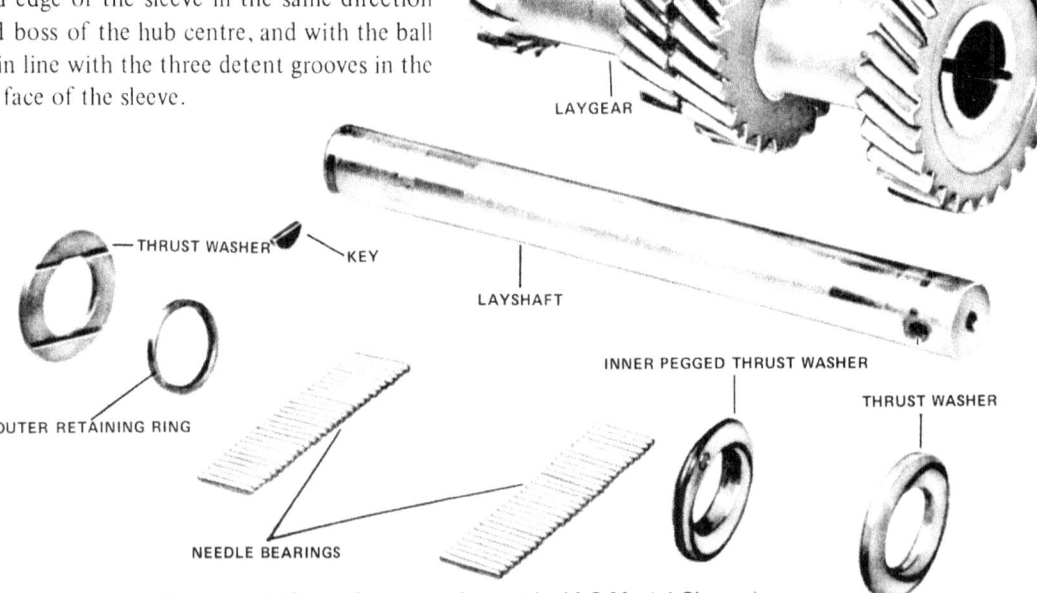

Dismantled View of Laygear Assembly (4.2 Model Shown).

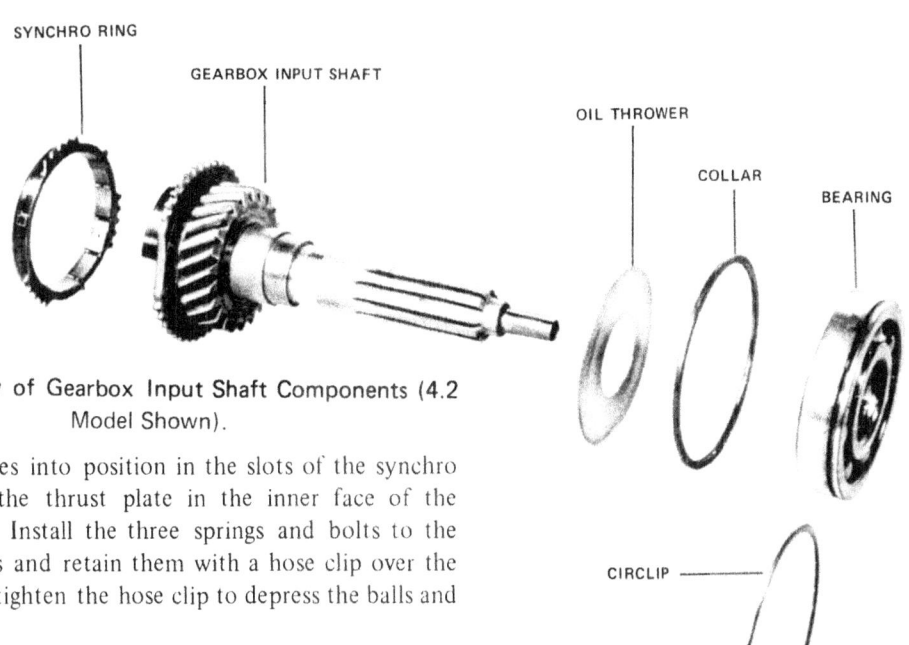

Exploded View of Gearbox Input Shaft Components (4.2 Model Shown).

and thrust plates into position in the slots of the synchro hub engaging the thrust plate in the inner face of the selector sleeve. Install the three springs and bolts to the remaining holes and retain them with a hose clip over the hub and balls, tighten the hose clip to depress the balls and thrust plates.

(15) Holding the operating sleeve in contact with the hose clip remove the packing from under the hub centre and place the assembly back on the bench supported by the bottom edge of the operating sleeve.

(16) Exert slight downward pressure on the hub centre and by using a screwdriver push down the thrust plates until they locate in the groove in the centre of the selector sleeve inner face. Additional pressure or a gentle knock on the hub centre will enter the spring loaded balls in the sleeve inner face and a click will be heard as they engage in the centre groove. With the synchro hub positioned fully in the selector sleeve the hose clip will detach from the assembly. Carry out operations (12), (13), (14), (15), and (16) to assemble first and second gear synchro hub assembly.

(17) Install 106 needle rollers coated with grease to the bearing sleeve on the forward end of the mainshaft with the spacer fitted between the two roller sections.

NOTE: As stated on dismantling the needle rollers are in sets and must be refitted in their original location as a set. 53 needle rollers are mounted at each side of the spacer. The third gear has a groove to identify it machined around the periphery of the gear.

(18) Slide the third gear over the needle rollers on the mainshaft with the fixed synchro cone on the gear pointing forward, install a loose synchro cone in position on the fixed gear synchro cone, followed by the synchro hub assembly with the wide chamfered edge of the selector sleeve pointing forward. Fit and tighten the locking washer and securing nut retaining the assembly to the front of the mainshaft, knock over the lock washer to secure. Position the loose synchro cone at the end of the synchro hub and retain in that position.

(19) Install 106 needle rollers coated with grease to the bearing sleeve on the rear end of the mainshaft, with the spacer fitted between the two roller sections.

NOTE: Ensure that the correct needle roller set is fitted.

(20) Slide the second gear over the needle rollers on the mainshaft with the fixed synchro cone on the gear pointing to the rear, install a loose synchro cone in position on the fixed synchro cone, followed by the synchro hub assembly with the wide chamfered edge of the selector sleeve pointing to the rear. Install a second loose synchro cone to the end of the synchro hub.

(21) Coat 120 needle rollers with grease and fit 60 rollers at each side of the spacer in the first gear centre bore, insert the loose bearing sleeve into position in the bore. Slide the first gear complete with sleeve and bearings into position on the mainshaft with the fixed synchro cone on the gear engaging the loose synchro cone at the end of the synchro hub assembly.

(22) Install the reverse gear on the mainshaft with the chamfered edge of the teeth pointing forward, tie a piece of string or fit a hose clip on the mainshaft at the rear of the reverse gear to prevent the gear from falling off during mainshaft installation.

(23) Assemble the gearbox input shaft, fitting the oil baffle followed by the bearing complete with collar and circlip, install and tighten the lock washer and securing nut, knock down the lock washer tab to secure.

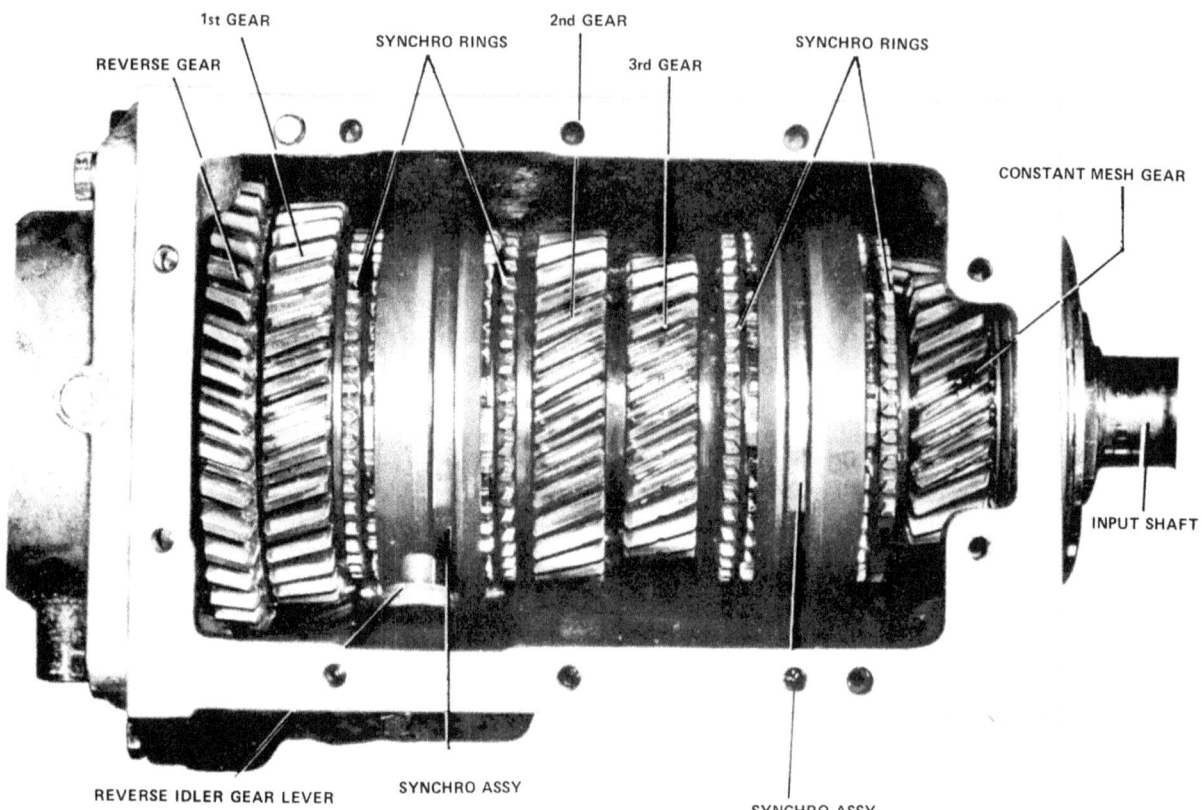

View of Gearbox Mainshaft Assembly (4.2 Model Shown).

(24) Install the mainshaft assembly through the top of the gear case with the tail end of the mainshaft through the rear bearing hole.

(25) Position a new gasket on the front face of the gear case, enter the gearbox input shaft with the cutaway section of the gear parallel with the top and bottom of the gear case.

(26) With the gearbox input shaft bearing knocked into position in the gear case, engage the mainshaft spigot in the roller bearing located in the input shaft centrebore. Remove the hose clip or string from the rear of the mainshaft.

(27) Install the rear bearing over the end of the mainshaft, and with the gearbox input shaft held in position, knock the rear bearing evenly into the gear case until the circlip is against the rear face.

NOTE: *Before proceeding any further the end-float clearances for first, second and third gear should be checked. The specified clearances for each gear are stated in the SPECIFICATION section. If end-float is found in excess of the specified clearance new parts as necessary must be fitted to rectify.*

(28) Bring the laygear up into position, engaging the laygear and mainshaft gear by lifting the laygear with the two pieces of string, align the thrust washers and centre bore of the laygear with the layshaft holes at each end of the gear case. Insert the layshaft and press through the assembly ensuring that none of the needle rollers or thrust washers are dislodged. Remove the pieces of string.

(29) Tighten the reverse idler relay lever retaining bolt at the side of the gear case and secure by knocking over the tab on the locking washer.

(30) Install the gears to the oil pump, lubricating the pump body and gears with oil. Ensure that the gears are fitted in their original position as marked on dismantling. Install the three countersunk screws and secure the pump housing, stake the screws to lock them in position.

(31) Install the woodruff keys locating the ends of the layshaft and reverse idler shaft in the rear of the gear case. Position a new gasket on the casing rear face.

(32) Install the spacer and oil pump driving pin, position the rear cover assembly on the gear case fitting and tighten evenly the securing bolts.

(33) Slide the speedometer driving gear into position on the mainshaft, insert the speedometer driven gear and align the hole in the gear body with the hole in the casing, install and tighten the securing bolt.

(34) Position a new gasket at the rear of the rear cover assembly, install a new oil seal in the rear cover plate, fit the rear cover plate to rear cover assembly ensuring that the securing bolt holes are in line with the casing holes. Fit and tighten the securing bolts.

Oil Pump Assembly fitted to 4.2 Models.

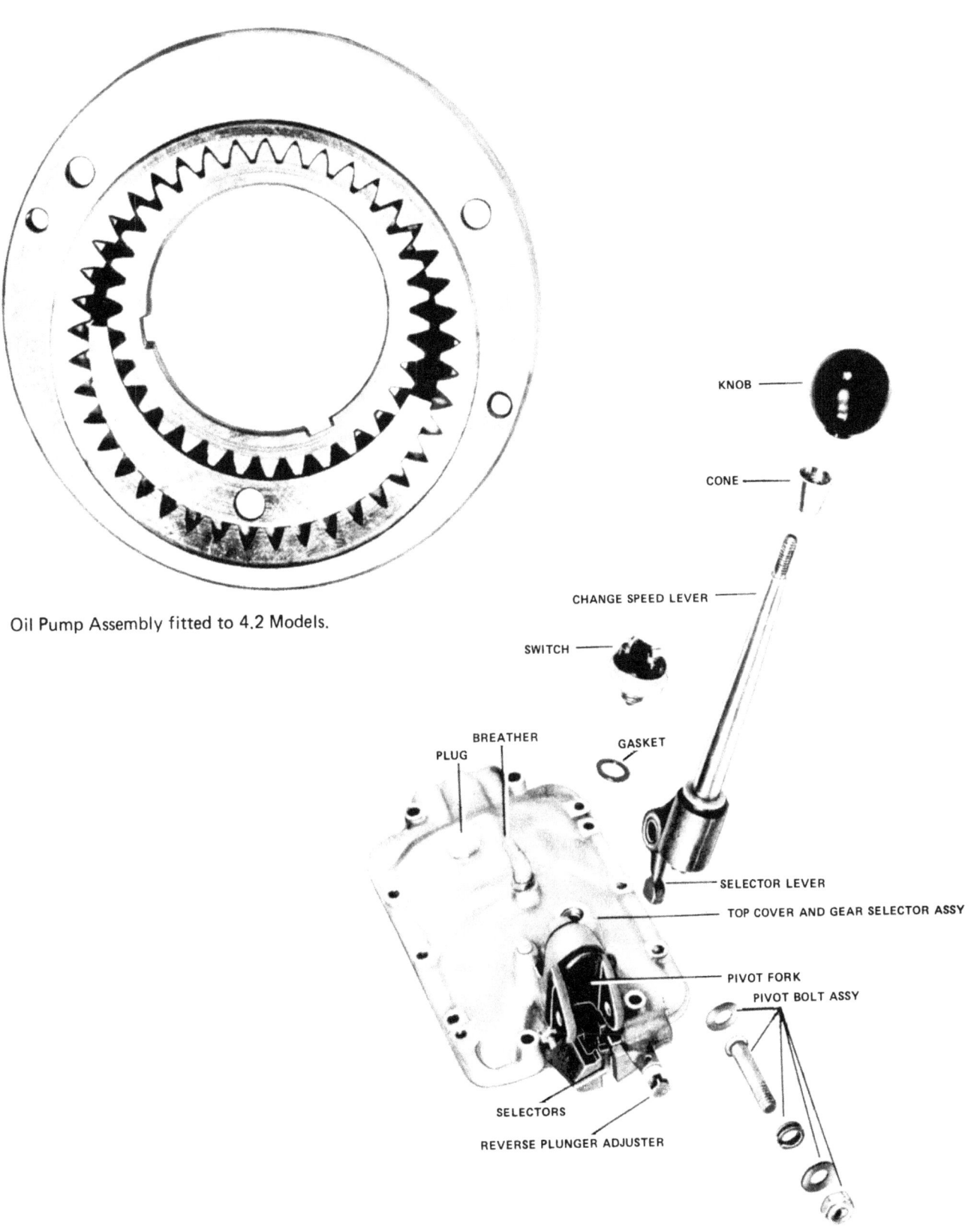

Dismantled View of Top Cover External Components (4.2 Model Shown).

(35) Slide the gears into first and reverse to lock the mainshaft, install the propeller shaft driving flange and secure with the flat washer and castellated nut, fit a new split pin to the nut. Disengage first and reverse gears.

(36) Install a new oil seal in the clutch bellhousing and fit the housing to the front of the gear case, install and tighten the lock plates and securing bolts, knock over the lock plate tabs and wire the heads of the securing bolts adjacent to the clutch throw-out fork trunnions.

(37) Install the clutch throw-out fork in the clutch housing and insert the pivot shaft, fit and tighten the Allen screw and secure with the locknut.

(38) Position the clutch throw-out bearing in the fork and secure with the two retaining springs.

(39) If the clutch slave cylinder has been removed, install on the clutch housing studs and secure with the nuts.

(40) Position a new gasket on the gear case top face, with the gear selector forks and the gear selector sleeves in the neutral position including the reverse idler, locate the selector forks in the sleeve grooves when installing the top cover. Fit and tighten the top cover securing bolts ensuring that the correct length bolts are fitted in the appropriate positions.

(41) Check that all gears can be engaged by selection with the gear shift lever, fill the gearbox to the correct level with the recommended oil and install the assembly in the vehicle as previously described.

3. PROPELLER SHAFT

DESCRIPTION

The propeller shaft is of the open type and is fitted with a needle roller and trunnion type universal joint at each end. A splined sliding sleeve is employed behind the front universal joint operating on mating splines on the front of the shaft. The needle roller bearing assemblies are retained in the universal joint yokes by circlips located in grooves machined in the bore of the yokes.

The propeller shaft and universal joint assembly is balanced and the tubular shaft must not be dented or otherwise damaged.

On earlier models a grease nipple is provided for lubrication at each of the universal joints and the splined sliding joint. On later models the universal joints and sliding joint do not require lubrication being prepacked on manufacture and assembly.

TO REMOVE AND INSTALL

(1) To remove the propeller shaft it is necessary to first remove the rear suspension assembly. For a description of this operation see *REAR SUSPENSION – TO REMOVE AND INSTALL.*

(2) Take out the two front seat cushions and the four securing nuts attaching each front seat to the seat slides, remove the front seats.

(3) Take out the screws located at each side of the radio control panel which retains the ash tray, take out the two screws which attach each side of the radio control panel casing to the supports under the dash and withdraw the casing.

(4) Take out the three securing screws attaching the shaft tunnel cover to the body.

(5) With the handbrake fully on and the gearshift lever pushed forward, slacken the gearshift lever knob locknut and remove the knob and locknut. Maneuver the shaft tunnel cover over the handbrake and gear levers and out of the vehicle.

(6) Unscrew the twelve securing screws and washers attaching the plastic gearbox cover to the body and remove the cover.

(7) Loosen and remove the four self locking nuts attaching the front universal joint to the gearbox drive flange and withdraw the propeller shaft at the rear end of the shaft tunnel.

Installation is a reversal of the removal procedure.

TO DISMANTLE AND ASSEMBLE

NOTE: The universal joints should not be dismantled unless the components are to be renewed. If needle rollers or trunnion journals are worn, they should be replaced as a kit. A maximum of .004" wear is allowed on the splined sliding sleeve and splined end of the shaft, this is measured on the outside diameter of the spline and relates to circumferential movement. If there is excessive wear in the splined sliding joint or the bearing cap holes in the yokes then the propeller shaft should be renewed.

Remove the front sliding joint from the propeller shaft.

(1) Compress and remove the two circlips securing two opposed needle roller bearings in one of the yokes of the front universal joint.

(2) Holding the joint in a vice, and using a soft metal drift, tap one of the bearing cups in to drive the other bearing out of the yoke. Lift the bearing out with the fingers to avoid dislodging the needle rollers.

(3) Again using a soft drift, tap the end of the trunnion of the bearing just removed to drive the other bearing out

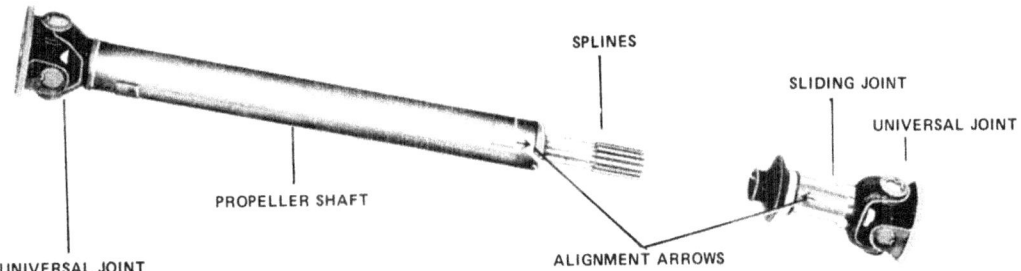

Align the Arrows when Replacing the Sliding Joint.

of the yoke and again carefully remove with the fingers to avoid dislodging the needle rollers.

(4) Maneuver the yoke over the ends of the trunnion and withdraw the yoke from the shaft assembly.

(5) Treat the other two bearings of the front universal joint and the four bearings of the rear universal joint in a similar manner to completely dismantle the propeller shaft.

(6) Check the needle roller bearings and trunnion journals for wear. If wear is apparent, renew the trunnion and bearings as a kit. Never renew individual needle roller bearing assemblies or fit old bearings to a new trunnion. Always use new bearing retaining circlips and bearing seal washers.

Reassembly is a reversal of the dismantling procedure.

Do not force an excessive amount of lubricant into the universal joint after assembly or damage to the seals may result.

When installing the sliding joint to the propeller shaft, engage the splines so that the arrows marked on the shaft and sliding joint are in line.

4. MANUAL TRANSMISSION FAULT DIAGNOSIS
GEARBOX

1. **Difficult gear change.**

   Possible cause
   (a) Maladjustment of selector mechanism.
   (b) Faulty gear synchroniser mechanism.
   (c) Faulty clutch or clutch release mechanism.
   (d) Faulty clutch hydraulic system.

   Remedy
   — Check and adjust selector mechanism.
   — Overhaul gearbox.
   — Check and overhaul clutch and/or adjust release mechanism.
   — Overhaul and bleed clutch hydraulic system.

2. **Gear clash on changing down.**

   Possible cause
   (a) Faulty clutch or clutch release mechanism.
   (b) Faulty synchro rings and cones.
   (c) Broken or incorrect positioning of synchro bar retaining springs.
   (d) Faulty clutch hydraulic system.
   (e) Gearbox lubricating oil too heavy.

   Remedy
   — Overhaul clutch and/or adjust release mechanism.
   — Check and overhaul gearbox, renew components as required.
   — Check and overhaul gearbox, renew components as required.
   — Overhaul and bleed clutch hydraulic system.
   — Drain gear case and refill with correct quantity and grade of oil.

3. **Slipping out of gear (1st and 2nd)**

   Possible cause
   (a) Weak or broken selector shaft detent spring.
   (b) Worn mainshaft sliding gear or laygear.
   (c) Excessive end-float of laygear.
   (d) Worn main drive gear, or main shaft ball bearings.
   (e) Incorrectly adjusted gear change mechanism.

   Remedy
   — Renew faulty components.
   — Check and renew faulty components.
   — Check and renew worn thrust washers.
   — Check and renew worn components.
   — Check and re-adjust as necessary.

4. **Slipping out of gear (3rd and top)**

   Possible cause
   (a) Weak or broken selector shaft detent spring.
   (b) Worn synchro teeth on third or top speeds.
   (c) Excessive end-float of laygear.
   (d) Worn ball bearings on main drive gear or mainshaft.
   (e) Incorrectly adjusted gear change mechanism.

   Remedy
   − Check and renew faulty components.
   − Check and renew worn components.
   − Check and renew worn thrust washers.
   − Check and renew worn bearings.
   − Check and re-adjust as necessary.

5. **Gearbox noise (in neutral)**

   Possible cause
   (a) Worn main drive ball bearing.
   (b) Chipped or pitted constant mesh gears (laygear, main drive gear or 2nd and 3rd speed mainshaft gear).
   (c) Excessive laygear end-float.
   (d) Lack of sufficient lubricant.

   Remedy
   − Overhaul and renew bearing.
   − Overhaul and renew components as necessary.
   − Check and renew laygear thrust washers.
   − Drain and refill gear case with correct quantity and grade of oil.

6. **Gearbox noise (forward gears engaged)**

   Possible cause
   (a) Worn main drive or mainshaft ball bearing.
   (b) Chipped or pitted constant mesh gears (laygear, main drive gear or 2nd speed or 3rd mainshaft gear).
   (c) Excessive laygear end-float.
   (d) Chipped or pitted reverse idler gear.
   (e) Lack of sufficient lubricant.

   Remedy
   − Overhaul and renew bearings.
   − Overhaul and renew components as necessary.
   − Check and renew laygear thrust washers.
   − Check and renew components as necessary.
   − Drain and refill gear case with correct quantity and grade of oil.

PROPELLER SHAFT

1. **Shaft vibration.**

   Possible cause
   (a) Bent propeller shaft.
   (b) Excessive wear in universal joint trunnion and bearings.
   (c) Propeller shaft out of balance.
   (d) Excessive wear of front sliding joint.
   (e) Universal joint to pinion flange bolts loose.

   Remedy
   − Renew shaft.
   − Renew complete universal joint (trunnion and bearings).
   − Renew complete propeller shaft.
   − Renew if necessary.
   − Renew and tighten loose bolts.

2. **Excessive backlash.**

   Possible cause
   (a) Worn universal joint trunnion and bearings.
   (b) Worn mainshaft and universal joint sleeve splines.

   Remedy
   − Renew joint trunnion and bearings as assembly.
   − Renew worn components.

AUTOMATIC TRANSMISSION 2+2 MODELS

SPECIFICATIONS

Type	3 forward speeds and reverse, epicyclic gear train with torque converter
Operation	Automatic, hydraulic
Ratios:	
Low	2.40:1
Intermediate	1.46:1
High	1.00:1
Reverse	2.00:1
Maximum ratio of torque converter	2.00:1
Lubricant type	Automatic Transmission Fluid Type A, or Type A Suffix A
Capacity with cooler	16 Imp pt from dry

Shift speeds on 2.88:1 final drive; with gearshift at D1:

Upshift speeds – light throttle:	
Low to intermediate	8 ± 1 mph
Intermediate to high	14 ± 2 mph
Upshift speeds – full throttle:	
Low to intermediate	41 ± 3 mph
Intermediate to high	69 ± 3 mph
Upshift speeds – on kickdown:	
Low to intermediate	54 ± 2 mph
Intermediate to high	85 ± 4 mph
Downshift speeds – light throttle:	
High to intermediate	11 ± 3 mph
Intermediate to low	6 ± 2 mph
Downshift speeds – full throttle:	
High to intermediate	30 ± 7 mph
Downshift speeds – on kickdown:	
High to intermediate	77 ± 4 mph
High to low	22 ± 2 mph
Intermediate to low	22 ± 2 mph

With gearshift at D2:

Upshift speeds – light throttle:	
Intermediate to high	14 ± 2 mph
Upshift speeds – full throttle:	
Intermediate to high	69 ± 3 mph
Upshift speeds – on kickdown:	
Intermediate to high	85 ± 4 mph
Downshift speeds – light throttle:	
High to intermediate	11 ± 3 mph
Downshift speeds – full throttle:	
High to intermediate	30 ± 7 mph
Downshift speeds – on kickdown:	
High to intermediate	77 ± 4 mph

With gearshift at L:

Downshift speeds – nil throttle:	
High to intermediate	60 mph
Intermediate to low	16 ± 4 mph

Shift speeds on 3.3:1 final drive; with gearshift at D1:

Upshift speeds – light throttle:	
Low to intermediate	7 ± 1 mph
Intermediate to high	12 ± 1 mph
Upshift speeds – full throttle:	
Low to intermediate	37 ± 4 mph
Intermediate to high	60 ± 2 mph
Upshift speeds – on kickdown:	
Low to intermediate	47 ± 2 mph
Intermediate to high	74 ± 4 mph
Downshift speeds – light throttle:	
High to intermediate	10 ± 3 mph
Intermediate to low	5 ± 2 mph
Downshift speeds – full throttle:	
High to intermediate	26 ± 7 mph
Downshift speeds – on kickdown:	
High to intermediate	67 ± 4 mph
High to low	19 ± 2 mph
Intermediate to low	19 ± 2 mph

With gearshift at D2:

Upshift speeds – light throttle:	
Intermediate to high	12 ± 1 mph
Upshift speeds – full throttle:	
Intermediate to high	60 ± 2 mph
Upshift speeds – on kickdown:	
Intermediate to high	74 ± 4 mph
Downshift speeds – light throttle:	
High to intermediate	10 ± 3 mph
Downshift speeds – full throttle:	
High to intermediate	26 ± 7 mph
Downshift speeds – on kickdown:	
High to intermediate	67 ± 4 mph

With gearshift at L:

Downshift speeds – nil throttle:	
High to intermediate	60 mph
Intermediate to low	14 ± 4 mph
Forward speed band adjustment	* Tighten adjusting screw to 10 in/lb and secure with locknut.

* With .25" spacer inserted between servo piston pin and adjusting screws.

Reverse speed band adjustment — Tighten adjusting screw to 10 ft/lb, back off 1.5 turns and secure with locknut.

TORQUE WRENCH SETTINGS

Oil pan drain plug	30 ft/lb.
Oil pan screws	13 ft/lb.
Extension housing to transmission case	33 ft/lb.
Transmission case centre mounting	25 ft/lb.
Forward speed band adjusting screw locknut	25 ft/lb.
Reverse speed band adjusting screw locknut	40 ft/lb.

1. DESCRIPTION

The automatic transmission combines a torque converter with a fully automatic three speed epicyclic gear system. The torque converter housing and the transmission case are separate castings.

The transmission provides three forward ratios and one reverse, with the forward ratios automatically selected in relation to the car speed and throttle position. By selecting L (lockup), over-riding is controlled by engine braking. The speed selector quadrant, attached to the shaft tunnel cover, is marked L (lockup), D1 (drive one), D2 (drive two), N (neutral), R (reverse) and P (park). A reversing lamp switch and starter cut-out switch are located on the selector quadrant. The starter cut-out switch is a safety measure to prevent the driver from starting the engine in ranges other than P (park) and N (neutral) positions.

The hydraulic system consists of a front pump and rear pump, with a hydraulic governor operating a valve arrangement. The valves control the fluid flow and direct the pressure to the selected transmission components. When the engine is running the front pump, driven by the converter impeller, supplies the transmission with hydraulic pressure while the vehicle is at low speed or brought to a halt. Drive for the rear pump is obtained from the output shaft of the transmission and operates effectively at speeds in excess of approximately 20 mph. A transmission fluid cooler unit is located at the radiator block. Fluid level in the transmission is checked by a dipstick type indicator located in the oil filler tube positioned adjacent to the bulkhead on the right hand side of the engine compartment.

The torque converter is rigidly attached by bolts to the engine drive plate which replaces the conventional flywheel, the converter replacing the conventional clutch assembly. Power from the engine is transferred smoothly to the transmission and so to the driving wheels through the torque converter. The converter also supplies a range of engine torque multiplication to low and intermediate gears, with very low speed flexibility with the transmission in high gear and consequently good acceleration without causing a downshift in the transmission.

The level of fluid in the transmission should be checked at 3,000 mile intervals, and only with the unit at normal operating temperature, the handbrake applied and the engine idling with P (park) selected on the gearshift quadrant.

2. HYDRAULIC FLUID

Only a recommended Automatic Transmission Fluid Type A or Type A, Suffix A, should be used in the transmission when topping up or changing the fluid in the system.

The fluid level in the transmission case should be checked at regular intervals of not greater than 3,000 miles and it is good policy to check the fluid level at each lubrication service.

Every 21,000 miles, the fluid in the transmission should be drained off while the transmission assembly is at operating temperature.

As it is necessary to remove the oil pan in order to adjust the forward speed band, the band checking and adjusting procedure should be carried out at the same time as the pan is removed for cleaning.

TO CHECK AND TOP UP

(1) Place the vehicle on a level floor and open the engine bonnet.

(2) Carefully clean around the top of the transmission case filler tube and dipstick, to ensure that no dirt or foreign matter can enter the filler tube as the dipstick is withdrawn.

(3) Place the selector lever in the P (park) position on the selector quadrant and firmly apply the handbrake.

(4) Start the engine and run at a fast idle to bring the engine and transmission assembly to normal operating temperature.

NOTE: As an alternative to operation (4), run the vehicle on the road for approximately 5 miles.

(5) Return the engine to the correct idling speed, remove the dipstick and wipe clean, insert the dipstick fully into position and withdraw immediately and check the level indicated on the dipstick.

(6) If necessary, add sufficient fluid to the transmission case via the filler tube to bring the level to the FULL mark on the dipstick.

NOTE: As a guide the difference between LOW and FULL marks on the dipstick is approximately 1.5 Imp pts. Use only the recommended Automatic Transmission Fluid Type A and do not overfill, or foaming and unsatisfactory operation of the assembly will result.

(7) Replace the dipstick in the filler tube, ensuring that no dirt or dust can enter the transmission case.

TO DRAIN AND REFILL

(1) Bring the transmission to the normal operating temperature and raise the vehicle on a hoist, or place it over a pit so that the transmission case is reasonably level.

(2) Unscrew and remove the transmission case oil pan drain plug and drain the hydraulic fluid into a suitable container.

NOTE: The fluid may be very hot particularly after a long run, use care to avoid scalding.

(3) Clean around the transmission case oil pan, take out the securing screws, detach the oil pan and gasket.

NOTE: Thoroughly clean out the oil pan ready for installing. Carry out the procedures for adjusting the forward speed band described under the appropriate heading.

(4) Install the oil pan with a new gasket, tighten the securing screws to a torque of 13 ft/lb. Fit the drain plug and tighten to a torque of 30 ft/lb.

(5) Refill the transmission case with the correct grade and quantity of fluid as recommended, start the engine and bring it to the normal operating temperature.

(6) Check the fluid level on the dipstick and top up, if necessary, as described in *TO CHECK AND TOP UP*.

3. FORWARD SPEED BAND

TO ADJUST

This service operation should be carried out every 21,000 miles, or on indication of a harsh shift pattern, or a loose adjusting screw locknut.

It is necessary to drain the fluid and remove the oil pan in order to adjust the forward speed band. The oil pan should be thoroughly cleaned and refilled with new fluid of the correct grade after the adjustment procedure has been completed.

(1) Carry out operations (1), (2) and (3) in *TO DRAIN AND REFILL*.

(2) Release the forward speed band adjusting screw several turns.

(3) Hold the servo lever out at the top and place a .25" thick spacer between the servo piston pin and the adjusting screw.

(4) Using a suitable tension wrench, tighten the adjusting screw to a torque of 10 in/lb and secure the screw by tightening the locknut to a torque of 25 ft/lb. Remove the spacer from between the servo piston pin and the adjusting screw.

(5) Clean the mating faces of the transmission case and oil pan, instal the pan using a new gasket and tighten the securing screws to a torque of 13 ft/lb.

(6) Refill the transmission case with fluid as described in *TO DRAIN AND REFILL*.

4. REVERSE BAND

TO ADJUST

This service operation should be carried out every 21,000 miles, or on indication of a harsh shift pattern, a loose adjusting screw locknut, or no drive in reverse. The band adjusting screw is located on the right hand side of the transmission case and access can be obtained through a hole in the shaft tunnel.

(1) Remove the carpets and hole cover on the right hand side of the shaft tunnel to expose the adjusting screw.

(2) Clean around the band adjusting screw and locknut on the right hand side of the transmission case.

(3) Slacken back the adjusting screw locknut several turns.

(4) Tighten the adjusting screw to a torque of 10 ft/lb and then back off the adjusting screw exactly 1.5 turns.

(5) Hold the adjusting screw in this position and tighten the locknut to a torque of 40 ft/lb.

(6) Install the tunnel cover and floor coverings.

5. TRANSMISSION SHIFT LINKAGE

TO ADJUST

(1) Working at the lefthand side of the gearbox tunnel, remove the trimmings and carpets to expose the cover plate, take out the securing screws and detach the cover plate.

(2) Slacken the locking assembly at the ball joint end attached to the gear operating lever at the side of the transmission case, ensure that the inner cable is free to slide in and out of the ball joint assembly.

(3) Position the gear operating lever right forward to engage the lockup detent, move the gearshift selector lever in the gear quadrant to the L (lockup) position.

(4) With both the gear operating lever and gearshift lever held in the above positions tighten the locking assembly at the end of the ball joint.

(5) Move the gear operating lever through all speed detent positions and ensure that the gearshift lever fully engages the appropriate gate in the gear change quadrant.

(6) Install the coverplate, carpets and trimmings.

6. CARUBURETTOR AND DOWNSHIFT VALVE LINKAGE

As an indication that adjustment is required, run the car along a flat road at very light throttle with D1 or D2 selected. At 1,150 rpm ± 50 rpm the intermediate to high upshift should take place, any variation indicates incorrect pressure. At full throttle an erratic intermediate to high upshift, or with D1 selected and bringing the car to a halt, a sharp intermediate to low downshift also indicates incorrect pressure. Before adjustment, ensure that the cable is in serviceable condition and not acutely bent or binding.

TO ADJUST

(1) Connect a pressure test gauge calibrated to 300 lb/sq. in. to the pressure take off point at the left hand side of the transmission case.

(2) With the engine and transmission assembly at normal operating temperature, firmly apply the handbrake and select D1 or D2 with the gearshift selector lever.

(3) Increase the engine idling speed to 1,250 rpm and check the pressure gauge reading which should be 72.5 ± 2.5 lb/sq. in.

(4) If adjustment is required, stop the engine, loosen the locknut at the cable yoke end on the engine side of the bulkhead, take out the split pin and clevis pin and turn the yoke in the direction required to effect an alteration in pressure.

NOTE: Turning the yoke clockwise will lower the pressure and turning the yoke anti-clockwise will lift the pressure, one complete turn of the yoke will cause a 9 lb/sq. in. variation. Excessive adjustment should be avoided otherwise loss of kickdown or an increase in gearshift speeds will occur.

(5) Install the yoke, clevis pin and new split pin, tighten the yoke locknut to secure.

(6) With the transmission still at normal operating temperature and the engine idling at 1,250 rpm recheck the pressure. If necessary effect further slight adjustment to obtain the correct pressure.

(7) Reset the engine idling speed to 500 rpm, and ensure that the butterfly valve plates are closed.

(8) Remove the pressure test gauge from the take off point.

TO REMOVE AND INSTALL CABLE

(1) Take out the split pin and clevis pin and disconnect the yoke at the rear of the cylinder head.

(2) Take out the securing screw and remove the cable retaining clip.

(3) Working on the left hand side of the gearbox tunnel, remove the trimmings and carpets to expose the cover plate, take out the six securing screws and remove the cover plate.

(4) Take out the Allen screw and washer attaching the outer conduit in the transmission case.

(5) Pull out the outer conduit and note the spring clip attaching the inner cable to the rod operating the kickdown cam. Prise open the clip and extract the inner cable.

Installation is a reversal of the removal procedure with attention to the following points:

With the new cable assembly installed, adjust the yoke position to give a length of 3.312" on the inner cable, measured between the end of the outer conduit and the centre of the clevis pin.

Ensure that the butterfly valve plates are closed, and carry out the procedure for adjustment as described earlier.

7. TRANSMISSION ASSEMBLY

TO REMOVE AND INSTALL

The transmission assembly can only be removed from the vehicle by taking out the engine and transmission assembly. This operation is described under *ENGINE – TO REMOVE AND INSTALL*.

(1) With the engine and transmission assembly removed from the vehicle, drain off the transmission fluid into a suitable container, if not already done.

(2) Take out the split pin and clevis pin and detach the cable yoke at the rear of the cylinder head. Remove the securing screw and detach the cable conduit retaining clip.

(3) Loosen and remove the securing bolts attaching the transmission case to the torque converter housing and remove the transmission case assembly.

NOTE: If removal of the torque converter and flywheel is required, proceed as follows:

(4) Detach the cover located at the front of the converter housing.

(5) Loosen and remove the starter motor taking out the securing bolts.

(6) Take out the securing bolts attaching the converter housing to the engine, and remove the housing.

(7) Working through the starter motor aperture, loosen and remove each of the securing bolts attaching the converter to the flywheel. It will be necessary to turn the engine to bring each of the four bolts in line with the starter motor aperture. Detach the converter from the flywheel.

(8) Prise or knock back the locking plate tabs and loosen and remove the securing bolts attaching the flywheel to the crankshaft flange. Mark the position of the flywheel on the crankshaft flange and remove the flywheel.

Installation is a reversal of the removal procedure with attention to the following points:

Ensure that the converter is fully engaged in the front of the transmission with the driving lugs of both impeller hub and pump drive correctly aligned for engagement. Check that the converter spigot engages in the bearing in the rear of the crankshaft. Ensure that the attachment faces of the converter housing and the rear of the engine are both clean and free of any burrs.

Tighten the flywheel securing bolts and the converter to flywheel bolts evenly.

Fill the transmission with the correct grade and quantity of hydraulic fluid.

8. AUTOMATIC TRANSMISSION FAULT DIAGNOSIS

The following transmission operating faults can be caused by conditions that may be rectified within the scope of the information given in this section.

(1) No drive in D range.

Possible cause
(a) Low fluid level in transmission.
(b) Incorrectly adjusted manual linkage.
(c) Incorrect transmission fluid in unit.

(d) Incorrectly adjusted downshift valve control cable.

Remedy
– Check fluid level and top up.
– Check and readjust manual linkage as detailed.
– Drain and refill with recommended grade of fluid (see specifications).
– Check and adjust cable as detailed.

(2) No reverse drive in R on quadrant.

Possible cause
(a) Low fluid level in transmission.
(b) Incorrectly adjusted manual linkage.
(c) Reverse band incorrectly adjusted.

Remedy
– Check fluid level and top up.
– Check and adjust manual linkage as detailed.
– Adjust reverse band as detailed.

(3) Slipping or rough in up-shift.

Possible cause	Remedy
(a) Incorrectly adjusted throttle linkage.	– Check and adjust linkage as detailed.
(b) Incorrectly adjusted downshift valve control cable.	– Check and adjust cable as detailed.

(4) Slipping in all speeds.

Possible cause	Remedy
(a) Low fluid level in transmission.	– Check fluid level and top up.
(b) Incorrect grade of fluid in unit.	– Drain and refill with recommended grade of fluid (see specifications).
(c) Incorrectly adjusted selector rod.	– Check and adjust selector rod as detailed.

(5) No transmission kickdown.

Possible cause	Remedy
(a) Incorrectly adjusted carburettor and accelerator linkage.	– Check and adjust linkage as detailed.
(b) Incorrectly adjusted downshift valve control cable.	– Check and adjust cable as detailed.

(6) Engine will not start in P or N positions, or will start in any range.

Possible cause	Remedy
(a) Neutral safety switch incorrectly adjusted.	– Check and adjust switch as detailed.
(b) Neutral safety switch faulty.	– Check and renew switch.
(c) Incorrectly adjusted selector rod.	– Check and adjust selector rod as detailed.

REAR AXLE

SPECIFICATIONS

Type	Salisbury 4HU with Thornton Powr-Lok Limited slip differential unit
Output shaft end float	.001" – .003"
Differential bearing pre-load	.006" – .010" shim thickness
Pinion bearing pre-load	8 in/lb – 12 in/lb
Backlash	.004" minimum and for maximum refer to drive gear marking

Axle ratios:
3.07:1
3.31:1
3.54:1

Oil capacity	2.75 Imp pt
Grade of oil	SAE90 Hypoid

TORQUE WRENCH SETTING

Drive pinion nut	125 ft/lb
Drive gear bolts	75 ft/lb
Differential bearing cap bolts	63 ft/lb
Powr-Lok differential bolts	43 ft/lb

1. DESCRIPTION

The Salisbury 4HU rear axle unit is fitted with a Thornton Powr-Lok limited slip differential with hypoid final drive gears.

The rear axle unit is mounted within a box type cross member and connected to the wheel hubs by means of short tubular axle shafts fitted with universal joints at each end.

These tubular axle shafts also serve as upper arms for the rear wheel assemblies.

Clutch friction discs and friction plates are positioned between the differential case and side gear ring at each side of the assembly. The bevel side gears are mounted within the side gear rings. Two pinion shafts each with two gears are mounted at right angles to each other and are meshed with the bevel side gears.

Load is imposed upon the clutch assemblies when road wheel resistance to turning, forces the pinion shafts and side gears apart and thereby bringing together the clutch disc and friction plates. The amount of clutch action is dependant upon the amount of torque transmitted when the vehicle is being driven in the straight ahead position. This action enables the two pinion shafts with their respective pinion gears as well as the differential side gears to come into action as one unit. On cornering the differential reverts back to the conventional type allowing the two rear road wheels to rotate at different speeds.

The crownwheel and differential case assembly is supported in the carrier by two bearings, the bearing preload and crownwheel backlash is adjusted by means of shims.

The drive pinion is supported in the carrier by two tapered bearings, the bearing preload and the pinion position in relation to the crownwheel is adjusted by means of shims.

Due to the action of the limited slip differential it is essential that the rear wheels are not driven while the vehicle is jacked up unless both wheels are clear of the ground.

2. REAR AXLE ASSEMBLY

TO REMOVE AND INSTALL

(1) Raise the rear of the vehicle on a lifting jack, but use a block of wood between the jack and rear suspension tie plate. Place stands on either side just ahead of the radius arm front mountings. To prevent damage, place blocks of wood between the stands and underbody.

(2) Unscrew the hub caps and remove both rear road wheels.

(3) Disconnect the exhaust tail pipes from the silencers by loosening the two clamp bolts and removing the nuts and bolts retaining the pipes to the centre mounting. Withdraw the pipes.

(4) Loosen off and detach both radius arms at the under-floor mountings.

(5) Disconnect the stabilizer bar at both links by removing the two self-locking nuts and bolts.

(6) Disconnect the hydraulic brake hose and plug the

connection to prevent the entry of dirt into the system.

(7) Disconnect the handbrake cable from the compensator linkage by removing the split pin and clevis pin, release the locknut and unscrew the threaded end of the outer conduit from the block in the linkage.

(8) Remove the four nuts and bolts retaining the rubber mountings at the forward end of the crossmember to the body frame.

NOTE: Establish the position and number of shims between the mountings and frame to facilitate reassembly.

(9) Similarly the rear rubber mountings should be removed by taking out the six self-locking nuts and four bolts.

(10) Disconnect the propeller shaft from the rear axle by removing the four self-locking nuts and bolts.

(11) By means of the jack carefully lower the assembly and remove from beneath the vehicle.

(12) Place the complete assembly on a work bench with the tie-plate facing upwards and take out the tie-plate securing nuts and bolts and remove the plate.

(13) Remove the four shock absorber and coil spring units.

(14) Disconnect the half shaft universal joint from the brake disc and output shaft flange by removing the four self-locking nuts from the output shaft flange studs.

NOTE: The locking nuts used on the output shaft flange studs should be the metal type and not nylon, due to the heat radiated by the brake disc.

(15) The shaft flange and brake disc should be separated and while doing so, the number of shims should be carefully noted as these effect the camber.

(16) From one end of the inner suspension arm fulcrum shaft remove one self-locking nut and tap out the fulcrum shaft.

(17) Detach the wheel hub, suspension arm, half shaft and radius arm from the assembly.

(18) Carry out the same procedure at the other side of the assembly.

(19) Remove the handbrake compensator linkage securing bolts and detach linkage. Disconnect the brake calliper hydraulic feed pipes.

(20) Remove the locking wire from the four differential carrier mounting bolts and take out the bolts. Separate the cross member from the differential carrier.

Installation is a reversal of the removal procedure.

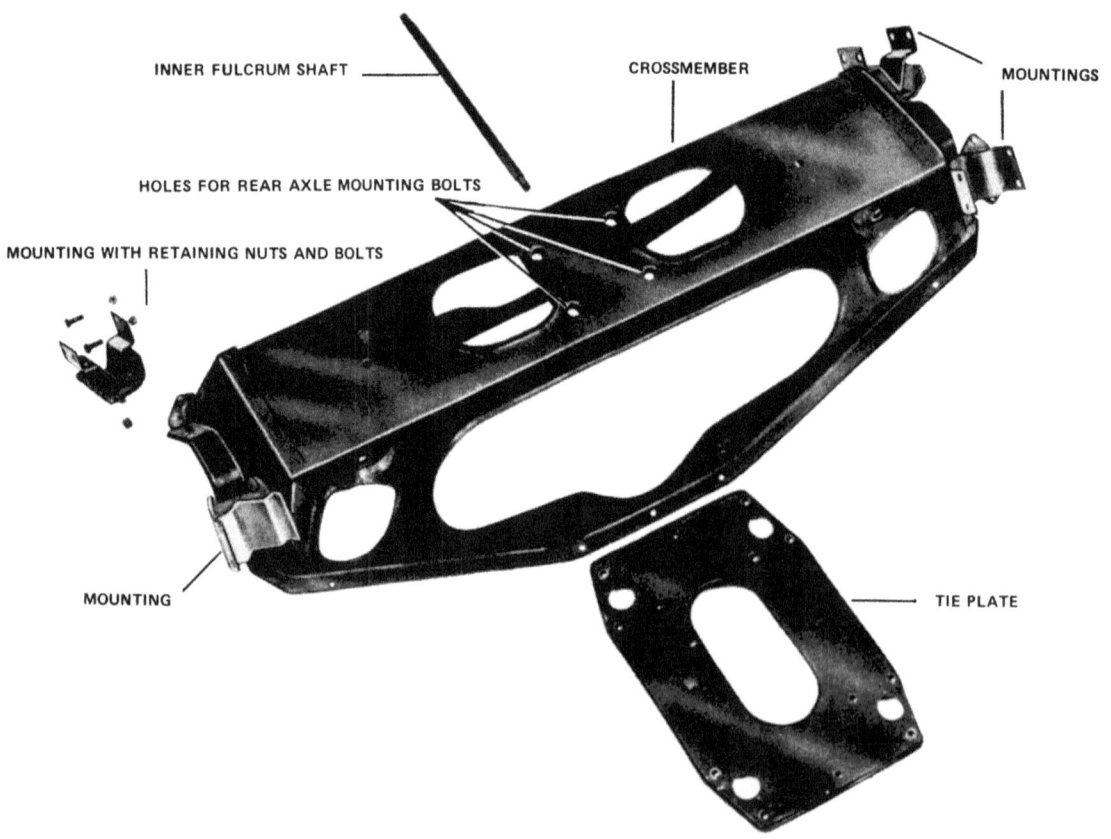

View of Crossmember in which Rear Axle is Mounted.

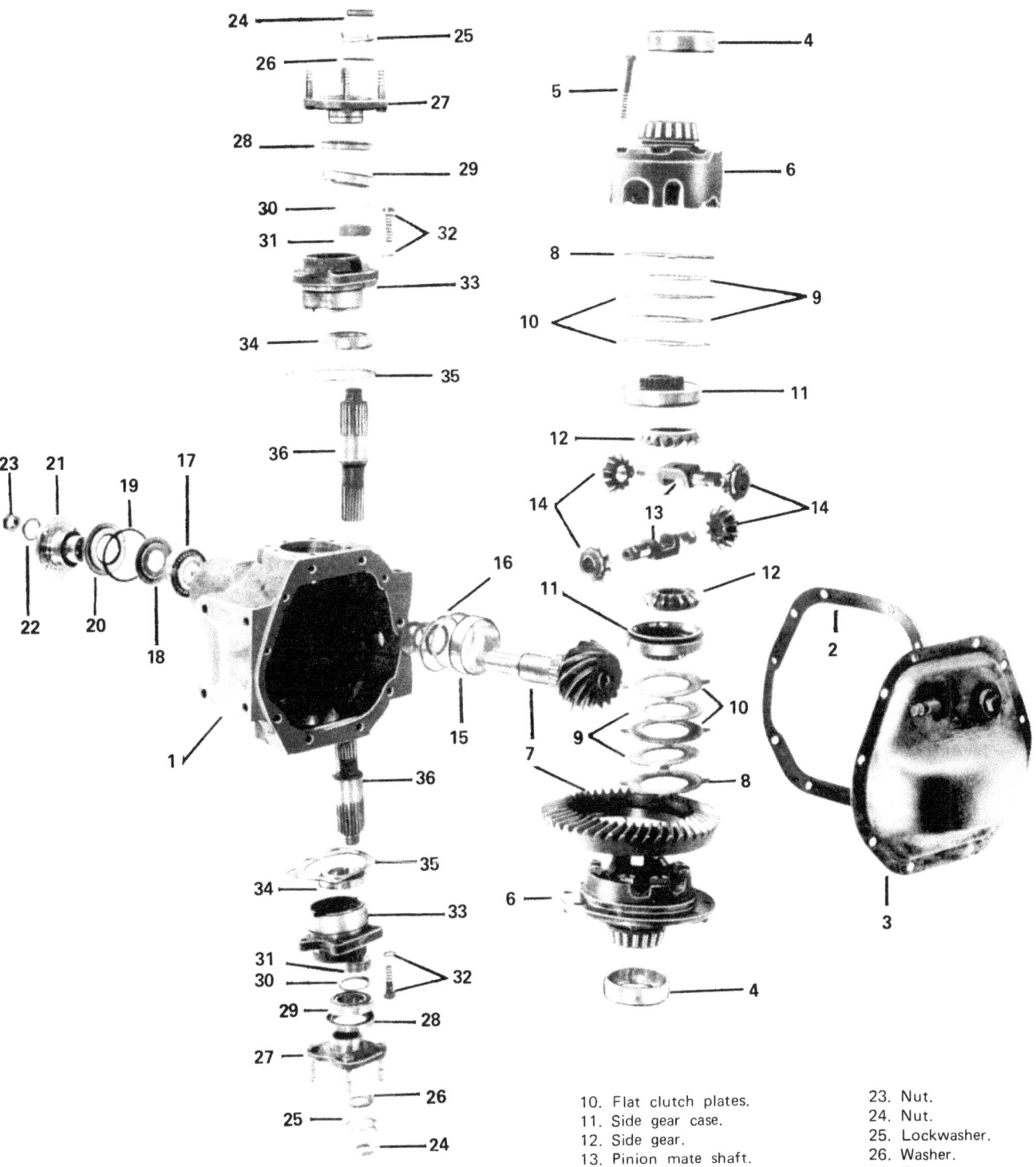

Exploded View of Rear Axle Components.

1. Differential carrier.
2. Cover gasket.
3. Rear cover.
4. Outer races.
5. Bolt.
6. Differential case and bearing.
7. Crownwheel and pinion.
8. Dished clutch plate.
9. Clutch discs.
10. Flat clutch plates.
11. Side gear case.
12. Side gear.
13. Pinion mate shaft.
14. Pinion mate gear.
15. Outer race.
16. Shims.
17. Bearing.
18. Oil thrower.
19. Gasket.
20. Oil seal.
21. Drive flange.
22. Washer.
23. Nut.
24. Nut.
25. Lockwasher.
26. Washer.
27. Flange.
28. Oil seal.
29. Bearing.
30. Shim.
31. Distance piece.
32. Bolt and washer.
33. Bearing housing.
34. Bearing.
35. Shim.
36. Output shaft.

3. DIFFERENTIAL ASSEMBLY

TO REMOVE FROM CARRIER

(1) Remove the axle assembly as described under *TO REMOVE AND INSTALL.*

(2) Release the lock washer tabs and take out the brake calliper supporting bolts.

(3) When removing the brake calliper, make a note of the number of small round shims installed between the calliper and the differential housing.

(4) Drain the oil from the housing, take out the nine securing bolts and remove the differential rear cover.

(5) Withdraw the output shaft bearing assembly, comprising output shaft, housing, bearings and adjustment shims, after removing the five securing bolts.

NOTE: Carefully note the number of pre-load shims installed.

Repeat the same removal procedure when removing the other output shaft.

(6) Take out the securing bolts from each bearing cap and carefully remove the differential assembly from the carrier.

NOTE: The bearing caps and the carrier face bear markings which should be noted to facilitate correct assembly.

TO DISMANTLE DIFFERENTIAL

(1) Prior to separating the two halves of the differential casing, scribe two marks, i.e. one on each half casing and directly opposite one another, to facilitate correct assembly.

(2) Take out the eight bolts joining the two half casings and separate the casings.

(3) Remove from one half casing the bevel side gear and gear case and take out the three clutch plates and two discs.

(4) From the remaining half casing, remove the pinion mate shafts and the four pinion gears, the bevel side gear and gear case followed by three clutch plates and two discs.

(5) Should it be necessary to remove the crownwheel, knock back the tabs of the lockwasher and loosen off and remove the crownwheel to differential casing securing bolts.

NOTE: If the crownwheel and pinion are to be renewed it is essential that they are replaced as a mated pair and not as individual components.

TO ASSEMBLE DIFFERENTIAL

(1) Install into the flange half of the differential casing the clutch plates and discs. Ensure that the dished plate is fitted first with the convex side against the casing.

NOTE: There are three plates (including the dished plate) and two discs in each half of the casing and they must be fitted alternatively.

(2) Engage the serrations of the side gear case with the serrations of the two clutch discs, and install the bevel side gear in the gear case so that the splines of the gear and case align.

(3) Mount the pinion gears on the pinion mate shafts and fit the shafts together.

(4) Install the pinion shafts and gears assembly into the casing so that the ramps on the shafts and casing are mated.

(5) Install the clutch plates, discs, side gear case and bevel side gear in the same manner to the remaining half casing.

(6) Bring together the two half casings aligning the marks made on dismantling. Check that the tongues of the clutch plates are in line with the grooves in the differential case. Install the eight casing bolts but do not tighten.

(7) Enter into position the two output shafts so that the splines of each shaft are inserted through the splines of the gear case and bevel side gear. Tighten the casing bolts evenly and progressively to a torque of 40 ft/lb.

NOTE: The above operation is essential to ensure that the splines of each side case and gear are aligned otherwise difficulty will be encountered at a later stage of assembly.

(8) If the crownwheel has been removed, check that the contact faces of the crownwheel and casing are clean, instal the crownwheel with new lockwashers and tighten the securing bolts to a torque of 75 ft/lb.

TO INSTALL AND ADJUST

(1) With the drive pinion located in the carrier but without the oil slinger and oil seal at this stage, install the differential in the carrier.

(2) Check the markings on the bearing caps with those on the housing face and install them in their correct location. Fit and tighten the securing bolts.

(3) Check the run-out of the crownwheel by mounting a dial gauge on the housing with the gauge plunger in contact with the rear face of the crownwheel. Turn the pinion by hand and note the reading, if the reading is more than .005", remove the assembly and clean the carrier bearings where they contact the housing.

(4) To facilitate setting the correct backlash, install the output shaft assemblies at each side of the housing but without any shims.

(5) Using a dial gauge mounted on the housing and with the plunger in contact with a tooth on the crownwheel, move the crownwheel by hand and note the backlash reading. The backlash should correspond with the specified marking on the crownwheel.

(6) Should adjustment be necessary, move the crownwheel in or out of mesh with the drive pinion by releasing the bearing housing bolts on one side and tightening them on the opposite side.

(7) Having got the correct setting, the gaps on either side between the differential housing and the crownwheel bearing housing should be checked with a feeler gauge and suitable shims fitted to maintain the backlash between the crownwheel and drive pinion.

(8) It is necessary to make an allowance for a preload of .003" from the feeler gauge reading between the differential housing and the crownwheel bearing housing on either side subtract this amount before installing shims.

NOTE: Shims are serviced in thicknesses of .003", .005", .010" and .030".

(9) Install the output shaft assemblies and necessary shims, fit and tighten the five securing bolts at each side.

(10) Place the differential housing on a bench with the drive pinion flange uppermost and remove the pinion shaft nut with washer and the flange.

(11) Install the oil slinger and a new drive pinion oil seal, pull the oil seal into position in the housing with special tool No. SL4P/B.

NOTE: On later model cars the oil seal is the metal case type used in conjunction with a gasket.

(12) Install the flange, washer and pinion shaft nut and tighten the nut to a torque of 125 ft/lb.

(13) Check the tooth contact of the crownwheel and drive pinion by applying a thin coating of red lead or engineers blue to both sides of approximately one third of the crownwheel teeth.

With the coated teeth in mesh with the drive pinion, rotate the pinion both ways until a good marking of the tooth contact is obtained.

NOTE: If the bearing pre-load and backlash have been correctly set, the margins above and below the area of contact should be the same and the contact margin should run approximately three quarters of the tooth length.

(14) Install the housing rear cover with a new gasket.

(15) Fit the drain plug and fill the unit with oil according to specifications. Install the filler plug.

(16) Install the brake disc and calliper with the small round shims used for centralising. Fit the retaining bolts with new lock washers and tighten to a torque of 55 ft/lb. Lock the bolts in position with the lockwasher tabs.

TO DISMANTLE OUTPUT SHAFTS

(1) Release the lockwasher and remove the securing nut, lock washer and plain washer.

(2) Using a press, remove the output shaft complete with inner bearing inner race, distance piece and end float shims by pressing from the bearing housing.

(3) Where replacement of the bearing is necessary, remove the shims and distance piece and using a suitable puller withdraw the inner bearing inner race from the shaft

Location of Differential Cap Bearing Marks.

and drive out the inner bearing outer race from the housing.

(4) Using a piece of metal pipe about the same bore as the outer race, press out the outer bearing and oil seal.

TO ASSEMBLE OUTPUT SHAFTS

(1) Install the new outer races at each end of the bearing housing, with the taper of the bearing surface facing outwards in each case. Ensure that the races are fully seated in the housing.

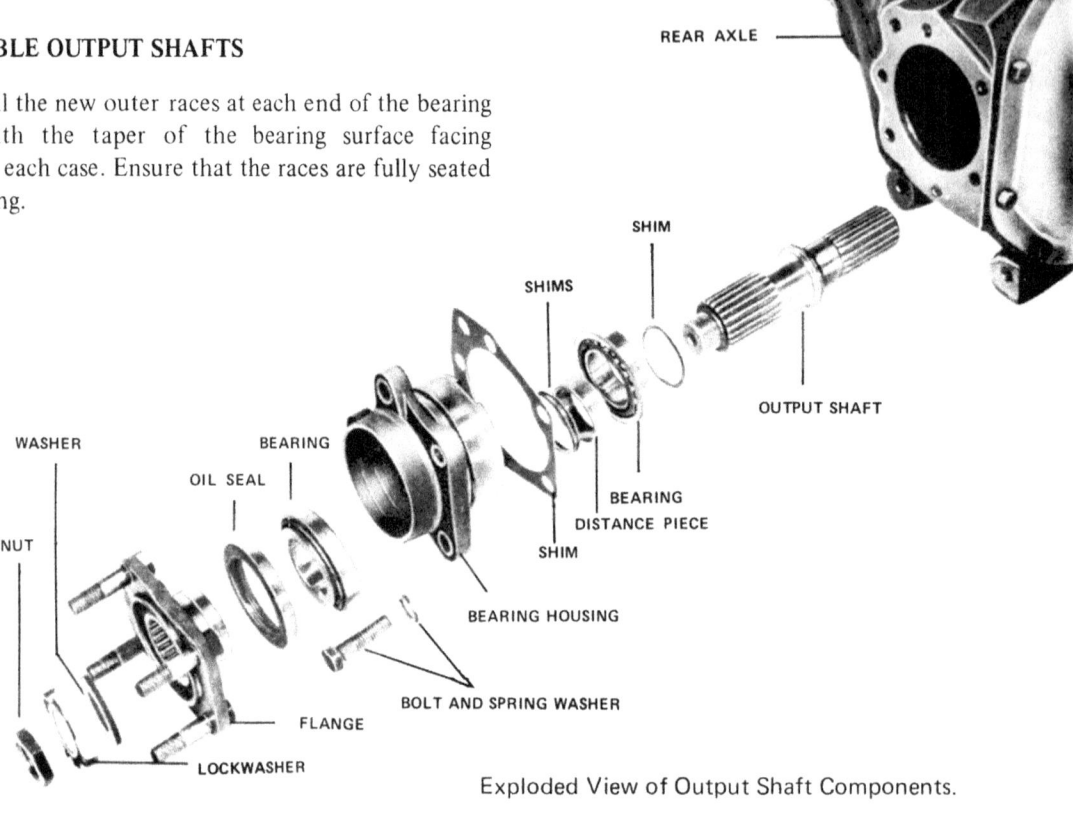

Exploded View of Output Shaft Components.

(2) Install the inner bearing inner race on the output shaft with the taper in the correct direction and press on the bearing until it abuts the shoulder on the shaft.

(3) With the distance piece and shims installed on the shaft enter the shaft and inner bearing into the housing.

(4) Press over the shaft and into the bearing housing the new outer bearing inner race. Do not fit the oil seal until the shaft end float adjustment has been effected.

(5) Install the output shaft flange together with the plain and lock washers, fit and tighten the securing nut.

(6) By means of a dial gauge, check the end float which should be .002" ± .001". If adjustment is required remove the securing nut, washers and flange, take out the outer bearing inner race and add to or remove from the shims as necessary.

NOTE: Add shims to increase the end float, remove shims to decrease the end float.

(7) When the specified end float is obtained, install the outer bearing inner race and a new oil seal. Ensure that the lip of the oil seal faces into the housing and that the outer face of the seal is flush with the housing edge.

(8) Install the flange together with the plain and tab washers, tighten the securing nut and lock in position by turning the tabs against the nut.

(9) The procedure described above is applicable to both output shaft assemblies.

4. DRIVE PINION

TO REMOVE

(1) With the differential removed from the carrier as already described, loosen off and remove the drive pinion nut and washer and with a puller, withdraw the flange.

(2) To avoid damage to the bearing, press the drive pinion through the bearing and out of the housing.

NOTE: Take note of the number of shims installed.

(3) Take out the pinion oil seal, oil slinger and outer bearing cone, examine the bearing outer race and only remove if replacement is necessary.

NOTE: A special puller is necessary to extract the outer race if it is to be used again. However if the race is to be renewed, the old race can then be driven out and discarded.

(4) If the pinion inner bearing outer race requires renewing or the drive pinion requires adjustment, use the method described according to the note above. Take particular note of the shims installed between the bearing cup and housing.

TO ASSEMBLE AND ADJUST

(1) Using special tool SL12, install the pinion outer bearing outer race.

(2) Using the original adjusting shims removed while dismantling the assembly place them in position and install the drive pinion inner bearing outer race.

(3) By means of a piece of metal pipe, the bore of which is the same as the inner race, and a suitable press, fit the inner bearing inner race in position on the pinion shaft.

NOTE: It is very important to ensure a high degree of accuracy in the adjustment of the drive pinion before proceeding further in assembling the unit.

(4) By checking the drive gear, it will be observed that on the machined face, the correct setting has been stamped and this, apart from serving as a guide at the time of assembling, also indicates that the mated crownwheel should bear similar markings, as these two components are lapped together and must be fitted in mated sets.

NOTE: Drive pinion settings for guidance:

(a) Pinion drop .... 1.5"
(b) Zero cone setting .... 2.625"
(c) Mounting distance ...... 4.312"
(d) Centre line to bearing
     housing .... 5.495" to 5.505"

(5) The letter stamped on the left, i.e. looking at the gear end with all markings in a vertical position, is merely a factory code number and is not intended to serve any purpose during the assembling process.

(6) On the right will be noticed a letter as well as a number. This mark indicates the dimension between the centre of the crownwheel and the centre of the drive pinion which will be found marked on the outer facing of the crownwheel carrier housing.

(7) The number stamped at the lower end of the drive pinion face indicates the dimension between the centre line of the crownwheel and the machined face of the drive pinion which can be plus or minus and this is adjustable by means of the drive pinion adjusting shims. For instance, since the zero cone setting is 2.625", i.e. the distance between the centre of the crownwheel and the face of the drive pinion, a (−2) marking will reduce the zero cone setting to 2.625" −2 = 2.623" and for a +2 will be 2.625 +2 = 2.627".

(8) After the drive pinion bearing cups have been installed with the shims removed at the time of dismantling, position the drive pinion, with the inner bearing cone, in the carrier.

(9) The carrier may be turned over with the drive pinion facing down and, between the work bench surface and the face of the pinion, position a block of wood to fit snugly in between.

NOTE: If a drive pinion bearing distance piece is a part of the assembly being worked upon, the same should be fitted at this stage.

(10) The outer bearing shims should be positioned on the drive pinion shaft according to the type of assembly being worked upon (see NOTE above).

(11) At this stage do not fit the oil slinger and oil seal assembly but only the drive pinion outer bearing inner race, companion flange, washer and nut.

(12) A special pinion cone setting gauge (Tool No. SL.3P) is required to check the setting distance, without the gauge no degree of accuracy can be obtained.

NOTE: Operations (13) to (18) relate to use of the special gauge for checking the pinion cone setting.

(13) Carry out the necessary adjustments on the dial indicator adjustable bracket for the differential being checked.

(14) With the setting block and dial indicator on a surface plate, position the dial indicator plunger on the 4HA setting and zero the gauge.

(15) Engage the dial indicator on the non-adjustable spindle of the gauge assembly clamp.

(16) Install the gauge assembly in position on the gear carrier, with the post of the dial indicator on the pinion head and the adjustable spindle of the gauge clamp located centre of the pinion threaded end. Secure the adjustable spindle with the thumb screw below the gear carrier.

(17) With the dial indicator plunger in contact with the differential bore, check the gauge reading. If the gauge reading is zero then the pinion setting is correct.

(18) If the gauge reading is not zero, note the direction and amount indicated on the gauge to determine whether shims are to be added or removed.

NOTE: Adjustment shims are serviced in thicknesses of .003", .005" and .010".

(19) When satisfied that the correct pinion setting has been obtained, after checking for a slight drag while rotating and also that there should be no end play of the pinion, check the pinion bearing pre-load which should be 8 in/lb to 12 in/lb.

NOTE: If the pre-load is less than specified it will cause too much deflection of the drive pinion while under load and if pre-load is excessive, pitting and failure of the bearings will result.

(20) The pinion oil seal assembly and the oil slinger should be fitted after adjustment of the differential has been carried out.

5. FAULT DIAGNOSIS

(1) Rear Wheel Noise.

Possible cause

(a) Wheel loose on axle flange.

(b) Bent tubular half shaft.
(c) Wheel out of balance or bent.

Remedy

— Check condition of axle and tighten or renew components.
— Replace component.
— Check and rectify wheel balance or renew or true up.

(2) Final Drive Gear Noise.

Possible cause

(a) Faulty pinion bearings.
(b) Faulty differential carrier bearings.
(c) Lack of lubrication.
(d) Incorrectly adjusted crownwheel and pinion.

(e) Incorrectly adjusted bearing pre-load (pinion or carrier bearings).
(f) Excessive noise or grind under load.
(g) Excessive noise on coast.

Remedy

— Renew pinion bearings and readjust gears.
— Renew carrier bearings and readjust gears.
— Check condition of assembly, flush and renew oil.
— Check condition of gears and readjust or renew as mated pair.
— Check condition of assembly, adjust bearing pre-load or renew faulty components.
— Overhaul assembly and renew faulty components.
— Faulty final drive gears and adjustment. Renew and readjust.

(3) Excessive Backlash in Differential.

Possible cause

(a) Looseness between axle shaft and differential side gear splines.
(b) Excessive backlash between differential side gears and pinions.
(c) Excessive wear between differential shaft and pinions and/or shaft bore in carrier housing.

Remedy

— Check and renew axle shafts and/or side gears.

— Check condition of gear and pinion teeth and renew.
— Check and renew faulty components.

(4) Pinion Shaft Rotates but will not drive Vehicle.

Possible cause

(a) Broken output shaft.
(b) Broken tubular half shaft.

Remedy

— Check and renew shaft.
— Check and renew shaft.

(5) Loss of Rear Axle Lubricant.

Possible cause

(a) Faulty final drive pinion oil seal.
(b) Leaking gasket between differential carrier and output shaft bearing housing.
(c) Incorrect type of lubricant causing excessive foaming.

Remedy

— Check and renew oil seal.
— Check and renew oil seal.

— Drain, flush and refill axle housing to correct level with recommended lubricant.

STEERING
SPECIFICATIONS

Type	Rack and pinion	Toe-in (wheel alignment)	.0625" to .125"
Steering wheel turns, lock to lock	2.50	End float at damper plunger	.006" to .010"
Turning circle	37 ft.	Load at rack ball joints	7 lbs.

1. DESCRIPTION

Rack and pinion type steering is utilised on both vehicles. Located at each end of the rack is a ball joint which is attached to the tie-rod operating the steering arms. The ball joint and a portion of the tie-rod is enclosed within a rubber gaiter which is secured to the rack housing and the tie-rod. The gaiter protects the ball joint and rack during operation from ingress of dust, dirt etc. The opposite end of the tie-rod is threaded for adjustment and attached to a ball joint assembly which is connected to the steering arm.

A damper pad is inserted at the steering rack and controls the amount of lash between the pinion and steering rack, adjustment is by shims under the damper pad cover.

Lubrication in service is required every 2,500 miles, a grease nipple is provided at the right hand side of the steering rack housing, a grease of the type specified should be used. When lubricating the steering rack and pinion, or ball joints, do not over lubricate to the extent that grease is forced from the rubber dust seal covers or gaiters.

View of Steering Column Assembly.

2. STEERING WHEEL

TO REMOVE

(1) Disconnect the battery.

(2) Take out the three grub screws located behind the steering wheel in the center hub, this will allow the horn assembly to be withdrawn from the steering wheel center.

(3) Remove the locking nut from the end of the steering column at the steering wheel center, loosen and remove the securing nut and flat washer.

(4) The steering wheel can now be removed by a sharp tap or pressure at the rear of the center hub, ensure that the two halves of the split cone are collected.

TO INSTALL

(1) Loosen the steering column adjuster nut, pull out the sliding section of the inner column and retighten the steering column adjuster.

(2) Smear grease into the split cone groove on the inner column, position the split cones with the thin end of the cone towards the steering wheel.

(3) With the front road wheels in the straight ahead position, engage the steering wheel on the steering column splines with the center spoke at the 6 o'clock position. Press the steering wheel down the splines.

(4) Install the flat washer and securing nut and tighten, refit the locknut but do not overtighten.

(5) Install the horn assembly with the head of the Jaguar upright, refit the grub screws and secure the assembly. Reconnect the battery.

3. STEERING COLUMN

TO REMOVE

(1) Disconnect the battery.

(2) Disconnect the indicator switch wires at the connector box located behind the side facia panel. Mark the respective wire connections to facilitate reassembly.

(3) Disconnect the horn push wire at the connector located at the base of the steering column tube.

(4) Loosen and remove the clamp bolt, nut and washer attaching the top universal joint to the splined end of the steering column.

(5) Loosen and remove the two securing bolts, locknuts and washers attaching the steering column to the lower support bracket.

(6) Take out the bolt, nut, washer and spacer attaching the steering column to the upper support bracket, positioned behind the side facia panel.

(7) Pull the steering column from the universal joint splines and remove from the vehicle.

TO DISMANTLE

(1) Remove steering wheel assembly as previously described.

(2) Remove the spring loaded indicator switch cover located nearest to the center of the car, take out the two screws, washers and clamp attaching the indicator switch assembly to the steering column and remove the switch assembly.

(3) Loosen the steering column adjuster nut and remove complete with split collet and circlip from the end of the inner column.

(4) Remove the horn push contact rod, spring and insulating bush from the center of the steering column.

(5) Take out the two screws attaching the indicator cancelling striker to the inner column and remove.

(6) Unscrew the stop button located in the inner column tube and withdraw the splined sliding shaft.

(7) Disconnect the earth contact from the bracket located on the steering column.

(8) Take out the bolt and nut retaining the slip ring contact to the contact holders.

(9) Gently tap the inner column tube up and out of the outer column tube.

(10) Remove the circlips, washers and felt bushes from each end of the outer column tube.

(11) Prise up the slotted end of the slip ring and remove from the splined end of the column, (this is only necessary if the slip ring is to be replaced), ensure that the contact and spring located in the bottom half of the rubber insulator are not lost.

NOTE: To remove the lower steering column operating shaft complete with universal joints see under next operation RACK and PINION ASSEMBLY AND LOWER STEERING COLUMN OPERATING SHAFT.

TO ASSEMBLE

(1) If the slip ring has been removed, refit new slip ring to the splined end of the column with the serrated edge of the slip ring towards the splined end of the column. Ensure that the contact and spring are located in the bottom rubber insulator before positioning the slip ring.

(2) Install new felt bushes in the outer column tube at both ends, install in the following order:- one retaining washer, felt bush, second retaining washer followed by the circlip.

(3) Install the inner column tube within the outer column tube.

(4) Refit the slip ring contact to the contact holders and install bolt and nut.

(5) Refit the earth contact to the bracket located on the steering column.

(6) Install the splined shaft in the inner column tube and refit the stop button.

(7) Refit the indicator cancelling striker to the inner column and install the securing screws.

NOTE: The direction indicator cancelling striker is slotted at either side to provide adjustment, with the road wheels in the straight ahead position the striker should be adjusted to a central position between the trip levers on the indicator switch assembly.

(8) Install the horn push contact rod with the spring fitted over the insulated bush and positioned beneath the head of the contact rod, ensure that the lower insulated bush is positioned at the base of the inner column.

(9) Screw the steering column adjuster nut complete with split collet and circlip into position on the inner column tube.

(10) Install the indicator switch assembly to the steering column and refit clamp and securing screws and washers. Refit the switch housing by springing over the spring clips.

(11) Refit steering wheel assembly as previously described.

TO INSTALL

(1) With the front road wheels in the straight ahead position and the steering wheel center spoke at 6 o'clock engage the splines of the steering column end in the splines of the universal joint.

(2) Install the bolt, nut, washer and spacer in the upper support bracket positioned behind the facia panel.

(3) Install the two securing bolts, locknuts and washers attaching the steering column to the lower support bracket.

(4) Tighten the securing bolts in both upper and lower support brackets evenly.

(5) Refit the clamp bolt, nut and washer to the top universal joint and tighten in position.

(6) Connect the horn push wire at the connector located at the base of the steering column tube, and connect the indicator switch wires at the connector box, in the positions marked on removal.

(7) Connect battery and test the operation of the horn and indicator switch.

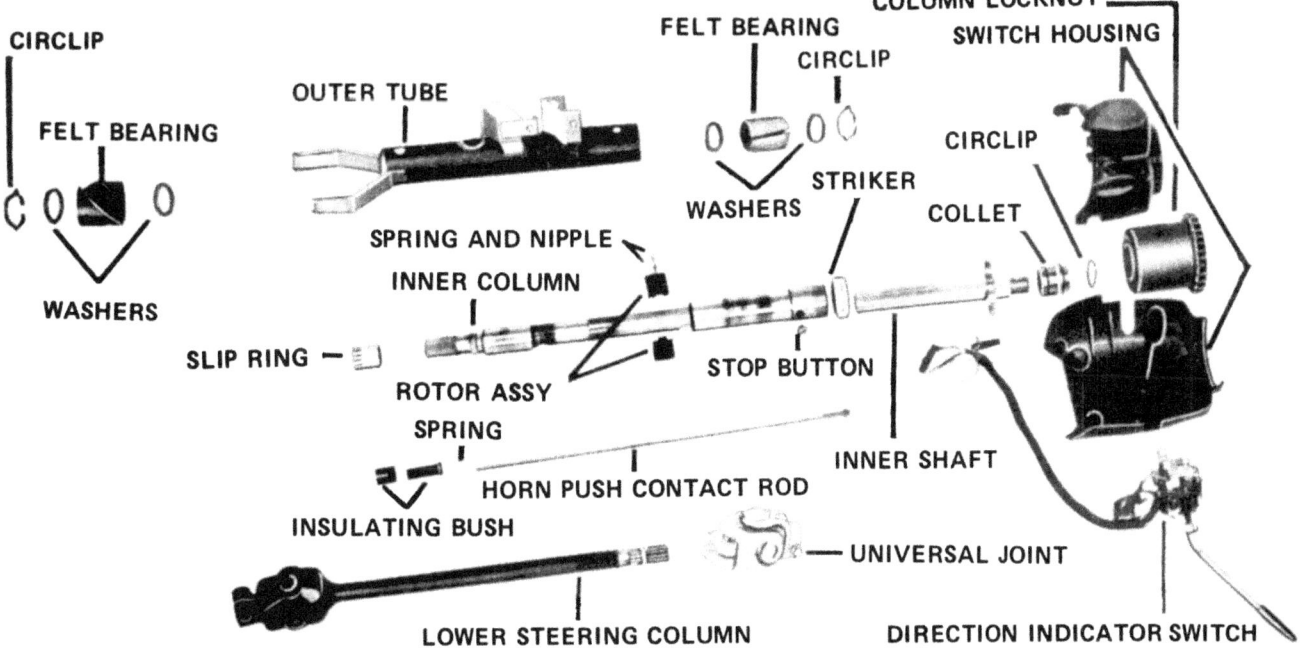

Exploded View of Steering Column Components (Typical).

Front View of Steering Arrangement (4.2 Model Shown).

4. RACK AND PINION ASSEMBLY

TO REMOVE

(1) Loosen the hub caps securing the front wheels, raise the vehicle on a jack and place axle stands under the support brackets located at the lower wishbone rear fulcrums. Remove the front wheels.

(2) Drain the radiator and remove as described in the *COOLING SYSTEM* section.

(3) Take out the split pin and remove the securing nut from both steering tie-rod ball joints at the steering arms. Using a suitable extractor separate the ball joints from the steering arm tapers.

(4) Take out the Allen screw securing the lower steering column universal joint to the pinion.

(5) Working at the steering pinion housing side of the assembly, loosen and remove the two inner self-locking nuts, and the centre bolt with self-locking nut, attaching the steering housing to the flexible mounting.

(6) Loosen and remove the upper and lower outer self-locking nuts and extract the bolts, noting the two spacers fitted between the mounting bracket and frame.

(7) Carry out the same operation for the opposite side mounting, noting that no spacers are fitted but are replaced by two adjusting locknuts.

(8) The rack and pinion assembly can now be removed from the frame by sliding it off the lower universal joint splines.

NOTE: The operating shaft connecting the steering column to the rack and pinion can be removed by taking out the clamp bolt, nut and washer attaching the top universal joint to the splined end of the steering column. Slide the universal joint off the steering column splines and remove from the vehicle.

TO DISMANTLE

(1) Slacken the ball joint locknuts and unscrew the ball joints and the locknuts from the ends of the tie-rods.

(2) Slacken the hose clips securing the rubber gaiters to the steering housing and tie-rods and remove.

NOTE: On the steering box pinion housing the gaiter is secured by means of a wire and not a hose clip.

(3) Prise back the locking tabs on the ball housing nuts at each end of the rack, unscrew the housing nuts and remove the tie-rods and housings, the ball sockets and socket springs, and the lock plates and lock nuts.

(4) Take out the three securing bolts and washers at the pinion end of the steering housing, remove the holding plate following by the O sealing ring and flexible mounting support plate.

(5) Pull out the pinion shaft complete with the bearing thrust plate.

(6) Using circlip pliers, remove the circlip at the damper pad housing and take out the disc, washer, shims and plunger from the housing.

(7) Slide the rack through the bearings and out of the housing, taking care not to damage the bearing faces with the rack teeth.

TO CLEAN AND INSPECT

(1) Wash all components in clean solvent and blow dry with compressed air.

(2) Check the condition of the rack and pinion teeth, ensure that there is no damage, wear or burrs.

(3) Check the bush type bearing fitted in the end of the rack housing, if worn or damaged, replace.

(4) Check the condition of the two pinion bearings and replace if necessary.

(5) Examine the ball housings and sockets, replace if worn.

(6) Check ball joints, if there is any signs of wear replace complete joint.

(7) Examine the rubber gaiters and ball joint dust seals for deterioration or splits, replace as required.

TO ASSEMBLE

(1) If a new bush type bearing is to be fitted in the end of the rack housing, soak the new bush in oil for a time. Using a long drift, from the opposite end of the rack housing drift out the old bush. Using a shouldered drift install the new bush until it is flush with the end of the rack housing.

(2) Cover the rack with a grease of the recommended type and slide into position in the housing.

(3) Lubricate the pinion bearings and insert the pinion shaft engaging the rack teeth.

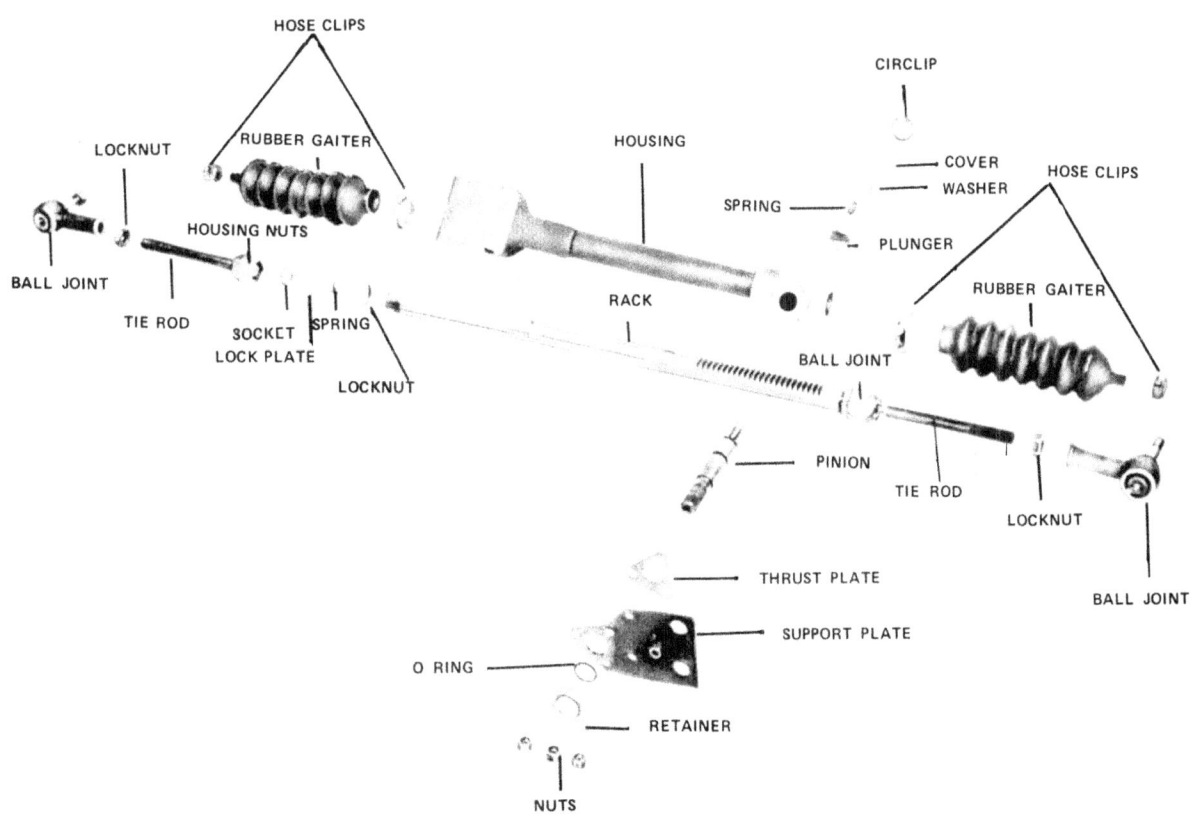

Exploded view of Rack and Pinion Housing Components.

(4) Install the pinion bearing thrust plate, and the mounting support plate, fit new O sealing ring and refit the holding plate and securing bolts and washers. Tighten into position.

(5) Install the damper plunger, disc and circlip, but do not install the shims or washer until the next operation has been effected.

(6) Mount a dial gauge on the steering housing with the plunger bearing on the center of the damper disc. Press the disc down as far as possible ensuring that the pinion teeth are fully meshed with the rack. Zero the dial gauge. Lift the rack up to remove all end float in the damper plunger and to bring the disc in contact with the circlip. Check the reading now on the dial gauge, deduct the thickness of the washer which remains to be fitted plus an additional .006" to .010" for the required end float. The remaining figure represents the thickness of shims required for correct adjustment.

(7) Remove the circlip and disc, install the shims of required thickness, fit the washer and disc and secure in position with the circlip.

NOTE: On later models a coil spring is fitted between the damper plunger and end cover in place of the adjustment shims.

(8) Screw the locknuts onto the rack, fit new lock plates, lubricate with grease the ball housing nuts and ball sockets. Fit the socket spring into position in the end of the rack and the ball socket over the ball.

(9) Position the ball joint at the end of the rack and screw up the housing nut until all end float is taken up.

(10) Install the tie-rod locknut and ball joint but do not tighten.

(11) Using a spring balance attached to the tie-rod ball joint, adjust the ball housing nut until a 7 lb reading on the spring balance is required to move the tie-rod in any direction from a centre position. When this is obtained lock the housing nut into position with the locknut and secure with the lockplate tabs.

(12) Remove the tie-rod ball joints and locknuts and fit steering housing gaiters, securing them with the hose clips.

NOTE: The large end of the gaiter fitted to the steering housing is secured by a wire and not a hose clip.

(13) Install the tie-rod locknuts and ball joints threading them on the tie-rod an equal number of turns.

TO INSTALL

(1) If the lower steering column operating shaft has been removed, install prior to fitting rack and pinion assembly.

(2) Position the assembly in the frame and engage the lower universal joint on the pinion splines.

NOTE: To ensure that the steering is connected in the straight ahead position, check that the front wheels are pointing straight ahead, fit the tie-rod ball joints to the steering arms, turn the steering wheel from a full lock, 1.25 turns to a central position with the center spoke at 6 o'clock. Engage the universal joint with the pinion splines.

(3) Install the flexible mounting at the steering pinion housing side of the assembly, ensure that the spacers are fitted between the mounting bracket and the frame. Tighten all self-locking nuts, and outer bolts and self-locking nuts.

(4) Refit the flexible mounting at the opposite end of the housing and tighten the center bolt and two inner bolt locknuts.

NOTE: To adjust the two outer mounting bolts and adjuster nuts, tighten the two adjuster nuts retaining the two outer bolts until the flat washers located under the bolt heads can just be turned by hand, screw up and lock together with the adjuster locknut.

(5) Install the Allen screw securing the lower universal joint and tighten into position.

(6) Tighten both ball joint securing nuts at the steering arms and fit new split pins.

(7) Install radiator and hoses as described in the *COOLING SYSTEM* section.

(8) Lubricate the rack and pinion and tie-rod ball joints with the specified lubricant.

(9) Adjust the front wheel alignment (toe-in) as described in the *FRONT SUSPENSION* section and secure the ball joint locknuts.

(10) Ensure that the hub caps are fully tightened when the vehicle is lowered to the ground.

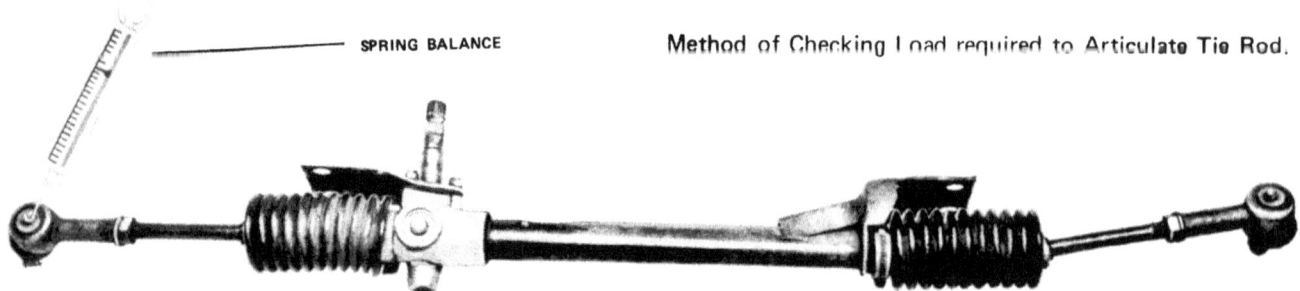

Method of Checking Load required to Articulate Tie Rod.

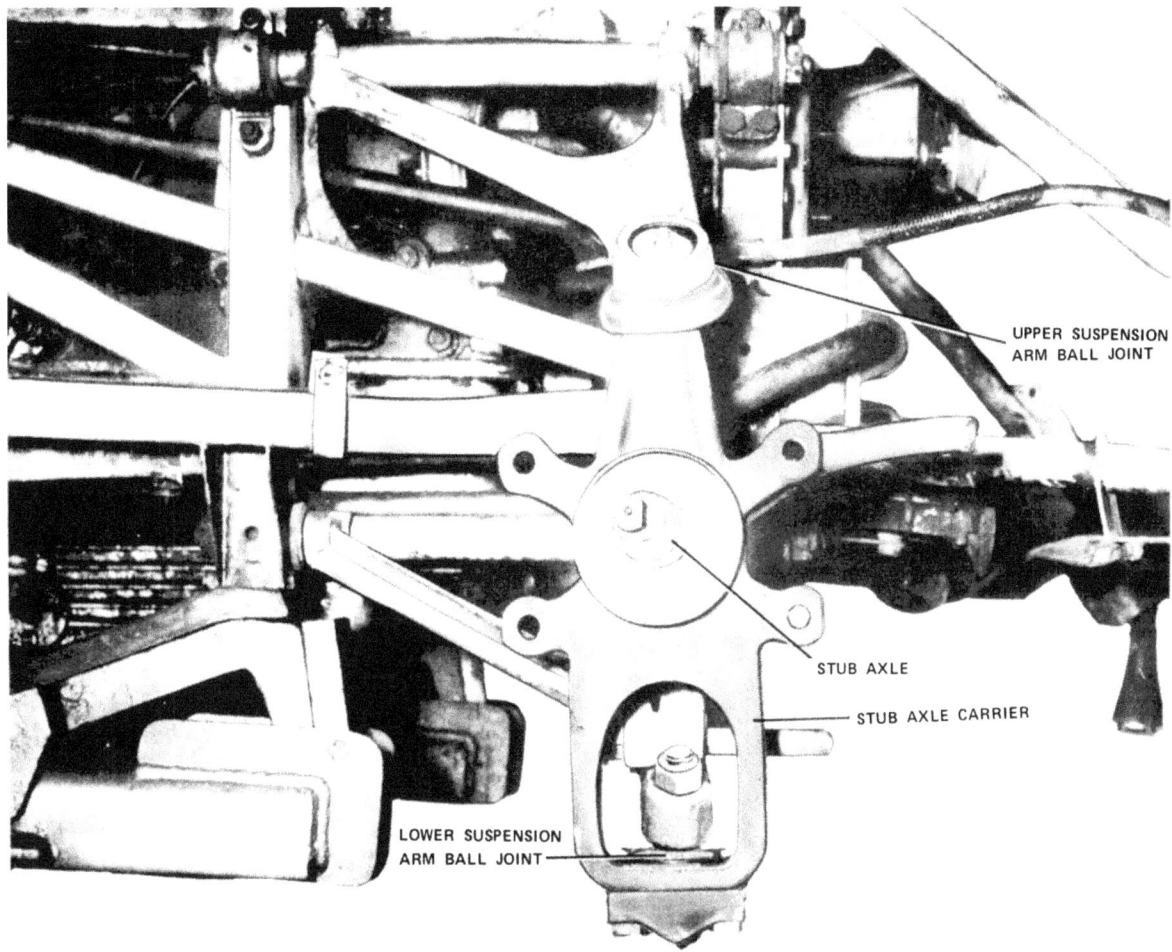

Showing Ball Joints on which Stub Axle Carrier Swivels.

5. LOWER STEERING COLUMN SHAFT

TO REMOVE AND INSTALL

(1) Disconnect the battery.

(2) Drain the radiator and remove as described in the *COOLING SYSTEM* section.

(3) Remove the bonnet assembly as described in the *BODY SECTION*.

(4) Disconnect the indicator switch wires at the connector box located behind the side facia panel. Mark the respective wire connections to facilitate reassembly.

(5) Disconnect the horn push wire at the connector located at the base of the steering column tube.

(6) Loosen and remove the clamp bolt, nut and washer attaching the top universal joint to the splined end of the steering column.

(7) Take out the Allen screw attaching the lower universal joint to the splined end of the pinion shaft.

(8) Loosen and remove the two securing bolts, locknuts and washers attaching the steering column to the lower support bracket.

(9) Take out the bolt, nut, washer and spacer attaching the steering column to the upper support bracket positioned behind the side facia panel.

(10) Withdraw the steering column from the upper universal joint splines, pull out the lower column shaft sufficiently to disengage the lower universal joint from the pinion shaft.

(11) Remove the steering column shaft through the front cross-members above the anti-roll bar.

Installation is a reversal of the removal procedure with attention to the following points:

Ensure that the universal joints are in a serviceable condition with no wear evident.

Install the spacer in the upper support bracket.

When engaging the splines of the universal joint at both pinion and steering column, ensure that the front wheels are in the straight ahead position with the steering wheel central and the center steering wheel spoke at 6 o'clock.

6. STEERING FAULT DIAGNOSIS

(1) Excessive lash or looseness in steering mechanism.

Possible cause	*Remedy*
(a) Rack and pinion worn/out of adjustment.	– Overhaul steering and readjust.
(b) Steering tie-rod ball joints worn/loose.	– Tighten or renew.
(c) Rack ball housing or socket worn/loose.	– Adjust or renew as necessary.
(d) Rack housing mountings broken/loose.	– Tighten or replace as necessary.
(e) Steering arm bolts/nuts loose on swivel hub.	– Check and tighten bolts/nut.

(2) Heavy steering.

Possible cause	*Remedy*
(a) Low or uneven tyre pressures.	– Check tyres and inflate to correct pressures.
(b) Rack and pinion incorrectly adjusted.	– Check and readjust.
(c) Lack of lubricant in rack housing.	– Check for leakage, rectify and lubricate.
(d) Rack assembly mounting bolts loose.	– Check and align housing and tighten bolts.

(3) Steering pulls to one side.

Possible cause	*Remedy*
(a) Uneven tyre wear or pressure.	– Check condition of tyres and inflate to correct pressure.
(b) Incorrect front end adjustment.	– Check front end alignment and adjust as necessary.
(c) Dragging front brakes.	– Check and rectify as necessary.
(d) Loose or incorrectly adjusted front hubs.	– Check and adjust front hub bearings.

(4) Front wheel wobble or shimmy.

Possible cause	*Remedy*
(a) Looseness in rack and pinion assembly.	– Check and readjust rack damper.
(b) Uneven tyre wear or incorrect tyre pressure.	– Check condition of tyres and inflate to correct pressure.
(c) Tyre and/or wheel unbalance.	– Check and balance wheels.
(d) Loose or incorrectly adjusted front hubs.	– Check and adjust front hub bearings.
(e) Incorrect front end adjustment.	– Check front end alignment and adjust as necessary.
(f) Loose or worn steering ball joints.	– Check and renew as required.

(5) Steering erratic or wandering.

Possible cause	*Remedy*
(a) Incorrect or uneven camber and/or caster setting.	– Check and adjust to rectify.
(b) Smooth front tyres.	– Check and renew as required
(c) Excessively low or high tyre pressure.	– Check and inflate tyres to correct pressure.
(d) Loose or incorrectly adjusted front hub bearings.	– Check and adjust front hub bearings.
(e) Excessive play in rack and pinion and/or ball joints.	– Check, adjust or renew as necessary.

FRONT SUSPENSION

SPECIFICATIONS

Type	Torsion bars and telescopic shock absorbers with control arms.
Shock absorber	Telescopic and sealed without any provision for adjustment.
Castor angle	2° ± .50° positive
Camber angle	.25° ± .50° positive
Swivel inclination	4°
Toe-in (Wheel alignment)	.0625" – .125"

Torsion bar – Checking:-
- 4.2 .... 3.5" ± .25"
- 2 + 2 .... 3.75" ± .25"

Between hole centres for Setting Links:-
- 3.8 .... 17.8125"
- 4.2 .... 18.0625"
- 4.2 (air conditioned) .... 17.780"
- 4.2 (2 + 2) .... 18.25"

NOTE: Commencing at chassis number IE 50875 (R.H. Drive) and IE 77407 (L.H. Drive) larger diameter torsion bars are fitted to 4.2 "E" Type 2 + 2 cars. The setting link necessary for these cars is 17.97" between hole centres.

1. DESCRIPTION

Each front suspension unit comprises a lower and an upper suspension arm, telescopic shock absorber, torsion bar and a stub axle carrier.

The shock absorber is attached at the lower end to the lower suspension arm and at the top to the end of the chassis frame.

The torsion bar, at the front end, is attached to the lower suspension arm and at the rear to the chassis frame by means of a bracket.

The stub axle carrier supports the stub axle assembly.

The upper and lower suspension arms are of two types. The lower arm inner end pivots on a fulcrum shaft in special silent block bushes. The outer end is secured to the stub axle carrier on the taper of a ball joint and secured in position by a self-locking nut. The upper suspension arm is one piece and the inner end is mounted on a fulcrum shaft and secured with two bolts. The fulcrum shaft is mounted on silent block bushes. The outer end of the upper arm also serves as a carrier for a ball joint which is secured to the stub axle carrier by the taper pin bolt and a self-locking nut.

The stabiliser bar is fitted to the lower suspension arms by means of link rods with rubber bushes. At the front end it is rubber mounted on two front cross members by means of two brackets.

The hubs of the front wheels are carried on inner and outer taper roller bearings on the stub axle shaft, the shaft inner end being secured to the stub axle carrier and secured with a self-locking nut.

2. FRONT HUB

TO REMOVE AND DISMANTLE

(1) Jack up the front of the vehicle and remove the wheel after slackening off the hub cap.

(2) Disconnect the hydraulic brake pipe at the connection on the frame and suitably plug the end to prevent the entry of dirt or possible fluid loss.

(3) Remove the brake calliper by taking out the wire from the two mounting bolts and removing the bolts.

NOTE: At the time of removing the brake calliper a special note should be made of the number of shims fitted between the mounting plate and the calliper.

(4) Take out the split pin from the castellated nut and remove the castellated nut and "D" washer from the axle shaft.

(5) Withdraw the hub assembly from the stub axle and remove the inner cone and roller assembly of the outer hub bearing.

(6) Carefully tap the inner cone and roller assembly out of the inner bearing together with the hub grease retainer.

(7) If the bearings are to be renewed, drive the two bearing cups out of the hub with a suitable tool.

TO CLEAN AND INSPECT

(1) Remove all the old grease and wash all the parts in cleaning solvent.

(2) Check the bearing rollers and cups for wear pitting or damage and renew as necessary.

NOTE: Individual parts of bearings should not be renewed. If any part of a bearing is faulty, the complete bearing must be replaced.

(3) Check the threads on the end of the stub axle and in the castellated nut for deterioration or damage. If the threads on the stub axle are unserviceable, the stub axle shaft should be replaced.

NOTE: Normally it should not be necessary to remove the stub axle shaft from the carrier unless it has to be renewed, in which case the self-locking nut on the inner side of the shaft may be removed and the shaft can then be removed by a few light taps with a soft metal drift.

TO ASSEMBLE AND INSTALL

(1) If the stub axle shaft has been removed, locate it in the appropriate aperture in the stub axle carrier, placing the correct end in position and secure it with a new self-locking nut.

(2) Install the two hub bearing cups into position in the hub so that their tapers are opposed to each other.

(3) Pack the space in the hub between the two bearings with wheel bearing grease, apply the grease to the roller of the inner bearing inner cone assembly and place it in position in the hub.

(4) Place a new grease retaining seal on the inner end of the hub and tap it into position.

NOTE: Always immerse a new grease retaining seal in light oil for a short period before fitting.

(5) Apply wheel bearing grease to the inner cone and rollers of the outer hub bearing, place the hub assembly on the stub axle and position the inner cone and roller assembly in the outer end of the hub.

(6) Fit the "D" washer and castellated nut on the stub axle and, while rotating the hub, tighten the nut until a slight preload is placed on the hub bearings. The correct end float is .004" ± .001" but this can only be accurately measured when a special dial gauge is available. In case a special gauge is not available, then fully tighten the axle nut and after doing so, slacken the nut back about one or two flats, at the same time fit a new split pin.

(7) Install the brake calliper and secure with the two mounting bolts and lock the bolt heads with wire.

NOTE: When installing the brake calliper ensure that the correct number of shims are fitted as were removed at the time of dismantling. If necessary refer to BRAKE SECTION.

(8) Connect the hydraulic brake pipe and bleed the brakes.

(9) Install the road wheel, tighten hub cap and lower the vehicle to the floor.

3. SUSPENSION UNIT

TO REMOVE

(1) Raise the front of the vehicle by first inserting a suitable size block of wood in the front cross member channel, the jack should be placed to take the weight of the vehicle on the wood and not on the channel, to avoid damage.

NOTE: It is advisable to have a suitable block of hard wood prepared corresponding to the measurements of the front crossmember channel and retain it with the tool kit of the car for use whenever required.

(2) With the vehicle raised, place a stand under the lower suspension arm fulcrum pivot bracket at the end of the front crossmember and on the side requiring attention.

(3) Slacken off the hub cap and remove the road wheel.

(4) From the connection on the frame, undo and remove the brake pipe and carrier bracket. To prevent dirt from entering the system, plug the end of the pipe.

(5) Disconnect the tie-rod from the steering arm by removing the split pin from the castellated nut on the ball pin and lightly tapping the steering arm near the pin.

(6) Separate the upper suspension arm ball joint from the stub axle carrier by removing the self-locking nut from the ball pin and lightly tapping the side of the carrier near the pin to dislodge it.

(7) Take out the two bolts and nuts attaching the upper suspension arm fulcrum shaft rear carrier bracket to the chassis frame. Withdraw the shims from between the bracket and frame and remove the stiffener plate positioned behind the two nuts on the frame inner face.

(8) Similarly from the front carrier bracket remove three bolts, the shims and stiffener plate. Detach the upper suspension arm.

NOTE: To ensure that the stiffener plates are not mistaken for shims, mark accordingly.

(9) Remove the self-locking nut from the ball joint retaining the lower suspension arm to the stub axle carrier, and separate the ball joint taper from the arm.

(10) Detach the stub axle carrier complete with brake and hub assembly.

(11) Raise the lower suspension arm with a jack sufficiently to take the weight of the vehicle but without lifting from the axle stands.

(12) Disconnect the stabiliser bar link from the lower suspension arm.

(13) Disconnect and remove the shock absorber from the lower suspension arm and the end of the chassis frame. Remove the jack.

(14) Take out the two bolts retaining the rear adjusting plate to the frame, move the plate forward until it disengages from the splines.

(15) Remove the bolt retaining the front end of the torsion bar in the lower suspension arm, push the bar to the rear to release the splines and withdraw from the front of the vehicle.

(16) Remove the two bolts attaching the fulcrum shaft rear carrier to the chassis frame and the four bolts attaching the front carrier to the frame. Detach the lower suspension arm.

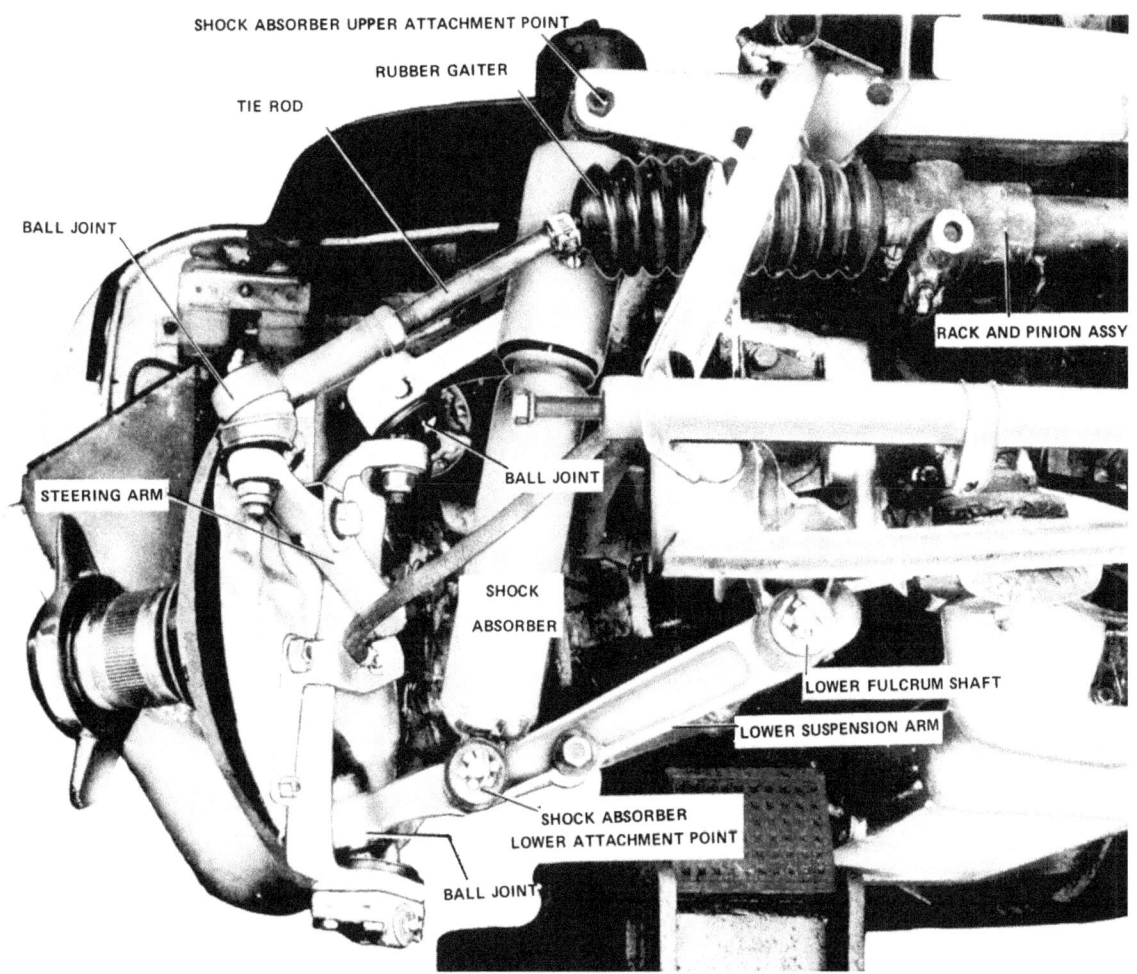

Front View of the Suspension and Steering Assembly.

TO DISMANTLE AND ASSEMBLE

Upper Suspension Arm

(1) Take out the split pins and remove the nuts at the ends of the fulcrum shaft and slide the brackets from the shaft.

(2) Remove the two bolts in the suspension arm retaining the fulcrum shaft in position, remove the shaft by rotating in a clockwise direction, (as viewed from the rear) until it can be withdrawn.

(3) Using circlip pliers, remove the circlip from the suspension arm ball joint and withdraw the disc, spring, socket and ball pin, if necessary remove the clip and detach the ball rubber gaiter from the suspension arm.

(4) If renewal of the bushes in the brackets is required, drift out the old bushes.

Assembly is a reversal of the foregoing procedure with particular attention to the following points.

Ensure that the fulcrum shaft bushes when fitted to the

brackets, extend by an equal amount from each side of the brackets.

Do not fully tighten the nuts at the ends of the fulcrum shaft until the vehicle weight is bearing on the suspension.

It will be necessary to readjust the castor and camber angles, see the appropriate section.

Check the clearance of the ball pin in the socket, .004" is required. Insert shims between the disc and upper ball socket until the ball is firmly held, when the disc and circlip are fitted without the spring. Remove one .004" shim and assemble with the spring. Renew components if wear is excessive, do not attempt to shim.

Lower Suspension Arm and Ball Joint

(1) Take out the split pins and remove the nuts at the ends of the fulcrum shaft and slide the brackets from the shaft.

(2) Working on the stub axle carrier, remove the ball joint rubber gaiter after releasing the circlip.

(3) Knock back the locking tabs and take out the four bolts attaching the ball pin cap to the carrier and detach the cap, shims, socket and ball pin.

Assembly is a reversal of the foregoing procedure with particular attention to the following points.

Ensure that the fulcrum shaft bushes when fitted to the brackets extend by an equal amount from each side of the brackets.

Check the clearance of the ball pin in the socket, .005" ± .001" is required. Remove the necessary shims until the ball is firmly held in its socket. Select and fit a shim to obtain the specified clearance which will allow movement of the ball pin by hand.

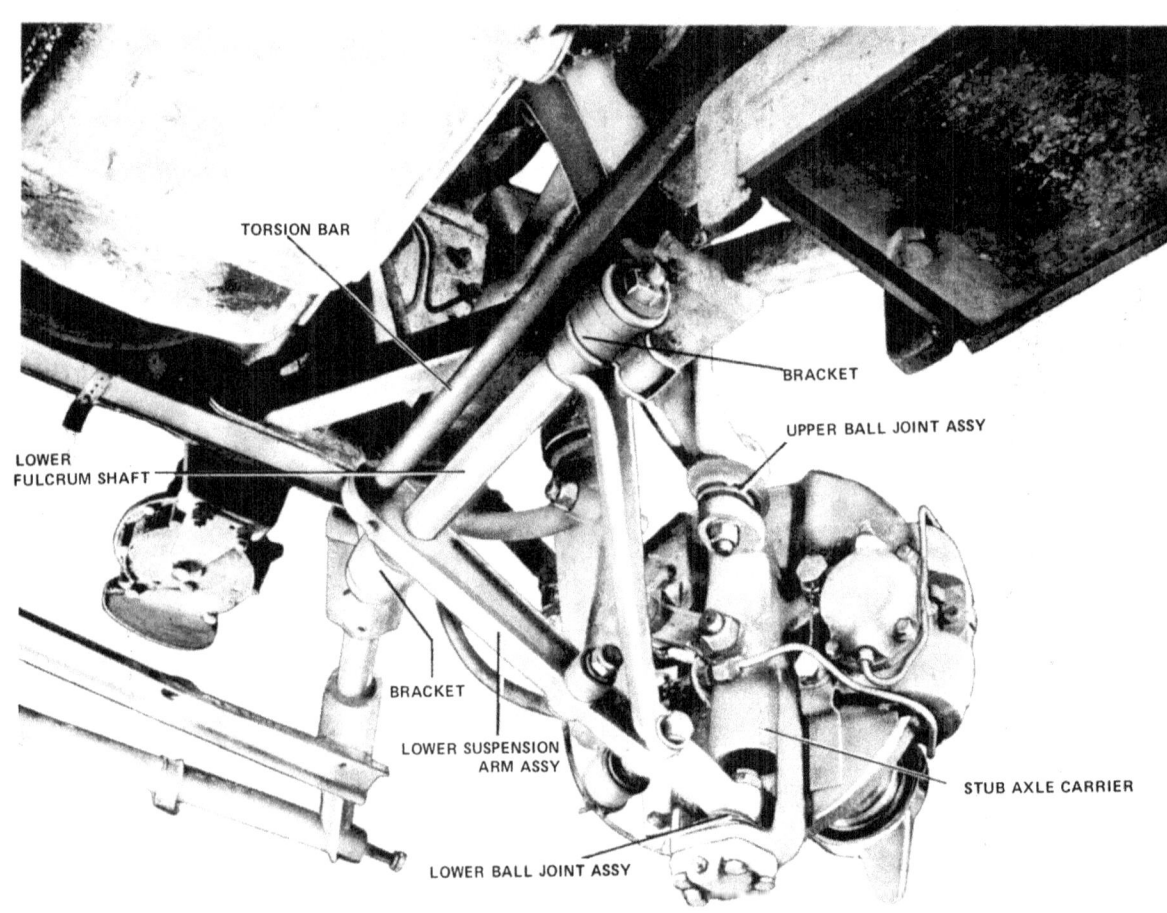

View of Lower Suspension Arm Assembly.

TO CLEAN AND INSPECT

(1) Wash components in solvent to remove grease and dirt, blow dry with compressed air.

(2) Rubber components should be cleaned in methylated spirits and examined for deterioration or damage and replaced as necessary.

(3) Check ball pins and sockets for wear or damage and replace as necessary.

(4) Examine the bearing surfaces and threads of the stub

axles and fulcrum shafts and replace if pitted or worn.

(5) Ensure that suspension arm and fulcrum shafts are not damaged or bent. It is essential that any effected components are replaced.

(6) Check that the shock absorbers are still in serviceable condition.

TO INSTALL

Installation is a reversal of the removal procedure with particular attention to the following points:

(1) Do not tighten the castellated nuts at the ends of the upper and lower fulcrum shafts until the weight of the vehicle is bearing on the suspension and the suspension is at its normal riding position. Fit new split pins.

(2) It will be necessary to adjust the torsion bar, see *TO CHECK AND ADJUST TORSION BAR.*

(3) Bleed the shock absorbers prior to fitting by holding in an upright position and operating in short strokes until all free movement is eliminated, follow with two strokes the full length of the units extension.

(4) Install the shims and stiffener plates in the appropriate positions when fitting the upper suspension arm.

(5) Bleed the brakes and carry out adjustment to the camber and castor angles as described under the appropriate headings.

TO CHECK AND ADJUST TORSION BAR

(1) Position the vehicle on a perfectly level surface with the front wheels in the straight ahead direction. Tyres should be inflated to the pressure specified for normal use. Petrol, oil and water levels should all be at the full mark to maintain correct loading.

3.8 Models

(2) Measure the distance from the surface on which the car is standing to the centre of the lower suspension arm fulcrum shaft. When correct this measurement should be 8.75" ± .25".

4.2 and 2 + 2 Models

(3) Measure the distance from the surface on which the car is standing to the centre of the lower suspension arm fulcrum shaft. Make a further measurement from ground level to a centre line taken through the stub axle and wheel assembly.

Subtract the first measurement from the second to give the dimension between the centre of the fulcrum shaft and the centre line through the stub axle assembly. When correct, this measurement should be: for 4.2 cars 3.50" ± .25" and for 2 + 2 cars 3.75" ± .25".

All Models

(4) If adjustment is necessary, jack up the vehicle and position stands under the lower fulcrum support brackets.

(5) Remove front road wheels.

(6) Disconnect as described earlier the upper arm ball joint at the stub axle carrier, the steering tie-rod ball joint and the stabiliser bar.

(7) Raise the lower suspension arm with a jack sufficiently to take the weight of the vehicle but without lifting from the axle stands.

(8) Take out the split pins and release the nuts retaining the lower suspension arm rubber mountings.

(9) Disconnect and remove the shock absorber. Lower the jack.

(10) Take out the two bolts retaining the torsion bar adjusting plate to the frame.

(11) Before adjustment can be effected, it will be necessary to make a setting gauge. This can be constructed from .25" x 1.0" mild steel strapping. Two holes should be drilled with the diameters of .453" and .640" respectively, with centres as follows:

3.8	17.8125"
4.2	18.0625"
4.2 (air conditioned)	17.780"
4.2 (2 + 2)	18.25"
4.2 (2 + 2) from chassis No. IE 50875 (R.H.D.) and IE 77407 (L.H.D.)	17.97"

(12) Attach the setting gauge to the upper and lower shock absorber mounting points, i.e. at the chassis frame and lower suspension arm. This will determine the lower suspension arm position.

(13) Check the alignment of the torsion bar adjusting plate bolt holes with the holes in the frame, if necessary disengage the plate from the splines and move to the appropriate position on the torsion bar splines.

NOTE: As the torsion bar has 25 splines on the rear end as against 24 splines on the front end, finer adjustment can be obtained, if necessary, by disengaging the front end splines from the lower suspension arm and selecting a new spline position.

(14) Secure both ends of the torsion bar when the adjuster plate bolts can be inserted without effort through the plate and frame holes.

(15) Support the lower suspension arm on a jack, remove the setting gauge and install the shock absorber.

(16) Connect the components in the reverse order of removal, but do not fully tighten or split pin the lower fulcrum shaft nuts and the shock absorber retaining nuts until the vehicle weight is on the suspension.

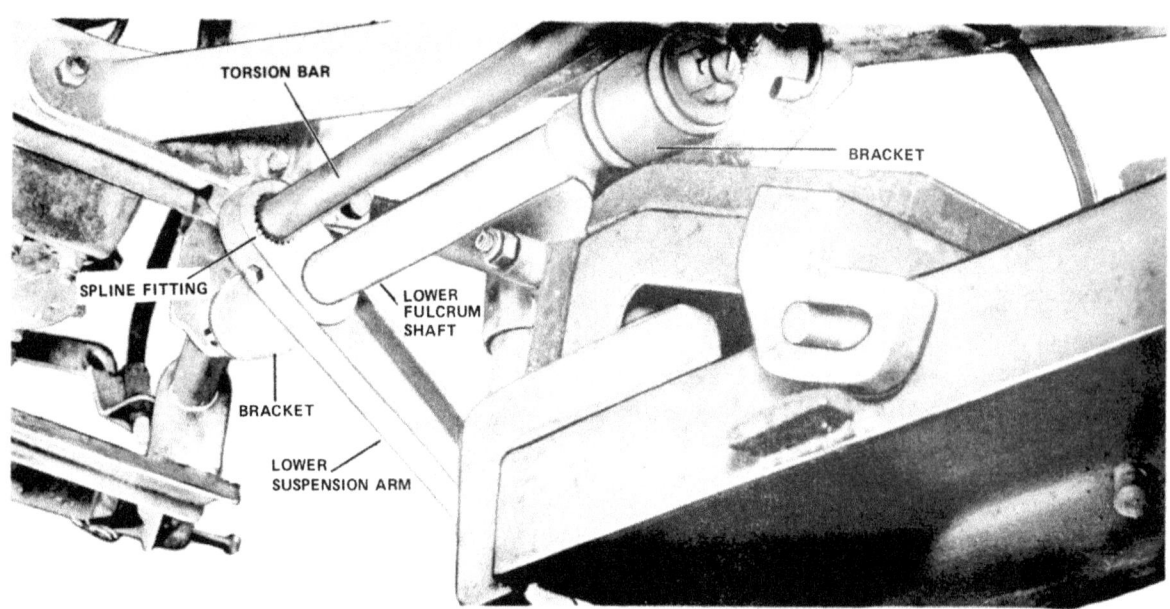

View of Lower Suspension Arm Fulcrum Shaft and Torsion Bar.

4. STABILISER BAR

TO REMOVE

(1) Raise the front of the vehicle on a jack and support on axle stands positioned under each lower suspension arm fulcrum mounting bracket.

(2) Take out the four bolts with nuts and washers securing the stabiliser bar brackets to the crossmember and remove the spacers and brackets.

(3) Disconnect the link arms at the lower suspension arms by removing the bolt and self-locking nut at each suspension arm.

(4) With the stabiliser bar detached from the vehicle take off the bracket rubbers which are split to facilitate removal, and remove the bolt and self-locking nut attaching each link arm to the stabiliser bar.

(5) If the link arm bushes are to be replaced press them out of the link arm eyes.

TO INSTALL

(1) Press new bushes into the link arm eyes so that an equal amount of the bush extends from each side of the eye.

NOTE: To assist in fitting the bushes, use soapy water as a lubricant.

(2) Install new bracket rubbers on the stabiliser bar.

(3) Connect the link arms to the ends of the stabiliser but do not tighten the nuts at this stage.

(4) Install the assembly on the chassis member with the spacers and brackets. Fit the bolts, nuts and washers but do not tighten.

(5) Connect the link arms to each lower suspension arm but do not tighten the holding bolts and nuts.

(6) Lower the vehicle to the ground so that the weight is on the suspensions.

(7) Fully tighten the bolts and nuts to secure the brackets and link arms in position.

5. SUSPENSION AND STEERING ANGLES

TO CHECK CASTOR AND CAMBER ANGLES

Before any attempt is made to check castor or camber angles or to check and adjust front wheel toe-in, the suspension unit should be thoroughly checked to ascertain that it is in a serviceable condition. The tread of the front tyres should be examined for excessive or uneven wear, as certain conditions of tyre wear are indicative of damaged or worn components in the suspension, steering linkage and/or wheels and bearings.

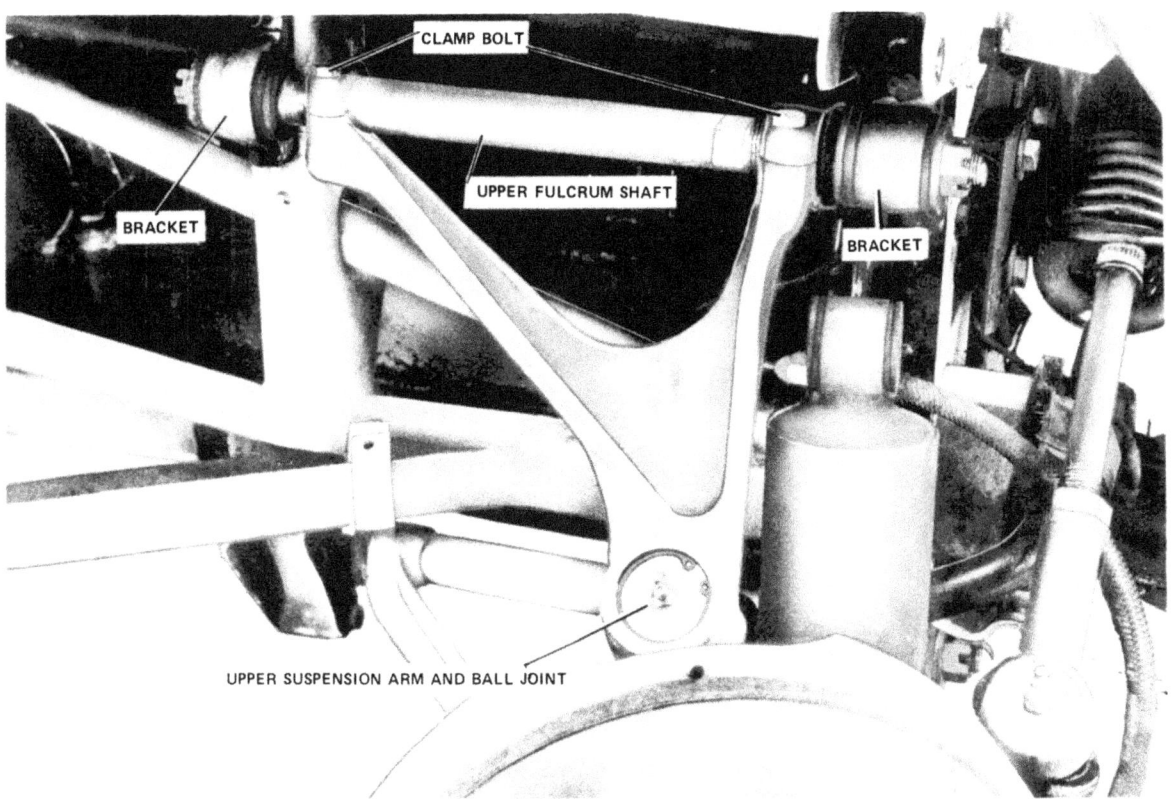

Adjust Castor Angle by Rotating the Upper Fulcrum Shaft, using a Spanner on the Flats Provided.

The vehicle should be unladen except for the normal quantity of fuel, water and engine oil, with the tyres inflated to specified pressures.

TO CHECK AND ADJUST TOE-IN

(1) Place the vehicle on a level floor.

(2) Check that the load in the car is normal i.e. full tank of petrol, full cooling system and full level of engine oil in the sump.

(3) Check that tyre pressure readings are according to specifications.

(4) Raise the front of the vehicle by placing a suitable size block of hard wood in the front crossmember channel, and lift so that the weight of the car is on the wooden block and not on the channel. Place stands below each lower suspension arm fulcrum mounting bracket.

(5) Rotate each wheel in turn and, using a piece of chalk, mark a line around the periphery of each tyre as near to the centre as possible.

(6) Lower the front of the vehicle to the floor and bounce the front and rear of the vehicle up and down and let it find its own height. Set the front wheels in the straight ahead position.

(7) Mark the centre chalk line on both tyres at points approximately 8" to 10" above the floor and in front of the front suspension.

(8) Using a suitable telescopic gauge, measure and record the distance between the two marks on the tyre centres.

(9) Maintain the wheels in a straight ahead position, roll the vehicle forward until the marks are the same distance above the floor but to the rear of the front suspension.

(10) Again use the telescopic gauge to measure and record the distance between the marks on the tyres. The distance measured at the front of the wheels must be .0625" – .125" less than the measurement taken at the rear of the wheels.

(11) In case adjustment is necessary, slacken the locking nuts at the end of both steering tie-rods and also to avoid damage to the rack rubber gaiters, slacken the two outer small securing clips.

(12) Turn each tie-rod by an equal number of threads in the direction required until such time as the toe-in is correct.

NOTE: It is important to make equal adjustments on each tie-rod to maintain the central position of the steering gear.

(13) Tighten the locking nuts at the end of each tie-rod and, after checking the rubber gaiter, tighten the two securing hose clips.

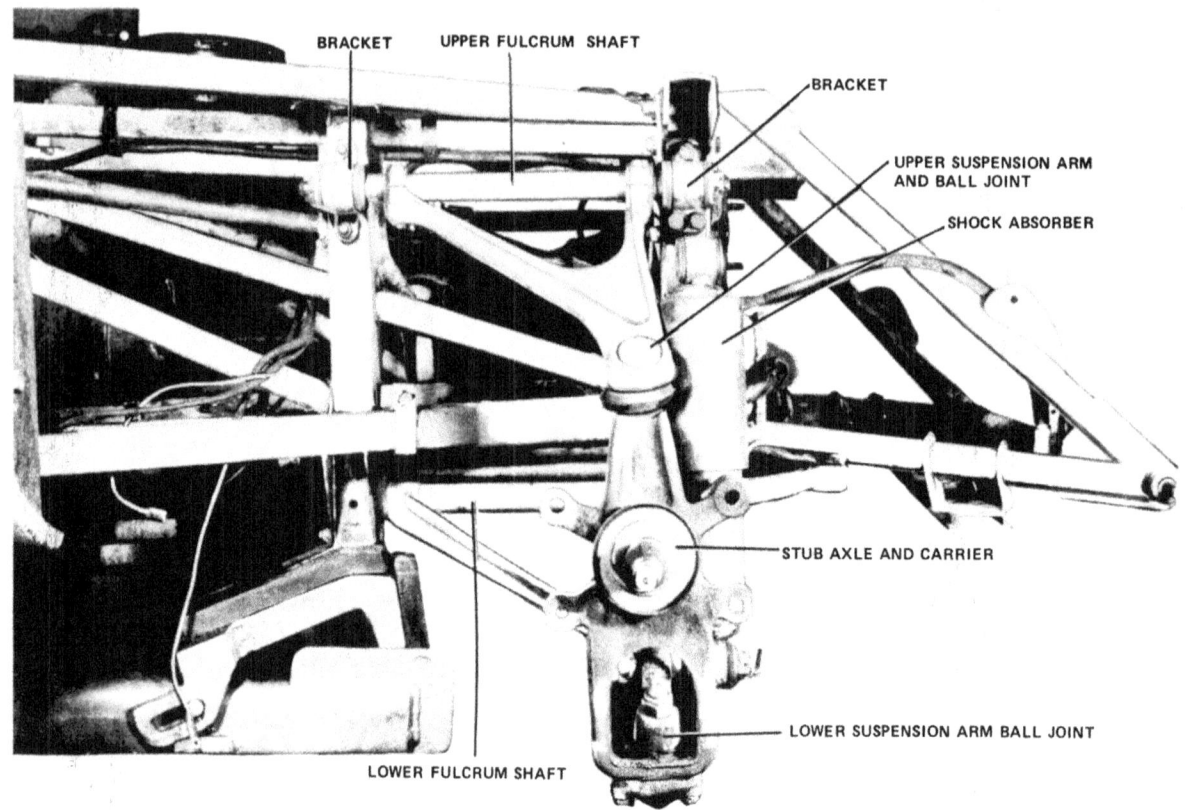

Adjust Camber Angle at Upper Fulcrum Shaft Brackets by Inserting or Removing Shims between the Brackets and Frame.

TO CHECK AND ADJUST CASTOR ANGLES

(1) Before adjustment can be effected, it will be necessary to make a setting link similar to that described in the section *TO CHECK AND ADJUST TORSION BAR* but with a dimension of 13.5" between the centres of the drilled holes.

(2) Disconnect and remove the shock absorber and install in its place the setting link. This will position the suspension at a mid-laden position.

(3) Install the rear suspension setting links as described in the section *REAR SUSPENSION*.

(4) Using a camber/castor gauge follow the equipment manufacturer's instructions and check the castor angle.

NOTE: The correct castor angle is 2 ±.5 positive, both wheels should be checked and the variation, if any, should not exceed .5 .

(5) If adjustment is necessary, take out the split pins and release the nuts at each end of the upper suspension arm fulcrum shaft.

(6) Release the clamp bolts in the upper suspension arm to allow the fulcrum shaft to be turned.

NOTE: When viewed from the front, the shaft should be turned in a clockwise direction to decrease positive castor angle and anti-clockwise to increase positive castor angle.

(7) Tighten the clamp bolts when the correct angle has been obtained, remove the setting link and refit the shock absorber. Remove the rear suspension setting link.

(8) With the weight of the vehicle on the suspensions, tighten and split pin the nuts at each end of the fulcrum shaft.

NOTE: Any adjustment to the castor angle may affect the front wheel toe-in setting, therefore check and adjust as described earlier.

TO CHECK AND ADJUST CAMBER ANGLE

(1) Before adjustment can be effected, it will be necessary to position front and rear suspensions in the mid-laden position.

(2) Using the setting links made for the castor angle adjustment, install them in the same manner.

(3) With the camber/castor angle gauge check the camber angle following the equipment manufacturer's

instructions. The correct camber angle is .25° ± .50° positive, both wheels should be checked and the variation, if any, should not exceed .50°.

NOTE: It is essential that the wheel being checked is parallel to the centre line of the vehicle.

(4) If adjustment is necessary, take out the bottom securing bolts in the upper suspension arm fulcrum shaft brackets and slacken back the top securing bolts. The top of the shims are slotted they can be removed or inserted with the upper bolt in position.

(5) Insert or remove shims as necessary, between the brackets and frame, to correct the angle.

NOTE: It is essential that shims of equal thickness are inserted or removed from both brackets to avoid affecting the castor angle. As a guide, note that a shim thickness of .0625" will alter the camber by .25 . Adding shims increases the positive camber angle and removing shims decreases the positive camber angle.

(6) Install and tighten the bracket securing bolts, remove the setting links and refit the shock absorber.

NOTE: Any adjustment to the camber angle may affect the front wheel toe-in, therefore check and adjust as described earlier.

6. SUSPENSION FAULT DIAGNOSIS

1. **Front End Noise**

    Possible Cause
    - (a) Loose upper mounting
    - (b) Noise in shock absorber
    - (c) Maladjusted front hub bearings
    - (d) Stabiliser link rod bushes worn
    - (e) Suspension arm bushes worn
    - (f) Stabiliser mounting bushes worn

    Remedy
    - Tighten mounting.
    - Renew shock absorber unit.
    - Readjust or renew hub bearings.
    - Renew bushes.
    - Renew bushes.
    - Renew bushes.

2. **Poor or Erratic Road Holding Ability**

    Possible Cause
    - (a) Low or uneven tyre pressure
    - (b) Defective shock absorber operation
    - (c) Incorrect front end alignment
    - (d) Loose or defective front crossmember
    - (e) Loose or defective front hub bearings
    - (f) Defective tyres or front wheel balance

    Remedy
    - Inflate tyres to recommended pressures.
    - Check and renew faulty unit.
    - Check and readjust alignment as necessary.
    - Check and tighten or renew member.
    - Adjust or renew hub bearings.
    - Renew defective tyres and balance front wheels.

3. **Heavy Steering**

    Possible Cause
    - (a) Low or uneven tyre pressure
    - (b) Incorrect front end alignment
    - (c) Lack of lubricant in steering gear and components
    - (d) Worn or damaged front suspension components
    - (e) Incorrect adjustment of steering gear

    Remedy
    - Check and inflate tyres to recommended pressures.
    - Check and adjust alignment.
    - Check oil level in steering and apply grease gun to all grease nipples.
    - Check and renew worn or damaged components.
    - Check and adjust steering gear.

4. **Front Wheel Wobble or Shimmy**

Possible Cause	*Remedy*
(a) Tyre and/or wheel unbalance	– Check and balance tyre and wheel as a unit.
(b) Rapid and uneven tyre wear	– Check front end alignment.
(c) Worn or loose hub bearing	– Check and renew or adjust hub bearing.
(d) Worn or damaged steering linkage	– Check, renew faulty components and adjust.
(e) Incorrect front end alignment	– Adjust and/or renew suspension components to restore alignment.
(f) Maladjusted or worn steering gear	– Renew and/or adjust steering gear components.
(g) Steering gear loose on frame mounting or off centre.	– Check and tighten mounting and/or centre steering gear.

5. **Vehicle pulls to one side**

Possible Cause	*Remedy*
(a) Low or uneven tyre pressure	– Check and inflate tyres to recommended pressures.
(b) Incorrect or unequal front end alignment	– Check and adjust to restore correct alignment.
(c) High road camber	– Avoid as far as possible.
(d) Weak or broken rear spring	– Renew faulty spring.
(e) Steering gear off center	– Check and re-center steering.

REAR SUSPENSION

SPECIFICATIONS

Type .... Dual coil springs enclosing double acting telescopic shock absorbers.

Spring: Early models   Later models
   Free length (approx.) ....   10.1"   10.5"
   Number of coils (approx.)   9.375   10
   Wire diameter ....   .432"

Track width .... 50.25"

Rear wheel camber .... .75° ± .25° negative

Road wheel movement from mid laden position:
   Full bump .... 3.125"
   Full rebound .... 3.125"

1. DESCRIPTION

The rear suspension comprises two coil springs on either side, each enclosing a double acting telescopic shock absorber, which are mounted, at the lower ends, on the lower suspension arm and at the top on the rear crossmember.

There are two tubular suspension arms, the lower at the outer end, pivots on the hub carrier and on the inner end it is mounted on the crossmember by means of a fulcrum shaft. The upper suspension arms are, in fact, the axle half shafts fitted with universal joints at either end.

The lower arm pivot bearings are placed at a distance apart to reduce flexibility in a lengthwise direction and thereby provide more stable riding conditions.

A box type crossmember frame serves as a carrier for the suspension assembly and is mounted at the top to the body on four 'V' shaped rubber mounting pads.

A radius arm has been provided at either side and is mounted at the outer end to the lower suspension arm and at the inner end it is mounted on the underbody.

The shock absorbers being the sealed type, adjustment or topping them up with fluid is not possible. In the event of any fault developing, replacement is the only solution.

2. SHOCK ABSORBERS

TO REMOVE AND INSTALL

(1) Raise the rear of the vehicle with a lifting jack by using a square block of wood an inch thick and ten inches square, placed between the jack and rear suspension tie plate. Place stands on either side just ahead of the radius arm front mountings. To prevent damage, place blocks of wood between the stands and underbody.

(2) Unscrew the hub caps and remove both road wheels.

NOTE: *Without removing the suspension assembly the coil springs and shock absorbers units can be removed from the vehicle.*

(3) From the lower mounting on the lower suspension arms, remove the two self-locking nuts and washers from each side.

(4) Using a suitable drift, tap out the shock absorber mounting pins.

(5) From the upper mounting on the crossmember, remove the self-locking nuts and the bolts. The springs and shock absorbers should now be taken out.

(6) With a special spring compressing tool, and with the unit held firmly in a vice, compress the spring until the split locking collar can be taken out from under the spring pad. Carefully release spring tension.

Installation is a reversal of the removal procedure.

TO TEST AND BLEED

The extent to which a shock absorber can be tested without special testing equipment, is limited to the following:-

(1) Mount the shock absorber upright in a vice by the lower mounting eye or stem, with the shroud to the top.

(2) Grasp the shroud firmly in both hands and commence by making six or eight strokes half way up and then down.

(3) After completing the short strokes give two long strokes and notice whether the movement is smooth or 'jerky'. If the movement is 'jerky' the unit should be replaced.

NOTE: *The resistance will be greater on the upward stroke.*

(4) In case the movement was smooth, next check the body of the shock absorber for dents or damage and also for traces of any fluid leakage. If found in good order, keep in a vertical position until ready to install.

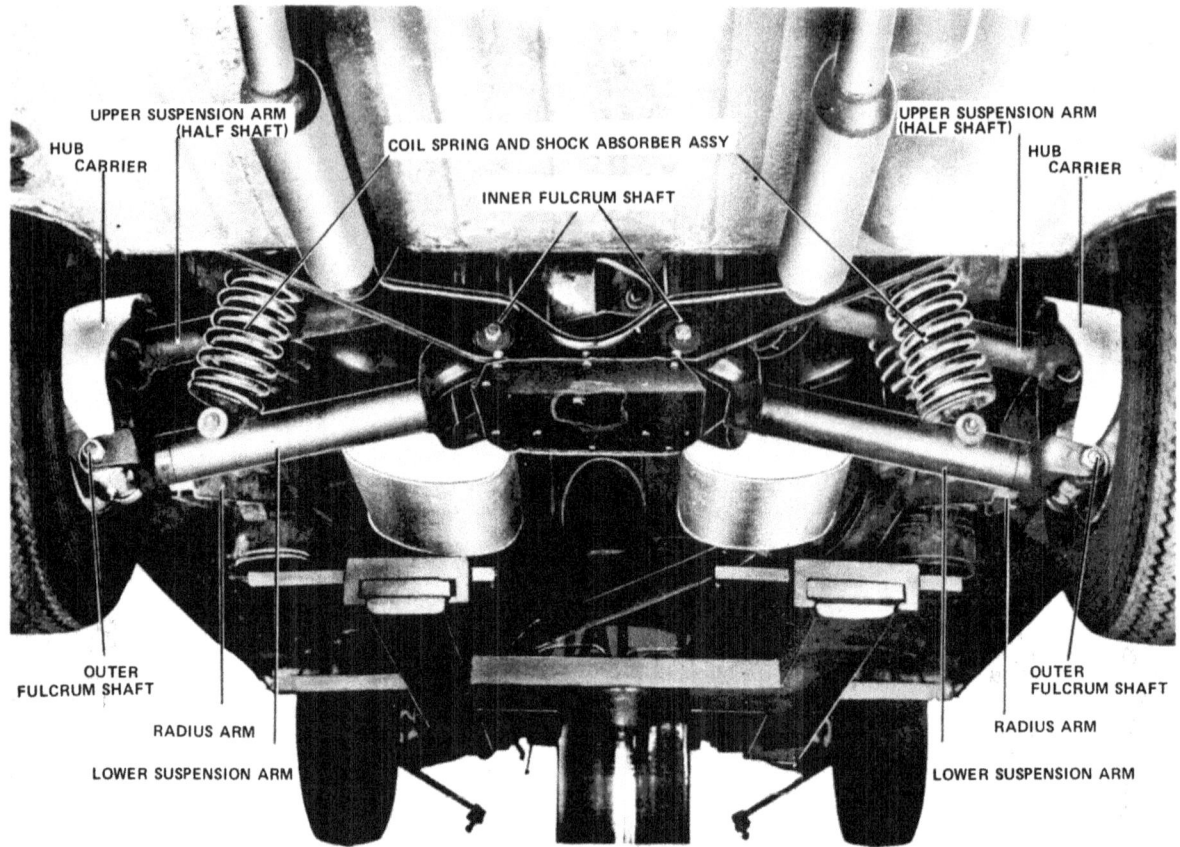

View of Rear Suspension Arrangement (Typical).

3. SUSPENSION UNIT

TO REMOVE

(1) Raise the rear of the vehicle with a lifting jack by using a square block of wood an inch thick and ten inches square between the jack and rear suspension tie plate. Place stands on either side just ahead of the radius arm front mountings. To prevent damage, place blocks of wood between the stands and the underbody.

(2) Unscrew the hub caps and remove both road wheels.

(3) Disconnect the tail pipes from the silencers by loosening the two clamp bolts.

(4) Take out from the tail pipe mounting, the two nuts, bolts and washers and remove the pipes.

(5) Disconnect the stabiliser bar from the link rod by unscrewing the two self-locking nuts and removing the bolts.

(6) Disconnect the hydraulic brake hose and plug the connection to prevent the entry of dirt.

(7) From the mounting on the crossmember, disconnect the handbrake cable from the handbrake calliper levers by taking out the split pin, washer and clevis pin.

(8) From the hand brake adjuster block, loosen the self-locking nut and take out the outer hand brake cable screw.

(9) Take out the four bolts and nuts retaining the crossmember front rubber mountings to the frame, noting the position and number of shims between the frame and mountings. Similarly the rear rubber mountings should be released by taking out six nuts and four bolts.

(10) Disconnect the propeller shaft from the pinion flange by removing the four nuts and bolts.

(11) Using the jack, the suspension unit can be lowered and removed from the vehicle.

Installation is a reversal of the removal procedure.

After connecting the hydraulic brake hose, bleed the system.

Check all rubber components for wear and deterioration and replace where necessary.

In case the radius arms were removed, the nuts securing them to the lower suspension arm should be fully tightened only when the suspension is at normal riding height.

When fitting the rear suspension mounting rubber, ensure that the rubbers are fitted with the cut-away flange towards the suspension unit.

4. RADIUS ARM

TO REMOVE

(1) From the safety strap and securing bolt, remove the locking wire.

(2) Remove the two self-locking nuts mounting the safety strap to the underside of the body.

(3) Remove the securing bolt and spring washer from the radius arm and take out the safety strap.

(4) From the mounting on the under-floor the radius arm should be removed.

(5) Disconnect the radius arm from the stabiliser bar link.

(6) Remove one nut from the hub bearing assembly fulcrum shaft securing it to the suspension arm.

(7) With a suitable drift, tap out the fulcrum shaft from the suspension arm and hub assembly.

(8) Remove the radius arm from the suspension arm by removing the self-locking nut and bolt.

(9) Check the condition of the radius arm rubber mountings and replace if necessary.

Installation is a reversal of the removal procedure.

NOTE: If the large mounting rubber requires renewing, ensure that the two holes in the rubber are fitted along the length of the radius arm. The rubber fitted in the other end of the radius arm should protrude equally on both sides.

When refitting the hub bearing assembly shaft, first fit in position with a dummy shaft.

5. SUSPENSION ARM

TO REMOVE

(1) Raise the rear of the vehicle with a lifting jack by using a square block of wood an inch thick and ten inches square, placed between the jack and rear suspension tie plate. Place stands on either side just ahead of the radius arm front mountings. To prevent damage, place blocks of wood between the stands and the underbody.

(2) Unscrew the hub caps and remove both road wheels.

(3) From the shock absorber lower mounting on the lower suspension arms, remove the two self-locking nuts and washers from each side.

(4) Using a suitable drift, tap out the shock absorber mounting pins.

(5) From the upper mounting on the crossmember, remove the self-locking nuts and remove the bolts. The springs and shock absorbers should now be removed.

(6) Release the crossmember from the tie plate by taking out the six self-locking nuts and bolts.

(7) Similarly, remove the tie plate from the mounting brackets of the suspension arm inner fulcrum by removing the eight self-locking nuts and bolts.

(8) From the fulcrum shaft securing together the suspension arm outer end to the wheel hub bearing assembly, remove a self-locking nut from one side and, drift out the fulcrum shaft and separate the hub bearing carrier from the suspension arm, after carefully noting the number of shims and their position.

(9) From the rear mounting of the radius arm on the suspension arm, take out the self-locking nut and special bolt and disconnect the radius arm.

(10) From the inner end of the suspension arm mounted on the crossmember, a self-locking nut should be taken off either end of the fulcrum shaft and drift out the fulcrum shaft.

(11) Disconnect the suspension arm and retrieve the oil seals and retainers with inner and outer thrust washers. Check the oil seals for wear and deterioration and renew if considered necessary.

(12) Take out the two bearing spacers.

NOTE: Usually it is not necessary to remove the large tubular spacer from between the ends of the inner fulcrum mounting bracket unless, for any reason, the bracket has to be replaced.

(13) Using a suitable drift, gently tap the needle containers out of the suspension arm if the needle rollers are to be removed with the spacer.

TO INSTALL

(1) Assuming that the needle rollers had been removed, press in position a roller container followed by the tubular spacer and the other roller container.

NOTE: The markings on the roller containers should be kept outward at the time of insertion.

(2) Position the tubular bearing spacers.

(3) Position the outer and inner thrust washers, oil seals and retainers after applying grease.

(4) Ensuring that the radius arm mounting bracket on the suspension arm is kept to the front and having a dummy fulcrum shaft at hand, place the suspension arm yoke between the ends of the mounting bracket and temporarily secure in position by pressing in the dummy fulcrum shaft.

(5) Liberally apply grease to the fulcrum shaft and gently tap it in position to replace the dummy shaft, and while doing so, check the egress of the dummy shaft.

Avoid dislodging the dummy shaft too quickly, otherwise a thrust washer or a spacer may drop out of position and if this should happen, it will entail having to commence assembly all over again.

(6) When the fulcrum shaft has been installed, fit new self-locking nuts and tighten to a torque of 55 ft/lb.

(7) Place the tie plate in position and first secure with the eight bolts and self-locking nuts. Then secure to the crossmember with the six bolts and self-locking nuts.

(8) Mount the rear end of the radius arm on the bracket on the outer end of the suspension arm and secure with the special bolt and a new self-locking nut.

(9) If the hub bearing housing components were dismantled, they should be positioned in the ends of the housing, placing them in the following order, two shims, tubular spacer, bearing, oil seal track, oil seal and two shims.

(10) The outer end of the suspension arm should now be positioned with the bearing hub assembly, and a dummy shaft temporarily fitted to hold them together with assembled components.

(11) Apply grease liberally to the fulcrum shaft and gently tap it into position to replace the dummy shaft. Care must be exercised while removing the dummy shaft to avoid dislodging a spacer in which case it will become necessary to repeat the operation of reassembling the components etc.

(12) Check the clearance between the hub carrier and the suspension arm lever and if the clearance at both ends is not the same, centralise by means of fitting shims.

(13) When adjustment is completed, fit new self-locking nuts and tighten to a torque of 55 ft/lb.

(14) The rear suspension camber angle should be checked.

(15) Further installation is a reversal of paragraphs 1 to 5 of this section.

6. SUSPENSION ARM OUTER PIVOT

TO REMOVE

(1) Raise the front of the vehicle with a jack after applying a wooden block as already explained previously in this section.

(2) Place a support below the bearing hub carrier and the suspension arm on the side concerned.

(3) Remove the road wheel.

(4) From either end of the outer fulcrum shaft, remove the self-locking nut and with a drift, tap out the fulcrum shaft. From between the ends of the hub carrier and the suspension arm, remove the shims, if fitted, and safely keep aside for fitting at the time of installation.

(5) Disconnect the suspension arm from the hub carrier.

TO DISMANTLE

(1) Take out the shims and oil seal track.
(2) Remove the oil seals.
(3) Remove the inner races of the taper roller bearing, the tubular spacer and the remaining shims.

CLEAN AND INSPECT

(1) Thoroughly clean all components.
(2) Check the bearings for wear and pitting.
(3) The oil seals should be replaced.
(4) Clean inside the housing.

TO INSTALL

(1) Install the roller bearing inner races.

(2) Install, two shims, tubular spacer, taper roller bearings and oil seal tracks only, as the oil seals and outer shims are not fitted at this stage.

BEARING ADJUSTMENT

(1) When it becomes necessary to adjust the taper roller bearings, first remove the hub as already described in the section *REAR AXLE*.

(2) Shims fitted between the two fulcrum shaft tubular spacers are there for the adjustment of the roller bearings, which is .000" − .002" preload. This is arrived at by increasing or reducing shims.

NOTE: Two sizes of shims are serviced, i.e. .004" and .007" thickness and the diameter is 1.125".

(3) Before commencing adjustment operations, it will be necessary to have readily available a small sheet of mild steel plate measuring 7" x 4" x .375". In the centre of the plate, drill and tap a hole the same diameter as the fulcrum shaft and with similar threads.

(4) Position the plate across the jaws of the vice and fix it.

(5) Into the threaded hole in the plate, screw one end of the fulcrum shaft and position one oil seal track, without the oil seal, onto the shaft.

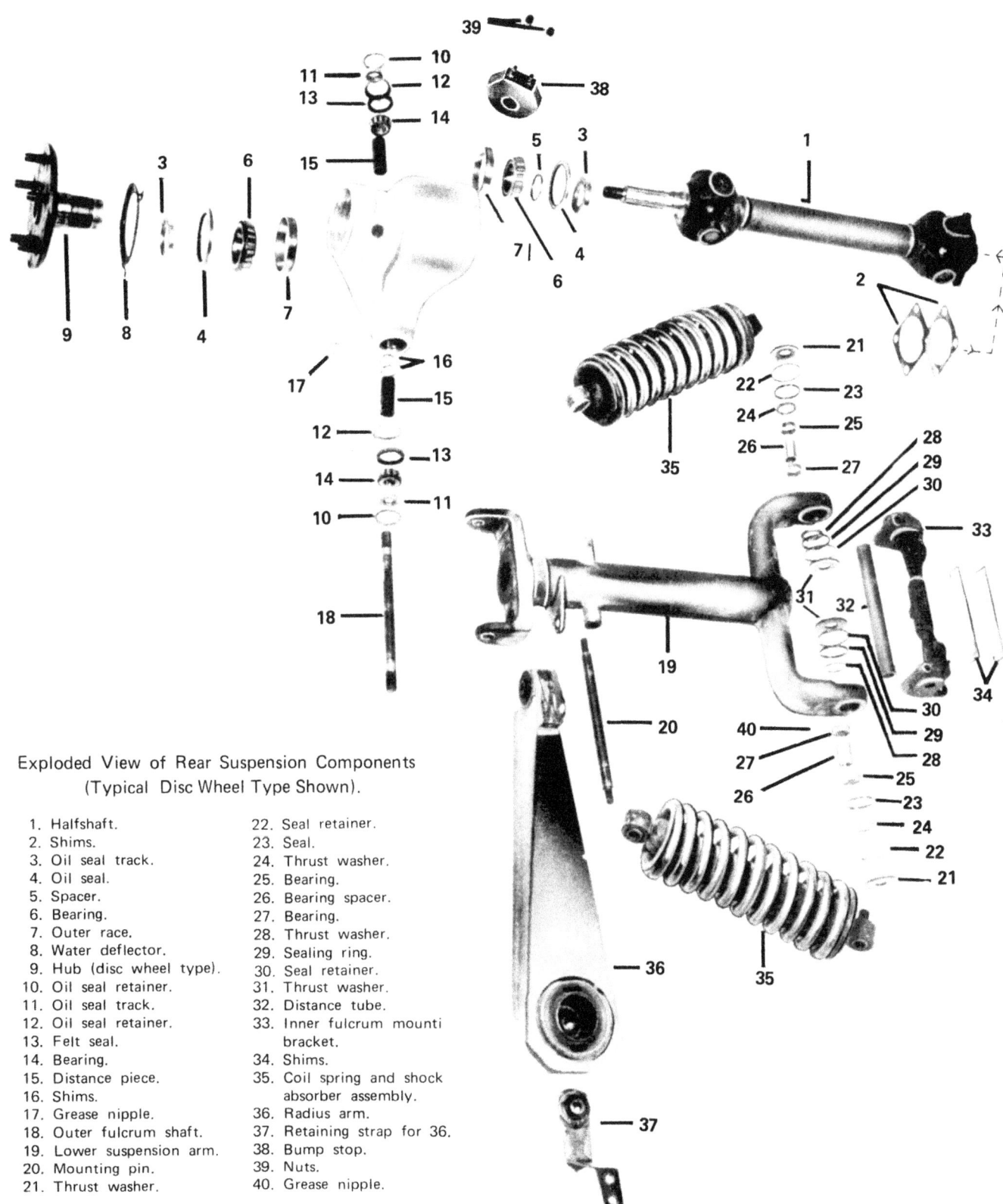

Exploded View of Rear Suspension Components (Typical Disc Wheel Type Shown).

1. Halfshaft.
2. Shims.
3. Oil seal track.
4. Oil seal.
5. Spacer.
6. Bearing.
7. Outer race.
8. Water deflector.
9. Hub (disc wheel type).
10. Oil seal retainer.
11. Oil seal track.
12. Oil seal retainer.
13. Felt seal.
14. Bearing.
15. Distance piece.
16. Shims.
17. Grease nipple.
18. Outer fulcrum shaft.
19. Lower suspension arm.
20. Mounting pin.
21. Thrust washer.
22. Seal retainer.
23. Seal.
24. Thrust washer.
25. Bearing.
26. Bearing spacer.
27. Bearing.
28. Thrust washer.
29. Sealing ring.
30. Seal retainer.
31. Thrust washer.
32. Distance tube.
33. Inner fulcrum mounti bracket.
34. Shims.
35. Coil spring and shock absorber assembly.
36. Radius arm.
37. Retaining strap for 36.
38. Bump stop.
39. Nuts.
40. Grease nipple.

(6) The assembly should now be positioned on the shaft with a counted number of shims, more than are usually fitted in between spacers.

(7) Position the outer thrust washer from the inner suspension arm yoke against the oil seal track. *NOTE:* washers should be placed in the remaining space to allow for securing the end with a nut. Tighten nut to a torque of 55 ft/lb.

(8) To form a good seat for accurate measuring with a feeler gauge, the assembly should be pushed towards the supporting plate in the vice with a slight twisting motion; to enable the bearing to seat itself.

(9) Continue to press the assembly towards the supporting plate and while doing so, check the clearance between the large washer and the assembly flat face by means of a feeler gauge.

(10) Instead of pressure towards the supporting plate, pull the assembly in the reverse direction and again, with a feeler gauge, take the same measurement between the large washer and the flat face of the hub carrier.

(11) To check if the preload is correct, the difference between the two measurements should be .000" ÷ .002". If the difference varies from the correct preload, remove shims to arrive at the figure.

(12) Having completed the adjustment, fit the half shaft to the bearing hub carrier as detailed under section *REAR AXLE*.

(13) Soak new oil seals in light oil, fit them with the lipside inward and position the fulcrum shaft in the bearing hub carrier.

(14) Place the bearing hub carrier and suspension arm in position and with the fulcrum shaft, push the dummy shaft through the other end, taking care not to dislodge thrust washers.

(15) To centralise the hub carrier in the suspension arm yoke, with a feeler gauge, check the distance between the suspension arm and the oil seal track and add or reduce shims to correct the position.

NOTE: Shims of the size .875" diameter and .004" are serviced for this operation.

(16) The fulcrum shaft self locking nuts should be tightened to a torque of 55 ft/lb.

(17) Install the road wheel.

(18) Remove the support from below the bearing hub carrier and the suspension arm.

(19) Lower the vehicle to the floor.

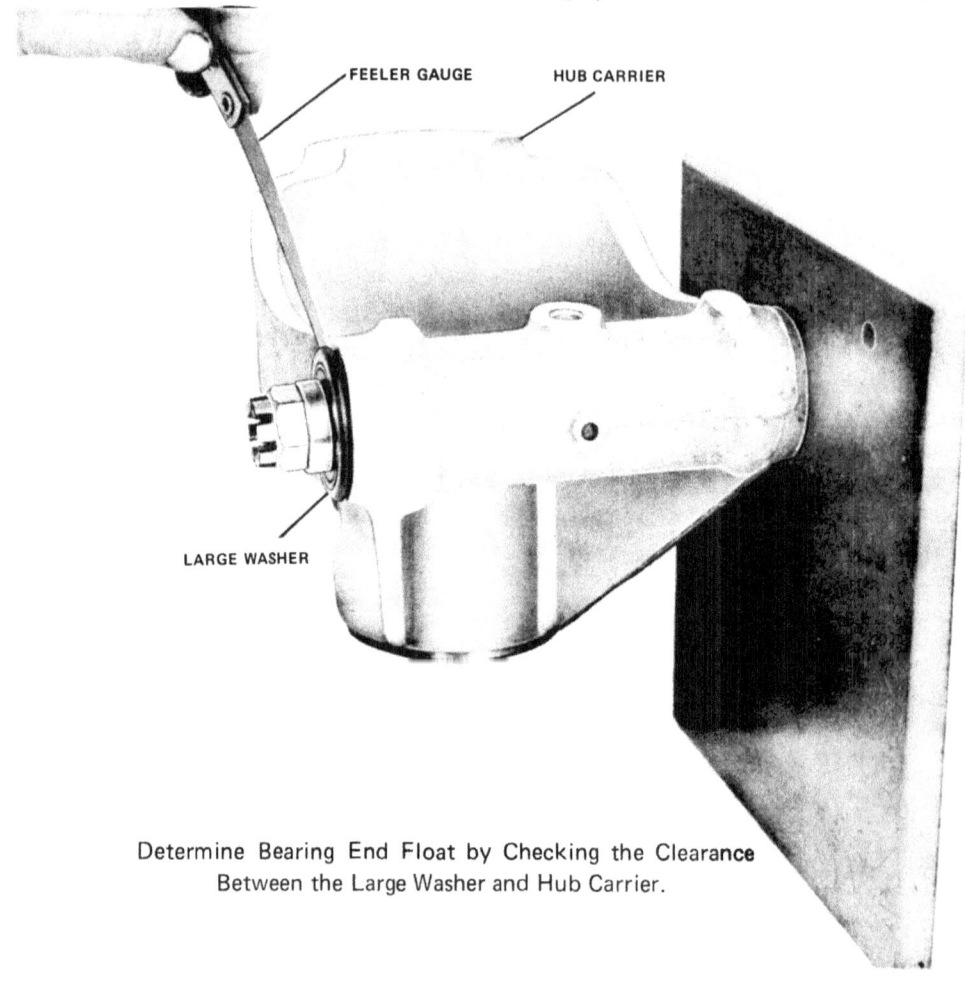

Determine Bearing End Float by Checking the Clearance Between the Large Washer and Hub Carrier.

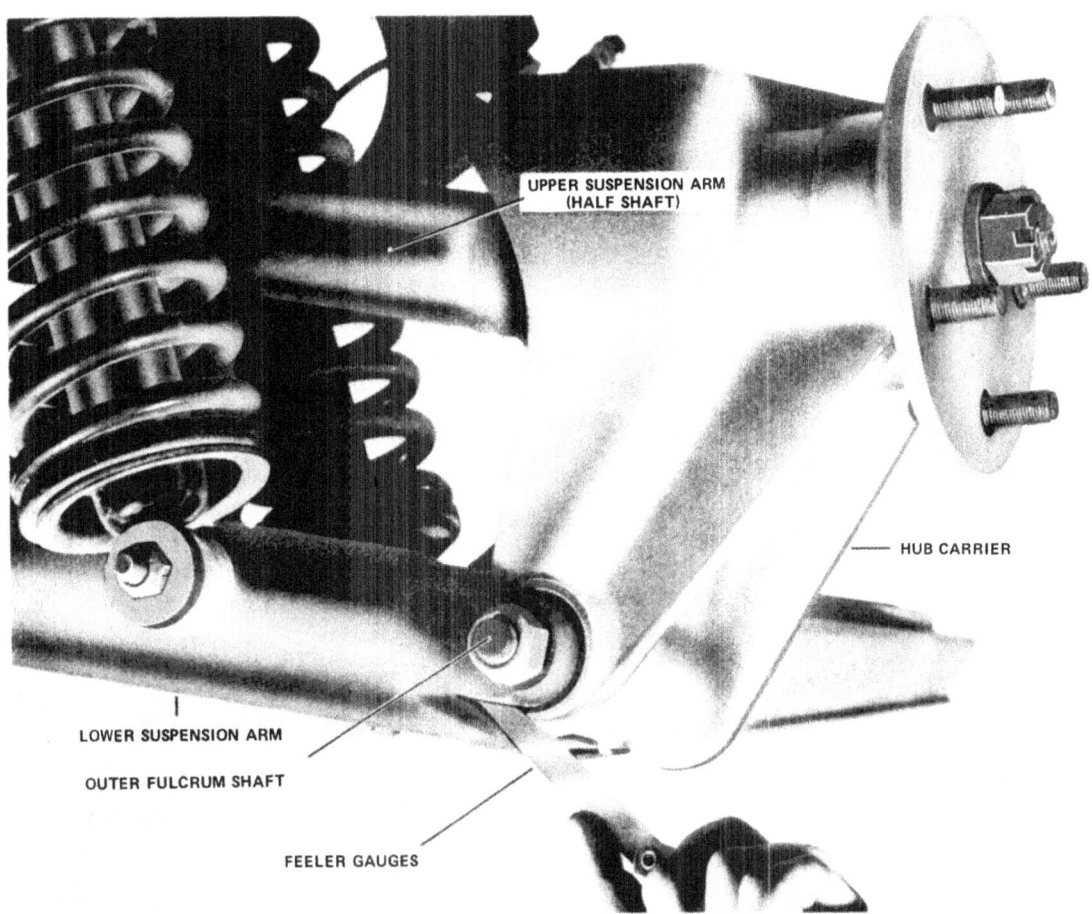

Method of Checking the Clearance between the Hub Carrier Oil Seal Tracks and Suspension Arm Fork (Typical).

7. INNER FULCRUM SUSPENSION MOUNTING BRACKET

TO REMOVE

(1) To remove the tie plate, take out eight bolts and locking nuts securing it to the inner fulcrum suspension arm mounting bracket and six bolts and self-locking nuts securing the tie plate to the crossmember.

(2) From one end of the fulcrum shaft, remove the self-locking nut and tap out the fulcrum shaft.

(3) Detach the yoke of the suspension arm from its location between the crossmember and the fulcrum mounting bracket.

(4) When removing the yoke, retrieve the bearing spacers, thrust washers, oil seals and retainers.

(5) Remove spacer from the fulcrum mounting bracket and take out the locking wire from the securing bolt heads.

(6) Remove the two securing bolts and detach the bracket from the differential unit, noting the number of shims between the bracket and differential.

TO INSTALL

(1) Position the fulcrum mounting bracket between the crossmember and insert the fulcrum shaft.

(2) Engage the bracket securing bolts a few threads into the differential casing and insert the necessary number of shims between the bracket and casing.

NOTE: Two sizes of shims are available, the thickness being .005" and .007" respectively.

(3) Tighten the securing bolts and secure with locking wire.

(4) Withdraw the fulcrum shaft from the bracket and crossmember and position the spacer between the bracket.

(5) In the correct order, place in the suspension arm yoke ends, spacer collars, needle roller bearings and spacers, inner and outer thrust washers, oil seals and retainers. The suspension arm yoke should be temporarily fitted to the mounting bracket and a dummy shaft fitted.

NOTE: Before fitting the suspension arm ensure that the radius arm mounting bracket is facing to the front of the vehicle.

(6) Apply grease liberally to the fulcrum shaft and commence replacing the dummy shaft by tapping the former through the crossmember, inner end of the suspension arm and inner fulcrum mounting bracket, during this operation ensure that the dummy shaft is not tapped through too fast otherwise a thrust washer or a spacer may become dislodged.

(7) With the fulcrum and other components in position, fit new self-locking nuts and tighten to a torque of 55 ft/lb.

(8) Secure the tie plate to the inner fulcrum suspension arm mounting brackets with the eight bolts and self locking nuts.

(9) Install the six bolts and self-locking nuts retaining the tie plate to the crossmember.

Installation of the rear suspension unit is a reversal of the procedure outlined in *SUSPENSION UNIT – TO REMOVE*.

8. REAR WHEEL CAMBER ANGLE — ADJUSTMENT

(1) To accurately check the wheel camber it is important that the vehicle is parked on a level surface, with tyre pressures at manufacturer's specifications.

(2) Setting links are necessary to retain the rear suspension in the mid-laden position. If necessary these can be fabricated from .281" diameter rod, form an eye at one end .594 radius and a hook at the opposite end, distance between the centres of eye and hook should be 8.1875".

(3) Install the setting links, one on each suspension so that the link eye is located over the hub fulcrum shaft rear securing nut and the hook is engaged in the lower hole of the rear axle crossmember mounting.

(4) With the links in position, from the lower suspension mounting pin on the suspension arm, remove the nut and washer and drive out the mounting pin to release the forward suspension unit.

(5) Using an approved type of gauge, take the camber angle readings of both rear wheels according to the manufacturers directions. The correct angle should be $-.75° \pm .25°$. If there is any variation between the two wheels or if one or both do not agree with the specified angle, this will require to be corrected by adding to or removing from the existing number of shims located between the half shaft inner flange and the brake disc.

NOTE: Shim thickness of .020" can alter the camber angle by about .25°.

(6) Jack up the side concerned using the same method of raising the car as described elsewhere in this section, and remove the wheel.

(7) From the upper mounting of the forward suspension unit, undo the self-locking nut and take out the bolt and remove the suspension unit.

(8) Separate the half shaft inner end flange from the brake disc by undoing the four self-locking nuts and drawing the flange and disc apart only far enough to remove or add shims as may be required.

NOTE: While adding or removing shims, care should be exercised not to damage the shims on the threads of the studs of the brake disc.

(9) After fitting the desired number of shims, the half shaft flange should be mounted on the brake disc studs and secured with the four self-locking nuts.

(10) Refit the forward suspension unit mounting on the crossmember and secure in position with the bolt and self-locking nut.

(11) Similarly the forward suspension unit should be refitted to the lower mounting on the suspension arm and after fixing the pivot pin, secure with a self-locking nut.

(12) Remove the setting links from each suspension.

(13) Install the road wheel.

(14) Lower the vehicle and remove the jack.

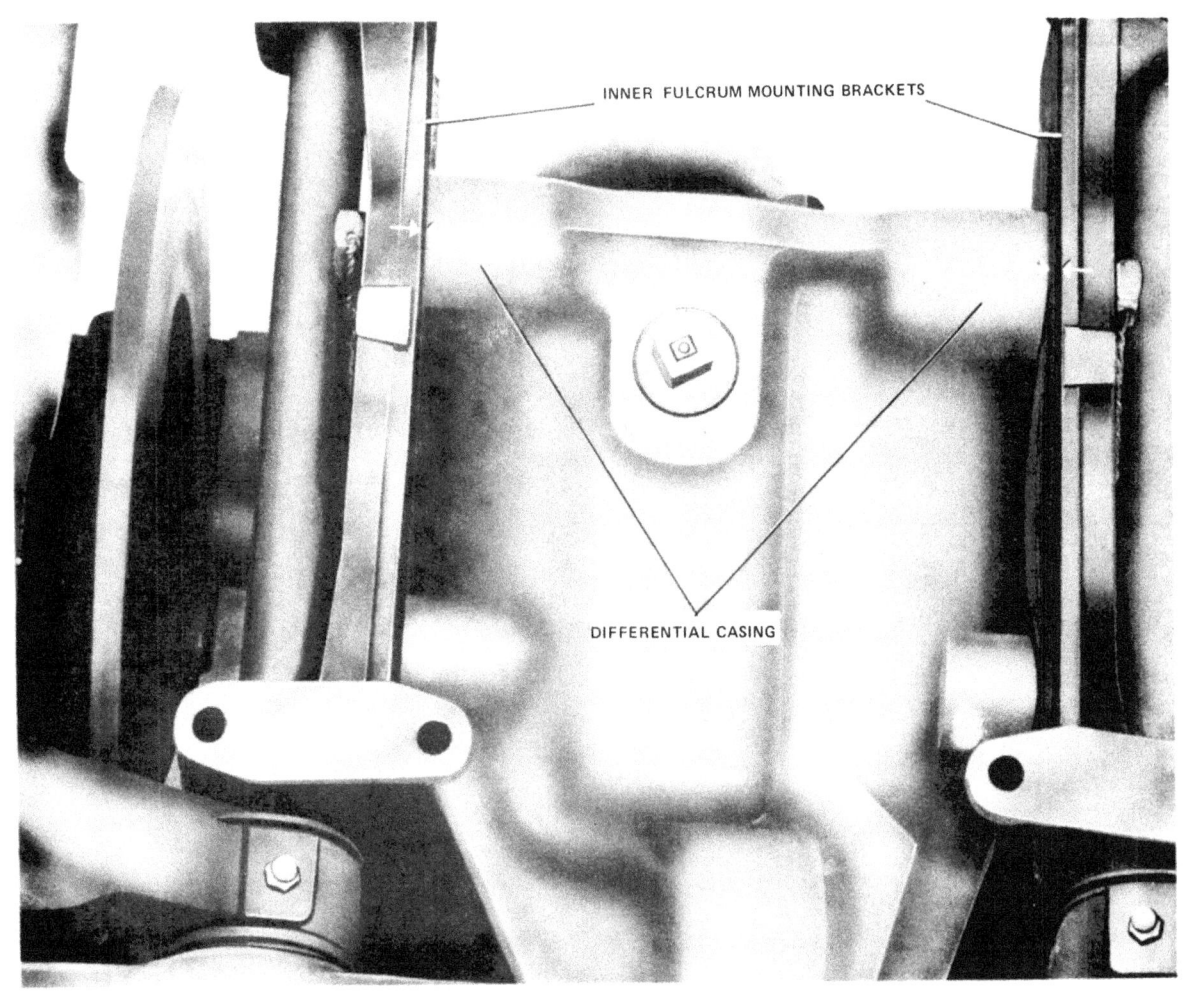

Check the Clearance between the Differential Casing and the Inner Fulcrum Mounting Bracket, at the Points Indicated by the Arrows.

9. REAR SUSPENSION FAULT DIAGNOSIS

1. **Noise in Suspension**

    Possible cause — *Remedy*
    - (a) Defective shock absorber and/or mounting. — Renew faulty components.
    - (b) Broken or loose coil springs. — Check, replace or tighten.
    - (c) Suspension arm/arms bent or damaged. — Check and renew if necessary.
    - (d) Loose or worn suspension bushes. — Check, replace or tighten.

2. **Rear Wheels Not In Alignment With Front Wheels.**

    Possible cause — *Remedy*
    - (a) Spring/s tension weak. — Renew springs.
    - (b) Bent tubular half shaft. — Renew.
    - (c) Distortion of body and frame. — Check and rectify body alignment.

NOTES

BRAKES

SPECIFICATIONS

3.8 MODEL

Make	Dunlop
Type:	
Front	Disc
Rear	Disc
Handbrake	Friction pad
Disc diameter:	
Front	11"
Rear	10"
Operation:	
Footbrake	Hydraulic with Dunlop bellows type vacuum servo
Handbrake	Mechanical on rear wheels
Adjustment:	
Footbrake	Self adjusting
Handbrake	Early models – adjuster bolt and handbrake cable. Later models – self adjusting
Master cylinder bore diameter	.625"
Master cylinder stroke:	
Upper master cylinder operating rear brakes	1"
Lower master cylinder operating front brakes	1.375"
Calliper piston bore diameter:	
Front	2.125"
Rear	1.75"
Pad lining type:	
Footbrake (early models)	Mintex M40 or M33
Footbrake (later models)	Mintex M59
Handbrake	Mintex M34
Hydraulic brake fluid	Castrol/Girling Crimson

4.2 MODEL

Make	Dunlop
Type:	
Front	Disc
Rear	Disc
Handbrake	Friction pad
Disc diameter:	
Front	11"
Rear	10"
Operation:	
Footbrake	Hydraulic with Lockheed dual-line servo system.
Handbrake	Mechanical on rear wheels
Adjustment:	
Footbrake	Self adjusting
Handbrake	Self adjusting
Master cylinder bore diameter	.875"
Master cylinder stroke	1.30"
Calliper piston bore diameter:	
Front	2.125"
Rear	1.75"
Pad lining type:	
Footbrake	Mintex M.59
Handbrake	Mintex M.34
Hydraulic brake fluid	Castrol/Girling Crimson

1. DESCRIPTION — 3.8 MODEL

Hydraulically operated disc brakes are fitted to front and rear wheels. The front discs are located on the front hubs with the calliper assemblies anchored to the front swivel axle units. The rear discs are located inboard adjacent to the rear axle casing with the calliper assembly anchored to the rear axle casing. No manual adjustment is required at the disc brake assemblies, adjustment being effected automatically during the operation of the footbrake by a self adjuster built into the calliper bores and pistons. The brake friction pads can be replaced without removing the calliper from its mounting as they are retained in position by a plate and securing bolt and nut.

Detachable piston housings are bolted to either side of the calliper body and house the piston assemblies which in turn are attached to the brake friction pads. A dust seal is incorporated in the piston assembly and fits into a groove in the housing. This is to prevent the entry of dirt and moisture. The piston body is fitted with a piston seal to prevent hydraulic fluid leakage from the pressure side of the piston. Later model cars are fitted with a modified type of piston and self adjusting mechanism.

The hydraulic system is fitted with twin master cylinders each supplied by its own reservoir. One master cylinder operates the front braking system while the other operates the rear braking system. A warning light situated on the dash indicates if either reservoir fluid level is low, provided, the handbrake has been released as the light also indicates that the handbrake is in the ON position.

A Dunlop bellows type vacuum servo unit operating with the hydraulic system provides pedal assistance in braking. A vacuum reservoir is fitted in the vacuum line between the inlet manifold and the servo unit, in the event of the engine cutting out power will still be available to operate the brakes. Power for the vacuum servo unit is supplied by the inlet manifold vacuum and atmosphere which expand or contract the bellows as the footbrake operates the valves within the unit.

The mechanically operated handbrake wheel assemblies are located above the calliper assemblies of the rear disc brakes. The handbrake units are attached to the calliper assembly with pivot bolts which allow movement of the friction pad housings. The friction pad is attached to each housing by a special bolt. At the opposite end to the pivot bolt on the inner friction pad housing is mounted the pivotted handbrake operating lever. On earlier models an adjuster bolt passes through the outer pad and engages the return spring and retaining nut located on the inner face of the inner pad housing, the adjuster bolt continues through the inner pad housing passing through the trunnion located in the operating lever and is finally secured by a self locking nut. Adjustment is provided for at the adjuster bolt which is fitted with a hexagonal recess in the bolt head for this purpose.

Later models are fitted with self-adjusting handbrake units at each rear wheel disc assembly. When wear takes place in the handbrake friction pads, an adjusting nut located in the operating lever is turned by means of a pawl adjacent to the adjusting nut which shortens the length of the adjusting bolt and draws together the friction pads situated at either housing.

2. MASTER CYLINDER — 3.8 MODEL

TO REMOVE AND INSTALL

(1) Disconnect the hydraulic brake pipes at the master cylinder ends. Plug the pipes to prevent dirt entering the hydraulic system and loss of fluid.

(2) Disconnect the hydraulic fluid supply pipes at the top of the master cylinders and drain off the brake fluid into a clean container.

(3) Loosen and take out the two securing bolts and locknuts attaching the upper master cylinder to the support bracket on the bulkhead.

(4) Slacken the locknut on the upper master cylinder push rod which is within the support bracket, screw the push rod out of the threaded forked connecting link and withdraw the upper master cylinder from the bracket.

(5) Loosen and take out the two securing bolts and locknuts attaching the lower master cylinder to the support bracket.

(6) Ease the lower master cylinder forward until the split pin can be removed from the clevis pin attaching the push rod fork, remove the clevis pin and the lower master cylinder can be withdrawn from the support bracket.

Installation is a reversal of the removal procedure with attention to the following points:

Adjust the upper master cylinder push rod at its threaded end to give .0625 free play when the cylinder operating piston is in the fully off position. Screw the threaded end of the push rod in or out of the threaded forked connecting link to effect this adjustment. Tighten the locknut, with the upper master cylinder push rod

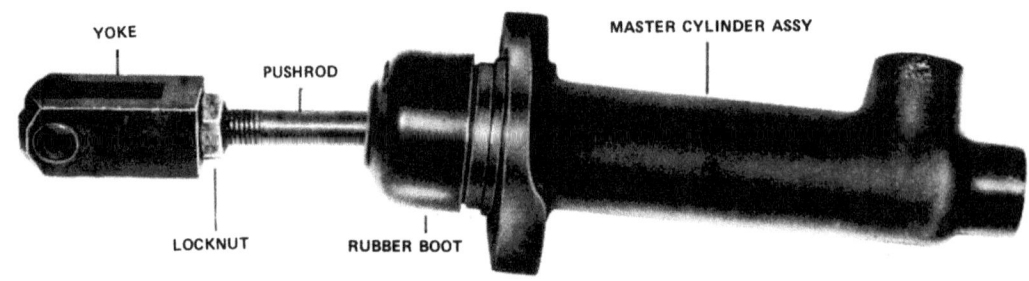

Upper Master Cylinder Assembly, Identified by Adjustable Pushrod (3.8 Model).

adjusted the requisite free play for the lower master cylinder push rod is compensated for by the connecting link between the master cylinder push rods.

Take care not to spill hydraulic fluid on any lacquered surface.

It will be necessary to bleed the braking system, see under operation *TO BLEED*.

TO DISMANTLE

(1) Pull the rubber boot off the open end of the master cylinder, remove the retaining circlip and dished washer and remove the push rod.

(2) Remove the piston complete with seals from the cylinder body, pull out the valve assembly complete with return spring and spring retainers.

(3) Use the same procedure to dismantle the other master cylinder.

TO CLEAN AND INSPECT

(1) Thoroughly clean the master cylinder components and the inside of the bore with methylated spirits. Do not use petrol or other mineral spirits.

(2) Check the inside of the bore for wear and/or pitting. If necessary, hone the cylinder bore.

(3) Check the piston for wear and renew the piston sealing ring and cup.

(4) Check the valve and fit new seal.

(5) Check the rubber boot and renew if it show signs of perishing or deterioration.

TO ASSEMBLE

(1) Dip the master cylinder components in clean hydraulic fluid and install the new cup seal on the piston with the lip of the seal facing towards the spigot end of the piston.

(2) Install a new seal ring on the piston body ensuring that it seats correctly in the groove.

(3) Install the valve seal on the valve stem and ensure that it locates correctly in the groove.

(4) Position the valve head into the slotted aperture of the front spring retainer.

(5) Install the piston into the rear return spring retainer.

(6) Install the valve head central in the piston bore and fit as a complete assembly to the cylinder bore.

NOTE: Do not install the valve, return spring and retainers into the cylinder bore without the piston, the assembly must be fitted complete.

Take care that the lips of the seals are not turned back or damaged on entry.

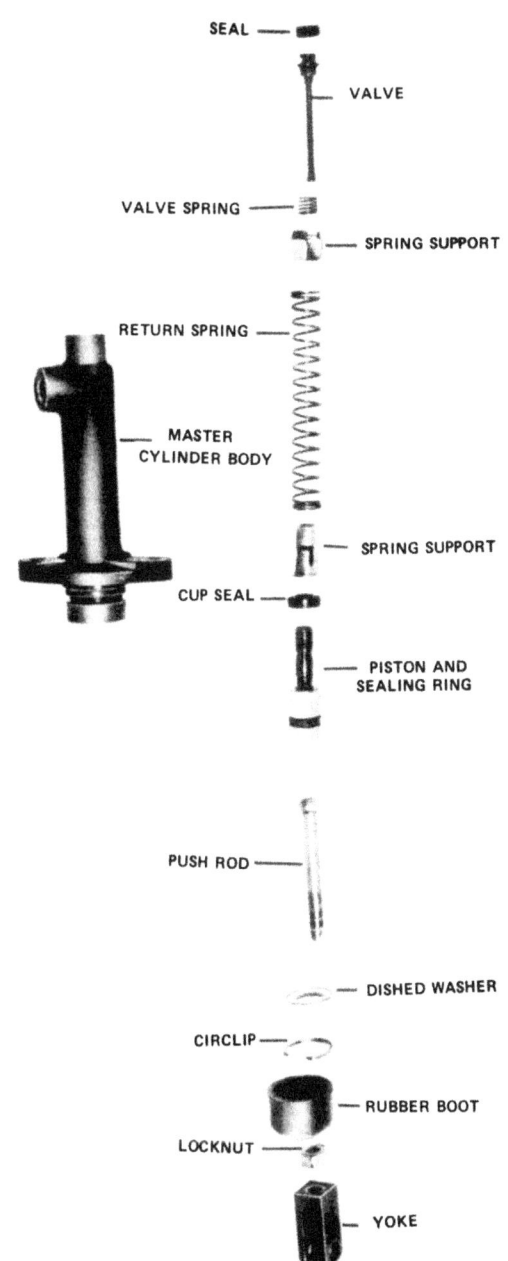

Exploded View of Master Cylinder Components (3.8 Model).

(7) Press in the piston assembly clear of the end of the cylinder bore and install the push-rod and dished retaining washer. Fit the circlip and ensure that it locates properly in its groove.

(8) Fill the rubber boot with Castrol Rubber grease and fit over the master cylinder end locating it in the groove.

3. FRONT WHEEL DISC BRAKES — 3.8 MODEL

TO REMOVE BRAKE CALLIPER

(1) Raise the front of the vehicle and remove the road wheel.

(2) Disconnect the hydraulic brake pipe at the calliper and plug the pipe to prevent entry of dirt into the system.

(3) Take out the locking wire from the heads of the two securing bolts, loosen the bolts and remove from the front suspension mounting.

NOTE: Shims are fitted between the calliper and mounting, note should be made of their position and quantity to facilitate reassembly.

(4) Slide the calliper assembly off the brake disc to remove from the vehicle.

TO INSTALL BRAKE CALLIPER

(1) Position the calliper assembly over the brake disc and refit securing bolts.

(2) Check the clearance between each side of the calliper and disc at both upper and lower positions. This clearance should not be exceeded by .010" at any point. Shims must be inserted between the calliper and mounting to correct this clearance and so that the assembly is central over the disc.

(3) After shim adjustment, tighten the securing bolts and rewire the bolt heads.

(4) Refit the hydraulic pipe to the calliper assembly.

NOTE: If the connecting pipe between the two calliper piston housings has been removed, install the pipe with the 'U' bend to the inner cylinder piston housing, i.e. nearest to the engine. The pipe is fitted with a sleeve marked "Inner Top".

(5) Bleed braking system, refit road wheel and lower vehicle.

TO REMOVE AND INSTALL BRAKE DISCS

(1) Raise the front of the vehicle and remove the road wheel.

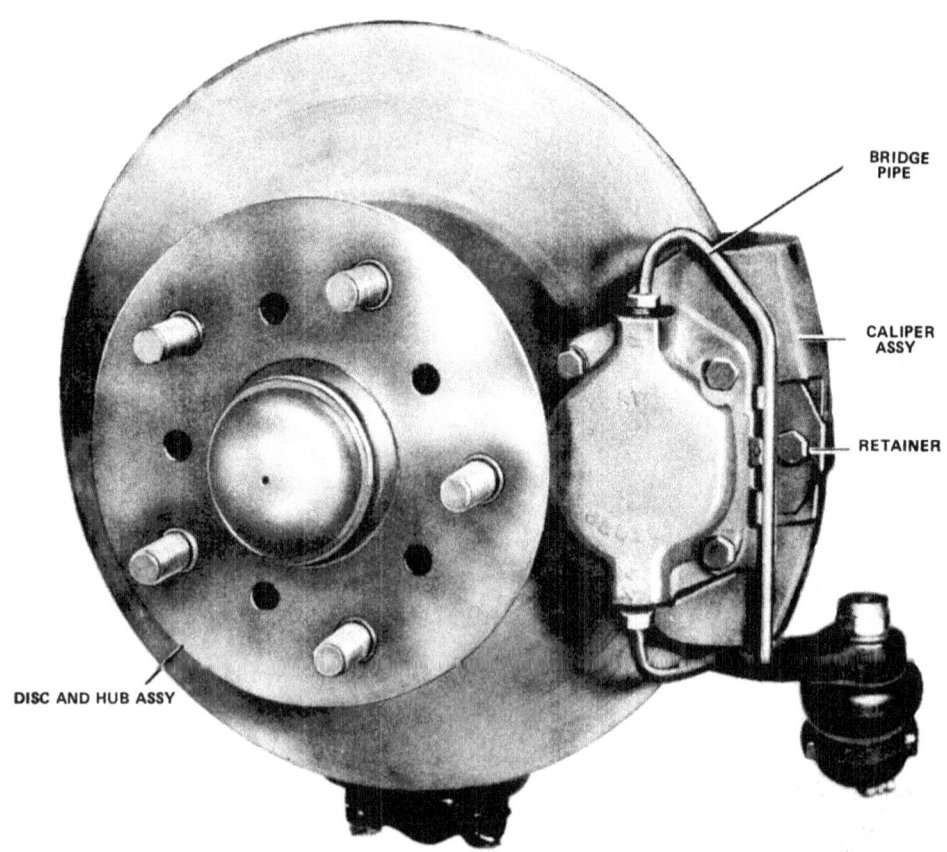

Front Brake Disc and Caliper Assembly (Typical).

(2) Disconnect the flexible hydraulic pipe at the support bracket and plug the pipe to prevent the entry of dirt or loss of fluid.

(3) Take out the locking wire from the heads of the two securing bolts and loosen and remove the bolts from the front suspension mounting.

NOTE: Shims are fitted between the calliper and mounting. Note should be made of their position and quantity to facilitate reassembly.

(4) Slide the calliper assembly off the brake disc and remove from the vehicle.

(5) Remove the front hub assembly as described in *FRONT SUSPENSION* for that operation.

(6) Loosen and take out the five securing bolts and self locking nuts attaching the disc to the front hub. Separate the disc from the hub.

Installation is a reversal of the removal procedure with attention to the following points:

Hub bearing end float should be adjusted correctly as described under *FRONT SUSPENSION*.

The calliper assembly should be adjusted and centralised by the shims as described earlier. Check the disc run-out with a dial indicator gauge mounted on the stub axle carrier and the plunger bearing on the disc face as near as possible to the centre of the pad track. Zero the dial gauge, rotate the hub and disc assembly on the stub axle and check that the disc run-out does not exceed .006". If a reading in excess of .006" is obtained, check the mating faces of the hub and disc for dirt, burrs or damage. Ensure that the front hub bearings are correctly adjusted.

Connect the brake pipe and bleed the braking system.

TO REMOVE AND INSTALL DISC PADS

(1) Raise the front of the vehicle and remove the road wheel.

(2) Loosen and remove the nut, lockwasher and bolt securing the brake pad retaining clip to the calliper body and remove the brake pad retainer clip.

(3) Draw out the disc pads by inserting a hook through the hole provided in the metal tab attached to the disc pad.

Installation is a reversal of the removal procedure with attention to the following points:

It will be necessary to move the calliper pistons back in the bore to allow entry of the new disc pads. A special tool is available for this purpose.

NOTE: Remove a quantity of brake fluid from the reservoir as forcing the pistons back may cause the fluid to overflow and damage the paintwork.

Install the disc pads into the calliper engaging the slot in the rear metal face of the pad with the button in the piston head.

Position the disc pad retaining clip and secure with the bolt, nut and washer.

Operate the footbrake on completion to implement the self adjusting action of the piston assemblies. Top up the brake fluid in the reservoir to the correct level.

TO DISMANTLE CALLIPER PISTON ASSEMBLY (EARLY MODELS)

(1) Remove the brake calliper and disc pads as described earlier.

(2) Disconnect the hydraulic brake pipe and plug to prevent the entry of dirt, disconnect the connecting pipe between the calliper housings.

(3) Take out the four securing bolts and lock washers attaching each piston housing to the calliper body at either side. Mark the housings in relation to the calliper body before separating.

(4) Remove the dust seal lip from the groove around the housing front. Apply low air pressure to the brake fluid inlet hole to ease out the piston assembly.

(5) Take out the two screws at the rear of the piston and remove the detachable plate, pull out the retractor bush from the piston bore.

(6) Remove the piston seal and cut away the dust seal from the piston body.

(7) Supporting the plate holding the dust seal to the main piston body, carefully press out the piston by applying pressure around the shouldered head of the disc pad locating button.

TO ASSEMBLE CALLIPER PISTON ASSEMBLY

(1) Clean all components, except the disc pads, in methylated spirits and examine them for wear. Discard the piston seals and dust seals.

(2) Install a new dust seal on the rear of the backing plate locating it on the lip and with the outer curved lip facing towards the rear of the piston.

(3) Position the backing plate over the disc pad locating button, with the dust seal between the backing plate and piston. With the piston properly supported press the backing plate over the shoulder and as far down as it will go.

(4) Install the retractor bush into the bore in the centre and rear of the piston.

(5) Dip a new piston seal in clean hydraulic fluid and install it in position on the rear piston face. Place the rear detachable plate on the piston next to the piston seal and fit the two securing screws, securely tighten the screws and peen in position.

(6) Lubricate the piston bore with clean hydraulic fluid and insert the piston engaging the retractor pin in the retractor bush.

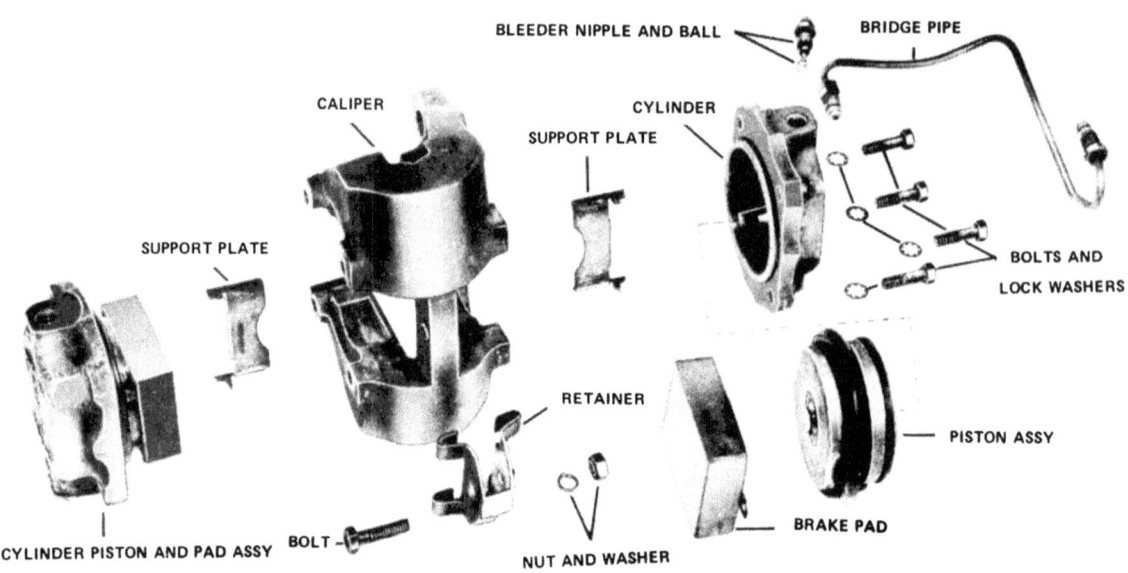

Exploded View of the Front Brake Caliper Components.

(7) With the piston correctly aligned with the bore press in the piston taking care not to turn back or damage the piston seal.

(8) Locate the outer curved lip of the dust seal in the groove around the cylinder housing face.

(9) Use the same procedure to assemble the other cylinder housing and piston.

(10) Check that the two support plates are still in position in their grooves in the calliper body.

(11) Install the cylinder housings to the calliper body mated with the marks made on dismantling. Install the securing screws and washers in each housing and tighten evenly.

(12) Connect the hydraulic brake pipe and the connecting pipe between the cylinder housings.

NOTE: *Install the brake pipe connecting the two housings with the 'U' bend of the pipe to the inner cylinder piston housing, i.e. nearest to the engine. The pipe is fitted with a sleeve marked "Inner Top".*

(13) It will be necessary to bleed the braking system, see under TO BLEED BRAKES.

TO DISMANTLE CALLIPER PISTON ASSEMBLY (LATER MODELS)

NOTE: *The later model cylinder housing assemblies can be identified by the letter 'C' located on the housing body adjacent to the brake pipe inlet hole.*

(1) Remove the brake calliper and disc pads as described earlier.

(2) Disconnect the hydraulic brake pipe and plug to prevent the entry of dirt, disconnect and remove the connecting pipe between the calliper housings.

(3) Take out the four securing bolts and lock washers attaching each piston housing to the calliper body at either side. Mark the housings in relation to the calliper body before separating.

(4) Remove the dust seal lip from the groove around the housing front. Apply low air pressure to the brake fluid inlet hole to ease out the piston assembly.

(5) Take out of the piston, the piston seal and dust seal.

NOTE: *Unlike the pistons fitted to earlier models which can be stripped down, this piston on later models is one piece and no further stripping can be done.*

(6) Check the piston and bore for scores or damage.

TO ASSEMBLE CALLIPER PISTON ASSEMBLY

(1) Clean all components, except the disc pads, in methylated spirits and examine them for wear. Discard the piston seals and dust seals.

(2) Dip a new piston seal in clean hydraulic fluid and install it in position on the piston, fit also a new dust seal and ensure that it is properly located.

(3) Lubricate the piston bore with clean hydraulic fluid and insert the piston engaging the retractor pin in the retractor bush.

(4) With the piston correctly aligned with the bore press in the piston, taking care not to turn back or damage the piston seal.

(5) Locate the outer curved lip of the dust seal in the groove around the cylinder housing front.

(6) Use the same procedure to assemble the other cylinder housing and piston.

(7) Check that the two support plates are still in position in their grooves in the calliper body.

(8) Install the cylinder housings to the calliper body mated with the marks made on dismantling. Install the securing screws and lock washers in each housing and tighten them evenly.

(9) Connect the hydraulic brake pipe and the connecting pipe between the cylinder housings.

NOTE: Install the brake pipe connecting the two housings with the 'U' bend of the pipe to the inner cylinder piston housing, i.e. nearest to the engine. The pipe is fitted with a sleeve marked "Inner Top".

4. REAR WHEEL DISC BRAKES — 3.8 MODEL

TO REMOVE BRAKE CALLIPER

(1) Remove and support the rear suspension unit as described under that operation in *REAR SUSPENSION* section.

(2) Take out the split pin and clevis pin connecting the handbrake linkage to the handbrake operating lever. Disconnect the hydraulic supply pipe at the branch union.

(3) Remove the disc pads from the calliper assembly as described under *TO REMOVE AND INSTALL DISC PADS*.

(4) Disconnect and remove the front hydraulic shock absorber and coil spring unit as described under *REAR SUSPENSION*.

(5) Remove the four self locking nuts from the halfshaft inner universal joint, pull the joint off the bolts allowing the hub carrier to move outwards and support the carrier in this position.

NOTE: Take note of the quantity and position of the shims fitted between the universal joint and the brake disc.

(6) Prise back the locking plate tabs and remove the swivel bolts attaching the handbrake pad carriers to the calliper body. Remove the locking plate and the forked retractor plate, and remove the handbrake pad carrier from the aperture at the rear of the crossmember.

(7) On the outside face of each handbrake pad carrier, loosen the securing nuts and slide the pads clear of the bolt heads.

(8) Turn the brake disc until the holes in the disc line up with the calliper mounting bolts, knock back the locking plate tabs and remove the mounting bolts.

NOTE: On earlier models locking wire instead of locking plates was used to secure the mounting bolts.

Take note of the quantity and position of the shims fitted to the mounting bolts between the calliper and the axle casing.

(9) Remove the calliper through the aperture at the front of the crossmember.

TO INSTALL BRAKE CALLIPER

(1) Position the calliper body over the disc and against the axle casing, install the shims between the calliper and axle casing in their original position.

(2) Install the mounting bolts and new locking plate if fitted, securely tighten the mounting bolts and lock in position with the locking plate or wire whichever is applicable.

(3) Install the handbrake pads to the pad carriers with the narrow face of the pad uppermost (towards the adjuster assembly end of the pad carrier), engage the securing bolt heads in the slot at the rear of the pad and tighten the securing nuts on the outside face.

(4) Position the handbrake pad carrier assembly on the calliper main body, engage the ends of the forked retractor plate in the locating holes in the pad carriers and install the locking plate and swivel bolts. Tighten the bolts and secure with the locking plate tabs.

(5) Engage the halfshaft inner universal joint on the four attaching bolts, installing the shims between the universal joint and brake disc in their original positions. Refit self locking nuts and securely tighten.

NOTE: It will be necessary to check that the calliper assembly is centrally situated over the brake disc. Follow the checking procedure as described under TO INSTALL FRONT BRAKE CALLIPER.

(6) Refit the front hydraulic shock absorber and coil spring unit as described under *REAR SUSPENSION*.

(7) Install the disc pads ensuring that the slot in the rear face of the pad engages the piston locating button. Refit the disc pad retaining clip and secure with the nut, bolt and washer.

(8) Connect the hydraulic brake pipe and the handbrake linkage to the operating lever, fit a new split pin to the clevis pin.

(9) Install the rear suspension unit as described under that operation in *REAR SUSPENSION SECTION*.

(10) It will be necessary to bleed the braking system.

NOTE: The procedure already described is applicable to either side rear brake calliper assembly.

TO REMOVE AND INSTALL BRAKE DISCS

(1) Carry out the operations 1 to 6 and 8 and 9 as described earlier under to *REMOVE REAR BRAKE CALLIPER*.

NOTE: It will be necessary to remove both front and rear hydraulic shock absorbers and coil spring units as described under REAR SUSPENSION.

(2) Gently knock back the four attaching bolts for the brake disc and inner universal joint.

(3) Move the halfshaft assembly, hub carrier and lower wishbone upwards to clear brake disc and to allow the disc to be detached from the attaching bolts.

Installation is a reversal of the removal procedure with attention to the following points:

Position the disc against the drive shaft flange and knock through the attaching bolts locating the heads against the rear of the drive shaft flange. Check that the calliper assembly is centrally situated over the brake disc, using the procedure as described under *TO INSTALL FRONT BRAKE CALLIPER*.

Check the disc run-out with a dial indicator gauge mounted on the crossmember and with the gauge plunger on the disc face as near as possible to the centre of the pad track. Zero the dial gauge, rotate the disc and check that the run-out does not exceed .006". If a reading in excess of .006" is obtained, check the mating faces of the hub and disc for dirt, burrs or damage.

Ensure that the end float in the axle drive shafts is correct as described under the *REAR AXLE SECTION*.

It will be necessary to bleed the braking system.

TO REMOVE AND INSTALL DISC PADS

(1) Loosen and remove the nut, lockwasher and bolt securing the brake pad retaining clip to the calliper body and remove the brake pad retainer clip.

(2) Draw out the disc pads by inserting a hook through the hole in the metal tab attached to the disc pad.

Installation is a reversal of the removal procedure with attention to the following points:

It will be necessary to move the calliper pistons back in the bore to allow entry of the new disc pads. A special tool is available for this purpose.

NOTE: Remove a quantity of brake fluid from the reservoir as forcing the pistons back may cause the fluid to overflow and damage the paintwork.

Install the brake pads in the calliper engaging the slot in the rear metal face of the pad with the button in the piston head.

Position the disc pad retaining clip and secure with the bolt, nut and washer.

Operate the footbrake on completion to implement the self adjusting action of the piston assemblies. Top up the brake fluid in the reservoir to the correct level.

TO DISMANTLE CALLIPER PISTON ASSEMBLY

(1) Remove the calliper assembly as described earlier.

(2) Carry out the procedure as described for front wheel disc brakes *TO DISMANTLE CALLIPER PISTON ASSEMBLY*.

(3) Identify the calliper piston type, i.e. early or late model, and treat accordingly.

TO ASSEMBLE CALLIPER PISTON ASSEMBLY

(1) Assemble calliper piston assembly as described for the front wheel disc brakes *TO ASSEMBLE CALLIPER PISTON ASSEMBLY*.

(2) Identify the calliper piston type, i.e. early or late model, and treat accordingly.

(3) Install the calliper assembly as described earlier.

5. HANDBRAKE ASSEMBLY — 3.8 MODEL

TO REMOVE AND INSTALL HANDBRAKE PAD CARRIERS

(1) Raise the car on a hoist or place over a pit.

(2) Release the handbrake, take out the split pin and clevis pin connecting the handbrake linkage to the handbrake operating lever.

(3) Prise back the locking plate tabs and remove the swivel bolts attaching the handbrake pad carriers to the calliper body. Remove the locking plate and the forked retractor plate.

(4) Move the handbrake pad carriers backwards around the disc and withdraw at the back of the rear suspension assembly.

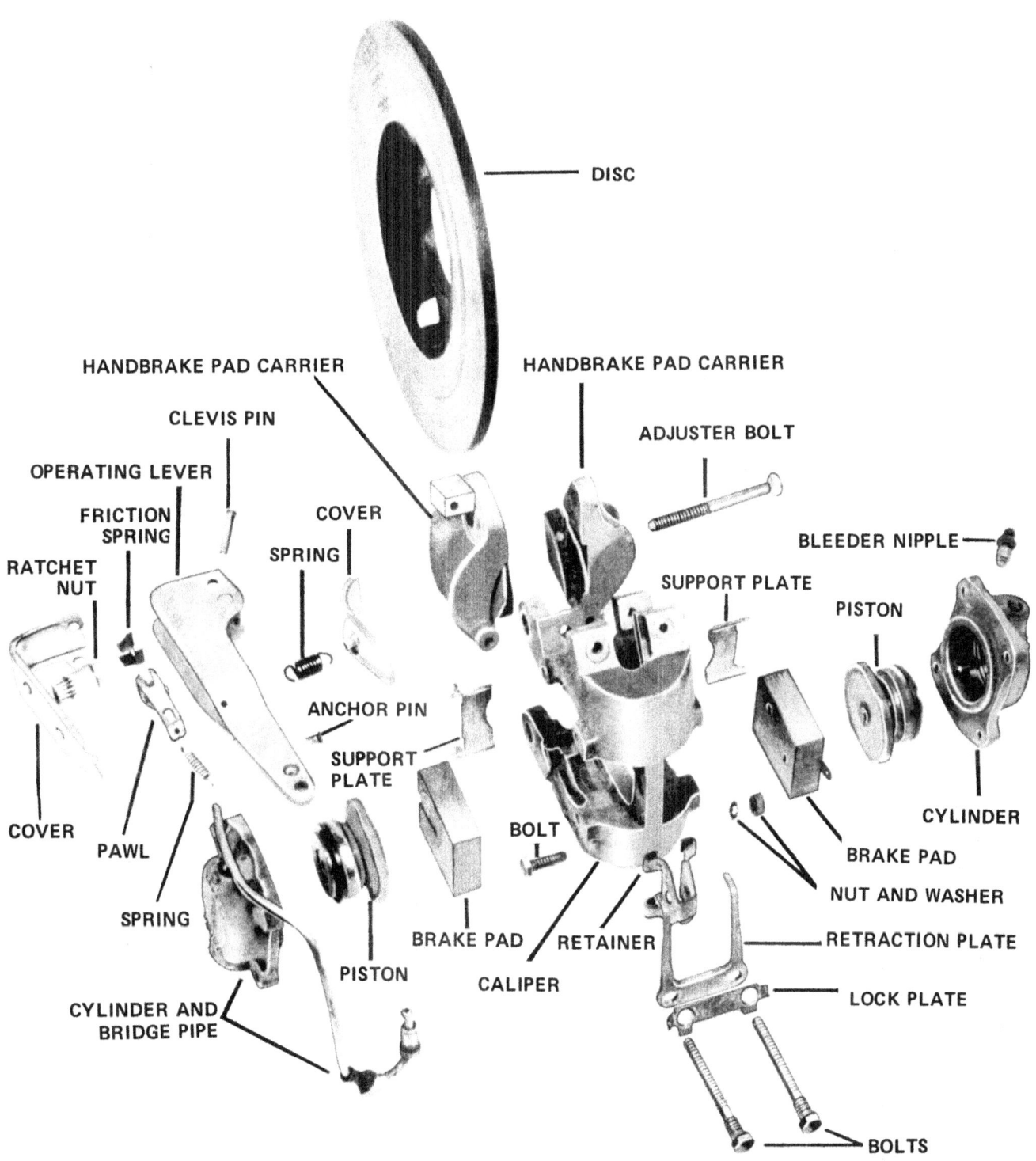

Exploded View of the Rear Brake Caliper Components (Typical).

(5) This procedure is applicable to either side handbrake carrier assembly.

Installation is a reversal of the removal procedure, with attention to the following points:

Fit new locking plates to the carrier swivel bolts.

Engage the ends of the forked retractor plate in the locating holes in the handbrake pad carrier. Adjust the handbrake pads to obtain the correct clearance between the pad and disc faces. This operation is described under *TO ADJUST HANDBRAKE CABLE AND PADS*.

TO DISMANTLE AND ASSEMBLE PAD CARRIERS (EARLY MODEL)

(1) Screw out the adjuster bolt, provided in this type for manual adjustment of the handbrake pads. Control the run of the self-locking nut located in the aperture of the operating lever.

(2) Take out the split pin and clevis pin attaching the pivot seat to the fork end of the operating lever.

NOTE: The spring and square nut within the retaining clip on the inside face of the pad carrier are not detachable. If damaged, or renewal required, replace the handbrake pad carrier. The trunnion fitted to the operating lever is positioned during manufacture and cannot be removed.

(3) Remove the operating lever and withdraw the pivot seat from its location in the end of the pad carrier.

(4) Remove the handbrake pads as described under *TO REMOVE AND INSTALL HANDBRAKE PADS*.

Assembly is a reversal of the dismantling procedure with attention to the following points:

Check that the trunnion operates freely in the operating lever, and that the pivot seat swivel pin is free in its location, and also that the head of the pivot seat is a sliding fit in the fork of the operating lever.

To preload the spring on the carrier inner face, pass the adjuster bolt through the outer pad carrier and thread into the square nut and spring. Install the operating lever and pivot assembly to the inner carrier, screw in the adjusting bolt until flush with the outer face of the trunnion. Insert a screwdriver blade between the square nut and the retaining clip, and lever against the spring pressure, again screw in the adjuster bolt until flush with the trunnion outer face. Position the self locking nut on the trunnion outer face and turn the adjuster bolt to engage the self locking nut thread immediately. Screw the adjuster bolt through the self locking nut until flush with the outer face of the nut and withdraw the screwdriver.

TO DISMANTLE AND ASSEMBLE PAD CARRIERS (LATER MODEL)

(1) Take out the cover securing bolt, split pin and clevis pin and remove the dust cover protecting the self adjusting mechanism in the operating lever.

(2) Take out the split pin locating the slot in the head of the adjuster bolt.

(3) Unscrew the adjuster bolt from the self adjuster nut located in the aperture of the operating lever, and remove the bolt and nut.

(4) Unhook the adjuster pawl return spring and detach the pawl from its positioning dowel.

(5) Unhook the operating lever return spring and remove the operating lever and lower dust cover, remove the pivot seat from its location in the pad carrier.

(6) Remove the handbrake pads as described under *TO REMOVE AND INSTALL HANDBRAKE PADS*.

Assembly is a reversal of the dismantling procedure with attention to the following points:

Ensure that the threads of the adjusting bolt and self adjuster nut are clean and not damaged.

Check that the trunnion operates freely in the operating lever, and that the pivot seat swivel pin is free in its location, and also that the head of the pivot seat is a sliding fit in the fork of the operating lever.

To adjust the self adjuster mechanism carry out the procedures as described under *TO ADJUST HANDBRAKE CABLE AND PADS*.

TO REMOVE AND INSTALL HANDBRAKE PADS

(1) Remove the handbrake pad carriers from the vehicle as described earlier.

(2) Loosen the handbrake pad securing nuts located in the recess of the carrier outer faces.

(3) Draw out the handbrake pads by inserting a hook through the hole provided in the metal tab attached to the handbrake pads.

Installation is a reversal of the removal procedure with attention to the following points:

Install the handbrake pads to the pad carriers with the narrow face of the pad uppermost (towards the adjuster assembly end of the pad carrier), engage the securing bolt heads in the slot at the rear of the pad and tighten the securing nuts on the outside face.

Install the handbrake pad carriers as described earlier and carry out the adjustment as described under *TO ADJUST HANDBRAKE CABLE AND PADS*.

TO REMOVE AND INSTALL HANDBRAKE CABLE

(1) Raise the car on a hoist or place over a pit.

(2) Take out the split pin and clevis pin attaching the rear end of the handbrake inner cable to the brake compensator mechanism.

(3) Loosen the locknut on the rear threaded end of the cable conduit and unscrew the conduit from the retaining block on the compensator mechanism.

(4) Release the spring supporting the cable clear of the propellor shaft.

(5) Working inside the car, loosen and remove the four securing nuts attaching each front seat to the seat slides and remove the seats.

(6) Take out the screw at each side of the radio control panel which secures the ashtray.

(7) Take out the two screws at each side of the radio

control panel attaching it to the brackets under the instrument panel and withdraw the radio control panel casing.

(8) Position the gear lever as far forward as it will go and loosen and remove the gear lever knob and locknut.

(9) Pull the handbrake to the fully on position.

(10) Take out the three screws attaching the propellor shaft tunnel cover to the body and maneuver the cover carefully over the gear and handbrake levers to remove.

(11) Take out the split pin and clevis pin attaching the front end of the inner cable to the handbrake lever assembly.

(12) Loosen and remove the clamp bolt securing the front end of the cable conduit in the retaining block. Note the position of the handbrake warning light switch and place to one side.

(13) Remove the rubber grommet and pull out the handbrake cable from the rear of the car.

Installation is a reversal of the removal procedure with attention to the following points:

Ensure that the handbrake inner cable operates freely in the cable conduit.

Fit the threaded sleeve of the cable conduit to the retaining block with the long end of the block pointing forward to the front of the vehicle.

Screw the threaded sleeve into the retaining block taking up any slackness in the cable and secure with the locknut.

Check the handbrake pad clearance as described under *TO ADJUST HANDBRAKE CABLE AND PADS.*

TO ADJUST HANDBRAKE CABLE AND PADS (EARLY MODEL)

(1) Remove the carpet from the luggage boot, take out the seven screws attaching the rear axle cover to the boot floor and remove the cover.

(2) Screw in the adjuster bolt at each rear handbrake pad carrier assembly until the pads bear hard against the brake disc.

(3) Position the handbrake in the fully off position.

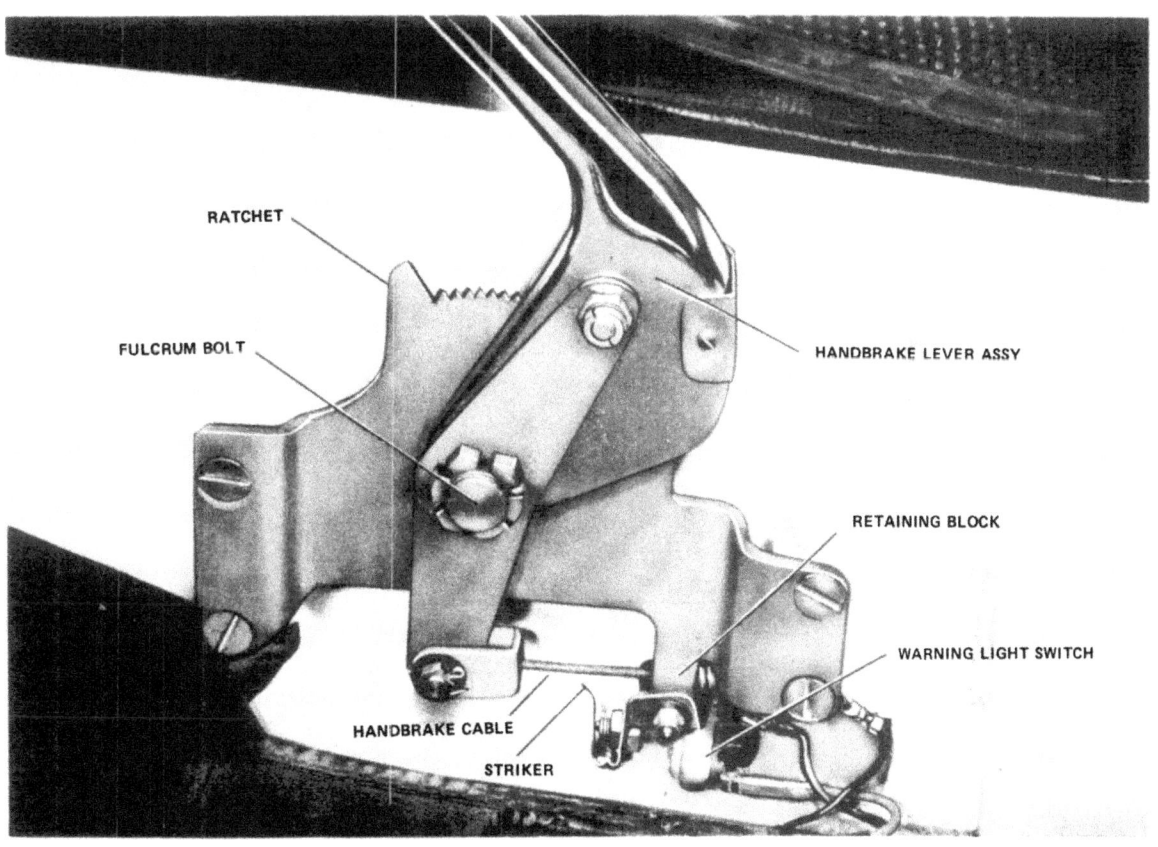

Handbrake Lever Assembly.

(4) Loosen the locknut on the threaded sleeve of the cable conduit where it enters the retaining block on the compensator mechanism.

(5) By screwing the threaded sleeve in the retaining block take up all cable slackness, without putting the compensator mechanism or cable in tension which may cause the brakes to bind.

(6) Secure the threaded sleeve after adjustment with the locknut.

(7) Slacken back the adjuster bolt until a .004" feeler gauge can be inserted between the face of the handbrake pad and disc.

(8) Remove the feeler gauge and rotate the disc to ensure that the handbrake pad is not binding at any point.

(9) Carry out the same procedure at the other side handbrake carrier assembly.

(10) Refit the rear axle cover and carpet in the luggage boot.

TO ADJUST HANDBRAKE CABLE AND PADS (LATER MODEL)

The handbrake pads are of the self adjusting type on later models, but require initial setting if the carrier assembly has been disturbed.

(1) Take out the split pin locating the slot in the adjuster bolt head. Release the handbrake to the fully off position.

(2) Adjust the brake pad clearance by screwing the adjuster bolt in or out until there is a clearance of .030" between the face of the pad and the disc at each side.

NOTE: If the carrier assembly is removed from the vehicle, set adjuster bolt to give a measurement of .437" between the faces of the handbrake pads, this comprises the thickness of the disc plus .062" which is the necessary clearance.

(3) With the assembly fitted to the car, operate the operating lever on and off several times, listen for the self adjuster mechanism operating, a distinct click will be heard. When the click is no longer heard the pads will have reached the correct adjustment with the necessary clearance between the pads and disc.

(4) Carry out the same procedure at the other side handbrake assembly.

(5) Position the handbrake in the fully off position.

(6) Loosen the locknut on the threaded sleeve of the cable conduit where it enters the retaining block on the compensator mechanism.

(7) Screw the threaded sleeve out of the retaining block but stop just prior to any movement of the operating levers. Check that no movement is transferred to the compensator mechanism when the operating levers are pressed towards the carriers.

NOTE: A slight amount of slackness will be present in the cable when correctly adjusted, do not attempt to adjust any further or put the cable in tension otherwise the brakes may bind.

6. BRAKE PEDAL ASSEMBLY — 3.8 MODEL

TO REMOVE AND INSTALL

(1) Remove the air cleaner elbow and the carburettor air intakes as described under *FUEL SYSTEM*.

(2) Loosen the rear carburettor float chamber banjo nut and bend the petrol supply pipe towards the float chamber.

(3) Remove the accelerator rods located above the servo unit bellows.

NOTE: Above operations required on right hand drive models only.

(4) Remove the servo vacuum pipe and securing clips.

(5) Drain the fluid from the brake and clutch reservoirs into suitable containers.

(6) Disconnect the fluid supply pipes from the brake and clutch master cylinders and plug the holes to prevent the entry of dirt.

(7) Disconnect the brake fluid warning light wires from the reservoirs and mark them to facilitate reassembly.

(8) Loosen and remove the brake and clutch fluid reservoirs from the securing clips.

(9) Disconnect the fluid pipes from the outlet ends of the master cylinders and plug to prevent the entry of dirt.

(10) Remove the two brake master cylinders as described under *MASTER CYLINDER – TO REMOVE AND INSTALL*.

(11) Working inside the car, remove the securing nuts attaching the footbrake and clutch pedal pads to the brake and clutch levers, remove the foot pads.

(12) Take out the securing screws and withdraw the under dash casing from its retaining clips.

(13) Loosen and remove the securing nuts attaching the servo assembly to the bulkhead.

(14) Squeeze the servo bellows together, lift and turn the assembly through 90° in a clockwise direction to permit the pedals passage through the aperture in the bulkhead. Remove the assembly from the car.

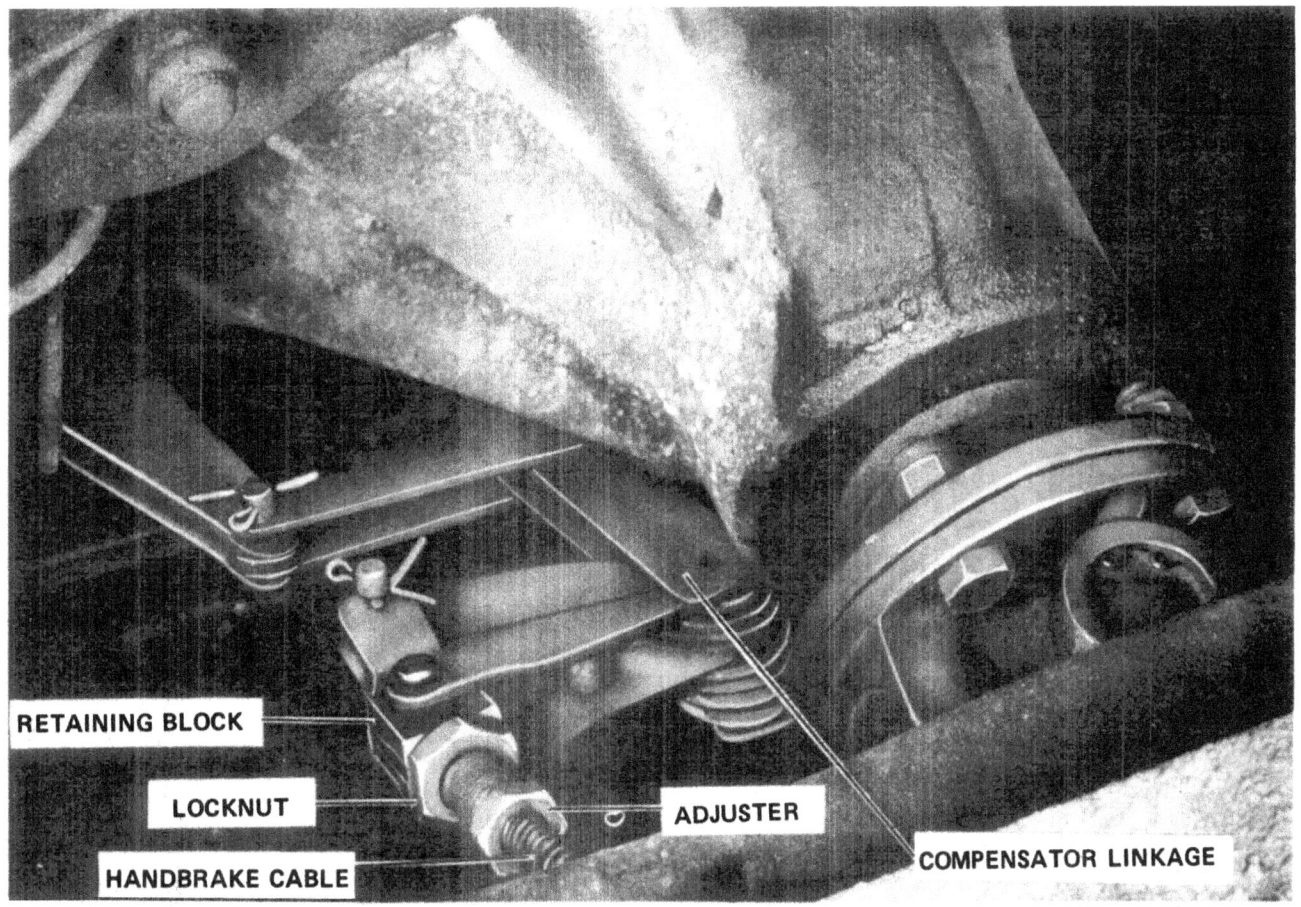

Showing Handbrake Compensator Linkage and Cable Adjuster.

Installation is a reversal of the removal procedure with attention to the following points:

Check that the rubber seal is positioned between the bellows and the bulkhead with the exhaust tube located in the centre.

When the assembly is positioned in the car fit the plain nut and lock washer on the shortest stud located at the centre front.

All clevis pins must be a sliding fit for the assembly to operate efficiently.

Reposition the petrol supply pipe before tightening the banjo union nut.

Connect the wires to the fluid reservoirs as marked on removal.

NOTE: One red/green wire and one black wire to each reservoir cap.

Bleed the brake and clutch hydraulic systems as described under appropriate headings.

TO DISMANTLE AND ASSEMBLE

(1) Remove the dust seal from the exhaust tube.

(2) Loosen and remove the four nuts and one screw securing the brake master cylinder mounting bracket.

(3) Loosen and remove the self locking nut from the end of the splined pin located at the bellows linkage, withdraw the spring and retaining washer.

(4) Take out the clamp bolt from the brake pedal at the pedal operating shaft end, and remove the circlip and washer from the pedal operating shaft at the side of the pedal housing.

(5) Remove the vacuum check point union located at the front valve housing.

(6) Withdraw the brake master cylinder support bracket complete with pedal shaft assembly and linkage from the pedal housing.

NOTE: Take note of the fibre washer positioned between the brake and clutch pedals when removing the pedal shaft assembly.

(7) On right hand drive models, remove the four securing nuts attaching the accelerator bell crank bracket.

(8) Loosen and remove the four self locking nuts attaching the servo assembly to the mounting bracket and detach the brake servo assembly.

(9) Take out the setscrew locating the brass bush in the side of the pedal housing and extract the bush.

(10) Take out the split pin and clevis pin from the clutch master cylinder push rod and remove the master cylinder. The clutch pedal can now also be removed.

(11) Loosen and remove the self locking nut at the pivot bolt located in the 'U' shaped pivot bracket, remove the bolt and the brake master cylinder support bracket.

(12) Disconnect the servo operating lever return spring, loosen and remove the castellated nut and off-centre barrel nut.

(13) Loosen and remove the locknut and washer from the bottom stud attaching the pedal shaft and detach the servo operating lever.

(14) Remove the dished washer, spacer, chamfered washer and rubber bush.

(15) Detach the power transfer arm from the pedal shaft assembly, remove the metal bush and nylon bush, press out the splined pin if renewal necessary.

(16) Loosen and remove the bolt and nut attaching the forked connecting arm to the 'U' shaped pivot bracket and master cylinders compensating link.

(17) Detach the upper master cylinder push rod fork by removing the split pin and clevis pin.

(18) Press out the spacer tubes from the 'U' shaped pivot bracket and master cylinders compensating link.

(19) Take out the grub screw securing the pin in the forked connecting arm, press out the pin.

(20) Loosen and remove the nuts and washers and separate the servo mounting bracket from the pedal housing.

Installation is a reversal of the removal procedure with attention to the following points:

Check all nylon bushes, bearings, pivots and clevis pins for wear and renew as required.

Ensure that all pivoted linkages are free to operate and that metal bearings are lubricated. Check that the fibre washer is positioned between the clutch and brake pedals in the pedal shaft assembly.

When installing the pedal shaft assembly on the pedal lever check that the pedal is lined up with the clutch pedal pad and does not engage the pedal housing when fully depressed.

It will be necessary to adjust the air valve at the off-centre barrel nut. This operation is described under *VACUUM SERVO ASSEMBLY.*

7. VACUUM SERVO ASSEMBLY AND VACUUM RESERVOIR — 3.8 MODEL

DESCRIPTION (VACUUM RESERVOIR)

The vacuum reservoir is installed on the bulkhead on the righthand side of the engine beneath the carburettor air intakes. It is connected by rubber hose to the inlet manifold and the vacuum servo unit. By holding a reserve of vacuum controlled by a check valve it allows the vacuum servo unit to work after the engine has stalled if braking should be required. Apart from the check valve and condition of the rubber hoses which should be checked periodically, no other service is required.

TO REMOVE AND INSTALL THE VACUUM RESERVOIR

(1) Take out the securing screws and nuts attaching the tray beneath the reservoir and remove the tray.

(2) Slacken the hose clips at the reservoir check valve and detach the two pipes from the check valve.

(3) Take out the four securing screws attaching the vacuum reservoir to the bulkhead and withdraw the reservoir from beneath.

(4) If the check valve is to be replaced unscrew it from the union on the vacuum reservoir.

Installation is a reversal of the removal procedure with attention to the following points:

Connect the rubber hose from the servo unit to the extension pipe on the check valve nearest to the threaded end, it can be further identified by two grooves in the pipe body.

Connect the rubber hose from the inlet manifold fitting to the extension pipe on the check valve nearest to the blank end of the valve, it can be further identified by two ribs in the pipe body.

DESCRIPTION (SERVO ASSEMBLY)

The servo unit is of the air-vacuum bellows type installed between the brake pedal and the master cylinders. Vacuum and air pressure are both controlled by valves located in the valve housing which are operated by brake pedal movement. Pressure on the brake pedal closes the air valve and opens the vacuum valve, air is drawn out of the bellows by the vacuum created in the inlet manifold, the action of the bellows contracting because of this provides power through the linkage to the master cylinder. When the pedal pressure is released the vacuum valve closes and the air valve opens allowing entry of air to the bellows which revert to the expanded position. If the pedal pressure is held in a semi-applied position both air and vacuum valves close maintaining the vacuum constant in the bellows until the pedal is released or additional pressure is applied.

Failure of the vacuum servo unit does not stop the brakes from being operated by normal hydraulic pressure.

The only items which normally require attention are:
(1) The check valve located on the vacuum reservoir.
(2) The air valve adjustment at the adjusting nut.
(3) The air filter located in the bellows unit.
(4) The rubber hoses and connections.

CHECK VALVE

The check valve is located on the vacuum reservoir and screwed onto a threaded connection. To replace, slacken the hose clips and detach the rubber pipes, unscrew the check valve from the connector on the reservoir. When installing a new check valve ensure that the hoses are connected to the correct check valve extension pipe, i.e. the rubber hose from the vacuum servo unit to the pipe nearest the threaded end of the check valve and with the two grooves in the pipe body, the rubber hose from the inlet manifold to the pipe nearest the blank end of the check valve and with the two ribs on the pipe body.

AIR VALVE ADJUSTMENT

To carry out this operation a vacuum gauge will be required reading 0-30" of mercury.

(1) Connect the gauge to the union on the valve housing face.

NOTE: On early models the union will be located on the rear mounting plate, whereas later models will have the union located on the front valve housing plate.

(2) With the engine running, apply the footbrake in the normal manner a full stroke, check the reading on the vacuum gauge which should be 20" of mercury. If adjustment is required proceed as follows:

(3) Disconnect the servo lever return spring which is located in the split pin hole, slacken back the castellated nut.

(4) Turn the head of the off-centre barrel nut until a reading of 20" of mercury is showing on the vacuum gauge. The air valve should now be closed and the vacuum valve fully open. Do not overadjust the barrel nut.

(5) Tighten the castellated nut, release the pedal pressure and the vacuum gauge reading should fall to zero, with the brakes perfectly free.

(6) Should the brakes not be free, turn the head of the off-centre barrel nut in the opposite direction to close the vacuum valve and free the brakes.

(7) Recheck the readings with the foot pedal applied and released. Ensure that the castellated nut is tight and refit the return spring.

(8) Switch off the engine, detach the vacuum gauge and shut the union.

AIR FILTER

To remove and clean the air filter it will be necessary to remove the bellows assembly from the car, the operation is described under *BRAKE PEDAL ASSEMBLY – TO REMOVE*.

(1) Using a padded vice, gently hold the pedal assembly.
(2) Squeeze the bellows to expose the end of the air intake tube and circlip.
(3) Detach the air intake baffle and draw out the air filter.
(4) Clean the air filter removing all dirt and foreign matter, install when clean and dry.

Installation is a reversal of the removal procedure.

RUBBER HOSES AND CONNECTIONS

Check to ensure that there are no air leaks at the connections and that the rubber hoses have not bulged or collapsed due to deterioration.

8. HYDRAULIC SYSTEM

TO BLEED

Bleeding the hydraulic system is not a routine maintenance operation and will only be required when some portion of the hydraulic equipment has been disconnected or fluid drained off, thereby allowing air to enter the system.

(1) Fill the master cylinders with clean hydraulic brake fluid of the specified type and maintain them at least half full throughout the bleeding operation.

(2) Commencing at the left hand rear brake assembly, attach a bleeder tube to the bleeder valve and allow the other end of the tube to be immersed in a small amount of fluid contained in a clean glass jar.

(3) Unscrew the bleeder valve one full turn.

(4) Depress the brake pedal slowly the full extent of its travel and allow it to return without assistance.

(5) Repeat operation (4) until a constant stream of clean fluid, without any air bubbles, is being discharged into the glass jar, hold the brake pedal down and tighten the bleeder valve.

(6) Carry out the operation on the other side rear wheel assembly and repeat for the front brakes.

NOTE: Do not allow the fluid level in the reservoirs to fall below the half full level at any time during the bleeding operation or air may enter the system and a fresh start will have to be made. Always use new fluid for topping up the reservoirs.

(7) Finally remove the bleeder tube, check that all bleeder valves are tight and top up the brake fluid in the reservoirs to the correct level.

9. DESCRIPTION — 4.2 AND 2+2 MODELS

Hydraulically operated disc brakes are fitted to front and rear wheels, the front discs are located on the front hubs with the calliper assemblies anchored to the front swivel axle units. The rear discs are located inboard adjacent to the rear axle casing.

No manual adjustment is required at the disc brake assemblies, adjustment being effected automatically during the operation of the footbrake by a self adjuster built into the calliper bore and piston. The brake friction pads can be replaced without removing the calliper from its mounting as they are retained in position by a plate and securing bolt and nut.

Detachable piston housings are bolted to either side of the calliper body and house the piston assemblies which in turn are attached to the brake friction pads. A dust seal is incorporated in the piston assembly and fits into a groove in the housings, this is to prevent the entry of dirt and moisture. The piston body is fitted with a piston seal to prevent hydraulic fluid leakage from the pressure side of the piston.

The mechanically operated handbrake wheel assemblies are located above the calliper assemblies of the rear disc brakes. The handbrake units are attached to the calliper assemblies with pivot bolts which allow movement of the **handbrake pad carriers. The handbrake pads are attached to the** pad carriers by means of a special headed bolt, to replace the handbrake pads it is necessary to remove the pad carriers from the vehicle. At the opposite end of the pad carrier pivot bolts is mounted the pivotted handbrake operating lever which incorporates the self adjusting mechanism. When wear takes place in the handbrake pads, an adjusting nut located in the operating lever is turned during brake operation by means of a pawl adjacent to the adjusting nut, which shortens the length of the adjusting bolt and draws together the friction pads situated at each carrier. A cable connects the operating levers through a compensator linkage to the handbrake. Provision for adjustment is made at the rear end of the handbrake cable.

The hydraulic system is fitted with a master cylinder employing a booster reaction valve and a tandem slave cylinder with integral vacuum booster. Brake fluid is supplied by twin reservoir to each unit. A warning light situated on the dash indicates if either reservoir fluid level is low, provided the handbrake has been released, as the light also indicates that the handbrake is in the ON POSITION.

The master cylinder consists of a main piston with piston seal operating in the main bore with the push rod located in one end. An intermediate piston is positioned in its own bore at the front of the master cylinder and in line with the booster reaction valve. The booster reaction valve assembly is attached to the front end of the master cylinder and the two control valves within the assembly are operated by the intermediate piston.

The tandem slave cylinder consists of two pistons with piston seals operating in line in the main bore, one piston serves the rear braking assemblies whilst the other piston serves the front braking assemblies. The slave cylinder is attached to the front face of the vacuum booster. A push rod engaged in the tandem cylinder piston is passed in line to the remote servo assembly where it is keyed in position.

Vacuum is fed to both vacuum booster and booster reaction valve from the engine manifold, when the system is not operating the vacuum causes constant exhausting of both units. Operation of the footbrake moves the master cylinder main piston which feeds fluid to the slave cylinder, the intermediate piston closes the diaphragm valve in the booster reaction valve so shutting off the vacuum from the air pressure side. As the intermediate piston moves further along its bore, it cracks the air control in the reaction valve allowing air to flow to the rear of the boost cylinder piston. The slave cylinder push rod, pushed by the boost piston, which has been activated by the introduction of air to the pressure side of the boost system so creating unbalance pressure, will operate the slave cylinder pistons and assisted by the master cylinder cause a fluid pressure feed to front and rear brake assemblies.

The braking system would still operate by hydraulic pressure in the event of an air or vacuum breakdown. The dual line system is so designed that in the event of a fluid pipe failure in the hydraulic system the car can still be brought to a halt.

NOTE: The following operations described apply to the 4.2 and 2+2 models only, any operation for these two models which is not described in this section will be found under the appropriate heading of the 3.8 model. These operations will be common to all models and the described procedure should be followed.

10. SLAVE CYLINDER AND VACUUM SERVO ASSEMBLY

TO REMOVE AND INSTALL

(1) Disconnect and remove the battery and the support bracket for the battery tray.

(2) Drain the hydraulic brake fluid from the reservoirs into a clean container.

(3) Disconnect the rubber hoses at the front and top of the servo unit, disconnect the metal brake pipes at the unions in the slave cylinder.

(4) Working inside the car, remove the left hand side trim on the floor aperture panel and expose the three securing nuts for the servo unit.

(5) Loosen and remove the three nuts attaching the servo unit to the bulkhead.

(6) Take out the bolt attaching the slave cylinder to the support bracket on the outer frame side section.

(7) Withdraw the slave cylinder and servo unit complete from the bulkhead.

Installation is a reversal of the removal procedure. It will be necessary to bleed the braking system on completion, for description of the bleeding operation see under *HYDRAULIC SYSTEM.*

TO DISMANTLE

(1) With the servo slave cylinder assembly removed from the vehicle, as already described, grip the slave cylinder in a padded vice.

(2) Remove the servo end cover by turning in an anti-clockwise direction until it can be released from the casing.

NOTE: Special tool No. J31 should be used for this purpose. Mark end cover in relation to the casing to ensure assembly in the correct position.

(3) Detach the diaphragm from its location on the diaphragm support.

(4) Remove the retaining key at the end of the push rod and withdraw the diaphragm support and support return spring.

NOTE: It may be necessary to shake the assembly to dislodge the retaining key.

(5) Release the locking plate tabs, take out the three retaining screws and remove the locking plate, abutment plate and servo casing from the end of the slave cylinder.

(6) Withdraw the bearing and seal from the open end of the slave cylinder followed by the spacer, push rod and cylinder piston assembly.

(7) Separate the push rod from the piston by moving back the spring clip around the piston to enable the retaining pin to be withdrawn.

(8) Take out the inlet pipe union from the cylinder body, ease the secondary piston up the bore to permit withdrawal of the stop pin from the bottom of the inlet union port.

(9) Remove the secondary piston and piston return spring from the cylinder bore. If necessary apply low air pressure to the inlet union port, blocking other outlets to facilitate removal.

(10) Take out the outlet pipe union from the cylinder body followed by the trap valve and spring.

NOTE: Do not distort the clip located within the trap valve body when separating.

(11) Remove the plastic spring retainer from the secondary piston followed by the seal and washer, remove the remaining seal from the opposite end of the piston.

TO INSPECT

(1) Wash all parts in hydraulic brake fluid or methylated spirits. Do not use petrol, kerosene or other cleaning solvent.

(2) Check the rubber components for deterioration or damage.

(3) Check the inside of the cylinder bore for wear, corrosion or pitting.

(4) Check both pistons for wear or damage.

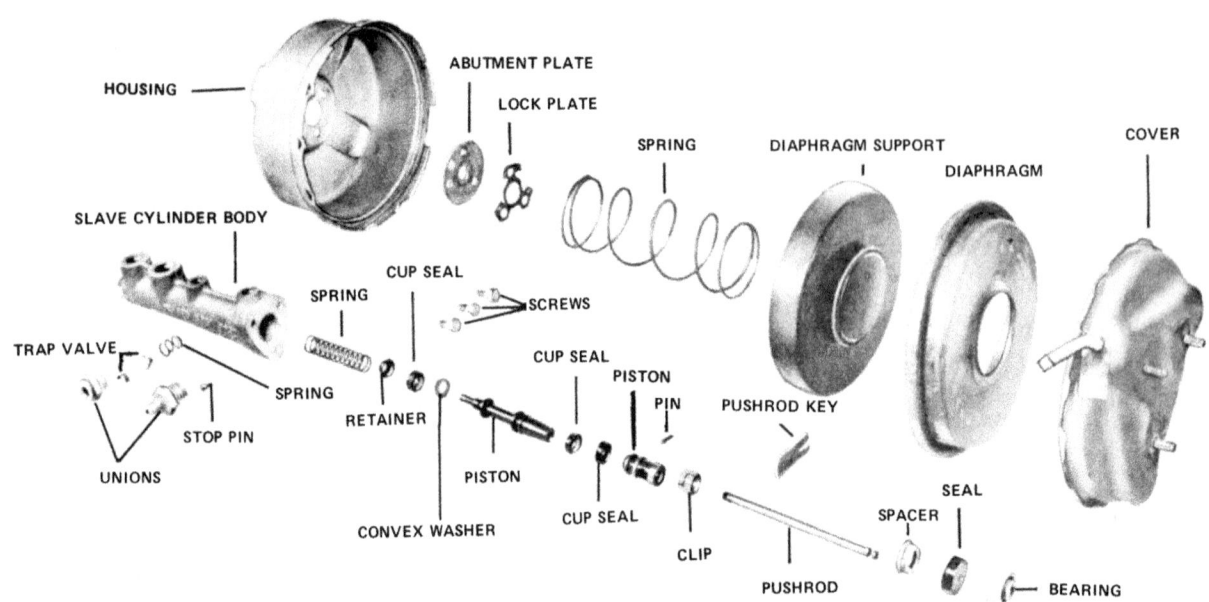

Exploded View of the Remote Servo and Slave Cylinder Components (4.2 Model).

TO ASSEMBLE

It is recommended that a repair kit containing all necessary parts for the overhaul of a slave cylinder is used at reassembly.

(1) Lubricate the components of the slave cylinder with clean hydraulic fluid during assembly.

(2) Install the dished piston washer on the secondary piston with the dished face towards the spigot end of the piston.

(3) Position two new rubber seals on the secondary piston with the lips of the seals towards the ends of the piston. Ensure that the seals locate correctly in the piston grooves.

(4) Install the plastic spring retainer on the spigot end of the piston followed by the return spring.

(5) Install the secondary piston assembly into the cylinder bore, spring first, taking care not to damage or turn back the lips of the seals on entry.

(6) Push the piston assembly down the bore until the flange on the piston clears the stop pin hole at the bottom of the inlet union port.

(7) Insert the piston stop pin and retain in position by installing the inlet pipe union with new copper gasket.

(8) With the clip installed in the trap valve body, install the trap valve and spring into the outlet port and retain in position by fitting the outlet pipe union with new copper gasket.

(9) Insert the push rod through the centre of the primary piston, compress the spring within the centre of the piston to allow the pin to be inserted. Ensure that the pin does not pass through the spring coils but that the spring is compressed between the heel of the piston and the pin.

(10) Slide the retaining clip along the piston into position around the small diameter of the piston body.

(11) Position a new rubber seal on the primary piston so that the lip of the seal will be towards the secondary piston. Ensure that the seal seats correctly in the piston groove.

(12) Install the primary piston assembly into the cylinder bore taking care not to turn back or damage the seal lip on entry.

(13) Position the spacer into the open end of the cylinder followed by the gland seal and plastic bearing. Allow the spigot end of the bearing to protrude from the end of the cylinder bore.

(14) With a new gasket on the end of the cylinder, engage the bearing spigot in the servo casing and install the abutment plate, locking plate and the three retaining screws. Tighten the three screws to a torque of 160 ins/lbs and lock in position by bending the tabs of the locking plate.

(15) Install the diaphragm support return spring so that it is centre of the casing, engage the diaphragm support on the push rod and with the slot in the support aligned with the groove of the push rod insert the retaining key.

(16) Mount the rubber diaphragm in position on the diaphragm support so that the bead around the inside of the diaphragm seats correctly into groove provided in the support.

NOTE: Ensure that the surface of the diaphragm is smooth when fitted and free of wrinkles. To facilitate fitting, coat the edges of the diaphragm with Lockheed disc brake lubricant.

(17) Align the marks on the casing and end cover made on dismantling and install the end cover using the special tool.

NOTE: When correctly fitted the end cover hose connections should line up with the inlet and outlet unions in the cylinder body.

(18) Install the assembly and bleed the system as previously described.

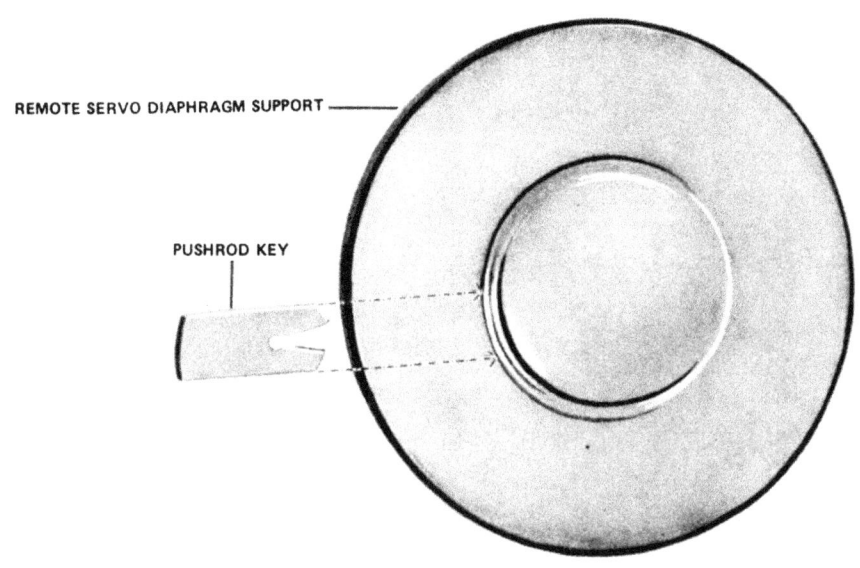

Showing Point of Entry in Diaphragm Support for Pushrod Key (4.2 Model).

11. MASTER CYLINDER AND BOOSTER REACTION VALVE ASSEMBLY

TO REMOVE AND INSTALL.

(1) Drain the hydraulic brake fluid from the reservoirs into a clear container.

(2) Disconnect the metal brake pipes at the unions in the master cylinder, disconnect the rubber hoses at the reaction valve.

(3) Take out the split pin and clevis pin attaching the master cylinder push rod to the brake pedal.

(4) Remove the domed air filter cover from the end of the reaction valve, note the position of the air filter components to facilitate reassembly.

NOTE: Operation (4) is not required on left hand drive vehicles as the master cylinder and booster reaction valve can be removed complete.

(5) Loosen and remove the two securing nuts attaching the master cylinder to the support bracket and withdraw unit.

Installation is a reversal of the removal procedure. It will be necessary to bleed the braking system on completion, for description of the bleeding operation see under *HYDRAULIC SYSTEM*.

TO DISMANTLE

(1) With the master cylinder and reaction valve assembly removed from the vehicle as already described, grip the master cylinder in a padded vice.

(2) Take out the bolt attaching the banjo union to the cylinder body and remove the union and gaskets.

(3) Take out the outlet pipe union from the cylinder body together with the trap valve, spring and washer.

(4) Detach the rubber boot from the end of the cylinder,

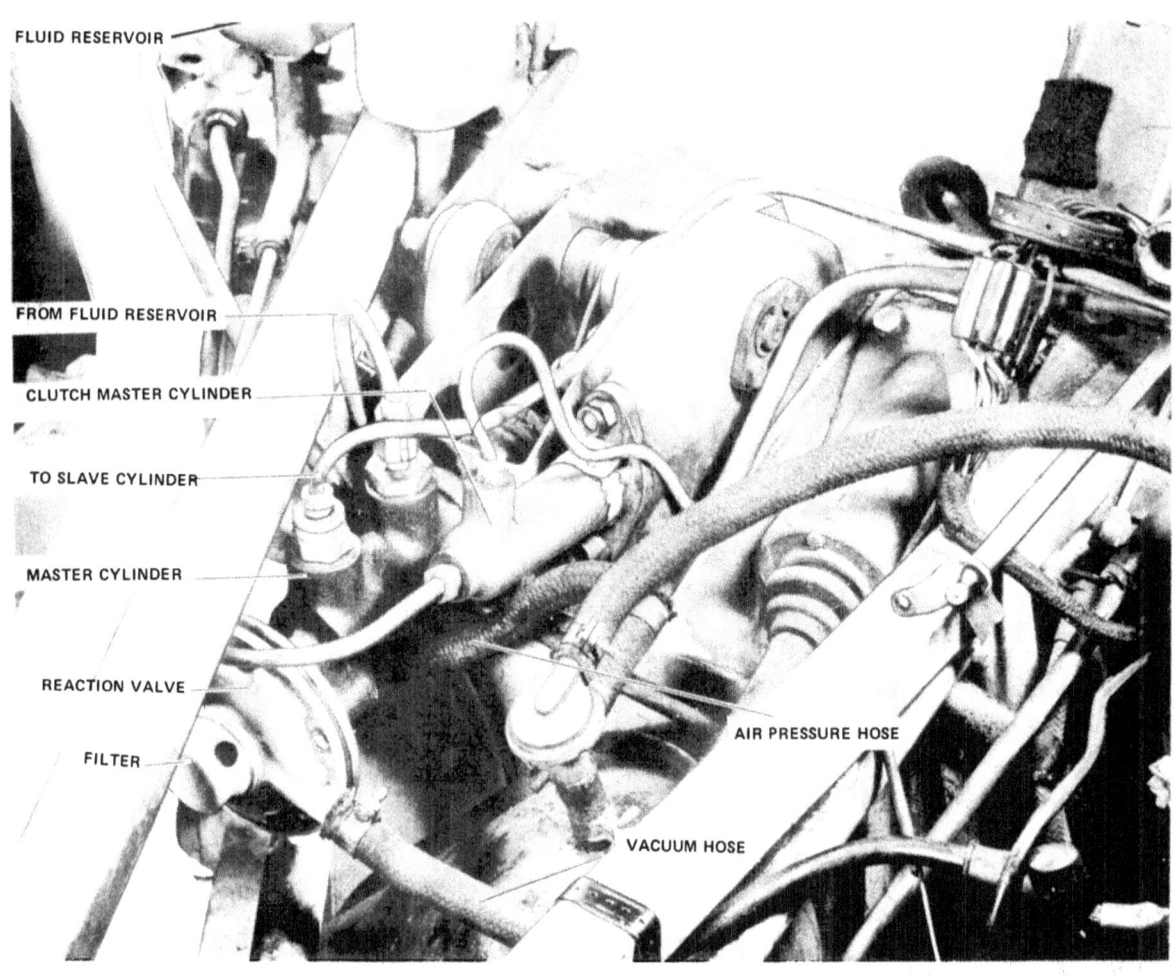

Showing Location of Master Cylinder and Connections (4.2 Model Shown).

compress the piston return spring and remove the spirolox circlip from the groove at the end of the piston.

(5) Withdraw the return spring retainer and return spring from the bore.

(6) Ease the piston assembly down the bore, and using circlip pliers remove the circlip at the open end of the bore, withdraw the piston assembly.

(7) Separate from the piston the plastic bearing together with the 'O' ring, secondary rubber cup and washer type plastic bearing.

(8) Remove the plastic spring retainer from the spigot end of the piston and detach the primary cup and dished piston washer.

NOTE: As the plastic retainer is an interference fit on the piston spigot it may be unavoidably damaged on its enforced removal. A new retainer is supplied with the repair kit.

(9) Withdraw the remaining return spring, steel retainer and lever from the cylinder bore.

(10) Take off the filter cover at the end of the reaction valve and remove the filter, washer and spring.

(11) Take out the five screws attaching the valve cover to the valve housing and detach the cover.

(12) Remove the retaining clip from the valve stem in the valve cover, take off the valve rubber and withdraw the valve from the cover. Remove the remaining rubber from the valve stem flange.

(13) Disengage the diaphragm from the diaphragm support.

(14) Take out the two screws and lock washers attaching the valve housing to the end of the master cylinder and separate the units.

(15) Remove the valve piston assembly located in the end of the cylinder by inserting a blunt probe in the

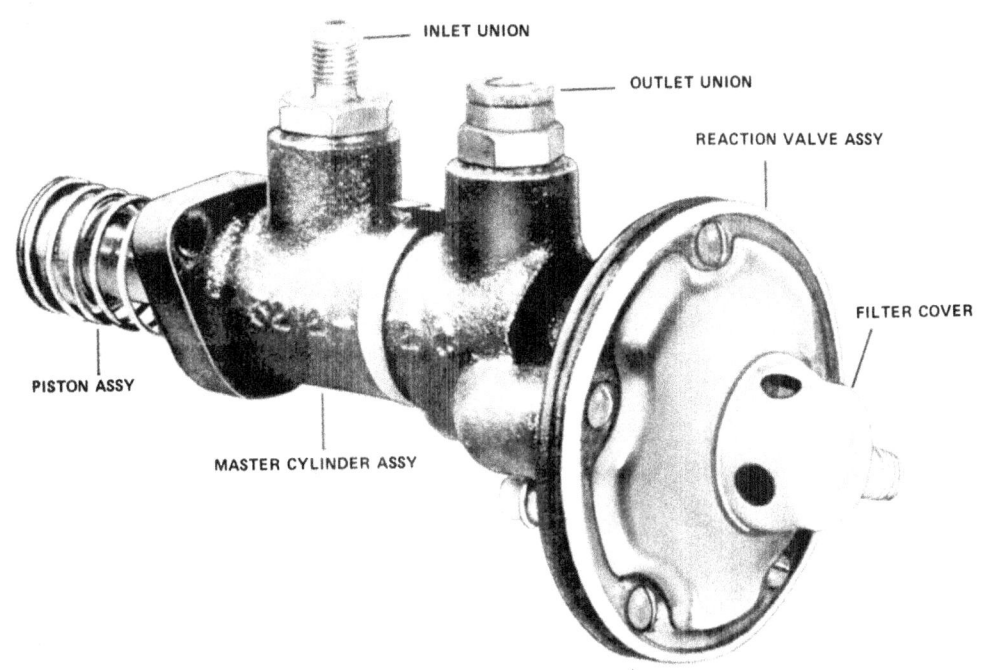

Master Cylinder and Reaction Valve Assembly (4.2 Model).

cylinder outlet port and moving the assembly out of location until it can be grasped and withdrawn.

TO ASSEMBLE

Prior to assembly inspect the components as described in *SLAVE CYLINDER – TO INSPECT*

It is recommended that a repair kit containing all necessary parts for the overhaul of a master cylinder is used at reassembly.

(1) With the exception of the reaction valve components, lubricate the master cylinder parts with clean hydraulic fluid during reassembly.

(2) Position the dished piston washer on the spigot end

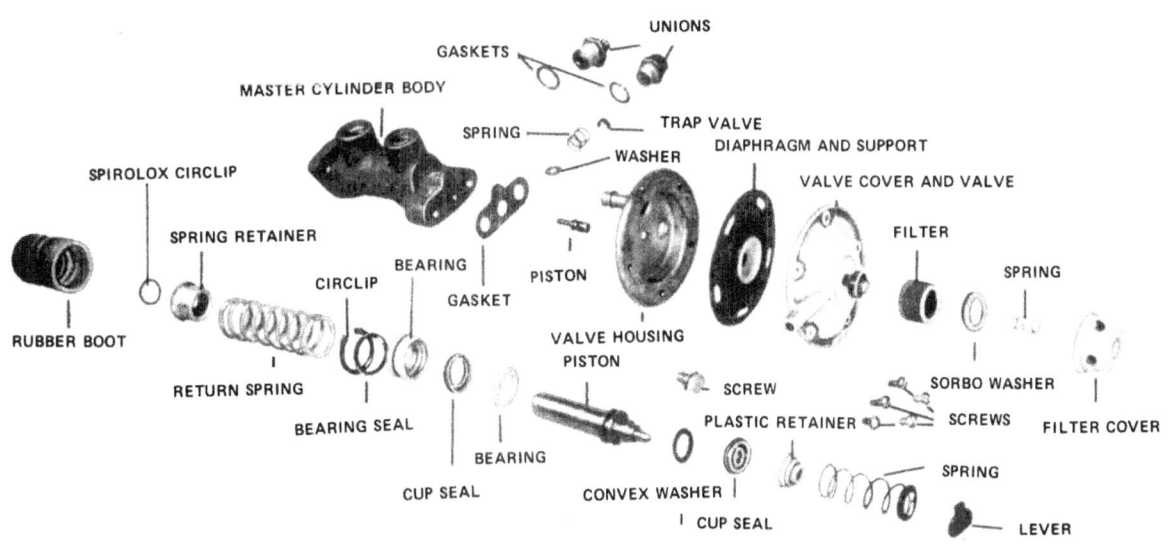

Exploded View of the Master Cylinder and Reaction Valve Components (4.2 Model).

of the master cylinder piston with the convex face against the piston flange.

(3) Install a new rubber primary cup on the spigot end of the piston with the seal lip towards the spigot end, press into position the new plastic spring retainer.

(4) With the master cylinder body held at an angle, install the lever, tab first, into the cylinder bore so that the tab engages in the recess at the bottom of the bore.

(5) Insert the steel spring retainer into the bore followed by the return spring ensuring that the lever tab is still correctly located.

(6) Install a new 'O' ring in the groove around the plastic bearing together with a new rubber secondary cup, located within the bearing with the seal lip facing towards the piston.

(7) Insert the piston assembly into the bore, making sure the seal lip is not turned back or damaged on entry, install the washer type plastic bearing followed by the bearing with the secondary cup and 'O' ring and push the assembly down the bore to enable the circlip to be fitted.

(8) Install the remaining piston return spring over the end of the piston followed by the spring retainer, push the retainer against the spring until the end of the piston is exposed and fit the spirolox circlip into the piston groove.

(9) Install a new valve seal and 'O' ring on the valve piston assembly and insert the assembly into the valve chamber taking care not to turn back or damage the seal on entry.

(10) With a new gasket positioned on the end of the master cylinder install the valve housing tightening the two retaining screws to a torque of 170 ins/lb.

NOTE: The hose connections on both the valve housing and valve cover should be in line at the bottom of the assembly when fitted.

(11) Install the diaphragm on the diaphragm support, ensuring that it seats correctly in the support groove, and insert the support stem through the hole in the valve housing to engage in the valve piston end.

(12) Fit a new valve rubber on the valve stem flange and insert the stem through the hole in the valve cover, install the remaining rubber and retaining clip.

(13) Position the valve cover on the valve housing and with the holes and hose connections in line install the five retaining screws.

(14) Install the spring on the valve stem retaining clip followed by the air filter and rubber washer, fit the air filter cover and press in until fully seated.

(15) With the clip installed in the trap valve body, install the trap valve, spring and washer into the outlet port and retain in position by fitting the outlet pipe union with a new copper gasket.

(16) Install the banjo union to the cylinder body using new gaskets between the bolt head and banjo and the cylinder body and banjo.

(17) Install the assembly as described previously together with the push rod and rubber boot. Bleed the system as described under the appropriate heading.

12. BRAKE PEDAL ASSEMBLY

TO REMOVE AND INSTALL

(1) Remove the air cleaner elbow and the carburettor air intakes as described under fuel system.

(2) Loosen the rear carburettor float chamber banjo nut and bend the petrol supply pipe towards the float chamber.

NOTE: Above operations required on right hand drive models only.

(3) Disconnect the rubber hoses at the reaction valve.

(4) Drain the fluid from the brake and clutch reservoirs into clean containers.

(5) Disconnect the fluid supply pipes from the brake and clutch master cylinders and plug the holes to prevent the entry of dirt.

(6) Disconnect the brake fluid warning light wires and remove the brake and clutch fluid reservoirs from the securing clips.

(7) Disconnect the oulet pipes from both brake and clutch master cylinders and plug to prevent the entry of dirt.

(8) Take out the five securing screws attaching the reaction valve assembly to the rear valve housing plate, remove the reaction valve assembly.

(9) Take out the two securing screws and lock washers attaching the rear valve housing plate to the end of the master cylinder. Take note of the gasket between the faces and ensure that the intermediate piston is not dislodged.

(10) Disconnect and remove the accelerator bell crank bracket.

NOTE: Operations (9) and (10) do not apply to left hand drive vehicles.

(11) Working inside the car, remove the securing nuts attaching the brake and clutch pedal pads to the levers and detach the foot pads.

(12) Take out the securing screws and withdraw the under dash casing from its retaining clips.

(13) Loosen and remove the securing nuts, the two distance pieces and the brake pedal stop plate. Note the position of the distance pieces for reassembly.

(14) Turn the brake pedal assembly through 90° to permit the pedals passage through the aperture in the bulkhead and withdraw from the car.

Installations is a reversal of the removal procedure with attention to the following points:

Use a new gasket between the faces of the rear valve housing plate and the end face of the master cylinder.

When the assembly is positioned in the car fit the plain nut and lockwasher on the shortest stud located at the bottom centre.

Position the petrol supply pipe before tightening the banjo unit nut.

Connect the warning light wires to the reservoirs with one red/green wire and one black wire to each reservoir cap.

Bleed the brake and clutch hydraulic systems as described under the appropriate headings.

13. BRAKE FAULT DIAGNOSIS

1. **Brake pedal hard.**

   Possible cause
   - (a) Incorrect disc pads fitted.
   - (b) Frozen pedal pivot.
   - (c) Restricted brake line from master cylinder.
   - (d) Frozen calliper piston/s.
   - (e) No vacuum from engine manifold.
   - (f) Fault in servo unit or reaction valve.
   - (g) Air valve incorrectly adjusted.

   Remedy
   - Check and replace pads with recommended type.
   - Check brake pedal bearing lubrication.
   - Check brake line and remove restriction or renew line.
   - Check free up or renew.
   - Check rubber hoses and connections, and reservoir check valve.
   - Overhaul of units required.
   - Check and adjust valve as described.

2. **Brake drag.**

   Possible cause
   - (a) Frozen calliper pistons.
   - (b) Handbrake pad carriers incorrectly adjusted.
   - (c) Handbrake cable or linkage frozen.
   - (d) Blocked air filter or air intake on servo.
   - (e) Air valve incorrectly adjusted.
   - (f) Master cylinder/tandem cylinder return ports/valves choked.
   - (g) Fault in servo unit or reaction valve.

   Remedy
   - Check free up or renew.
   - Adjust as described.
   - Check, free up or renew.
   - Check air intake ports, clean air filter.
   - Check and adjust valve as described.
   - Check and overhaul units.
   - Overhaul of units required.

3. **Low or spongy brake pedal.**

   Possible cause
   - (a) Master cylinder/tandem cylinder rubbers defective.
   - (b) Lack of fluid in reservoirs.
   - (c) Air in brake hydraulic system.

   Remedy
   - Overhaul hydraulic units fit new seals.
   - Check for leaks, replenish fluid to correct level.
   - Bleed hydraulic system.

4. **Brakes grab.**

   Possible cause
   - (a) Grease or brake fluid on pads.
   - (b) Incorrect disc pads fitted.
   - (c) Scored brake discs.
   - (d) Sticking calliper piston/s.

   Remedy
   - Clean or renew disc pads.
   - Check and replace pads with recommended type.
   - Check and renew as necessary.
   - Check and free up.

5. **Brake pedal pulsates.**

   Possible cause
   (a) Bent or eccentric brake disc.
   (b) Loose or worn front hub bearings.
   (c) Calliper assemblies not centralised over disc.

   Remedy
   – Check and renew as necessary.
   – Adjust or renew hub bearings.
   – Centralise as described.

6. **Brake fade at high speed.**

   Possible cause
   (a) Grease or brake fluid on pads.
   (b) Bent or scored brake disc/s.
   (c) Incorrect disc pads fitted.

   Remedy
   – Clean or renew disc pads.
   – Check and renew as necessary.
   – Check and replace pads with recommended type.

7. **Brakes overheat**

   Possible cause
   (a) No running clearance at disc pads.
   (b) Handbrake pad carriers incorrectly adjusted.
   (c) Handbrake cable or linkage frozen.
   (d) Air valve incorrectly adjusted.
   (e) Frozen calliper piston/s.
   (f) Blocked vent in reservoir caps.
   (g) Return flow of brake fluid restricted in master cylinder/tandem cylinder.
   (h) Fault in servo unit or reaction valve.

   Remedy
   – Check pistons and self adjusters for defect.
   – Adjust as required.
   – Check and free up.
   – Adjust as described.
   – Check and free up.
   – Check and clean vents.
   – Check and overhaul units.
   – Overhaul of units required.

ELECTRICAL SYSTEM

SPECIFICATIONS

BATTERY

Type	Lucas 12 volt 11 plate
Capacity	55 amp/h at 10 hour rate
	60 amp/h at 20 hour rate
Polarity	Negative to earth (3.8 – Positive)
Location	Left side of engine compartment

GENERATOR

EARLY MODELS

Type	C.45 PVS6
Maximum output	25 amps
Cut in speed	1300 rpm 13 volts
Brush tension – maximum	28 ozs. (new brushes)
minimum	20 ozs. (worn)
Field resistance	6 ohms

LATE MODELS

Type	C.42
Maximum output	30 amps
Cut in speed	1250 rpm at 13 volts
Field resistance	4.5 ohms
Brush tension – maximum	32 ozs. (new brushes)
minimum	16 ozs. (worn)

LUCAS A.C. SYSTEM (4.2 and 2 + 2 cars)

Type	Lucas 11
Maximum output	45 amps 6000 rpm
Cut in voltage	13 volts 500 rpm
Field resistance	3.770 ohms
Number of brushes	2
Brush length, new	.625"
worn (minimum)	.156"
Brush spring tension compressed to .78125" length	4 to 5 ozs.
Brush spring tension compressed to .40625" length	7 to 8 ozs.

GENERATOR REGULATOR

(Fitted in conjunction with C45 PV6 generator)

Type	RB310
Cut in voltage	12.7 – 13.3 volts
Cut out voltage	9.5 – 11 volts
Current regulator setting	24 – 26 amps
Open circuit voltage setting:	
50 F	15.1 – 15.7 volts
68 F	14.9 – 15.5 volts
86 F	14.7 – 15.3 volts
104 F	14.5 – 15.1 volts

(Fitted in conjunction with C42 generator)

Type	RB340
Cut in voltage	12.6 – 13.4 volts
Cut out voltage	9.25 – 11.25 volts
Current regulator setting	30 amps
Open circuit voltage setting	Same as RB310 regulator

LUCAS A.C. SYSTEM (4.2 and 2 + 2 cars)

Type	Lucas 4TR (Transistor)
Polarity	Negative to earth

DISTRIBUTOR

3.8 MODEL

Type	Centrifugal vacuum advance, DMBZ6A
Cam dwell angle	35° ± 2°
Contact breaker gap	.014" – .016"
Contact breaker spring tension	18 – 24 ozs.
Timing (8 to 1) compression	9° btdc
Timing (9 to 1) compression	10° btdc

4.2 and 2 + 2, ALSO FITTED TO LATER 3.8

Type	Centrifugal vacuum advance 22 D6
Cam dwell angle	34° ± 3°
Contact breaker gap	.014" – .016"
Contact breaker spring tension	18 – 24 ozs.
Timing (8 to 1) compression	9° btdc
Timing (9 to 1) compression	10° btdc

SPARK PLUGS

Type	Champion UN12Y
Size	14 mm
Electrode gap	.025"
Tightening torque	28 ft/lb
Firing order	1-5-3-6-2-4

STARTER MOTOR

3.8 MODEL

Type	Lucas 12 volt M45G inertia engagement
Lock torque	22 ft/lbs @ 430 – 450 amps
Lock torque voltage	7.8 – 7.5
Brush tension	30 – 40 ozs.
Brush length (new)	.625"
Brush length minimum	.3125"

4.2 E TYPE and 2 + 2 MODELS

Type	Lucas 12 volt M45G pre-engaged
Lock torque	22 ft/lbs 465 amps
Lock torque voltage	7.6 @ 465 amps
Brush tension (new brush)	52 ozs.
Brush length	.625"
Brush minimum length	.3125"
Solenoid closing resistance	.36 – .42 ohms
Solenoid hold on resistance	1.49 – 1.71 ohms
Solenoid model	Lucas 10S

1. BATTERY

MAINTENANCE

Maintenance consists mainly of regular inspection and servicing.

(1) Keep the battery and its surroundings clean and dry. Give the top of the battery particular attention to prevent electrical leakage between cell terminals.

(2) Remove the vent plugs and see that the vent holes are clear.

(3) Check the electrolite level and top up as necessary. The correct level is just over the top of the separators or perforated plate. Do not overfill or acid will escape through the vent holes with detrimental effect on the connections and adjacent parts of the car.

(4) Use only pure distilled water for topping up.

NOTE: Never use a naked light when examining the battery, as the gases given off by the battery can be dangerously explosive.

(5) If the battery requires an excessive amount of topping up, the cause should be sought. If over-charging is suspected, check the regulator setting. If one cell in particular is at fault, check the case for cracks. Never transfer electrolite from one cell to another.

(6) Keep the positive and negative terminals clean and apply a small amount of petroleum jelly to the terminals to prevent corrosion.

NOTE: Salt water, chlorinated, or chemically softened water must never be used.

2. GENERATOR AND REGULATOR

GENERATOR

DESCRIPTION

The generators are of a two pole, two brush shunt wound type unit arranged to work in conjunction with a current voltage control. The early model vehicles are fitted with Lucas C45PV6 generator controlled by a RB310 current/voltage regulator. Later models are fitted with Lucas C42 generators and RB340 regulators. These units can readily be identified by the markings on the body of the generators and covers of the regulator units.

Basically the construction of the units are the same. Variations in specifications etc. are covered in the appropriate sections.

Both generators are controlled by the regulator unit and dependent on both the state of charge of the battery and the loading of electrical equipment in use. The regulator controls the battery charge through the field windings of the generator providing a high output when the battery is in a low state of charge or when the electrical accessories are in use, adjusting the current rate to the demand conditions.

TO REMOVE AND INSTALL

(1) Loosen the generator link and mounting bolts and push the generator towards the engine.

(2) Slip the driving belt off the generator pulley and remove the terminal leads from the D and F terminals of

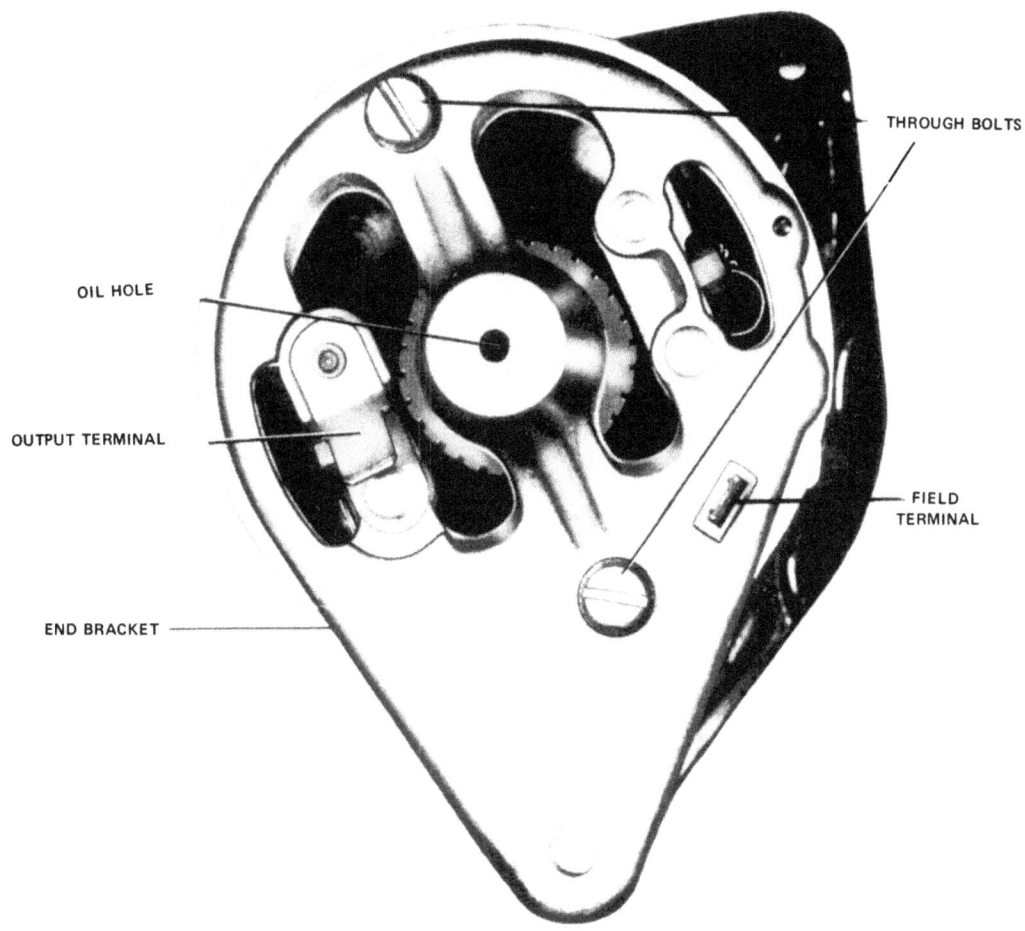

End View of Generator Showing Arrangement of Terminals.

the generator. Note that the heavier of the two leads is connected to the D terminal of the generator.

(3) Remove the adjusting link screw and the two mounting bolts and withdraw the generator from the vehicle.

Installation is a reversal of the removal procedure, but note that if the generator has been dismantled it will be necessary to polarise the generator before the engine is started.

This may be done by momentarily connecting the D terminal of the generator with a jumper lead to the positive terminal of the battery, to rotate the generator armature in the correct direction for a few revolutions, before fitting and adjusting the driving belt.

Adjust the drive belt until it is possible to flex the belt in and out approximately .500" with the thumb and forefinger on the longest run of the belt between pulleys.

NOTE: Care must be taken not to over tighten the drive belt as this will result in overload of the generator and water pump bearings. Always use a belt tension gauge if available.

TO DISMANTLE AND REASSEMBLE

(1) Remove the generator from the vehicle as previously described.

(2) Remove the nut and take off the drive pulley. Remove the Woodruff key from the armature shaft.

(3) Unscrew and remove the two through bolts at the commutator end plate and withdraw the armature and drive end plate assembly from the generator body.

(4) Remove the field terminal nut and insulating washers and withdraw the commutator end plate. Note the insulating sleeve and washer that will remain on the terminal attached to the field coils. It will not be necessary to remove the field coils and pole shoes unless the fields prove to be faulty under test, in which case proceed as follows:

(5) Mark the body and pole shoes so that they can be replaced in the position from which they were removed.

(6) Using a shoe expander and wheel operated screwdriver, remove the pole shoe attaching screws and withdraw the shoes together with the field coils.

NOTE: The insulating piece between the field coil connections and the body should be removed before the coils are detached from the body.

(7) Remove the drive end plate assembly from the armature, remove the bearing retaining plate rivets and withdraw the bearing, waved washer, felt washer and oil retainer washer.

NOTE: If a new commutator end bearing bush is to be fitted, it must be soaked in thin engine oil for 24 hours in order to fill the pores of the bush and provide lubrication. Where circumstances will not permit this period of time, the bush should be treated as follows:

Completely immerse in hot (212°F) engine oil where it should remain until the oil returns to normal temperature.

Reassembly is a reversal of the dismantling procedure but note the following points:

Use a shoe expander and wheel operated screwdriver when installing the field coils and pole shoes and lock the attaching screws with a centre pop at the screw slot.

Do not omit to replace the insulating piece between the field connection and the body.

The commutator end plate bearing bush must not be reamed to size, as reaming will destroy its porosity and oil retaining ability. Use a shouldered mandrel of the correct size to press in the bush.

When fitting the commutator end plate use a small screwdriver through the apertures in the body to raise the two bushes on to the commutator.

Note the steel ball in each end plate and the groove in each end of the body for correct alignment when reassembling the generator.

TO TEST IN POSITION

In the event of a fault in the charging circuit, adopt the following procedure to locate the cause of the trouble.

(1) Check that the drive belt is not slipping, and adjust if necessary.

(2) Check that the generator and regulator are connected correctly. The larger generator terminal D must be connected to the regulator terminal D and the smaller generator terminal F to regulator terminal F.

(3) Switch off all lights and accessories, disconnect the cables from the terminals of the generator and connect the two terminals with a short length of wire.

(4) Start the engine and set to run at normal idling speed.

(5) Clip the negative lead of a moving coil type voltmeter, calibrated 0-20 volts, to one generator terminal and the other lead to a good earthing point on the body.

(6) Gradually increase the engine speed, when the voltmeter reading should rise rapidly and without fluctuation. Do not allow the voltmeter reading to reach 20 volts and do not race the engine in an attempt to increase the voltage. It is sufficient to run the generator up to about 1,000 rpm. If there is no reading, check the brush gear. If there is a low reading of approximately .5 to 1 volt, the field winding may be at fault. If there is a reading of 4 to 5 volts, the armature may be at fault.

(7) Examine the commutator and brushes. Hold back each of the brush springs and move the brush by pulling gently on its flexible connector. If the movement is sluggish, remove the brush from its holder and ease the sides by gently polishing on a smooth file. Always replace brushes in their original positions. If the brushes are worn so that they do not bear on the commutator, new brushes must be fitted and bedded to the commutator.

(8) Test the brush spring tension with a spring scale.

(9) The tension of the springs when new is 28 oz. and the minimum of 15 oz. for worn brushes on generator C45PVS6 and 32 oz. new and 16 oz. worn on C42 generator. Fit new brushes or springs if tension is below these figures.

(10) If the commutator is blackened or dirty, clean it by holding a petrol moistened cloth against it while the engine is slowly turned. Re-test the generator; if there is still no reading on the voltmeter there is an internal fault, and the complete unit, if a spare is available, should be replaced. Otherwise the unit must be dismantled for internal examination.

(11) If the generator is in good order, remove the link from between the terminals and restore the original connections, taking care to connect generator terminal D to the regulator terminal D and the generator terminal F to the regulator terminal F.

(12) Remove the lead from the D terminal on the regulator and connect the voltmeter between the cable and a good earth on the vehicle.

(13) Run the engine as before and the reading on the voltmeter should be the same as that taken directly on the generator. No reading on the voltmeter indicates a break in the cable to the generator.

(14) Repeat the test on the F terminal of the regulator, connecting the voltmeter between the cable and earth, when the results should be the same.

TO TEST FIELD COILS

(1) Measure the resistance of the field coils, without removing them from the generator body by means of an ohmmeter connected between the field terminal and the body. The correct resistance is 6 ohms for the generator C.45PV-6 and 4.5 ohms for the C42 generator. A very high reading indicates a faulty connection or an open circuit in the field circuit, whilst a reduced reading indicates an

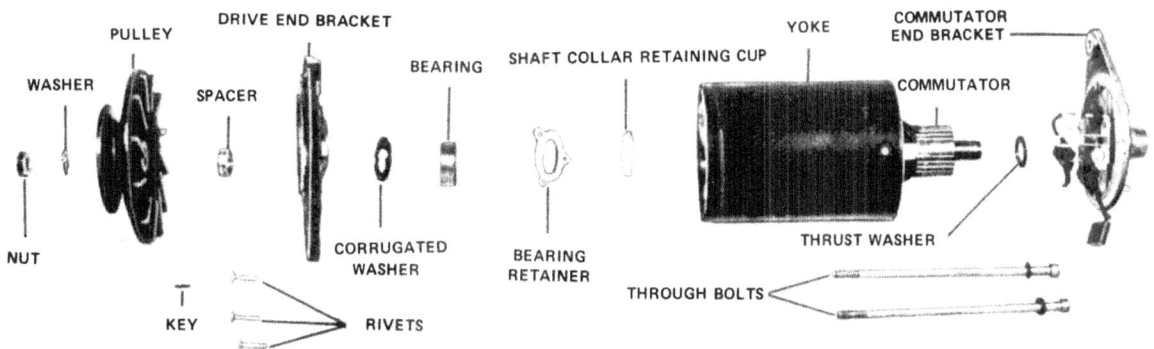

Exploded View of Generator Components (Fitted to Early Models).

earthed field coil. If an ohmmeter is not available, connect a 12 volt DC supply with an ammeter in series between the field terminal and generator body. The ammeter reading should be approximately 2 amperes. No reading on the ammeter indicates an open circuit in the field winding, and a higher reading indicates an earthed field coil.

(2) In either case, unless a replacement generator is available, the field coils must be replaced. To do this carry out the procedure outlined below, using a pole shoe expander and wheel-operated screwdriver.

(3) Remove the insulation piece which is provided to prevent the junction of the field coils from contact with the body.

(4) Mark the body and pole shoes in order that they can be fitted in their original positions.

(5) Unscrew the two pole shoe retaining screws by means of a wheel-operated screwdriver.

(6) Draw the pole shoes and coils out of the body and lift off the coils.

(7) Fit the new field coils over the pole shoes and place them in position inside the body. Take care to ensure that the taping of the field coils is not trapped between the pole shoes and the body.

(8) Locate the pole shoes and field coils by lightly tightening the fixing screws.

(9) Insert the pole shoe expander, open it to the fullest extent and tighten the screws.

(10) Finally tighten the screws by means of the wheel-operated screwdriver and lock them by staking.

(11) Replace the insulation piece between the field coil connections and the body.

(12) Re-solder the field coil connections to the field coil terminal tags and re-rivet the assembly to the body.

TO TEST ARMATURE

(1) Before proceeding with any test, clean the armature.

(2) To test for a short circuit, place the armature in a growler, and hold a piece of steel strip over the top of the armature in line with the shaft, slowly revolve the armature, keeping the steel strip in the same position.

If a short circuit exists, the steel strip will be heavily attracted towards the slot containing the faulty coil. Having located the fault on one side continue rotating the armature, when a second faulty slot will be found.

OPEN CIRCUIT TEST

(1) Such can occur in the commutator segments or in the armature windings and can be located by the following procedure:

Using a 12 volt battery and a voltmeter with test prods, connect one lead and prod to the negative pole of the battery and connect the voltmeter and other lead to the positive pole of the battery.

(2) Place the prods on each pair of adjacent commutator segments in turn and note the voltmeter readings. If the armature is in good order all readings will be similar. A pair of segments with a low or zero reading means that one or more adjacent coils are open circuited.

TO CHECK BRUSHES

(1) Check if the brushes are sticking. Clean them with petrol and lightly polish the sides on a smooth file. The brushes must be replaced in their original positions.

(2) Check the brush spring tension. If the tension is below that shown in specifications, renew springs or brushes as required.

(3) Renew the brushes if worn to a minimum length and bed the brushes to the commutator.

TO RECONDITION COMMUTATOR

(1) A commutator in good condition will be smooth and **free from pits or burned spots. Clean the commutator with** a petrol moistened cloth. If this is ineffective, polish with a strip of fine glass paper while rotating the armature. To remedy a badly worn commutator, mount the armature, with or without the drive end plate, in a lathe, rotate at high speed and take a light cut with a very sharp tool.

(2) Do not remove more metal than is necessary. Polish the commutator with very fine glass paper. Undercut the insulators between the segments to a depth of .03125" with a hacksaw blade ground down to the thickness of the insulator.

TO RENEW BEARINGS

The generator is fitted with a ball bearing at the drive end and a porous bronze bush at the commutator end.

Bearings that are worn to such an extent that they will allow side movement of the armature shaft, must be replaced.

To replace the bearing bush at the commutator end, proceed as follows:

(1) The correct method of removing the bush in these cases is to use a lipped expanding type extractor. Where such a tool is not immediately available the bush can be removed by screwing in a .625" tap for a few turns and withdrawing the bush and tap complete. Care should be taken to screw the tap squarely into the bush to avoid damage to the end plate.

(2) Press the new bearing bush into the end plate using a shouldered, highly polished mandrel of the same diameter as the shaft which is to fit the bearing. Porous bronze bushes must not be opened out after fitting, or the porosity of the bush may be impaired.

NOTE: Before fitting the new bearing bush, it should be allowed to stand for 24 hours completely immersed in thin engine oil. This will allow the pores of the bush to be filled with lubricant. In cases of extreme urgency, this period may be shortened by heating the oil to 212°, when the time of immersion may be reduced to 2 hours.

The ball bearing, which is a push fit in the drive end plate, is replaced as follows:

(3) Drill out the rivets securing the bearing retaining plate to the end plate.

(4) Push the bearing out of the end plate and remove the corrugated washer, felt washer and oil retaining washer.

(5) Before fitting the replacement bearing see that it is clean and pack it with high melting point grease.

(6) Place the oil retaining washer, felt washer and corrugated washer in the bearing housing in the drive end plate.

(7) Locate the bearing in the housing and push it home (hand pressure only is needed).

(8) Fit the bearing retaining plate. Insert the new rivets from the inside of the end plate and open the rivets by means of a punch to secure the plate rigidly in position.

(9) It is recommended that a piece of mild steel tubing 4" long with an internal diameter of 5/8", is used to support the inner race of the bearing when fitting the drive end plate to the armature shaft.

Under no circumstances is it permissible to use the drive end plate as a support. This could cause damage to the corrugated washer, and as a result the armature would not maintain its correct position and the brushes may overhang the edge of the commutator.

(10) The bearing and end plate should be thoroughly cleaned and repacked with high melting point grease immediately prior to reassembly.

REGULATOR

Each unit of the control box is correctly adjusted during assembly and it should not be necessary to make further adjustments. If, however, the battery does not keep in a charged condition, or if the generator output does not fall when the battery is fully charged, the settings should be checked and, if necessary, corrected.

It is important before altering the regulator settings to check that the low state of charge of the battery is not due to a battery defect or a slipping drive belt.

The early model vehicles are equipped with RB310 type regulators matching the C45PVS6 generator. Later model vehicles are fitted with RB340 regulators and C42 generators as indicated in the main electrical specification section. Although the internal circuits of the two regulators are somewhat different, the testing and setting procedures are identical with the exception of certain specifications as indicated in the appropriate parts of the text.

TO CHECK AND ADJUST VOLTAGE REGULATOR

The open circuit setting of the voltage regulator unit should be checked with the control box cover in position and at normal operating temperature.

All tests must be made as quickly as possible, to avoid overheating the regulator windings, in which case a **false** reading will result.

It is important that only good quality instruments are used in testing and adjusting the control box. These should comprise an 0 to 30 volt moving coil voltmeter and a 40-0-40 scale moving coil ammeter.

NOTE: A generator run at high speed on open circuit will build up a high voltage. Therefore, when testing and adjusting the voltage regulator increase the engine speed slowly until the regulator operates, otherwise a false setting will be made.

(1) Disconnect the wiring connection from the regulator terminal B.

(2) Connect the negative lead of the test voltmeter to the regulator terminal D or WL, and the positive lead to the regulator base.

(3) Start the engine and gradually increase the speed until the voltmeter needle flicks and then steadies (approximately 3000 generator rpm). This should occur at a voltmeter reading between 14.7 and 15.1 volts at 68°F (20°C).

Carefully note the ambient temperature and apply a correction for any temperature variation noted as follows:

For every 18°F (10°C) above 68°F (20°C) — subtract 0.20 volts.

For every 18°F (10°C) below 68°F (20°C) — add 0.20 volts.

NOTE: An unsteady reading may be caused by unclean contacts, incorrect mechanical setting, a loose fan belt or a faulty internal connection.

(4) If the voltmeter reading is steady but is not within the limits specified, the regulator is in need of adjustment. Increase the speed gradually until the maximum voltmeter reading is obtained. This should not be more than half a volt above the specified readings.

If the voltmeter reading continues to rise as the engine speed is increased, possibly swinging the needle right over, it is indicative that either the regulator points are not operating or there is a poor or no earth between the regulator and the body.

If the points are not opening, the regulator should be renewed, as it is possible that they are welded or shorted, or there is an open circuit in the shunt coil.

(5) Adjust the voltage regulator as follows: Stop the engine and remove the regulator cover.

(6) Re-start the engine and run at the speed where the voltmeter reading is steady (approximately 3000 generator rpm). Carefully check this reading — it should be between 14.7 to 15.1 volts at 68°F (20°C).

(7) Using the special Lucas type adjusting tool, (screwdriver in the case of RB310), slightly rotate the voltage regulator adjustment cam until the correct setting is obtained. Turn the tool clockwise to increase the voltage, or anti-clockwise to decrease the voltage. Turn the cam only a fraction at a time.

(8) Check the setting by stopping the engine, re-starting, and running the generator again at the test speed.

(9) Stop the engine, disconnect the voltmeter, re-connect the wiring to the B terminal and replace the regulator cover.

TO CHECK AND ADJUST CURRENT REGULATOR

When checking the current regulator on-load setting, the generator must develop its maximum rated output whatever the battery state of charge. The voltage regulator must therefore be made inoperative.

To do this, the voltage regulator contacts must be short-circuited by a convenient means such as a spring clip large enough to bridge the adjustable contact and the armature.

(1) Remove the regulator cover.

(2) Bridge the voltage regulator contacts as previously outlined.

(3) Disconnect the wiring connection from terminal B of the regulator and connect the test ammeter between this terminal and the disconnected cable.

(4) Start the engine, run the generator at approximately 4000 rpm (engine rpm 2700) and note the ammeter reading.

This should indicate a current equal to the maximum rated output of the generator ± 1½ amps.

NOTE: An unsteady reading may be due to dirty contacts, incorrect mechanical setting, a loose fan belt or a faulty internal connection.

(5) If the reading is steady but is outside the specified limits, adjust the current regulator as follows:

Using the special tool, (RB340 regulator — screwdriver RB310), rotate slightly the adjustment cam until the correct setting is obtained. Turn the tool clockwise to increase the current, or anti-clockwise to decrease the current.

(6) Switch off the engine, remove the spring clip from the regulator contacts, remove the ammeter, reconnect the wiring to the terminal B and replace the regulator cover.

TO CHECK AND ADJUST CUT-OUT ELECTRICAL SETTINGS

Cut-out Cut-in Voltage:

NOTE: As when testing and adjusting the voltage regulator, the electrical readings should be completed as quickly as possible to avoid errors due to the coils heating.

(1) Connect the negative lead of the test voltmeter to

the regulator terminal D or WL, and the positive lead to the regulator base plate.

(2) Connect a lamp load across the battery. This load is necessary to ensure the drop in voltmeter reading (see below), is immediately discernible.

(3) Start the engine and slowly increase the speed.

Note the maximum reading obtained on the voltmeter, this should be between 12.7 and 13.3 volts.

NOTE: After registering the maximum reading, the voltmeter needle should drop suddenly, indicating that the cut-out contact is closed.

(4) If necessary, adjust the cut-in voltage as follows:

Remove the regulator cover, ensure the engine speed is below cut-in speed and using the special tool, rotate slightly the cut-out adjustment cam in the appropriate direction. Turn the tool clockwise to increase the cut-in voltage or anti-clockwise to decrease the cut-in voltage. Re-check the voltage as previously outlined.

(5) Repeat the procedure until the correct value is obtained.

(6) Stop the engine, remove the lamp load, disconnect the voltmeter and replace the regulator cover.

Cut-out Drop-off Voltage:

(1) Disconnect the wiring connection from the regulator terminal B.

(2) Connect the negative lead of the test voltmeter to terminal B and the positive lead to the regulator base plate.

(3) Run the engine at about half throttle and then gradually decrease the engine speed, noting the voltage immediately after which the needle flicks back to zero, indicating that the cut-out contact is open.

This should occur between 9.3 and 11.0 volts (RB340 – 9.25 – 11.25 volts).

(4) If the drop-off voltage is outside these limits adjust the cut-out as follows:

(5) Stop the engine and remove the regulator cover.

(6) Carefully bend the cut-out fixed contact bracket to vary the contact gap.

Close the contact gap to increase the drop-off voltage.

Open the contact gap to reduce the drop-off voltage.

RB340 regulator – turn cam clockwise to increase, anti-clockwise to decrease voltage.

NOTE: There should be .010" to .020" moving contact follow through or blade deflection when the armature is pressed fully downwards.

(7) Start the engine and re-check as outlined in operation (3).

(8) Stop the engine, disconnect the voltmeter, re-connect the wiring to terminal B and replace the regulator cover.

TO CHECK AND ADJUST MECHANICAL SETTINGS

Air gap settings are accurately set during manufacture and should require no further attention.

If, however, the points have been removed for cleaning, it will be necessary to re-set them to obtain the correct armature to core air gap clearance.

After completing any mechanical setting, the regulator must be tested and the electrical settings adjusted as previously outlined.

Current and/or Voltage Regulator, Air Gap Adjustment:

(1) Remove the regulator from the car.

(2) Using the special tool, turn the adjustment cam to the position giving minimum lift to the armature spring, i.e. fully anti-clockwise.

(3) Slacken the adjustable point locknut and screw the point a few turns outwards.

(4) Insert a .045" feeler blade between the armature and the copper separation shim on the core face, taking care not to turn up or damage the copper shim. Position the feeler blade over the core as far as the rivet heads will allow and then press the armature firmly downwards.

(5) Whilst holding the armature down, screw the adjustable point inwards until it just touches the fixed point and then secure in this position by tightening the locknut.

(6) Release the armature and check the armature to core air gap, this should be .045" to .049".

(7) Carry out the electrical settings as previously outlined.

Cut-out Relay Air Gap:

The cut-out armature to core air gap should be .035" to .045" measured by means of a suitable feeler blade inserted as far as the rivet heads will allow.

If an adjustment is necessary, carefully bend the back stop as required. Carry out the electrical setting as previously outlined.

TO CLEAN UNIT CONTACTS

When truing the voltage or current regulator contacts, use a fine carborundum stone or silicone carbide paper and then clean the contacts with methylated spirits.

The cut-out contacts should be cleaned with a strip of fine glass paper. On no account use carborundum stone, paper or emery cloth on these contacts as they consist of a soft metal.

(1) Remove the regulator wiring connections, undo the three retaining screws and remove the regulator from the vehicle.

(2) Remove the voltage regulator and current regulator

adjustable contacts by slackening their respective locknuts and unscrewing the contacts from their mountings.

(3) Clean the contact points as previously outlined.

(4) Reassemble the adjustable contacts and re-set the armature air gaps as outlined earlier.

(5) Replace the regulator on the vehicle and reconnect the wiring.

(6) Check the regulator electrically and if necessary re-set as previously outlined.

3. ALTERNATOR AND REGULATOR

DESCRIPTION

The Lucas 11 AC alternator is designed to provide increased output at all engine speeds and consists of a rotor and field coil assembly rotating within a laminated stator and stator winding assembly which is held between two end plates, these in turn carry the rotor shaft bearings.

The stator consists of a 24 slot 3 phase star connected winding on a ring shaped laminated pack.

The rotor is of eight pole construction and carries the field windings connected to two slip rings and is supported by a ball type bearing at the drive end and a needle roller bearing at the slip ring end.

Two brushes, one positive and one negative are mounted on the rear end plate and bear on the concentric slip rings which are fitted to, but insulated from, the rotor shaft.

There are six silicon diodes mounted in the rear end plate, these are connected in a three phase bridge circuit and provide rectification of the generated alternating current output.

The cooling of the assembly is achieved by an air flow through the unit produced by a six inch fan which is fitted to the rotor shaft at the drive end of the alternator.

The alternator is controlled by a matching output unit model 4TR. A cut out is not included in the control unit because the diodes in the alternator prevent reverse current from flowing through the stator when the unit is stationary or charging less than the battery voltage.

No separate current limiting device is required owing to the inherent self regulating characteristics of the alternator.

The output control unit and the alternator field winding are isolated from the battery when the engine is stationary by a separate set of contacts in the ignition switch. Cars fitted with a steering column lock are also fitted with an isolating relay which replaces the ignition switch control.

Although the model 4TR control is an electronic unit, in effect its action is similar to that of the vibrating contact type voltage control unit, but the switching is achieved by transistors instead of vibrating contacts.

OPERATION

Alternator

With the ignition switch turned ON and the engine running, the flow of current through the rotor field coil winding energises the pole rotating electromagnet. The rotation of the motor will cause the stator windings to cut the magnetic lines of force of the rotor.

This induces an AC current voltage in the stator windings. The silicon rectifiers convert the alternating current to direct current at the output terminal, to carry the electrical load and charge the battery. The silicon rectifiers prevent the battery from discharging through the alternator.

As the rotor speed increases, the induced voltage in the stator windings increases causing more current to flow to satisfy the load requirements. However, there is another factor, commonly known as inductive reactance which has an important bearing on current control.

Inductive reactance is a counter-voltage (voltage of opposite polarity) which is also induced in the stator windings. The voltage tends to oppose the induced voltage in the stator windings. As the rotor speed increases, the counter-voltage also increases. This factor has been taken into consideration in the design of the alternator to take advantage of this factor. By designing the correct size and shape of the rotor and stator, the selection of the correct size and number of windings, the correct air gap between the rotor poles and stator, and other design features, the alternator permits inductive reactance to limit output current, therefore no current regulator is needed.

REMOVE AND INSTALL

(1) Disconnect the earth lead at the negative terminal of the battery. This is important to avoid accidentally reversing the polarity of the system and damaging the diodes in the alternator.

(2) Disconnect the leads from the B and E terminals and the F and IND connectors on the rear end of the alternator. Note the color of each lead and its position for correct installation.

(3) Loosen and remove the alternator adjusting bracket bolt, push the alternator towards the engine and remove the drive belt.

(4) Support the alternator, remove the mounting bracket bolt and remove the alternator from the vehicle.

NOTE: If air conditioning equipment is fitted it will be necessary to remove the compressor to gain access to the alternator. DO NOT disconnect the compressor hose unions. Support the compressor unit in the engine compartment after removing.

Installation is a reversal of the removal procedure with particular attention to the following points:

(1) Adjust the tension on the drive belt sufficiently to prevent slipping on the pulleys. Do not over tension the belt. When correctly adjusted the belt defection should be .500 with pressure applied between pulleys.

(2) Reconnect the wires to the correct terminals and instal the battery lead.

NOTE: When adjusting the drive belt, apply leverage to the drive end plate only and NOT to any other part of the alternator.

TO TEST IN POSITION

(1) Disconnect the battery.

(2) Remove the wires from the ammeter. (It will be necessary to partly remove the instrument panel to gain access). Connect the wires to a moving coil ammeter with a range of at least 70 amps.

(3) Remove the three wires from the control box and connect the Black and Brown/green wires together using a suitable jumper lead. The purpose of this arrangement is to connect the field windings across the battery terminals and also by-pass the control unit.

(4) Reconnect the battery lead, start the engine and gradually increase the engine speed to 2000 rpm. The ammeter should read around 40 amps. Low readings will indicate poor connections or faulty alternator. Check the condition of all associated connectors and then repeat the test.

(5) If the second test readings remain low, the field resistance of the rotor should be checked. To do this, connect an ohmmeter between the field terminal blades (external wire removed). The resistance should be in the vicinity of 3.78 ohms.

(6) This test can also be carried out using a DC power supply between the field terminals with an ammeter connected in series. The ammeter reading should be in close vicinity to 3.2 amps.

A zero reading on the ammeter or an infinity reading on the ohmmeter indicates an open circuit in the field winding circuit, i.e. winding, slip ring or brush assemblies.

If the current reading on the ammeter is much above 3.2 amps or the ohms resistance is much below 3.78 a short circuit in the rotor winding is indicated and in which case the rotor slip ring assembly must be changed or reconditioned.

NO LOAD TEST

(1) Remove all cables from the alternator terminals noting carefully the order of connection.

(2) Connect together terminals F and E.

(3) Connect the positive terminal of a 12 volt battery to alternator terminal IND and the battery negative terminal to terminal E.

(4) Connect the positive terminal of a good quality 0-20 voltmeter to terminal B and the voltmeter negative terminal to terminal E. A reading of battery terminal voltage at this stage (i.e. with the engine stationary) is indicative of one or more short-circuited field-feed diodes. Providing no reading is obtained temporarily disconnect the voltmeter, start the engine and allow to run at idling speed (500-600 rpm) then re-connect the voltmeter as before.

(5) Under these conditions a reading of approximately 13 volts can be expected. If so, disconnect the cable from the battery negative terminal, when the meter reading should rise to approximately 17 volts. If either of these readings is appreciably below the values given, the alternator must be dismantled for more detailed exami-

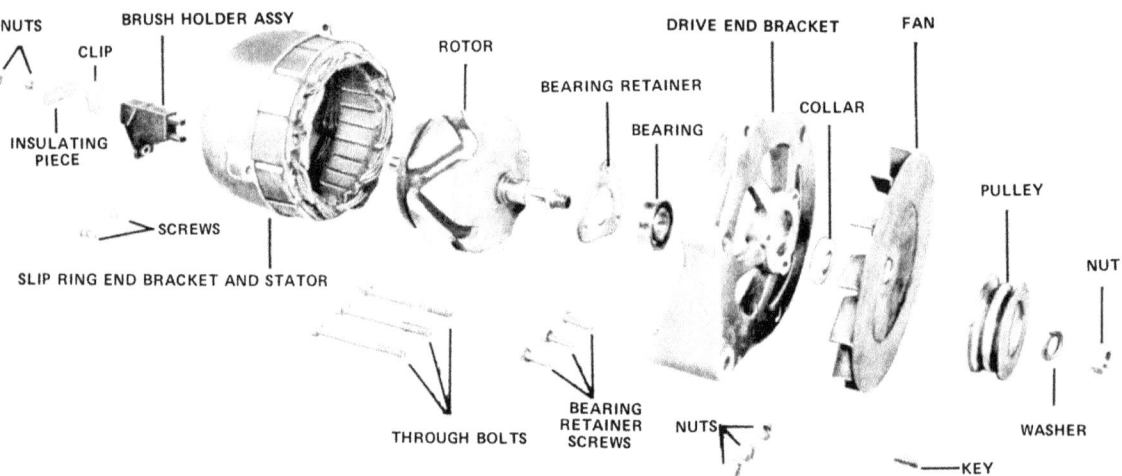

Exploded View of Alternator Components (Fitted to Later Models).

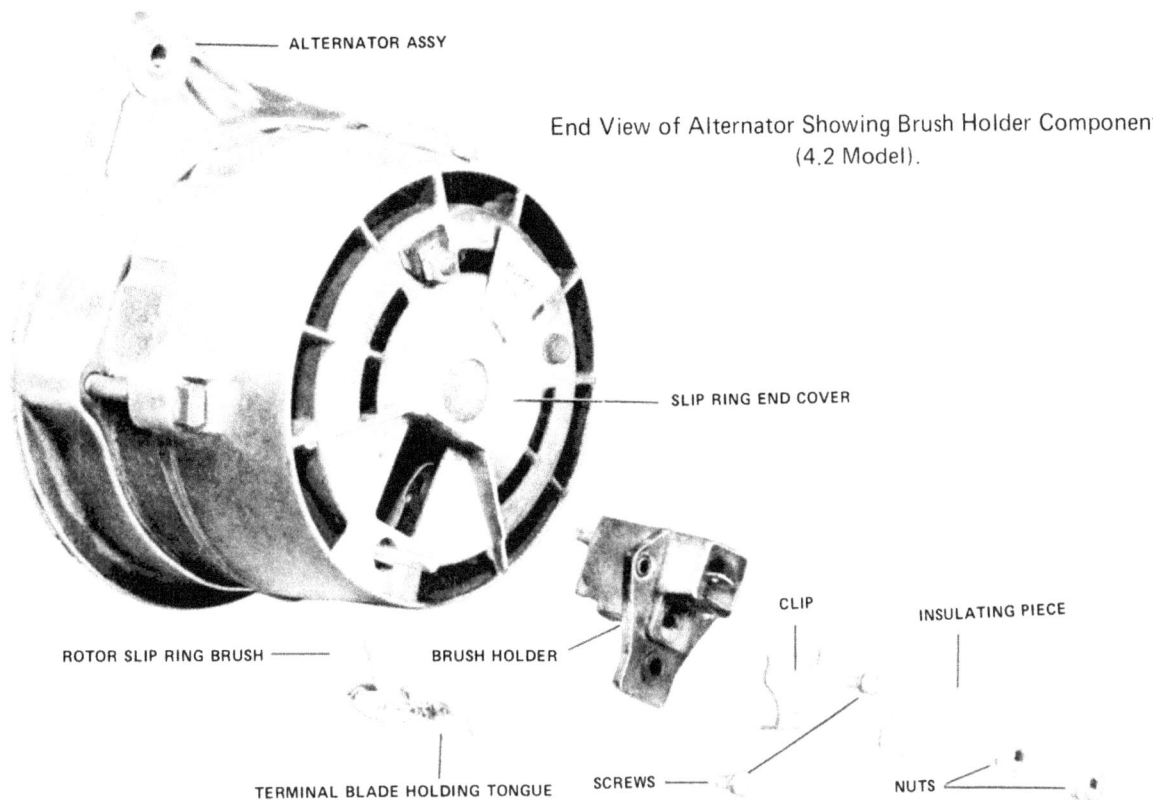

End View of Alternator Showing Brush Holder Components (4.2 Model).

nation. Providing, however, that the machine has performed satisfactorily in the *NO LOAD* test it should then be subjected to the *FULL LOAD* test as described in the following sub section.

FULL LOAD TEST

(1) Reconnect the battery negative cable.

(2) Disconnect the battery positive cable from terminal IND and connect it to a 60-0-60 ammeter, connecting the other ammeter terminal to terminal B.

(3) Connect an 0.4 ohm, 40 ampere load resistor across the battery terminals. An ammeter reading under these conditions (i.e. with the engine stationary) indicates either faulty output diodes or B terminal insulation.

(4) Start the engine and run the alternator at between 5000 and 6000 rpm. When the voltmeter is in the range 12.5 – 13.0 volts the ammeter should indicate a charge of 35-40 amperes. If the ammeter fails to register immediately momentarily link terminals B and IND.

WARNING: On completion of the FULL LOAD test the engine speed should be returned to 'idling' and the resistor disconnected from the battery BEFORE the engine is switched off. The resistor must not be disconnected from the battery whilst the alternator is delivering its full output.

If any of the foregoing tests have revealed poor alternator performance the machine must either be replaced with another of the same model or be dismantled for more detailed examination.

If however, the machine has performed satisfactorily and the charging circuit fault persists, attention should now be turned to checking the associated cables and output control unit.

DIODE TEST

Each diode can be checked as follows:

(1) Connect the diode in series with a 1.5 watt bulb across a 12 volt DC supply and then reverse the connections. Current should flow in one direction only.

(2) If the bulb lights up in both tests or does not light up on either test, then the diode is defective and the appropriate heat sink assembly must be replaced.

NOTE: The above procedure is adequate for shop service purposes. Accurate diode resistance cannot be obtained with a battery powered ohmmeter. Factory equipment is required for this purpose.

DISMANTLE AND ASSEMBLE

(1) Remove alternator from engine as described in *REMOVE AND INSTALL* section.

(2) Remove the nut and lock washer from the shaft and withdraw pulley.

(3) Remove the three nuts and withdraw the through bolts.

NOTE: The nuts are pinned to the through bolts and must be free before any attempt is made to remove them from the bolts.

(4) Suitably mark the end plates and body so that they can be reassembled correctly.

(5) Withdraw the end plate and rotor from the stator. It is not necessary to remove the end plate and bearing from the rotor and unless it is necessary to renew the bearing, end plate etc. it is advisable not to disturb these units. Where it is necessary to remove these assemblies a hand press should be used to press the bearing assembly from the shaft.

(6) Remove the terminal nuts, washers, insulating pieces, brush box screws and the two hexagon headed screws and remove the stator and heat sink assemblies from the slip ring end plate.

(7) Withdraw the brush spring and terminal assemblies from the moulded brush box.

TO ASSEMBLE

Assembly is the reversal of the dismantling procedure with particular attention to the following:

Care must be taken to ensure the alignment of the drive end plate, laminated pack and slip ring end plate.

The through bolts should be tightened evenly and to a maximum torque of 50 in/lbs.

INSPECTION OF BRUSHGEAR

(1) A new brush is .625" long. The brush is considered to be fully worn when no more than .15625" protrudes beyond the face of the brush box moulding with the brush spring in the uncompressed state, i.e. with the moulding withdrawn from the machine. This corresponds to approximately .3125" overall remaining brush length.

(2) The normal brush spring pressures are 4-5 oz. with the spring compressed to .78125" in length and 7½-8½ oz. with the spring compressed to .40625" in length.

(3) Check that the brushes move freely in their holders. If at all sluggish, clean the brush sides with a petrol-moistened cloth or, if this fails to effect a cure, lightly polish the brush sides on a smooth file. Remove all traces of brush dust before repositioning the brushes in their holders.

INSPECTION OF SLIP-RINGS

The surfaces of the slip-rings should be smooth and uncontaminated by oil or other foreign matter. Clean the surfaces using a petrol-moistened cloth or, if there is any evidence of burning, very fine glasspaper. On no account must emery cloth or similar abrasives be used. No attempt should be made to machine the slip-rings as any eccentricity

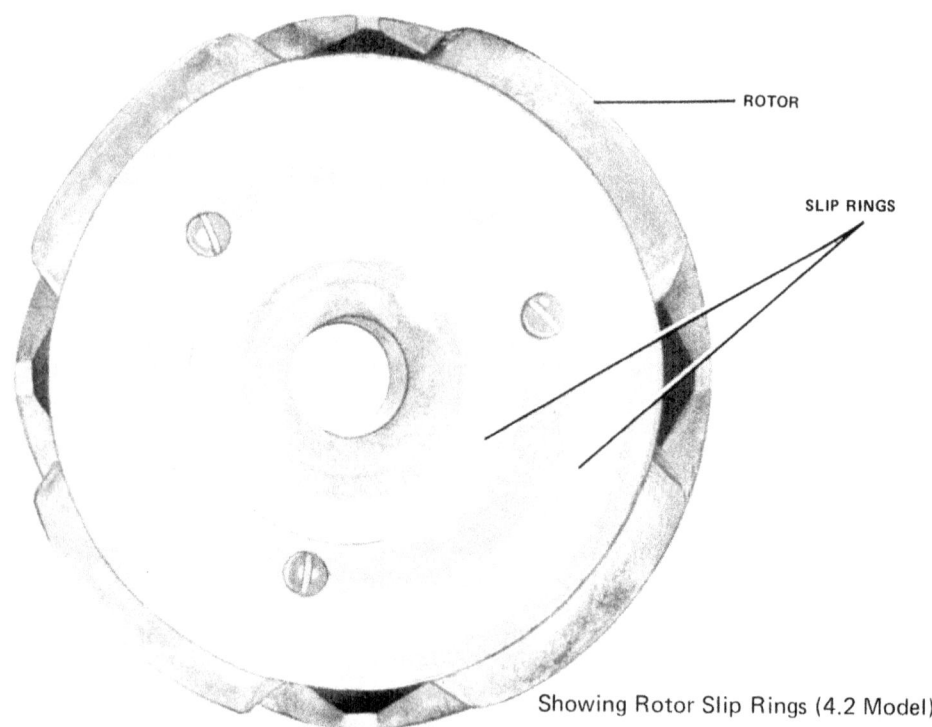

Showing Rotor Slip Rings (4.2 Model).

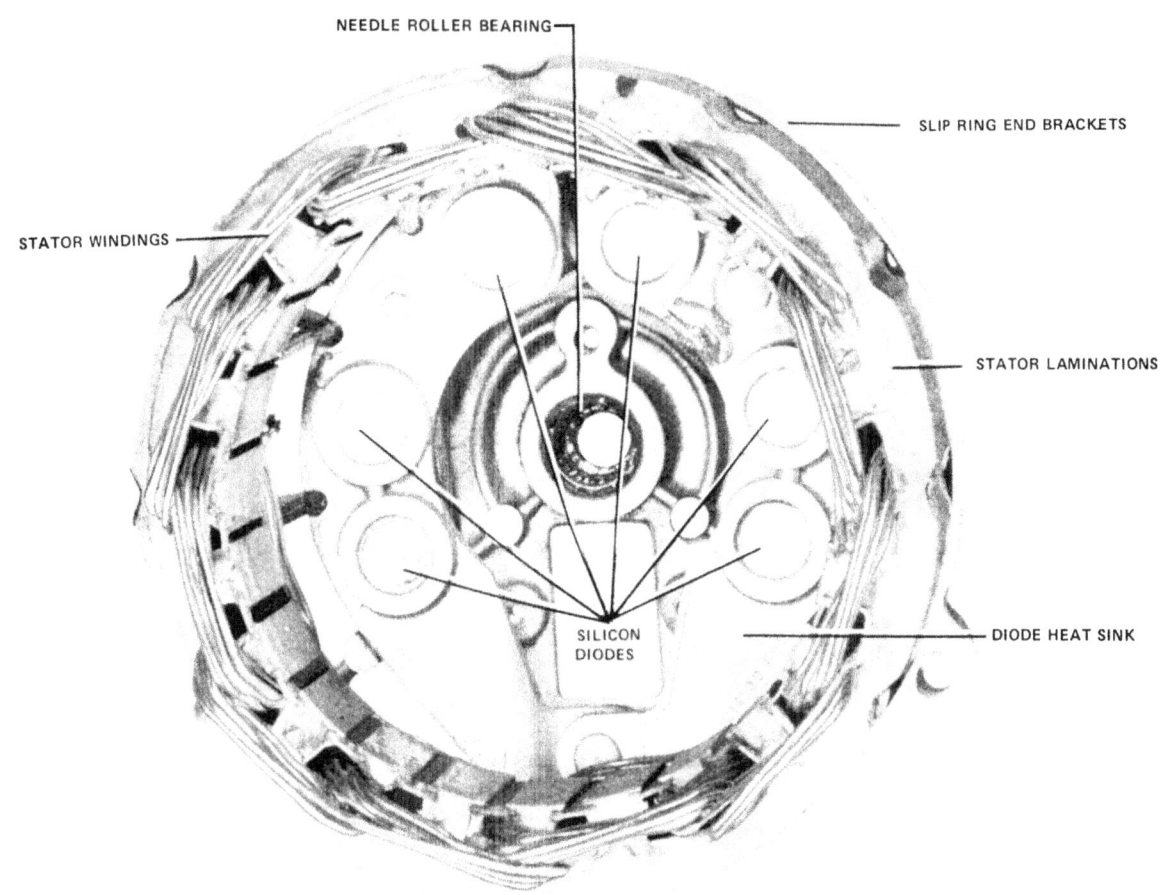

Showing Stator and Heat Sink Components (4.2 Model).

in the machining may adversely affect the high speed performance of the alternator. The small current carried by the rotor winding, and the unbroken surface of the slip-rings mean that the likelihood of scored or pitted slip-rings is almost negligible. Squealing brushes can be overcome by spraying the whole slip-ring assembly with CRC 2-26 formula compound which has beneficial effects on conductivity.

BEARINGS

Bearings which are worn to the extent that they allow excessive side movement of the rotor shaft must be renewed.

SLIP-RING END BRACKET BEARING REPLACEMENT

IMPORTANT: This operation will be undertaken with the stator and slip-ring end plate still joined. To ensure that the stator windings are not exposed to damage by crushing use a length of tubing, 1" in internal diameter and 4-6" in length, to contact the inner face of the end bracket (and thus to support the assembly) whilst pressing out the bearing and its end seal from the outside end of the end plate. The fitting pin must be either of tubular construction or concave-faced so that pressure is applied only to the periphery of the bearing.

Press in the replacement bearing from the same direction, until the distance from the open end of the bearing and the inner face of the plate is 0.170".

Finally, fit the replacement end seal flush with the face.

DRIVE-END BRACKET BEARING REPLACEMENT

To renew the drive-end ball bearing (following withdrawal of the rotor shaft from the drive-end plate) proceed as follows:

File away the roll-over on each of the three bearing retaining plate rivets and punch out the rivets.

Press the bearing out of the end plate.

Before fitting the replacement bearing see that it is clean and, if necessary, pack it with high melting point grease.

The bearing is shielded on one side. When the bearing is fitted this shielded side must be positioned towards the outside of the drive end plate.

Locate the bearing in the housing and press it home.

Refit the bearing retaining plate using new rivets.

REGULATOR

CHECK AND ADJUST

The regulator is adjusted by means of a screw situated in the base of the unit. To gain access to the screw it is necessary to remove the regulator from the holding bracket and scrape away the black sealing compound used to protect the adjustment screw. It is important that the seal is removed only while the engine is stationary and that a jumper lead is connected from the metal firing bracket to a good earth on the vehicle before the engine is started up.

The setting of the regulator can only be checked when the battery is in a good state of charge.

(1) Remove unit from holding bracket.

(2) Remove sealing to expose adjusting screw.

(3) Apply a load of approximately 2 amps, i.e. switch on side lights.

(4) Connect a jumper lead from the unit bracket to a good earth.

(5) Connect a voltmeter across the battery terminals.

(6) Start engine and run the alternator at 3000 rpm, (1500 engine rpm). Voltage should rise to 13.9 ± .2 volts.

(7) If the voltage is steady but outside these limits adjustment can be made by turning the adjustment screw

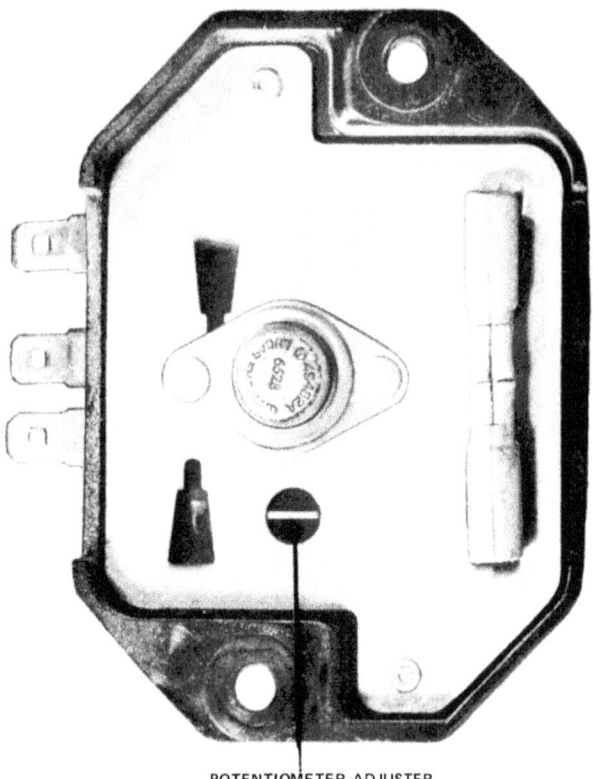

Rear View of Alternator Output Control Box Showing Potentiometer Adjuster (4.2 Model).

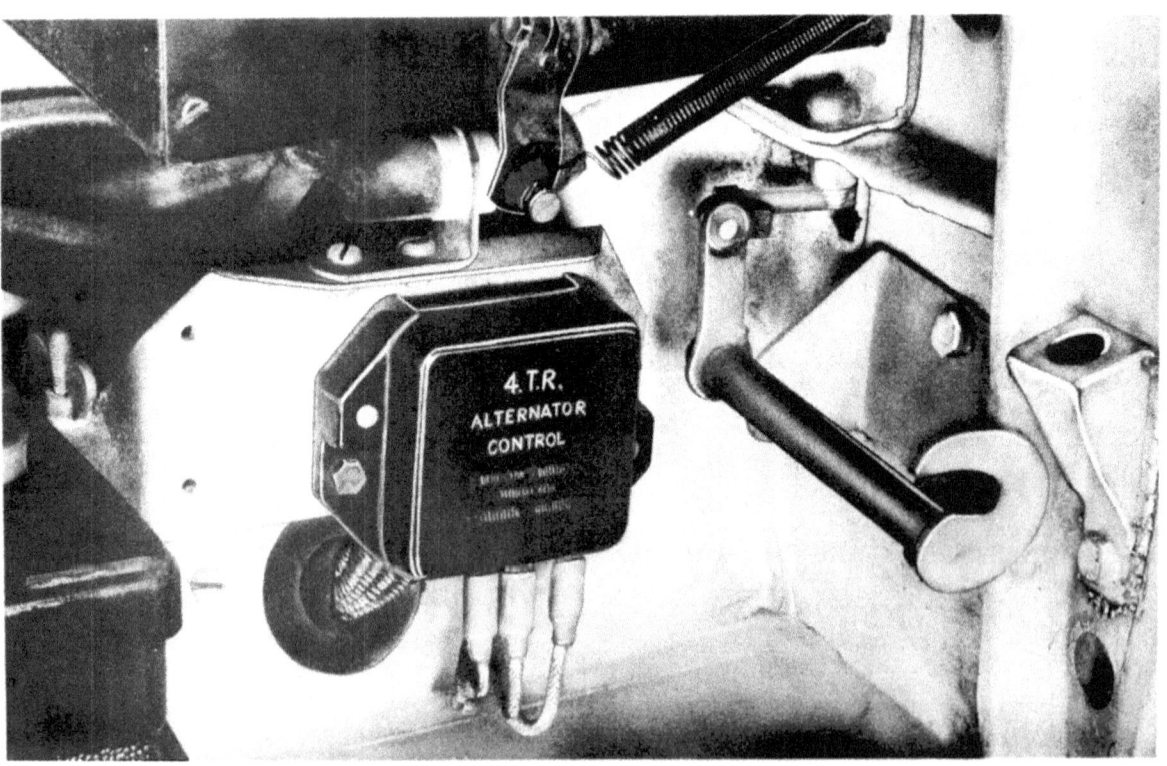

The Alternator Output Control Unit (4.2 Model).

clockwise to increase the setting or anti-clockwise to decrease it.

NOTE: If the correct adjustment tool (Lucas 62380157) is not available, the adjustment must only be turned when the engine is stationary.

Failure to observe this procedure will result in damage to the unit.

(8) After any adjustment re-check as described in the foregoing.

(9) Stop engine, remove jumper lead and refit unit to holding bracket.

4. WARNING LIGHT CONTROL UNIT

DESCRIPTION

Later model vehicles are fitted with a sealed device that works in conjunction with the ignition warning light to give indication that the alternator is charging. The unit is designated as a Model 3AW Warning Light Control Unit and it is connected to the centre point of one of the pairs of diodes in the alternator.

The unit is mounted near the regulator unit and is similar in appearance to the flasher unit but is an entirely different type of unit, consisting of an electrolytic polarised capacitor, a resister and a silicon diode. The unit can be identified by a distinctive green label attached to the aluminium case.

The unit being sealed is not adjustable and checking of the unit function is by substitution.

NOTE: A faulty diode in the alternator unit or an intermittent or open circuit can cause excessive voltages to be applied to the warning light unit.

TO RENEW

Before renewing a suspect unit, check the voltage between the AL terminal and earth as follows:

(1) Connect a voltmeter between terminal AL and a good earth.

(2) Run the engine at 1500 rpm, when the voltage should be 7 – 7.5 volts.

(3) If a higher voltage reading is obtained check that all associated circuits and connections are clean and tight and check the alternator diodes. Refer to *DIODE TEST* in the alternator section.

5. STARTER MOTOR

DESCRIPTION

The starter motor is a 12 volt four pole, four brush unit. Early model cars were fitted with the Lucas M45G inertia engagement type. Later models and the 4.20 and 2 + 2 cars were fitted with the M45G pre-engagement type starter unit.

With the exception of the pre-engagement apparatus and some minor specifications, the two starter units are basically the same in construction and operation.

TO TEST IN POSITION

Switch on the lamps and operate the starter control.

If the lights go dim, but the starter motor is not heard to operate, the indication is given that the current is flowing through the starter motor windings, but the armature is not rotating for some reason; possibly the pinion is locked in mesh with the geared ring on the flywheel. In this case the motor must be removed from the engine for examination.

Should the lamps retain their full brilliance when the starter switch is operated, check the circuit for continuity from battery to starter motor via the starter switch, and examine the connectors at these units. If the switch is found to be faulty, a new switch must be fitted. If the supply voltage is found to be applied to the motor when the switch is operated, an internal fault in the motor is indicated and the unit must be removed from the engine for examination.

Sluggish or slow action of the starter motor is usually caused by a poor connection in the wiring, giving rise to a high resistance in the starter motor circuit. Check as described above.

If the starter motor is heard to operate, but does not crank the engine, indication is given of damage to the drive.

TO REMOVE AND INSTALL

(1) Disconnect the battery earth lead.

(2) Disconnect the battery cable from the solenoid switch on the starter (inertia type, remove cable from starter terminal).

(3) Remove the distributor clamping plate retaining screw and withdraw the distributor.

(4) Remove the two bolts securing starter to the clutch housing. Carefully bend away fuel drain pipes and remove starter through chassis frame.

NOTE: The two holding bolts are accessible from beneath the car or through an access panel in the right hand side of the gear box tunnel.

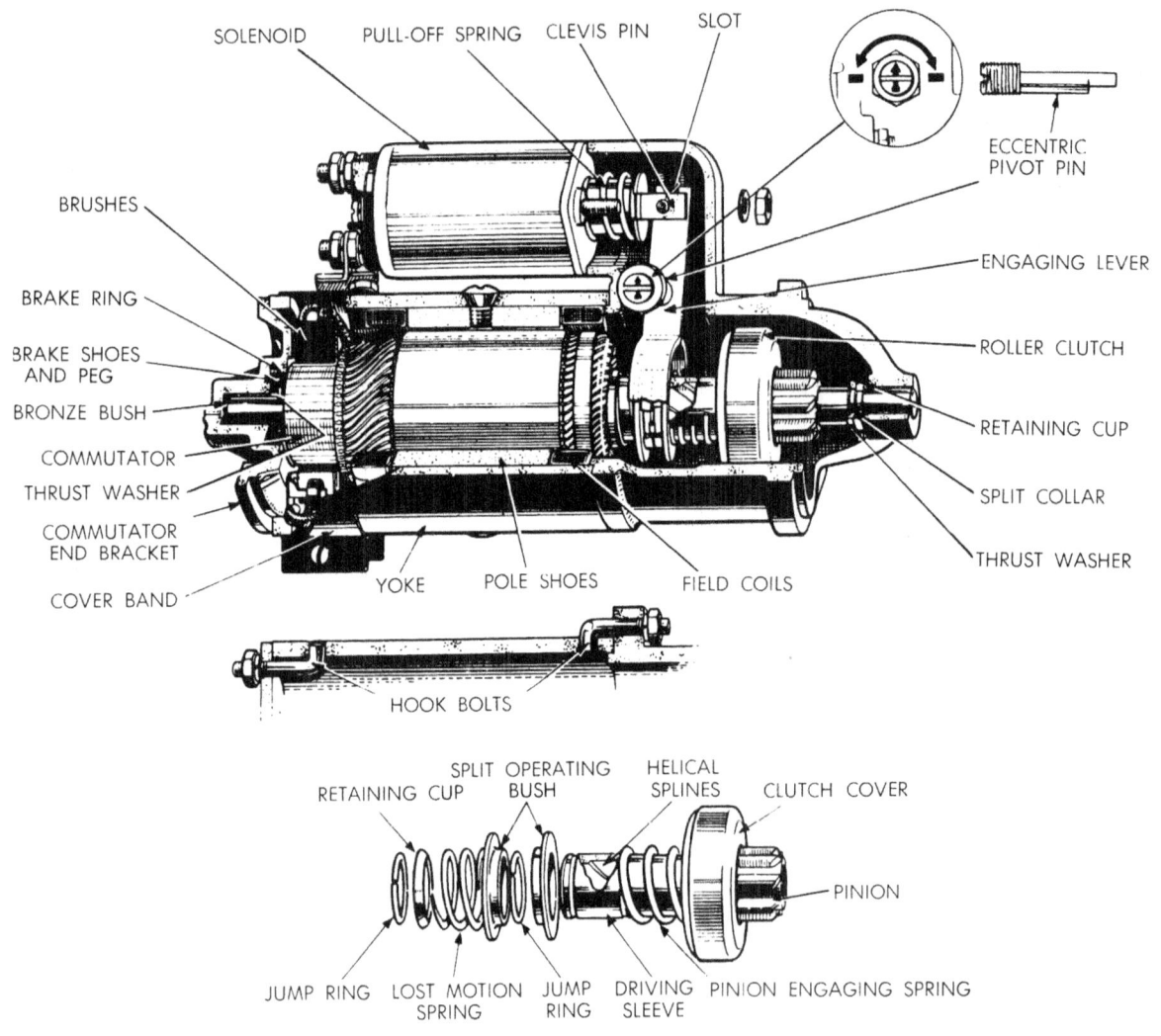

Sectioned View of the Pre-engaged Type Starter Motor (4.2 Model).

(5) Installation is the reversal of the foregoing procedure.

DISMANTLE AND REASSEMBLE

MG45 Pre-engagement.

(1) Disconnect the copper link between the lower solenoid terminal and the starter body.

(2) Remove the solenoid securing nuts. Disconnect the extension cables and withdraw the solenoid from the end casting, disconnect the solenoid plunger from the drive engagement lever.

(3) Unscrew the two through bolts from the commutator end plate. The commutator end plate and the body can now be removed from the intermediate and drive end brackets.

(4) Remove the rubber seal from the drive end plate slacken the nut securing the eccentric pin on which the starter drive engagement lever pivots. Unscrew and withdraw the pin.

(5) Remove the end plate from the armature and intermediate assembly.

(6) Remove the thrust washer from the end of the armature shaft using a mild steel tube of suitable bore size. Prise the jump ring from its groove and slide the drive assembly and intermediate end plate from the shaft.

(7) The drive can be further dismantled by prising off the jump ring retaining the operating bush and engagement spring.

(8) Assembly is the reversal of the dismantle procedure.

M45G Inertia.

(1) Loosen off and remove the cover band, lift each brush spring to allow the brushes to be withdrawn from their holders.

(2) Remove the terminal nuts from the post at the commutator end bracket and unscrew the two through bolts.

(3) Detach the commutator end bracket from the yoke and withdraw the drive end bracket complete with armature.

(4) Take out the split pin from the starter drive nut, hold the square at the commutator end of the shaft with a spanner and unscrew the shaft nut.

(5) Withdraw from the shaft the main spring, washer, pinion and sleeve, collar, restraining spring and sleeve in that order.

(6) Assembly is a reversal of the dismantle procedure.

TO TEST FIELD COILS

Test the field coils for continuity by connecting a 12 volt battery with a 12 volt bulb in series between the tapping points of the field coils at which the brushes are connected. Failure of the lamp to light indicates an open circuit in the wiring of the field coils.

Lighting of the lamp does not necessarily mean that the field coils are in order, as it is possible that one of them may be earthed to a pole shoe or to the body. This may be checked with a 110 volt test lamp, the test leads being connected to one of the field coil tapping points and to a clean part of the body. Should the lamp light, it indicates that the field coils are earthed to the body.

In either case, unless a replacement starter motor is available, the field coils must be replaced. To do this, carry out the procedure outlined below, using a pole shoe expander and a wheel-operated screwdriver.

(1) Remove the insulation piece which is provided to prevent the inter-coil connector from contact with the body.

(2) Mark the body and pole shoes in order that they can be fitted in their original positions.

(3) Unscrew the four pole shoe retaining screws by means of a wheel-operated screwdriver.

(4) Draw the pole shoes and coils out of the body and lift off the coils.

(5) Fit the new field coils over the pole shoes and place them in position inside the body. Take care to ensure that the taping of the field coils is not trapped between the pole shoes and the body.

(6) Locate the pole shoes and field coils by lightly tightening the fixing screws.

(7) Insert the pole shoe expander, open it to the fullest extent and tighten the screws.

(8) Finally tighten the screws by means of the wheel operated screwdriver.

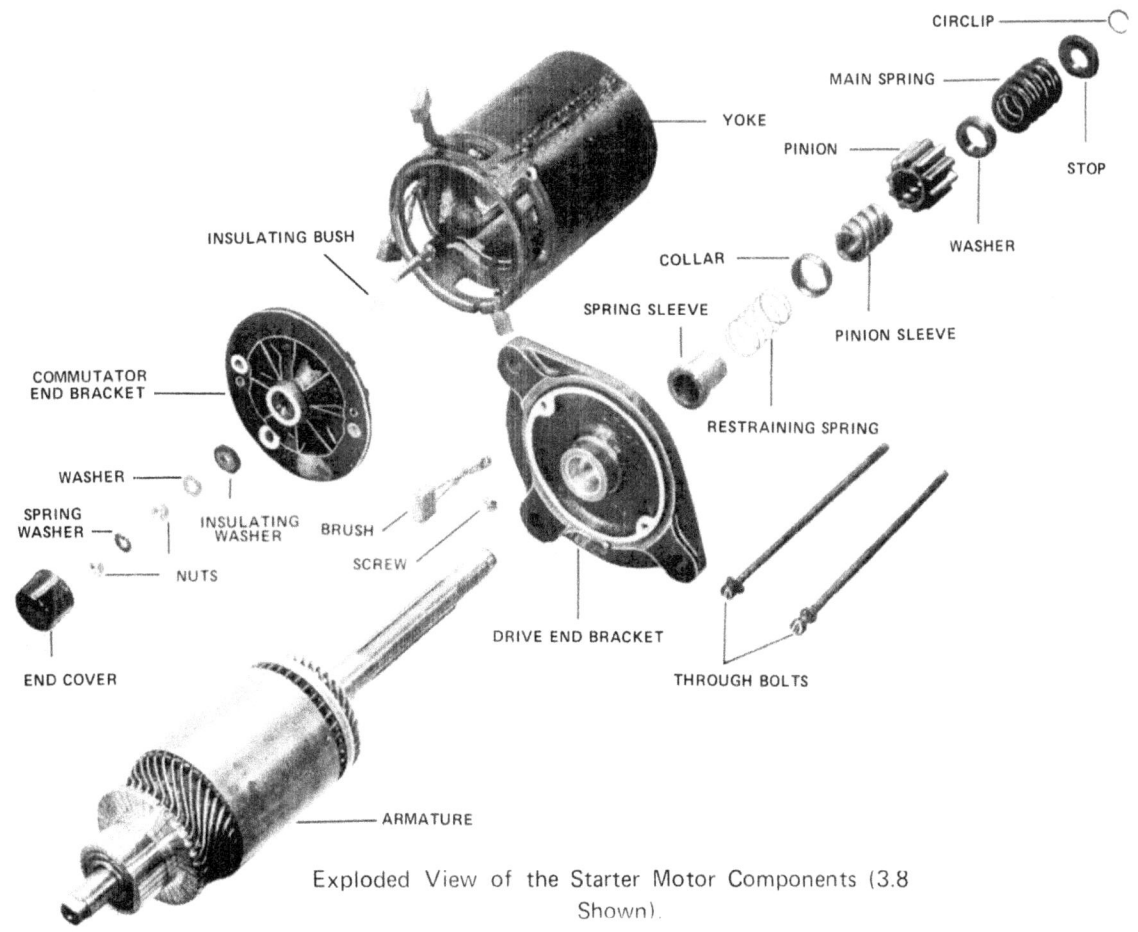

Exploded View of the Starter Motor Components (3.8 Shown).

(9) Replace the insulation piece between the field connection and the body.

TO CHECK ARMATURE

Examination of the armature may reveal the cause of the failure, i.e. conductors lifted from the commutator due to the starter being engaged while the engine is running and causing the armature to be rotated at an excessive speed. A damaged armature must in all cases be replaced.

No attempt should be made to machine the armature core or true a distorted armature shaft.

TO TEST ARMATURE

(1) Before proceeding further, clean the armature.

(2) To test for short circuit, place the armature in a growler, and hold a piece of steel strip over the top of the armature in line with the shaft, slowly revolve the armature, keeping the steel strip in the same position.

If a short circuit exists, the steel strip will be heavily attracted towards the slot containing the faulty coil. Having located the fault on one side continue rotating the armature, when a second faulty slot will be found.

OPEN CIRCUIT TEST

Open circuits can occur in the commutator segments or in the armature windings and can be located by the following procedure:

(1) Using a 12 volt battery and voltmeter with test prods, connect one lead and prod to the negative pole of the battery and connect a voltmeter and the other lead to the positive pole of the battery.

(2) Place the prods on each pair of adjacent commutator segments in turn and note the voltmeter readings. If the armature is in good order all readings will be similar. A pair of segments with a low or zero reading means that one or more adjacent coils are open circuited.

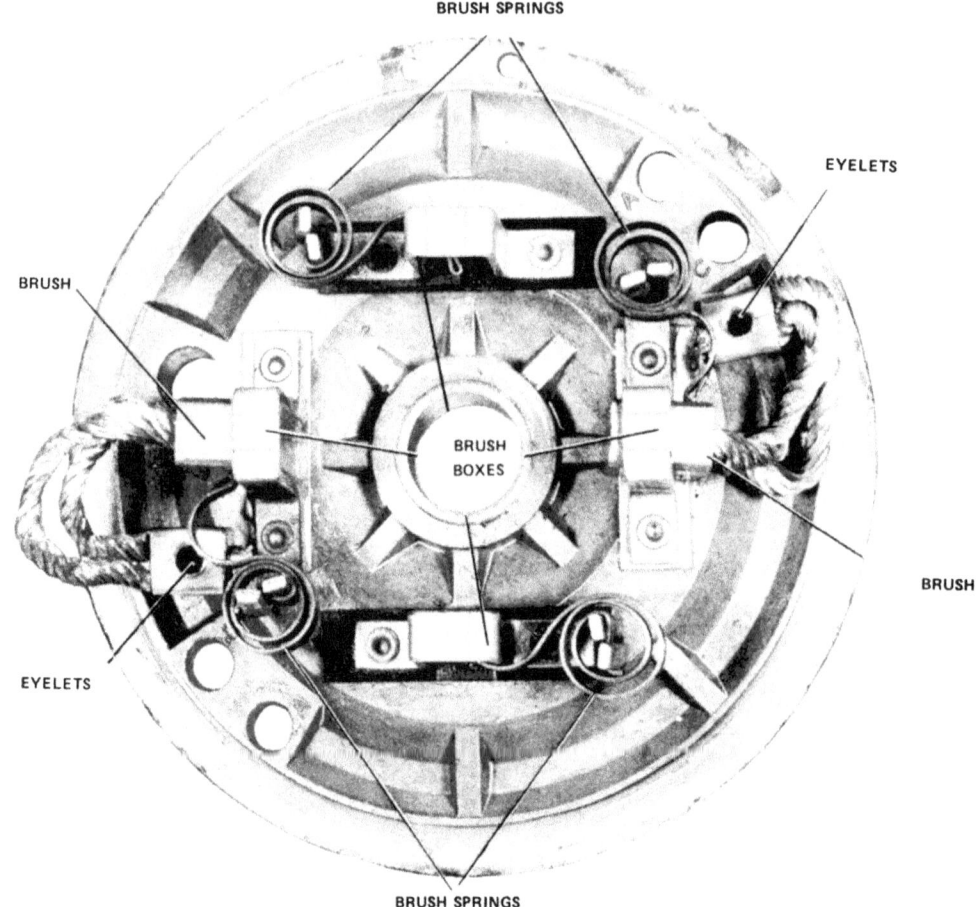

Showing Brush Arrangment on Commutator End Bracket
(3.8 Shown).

TO TEST BRUSH GEAR AND COMMUTATOR

If it is necessary to remove the motor from the engine, first proceed as follows:

(1) Disconnect the cable from the positive battery terminal to avoid any damage by causing short circuits.

(2) Disconnect the heavy cable from the starter motor.

(3) After removing the starter motor from the engine, secure the body in a vice and test by connecting it with heavy gauge cables to a 12 volt battery. One cable must be connected to the starter terminal and the other held against the body or end plate. Under these light load conditions, the starter should run at a very high speed.

(4) If the operation of the motor is unsatisfactory, remove the cover band and examine the brushes and commutator. Hold back each of the brush springs and move the brush by pulling gently on its flexible connector. If the movement is sluggish, remove the brush from its holder and ease the slides by lightly polishing on a smooth file. Always replace the brushes in their original positions. If the brushes are worn so that they will not bear on the commutator, or if the brush flexible connector is exposed on the running face, they must be replaced.

(5) Check the tension of the brush springs with a spring scale. The correct tension is 30 to 40 ozs. (inertia type) and 50 ozs. for pre-engaged unit (new brushes). A new spring should be fitted if the tension is low.

(6) If the commutator is blackened or dirty, clean it by holding a petrol-moistened cloth against it while the armature is rotated.

(7) Re-test the starter as described above, if the operation is still unsatisfactory, the unit must be dismantled for detailed inspection and testing.

TO RENEW BRUSHES

(1) Remove brushes from holders.

(2) Unsolder the two fixed brush leads that are attached to the field eyelets.

(3) Re-solder the two new brush leads to the eyelets.

(4) The other two brushes and leads can be removed by removing the two terminal screws.

(5) The brushes are pre-formed so that bedding to the commutator is not necessary.

TO RENEW BEARINGS

Bearings that are worn to such an extent that they will allow excessive side play of the armature shaft must be replaced. To replace the bearing bushes proceed as follows:

(1) Press the bearing bush out of the end plate.

(2) Press the new bearing bush into the end plate, using a shouldered, highly polished mandrel of the same diameter as the shaft which is to fit in the bearing. Porous bronze

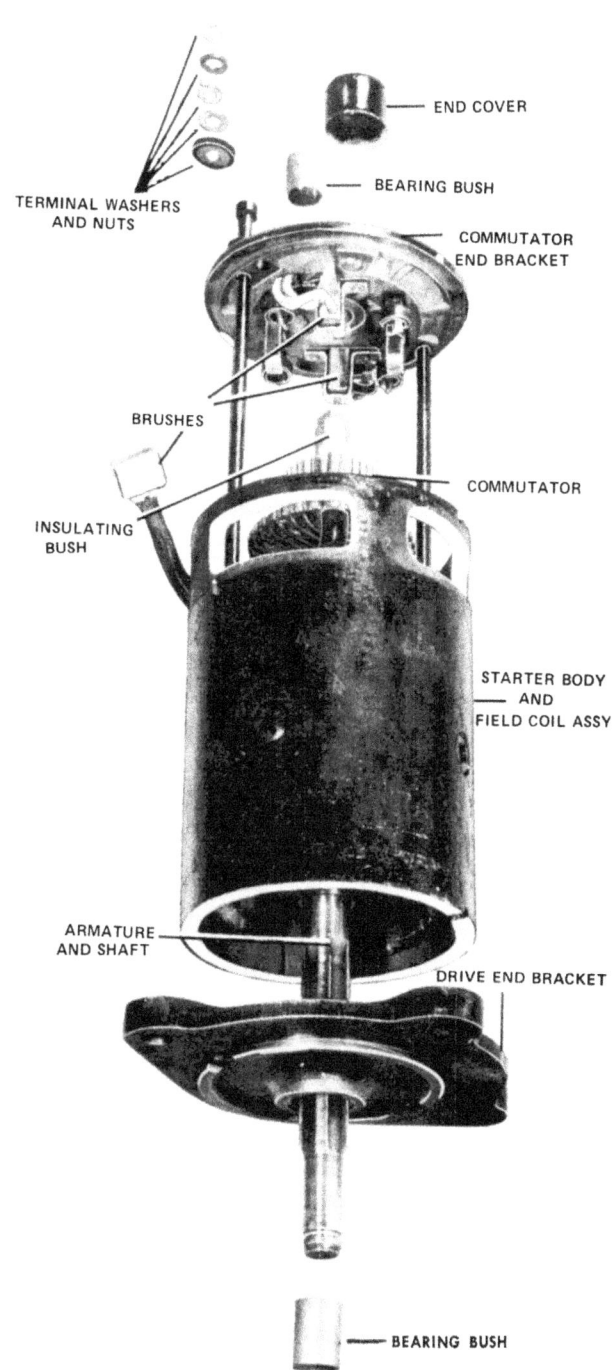

Exploded View of the Starter Motor Showing Bearing Bushes for End Brackets (3.8 Shown).

bushes must not be opened out after fitting, or the porosity of the bush will be impaired.

NOTE: Before fitting a new porous bronze bearing bush, it should be completely immersed for 24 hours in clean thin engine oil. In cases of extreme urgency this period may be shortened by heating the oil to 212°F, and allowing the bush to remain completely immersed until the oil returns to normal temperature.

TO CHECK AND ADJUST PINION MOVEMENT (PRE-ENGAGEMENT)

(1) Connect the solenoid terminal to a six volt supply. Connect the other side of the supply to the solenoid body.

(2) Application of this current will cause the switch to close, throwing the drive assembly forward and into drive position.

(3) Measure the clearance between the pinion and the thrust washer on the armature shaft extension. When taking this measurement, press the pinion slightly towards the armature to compensate for any slack in the engagement assembly. The correct clearance is .005" – .015".

(4) To adjust the setting, slacken the eccentric pivot pin securing nut and turn the pin until the correct clearance is obtained.

(5) After adjustment tighten the securing nut to retain the pin position.

NOTE: The arc of the adjustment is 180° and the head of the arrow marked on the pivot pin should be set only between the arrows on the arc scribed on the end of the body.

TO CHECK OPERATION OF STARTER SWITCH

The following tests are based on the assumption that the setting as described in *TO CHECK AND ADJUST PINION* are correct.

(1) Remove the copper link connecting the solenoid terminal 'STA' with the motor terminal.

(2) Connect a 10 volt DC supply through a switch on the series winding, i.e. between the solenoid bayonet terminal and large 'STA' terminal.

(3) Do not close the switch at this stage but connect a separately energised test lamp circuit across the solenoid main terminals.

(4) Insert a stop in the drive end bracket to restrict the pinion travel to that of out-of-mesh clearance, normally a nominal .125". The jaws of a spanner can be utilised for this purpose.

(5) Energise the shunt winding with a 10-volt supply and then close the switch with the series winding circuit. The solenoid contacts should close fully and remain closed, as indicated by the test lamp being switched on and emitting a steady light.

(6) Switch off power supply and remove stop. Switch on again and hold the pinion assembly in the fully engaged position. Switch off and observe the test lamp. The solenoid contacts should open, as indicated by the test lamp being switched off.

6. DISTRIBUTOR AND IGNITION CIRCUIT

TO REMOVE AND INSTAL

(1) If it is desired to remove the distributor for overhaul, without upsetting the ignition timing, do not release the clamp plate pinch bolt.

(2) Mark the location of the clamp plate on the crankcase to facilitate replacement.

(3) Turn the engine over until the distributor rotor arm is pointing to the cover segment for No. 1 cylinder plug lead and the 0 on the crankshaft damper is in line with the pointer attached to the front of the engine sump.

(4) With the cap removed, disconnect the low tension lead at the distributor terminal and remove the vacuum advance pipe.

(5) Remove the bolt securing the distributor clamp plate to the crankcase and withdraw the distributor. Do not rotate the crankshaft until the distributor has been replaced.

(6) Installation is the reversal of the foregoing procedure.

TO DISMANTLE

NOTE: It is extremely important that, before dismantling the distributor, a careful note is made of the relative positions of the various components to ensure correct replacement on reassembly. This will apply particularly to the rotor arm drive slot in the cam spindle in relation to the offset driving dog at the drive end of the spindle, to avoid assembling 180° out. Components of the centrifugal weight assembly need not be dismantled unless they are to be renewed.

(1) With the distributor cap removed, remove the rotor arm.

(2) Remove the nut and washer from the contact breaker arm spring anchor. Withdraw, in the following order: the insulating sleeve, condenser lead, low tension lead, contact breaker arm spring, at the same time sliding the contact breaker arm off its pivot pin and remove the large insulating washer from the pivot pin and the small one from the anchor pin.

(3) Remove the two screws with spring and flat washers and lift off the fixed contact. Slide out the low tension terminal and lead. Remove the vacuum diaphragm connecting link.

(4) Remove the condenser and contact breaker base plate, noting that one of the screws securing the base plate to the distributor body also secures the earth lead.

(5) Remove the screw from the centre of spindle and lift off the cam.

(6) Lift off the centrifugal weights as two assemblies. These assemblies need not be dismantled further unless the components are to be renewed.

(7) Release the circlip and remove the adjusting nut and spring and withdraw the vacuum advance unit, taking care not to lose the adjusting nut lock clip.

(8) Mark the position of the driving gear in relation to the shaft, drive out the pin retaining the driving gear and remove the driving gear and thrust washer.

Remove the shaft from the distributor body.

TO REASSEMBLE

Reassembling the distributor is a direct reversal of the dismantling procedure, with particular attention to the following:

(1) Check the rotor electrode and the distributor cap carbon brush for burning and looseness. Check that the contact breaker points are clean and serviceable. They must be flat and free from burning and pitting.

(2) Check all parts for wear and renew as necessary. If a new bush is to be fitted use a shouldered mandrel to instal the bush. The new bush should be allowed to stand in thin engine oil for 24 hours prior to fitting and should not be reamed to size.

(3) Inspect the top ball type bearing condition and lubricate. Renew if any side play is evident.

(4) Lubricate each component as necessary with thin engine oil and fit all components in their original positions in the centrifugal weight assemblies.

(5) Adjust the contact breaker point gap. (See Specifications).

TO INSTALL

Installation is a reversal of the removal procedure, but it is necessary that attention be given to the following points:

If the engine crankshaft has been rotated with the distributor removed it will be necessary to set No. 1 piston on the compression stroke and install the distributor as described in *TO TIME IGNITION*.

If the engine has not been disturbed with the distributor removed, carry out operation (3) to (10) inclusive as described in *TO TIME IGNITION*.

TO ADJUST IGNITION TIMING

Ignition adjustment is made on the micrometer adjusting nut at the end of the vacuum advance unit, which is calibrated at the opposite end of the adjusting spindle barrel, each calibration representing approximately 4° timing variation. Clockwise rotation of the adjusting nut advances, and anti-clockwise retards the ignition.

The micrometer adjustment range is normally sufficient to compensate for variations in fuel quality and it should not be necessary to disturb the distributor clamp bolt, unless the ignition timing has been lost during the distributor removal.

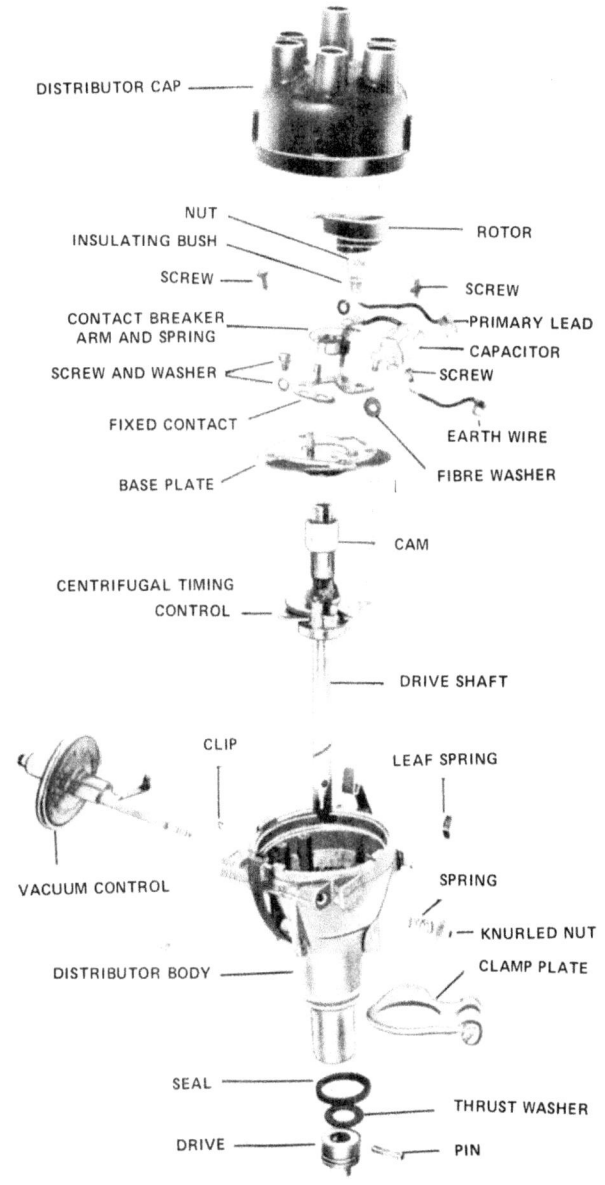

Exploded View of Distributor Components (3.8 Model Shown).

USING A STROBOSCOPE

(1) Ensure that the timing marks on the crankshaft damper are in a clean and visible condition. If necessary add white paint or chalk.

(2) Connect the instrument in accordance with type and make of the equipment.

(3) Start the engine and adjust the idle to 500 rpm at normal running temperature.

NOTE: It is most important that this setting be correct otherwise operation of the vacuum advance mechanism will cause inaccurate readings.

(4) Aim the light onto the timing pointer on the front cover and check that the appropriate marks appear to be in the correct position.

(5) If the mark is to the left of the correct position the timing is retarded. Advance the timing by turning the distributor body anti-clockwise If the mark is to the right of the correct position, turn the body of the distributor clockwise to retard.

(6) Stop the engine and reconnect the vacuum pipe to the distributor.

TO CHECK OPERATION OF VACUUM ADVANCE USING STROBOSCOPE

(1) Lubricate the advance mechanism and disconnect the vacuum advance feed pipe at the carburettor.

(2) Connect the instrument in accordance with type and make of equipment and start engine.

(3) Aim the light onto the crankshaft damper and observe the timing marks, gradually increase the engine speed from idle to approximately 3000 rpm. The distance between the mark on the pulley and the set pointer on the front cover should increase with the speed of the engine. This indicates that the centrifugal advance mechanism is operating. A jerky movement of the timing marks during increase or decrease of engine speed, indicates sticking mechanism and this should be corrected before proceeding further with the operation.

(4) Adjust the engine speed to approximately 1500 rpm and while still observing the marks on the crankshaft pulley, reconnect and disconnect the vacuum line to the carburettor several times. This should cause the vacuum advance to come in and out of operation. This will be

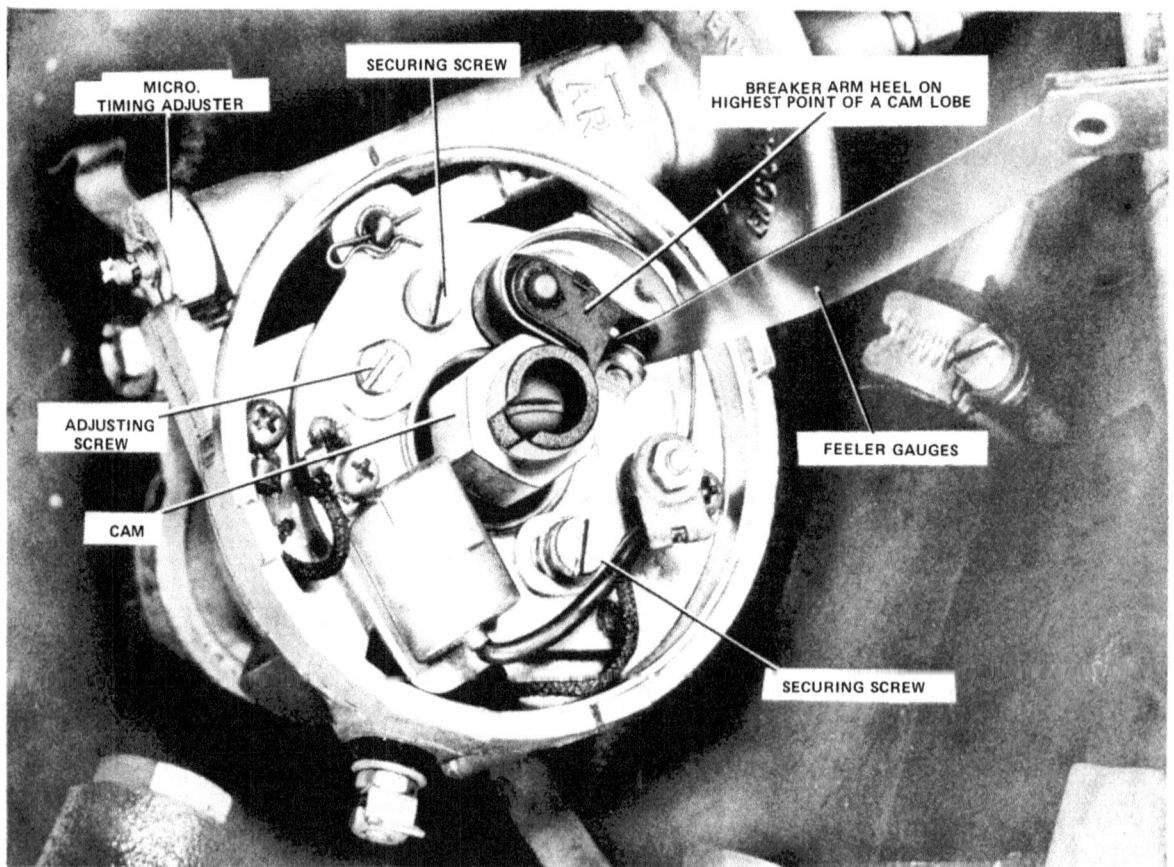

Using **Feeler Gauges** to Check the Points Gap.

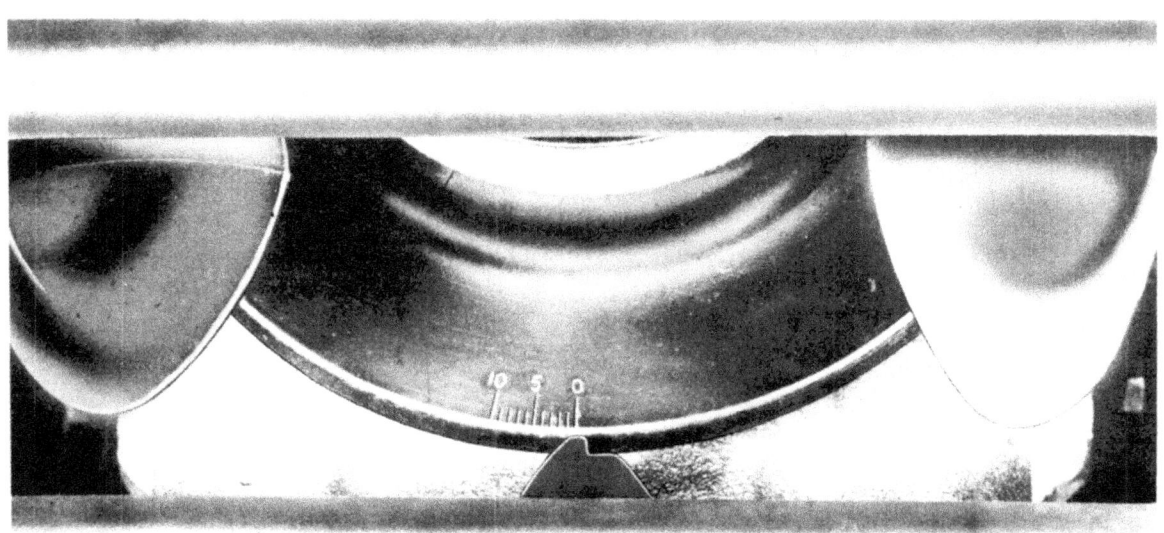

Ignition Timing Marks on Crankshaft Damper.

evident from the changing position of the timing marks on the crankshaft pulley.

(5) If there are no changes in the timing marks position during this operation, the unit will have to be removed and checked for sticking parts, blocked line, punctured diaphragm etc.

TO ADJUST CONTACT BREAKER POINTS

At intervals of approximately 6000 miles the contact breaker points should be removed and inspected.

Points that are badly pitted and burned should be renewed. Points that are still serviceable should be cleaned up to a smooth, square surface on a fine oil stone. Remove all traces of oil from the points by washing in petrol as oil or grease on the points will cause pitting and burning.

(1) With the distributor cap and rotor removed, turn the engine until the heel of the moving contact is on the highest point of a cam lobe. The contact points should now be at the point of maximum opening.

(2) Check the point gap with a feeler gauge. The gap should be from .014" to .016". The feeler gauge should be a sliding fit between the points.

(3) To adjust the gap, loosen the fixed contact lock screws, move the fixed contact in the required direction by turning the adjusting screw. Tighten the lock screw when the gap setting is correct.

(4) Apply a single drop of light engine oil to the moving contact pivot pin and, using a spring scale, check the contact breaker spring tension at right angles to the contact points. Spring tension at the points should be 18 to 24 ozs. Apply a slight smear of high melting point grease to the cam.

(5) Replace the rotor and distributor cap.

TO TIME IGNITION

Where engines are operating on premium grade fuels above 90 octane the correct static timing is on 8 to 1 compression ratio, 9° btdc, and 10° btdc on 9 to 1 compression ratio.

The following procedure should be used to reset the distributor when the original setting has been lost.

(1) Turn the engine in a clockwise direction as viewed from the front of the vehicle until the No. 6 piston approaches tdc on compression stroke.

(2) Continue to turn the engine until the timing pointer (attached to the end of the sump), is in line with the correct mark, i.e. 9 to 1 compression ratio models, the pointer should align with the 10° mark, on the crankshaft damper.

(3) Adjust the micrometer (octane selector) adjustment to the mid point, i.e. turn the adjustment to full extent in one direction then turn to full extent in the opposite direction, back off half the total distance.

(4) Rotate the rotor shaft until the rotor is in line with the No. 6 (front) cylinder electrode in the distributor cap.

(5) Insert the distributor in the crankcase aperture. It may be necessary to turn the rotor shaft or body slightly to locate the drive dog.

(6) Connect a 12 volt test lamp with one lead to the distributor terminal or the C.B. terminal of the coil and the other to a good earth.

(7) Rotate the distributor body until the points are just breaking. That is when the lamp lights.

(8) Tighten distributor clamping plate retaining screw.

(9) Reconnect the vacuum advance pipe and complete the assembly.

7. SPARK PLUGS

TO SERVICE

(1) The sparking plugs should be removed for inspection, cleaning and resetting at intervals of 3000 to 4000 miles. Sparking plugs removed from an engine in good mechanical condition, operating under normal conditions, should have light powdery deposit ranging in colour from light brown to greyish tan. After considerable service the electrodes will show signs of wear or normal burning.

(2) Sparking plugs showing a thick black oily deposit indicate an engine in poor mechanical condition or possibly that a plug with too low a heat range has been fitted.

(3) Sparking plugs showing a white or yellowish deposit indicate sustained high speed driving or possibly that plugs of too high heat range have been fitted, particularly when these deposits are accompanied by blistering of the porcelain and burning of the electrodes. Check the recommended heat range for the engine (see specifications) and select the correct heat range if operating conditions are abnormal.

(4) If the heat range is correct, clean the plugs on a sand blast machine and blow clean with compressed air. Set the electrode gap (see specifications) by bending the earthing electrode and test the plugs on a reliable testing machine.

NOTE: Never attempt to set the electrode gap by bending the centre electrode or a cracked insulator will result.

(5) Clean the sparking plug threads and, using new gaskets, fit the plugs, screwing up finger tight.

(6) Using a torque wrench, tighten the sparking plugs to the recommended torque.

8. HIGH TENSION CABLES

TO CHECK

The high tension cables between the sparking plugs and the distributor cap and the centre high tension terminal on the distributor cap and the ignition coil are of special manufacture and have a carbon impregnated core instead of the normal wire core.

This is to eliminate radio interference and care must be exercised when removing the cables from the sparking plugs to ensure that the cables are not damaged by stretching, which will break the core and render the cable unserviceable.

Always remove the cable from a sparking plug by pulling on the cable terminal. Use the same care when connecting the cable to the plug.

If a cable has a broken core it will cause misfiring.

Check the cables for perishing or cracking and renew as required. Never attempt to repair defective cables.

The cables may be carefully cleaned, using a cloth moistened with kerosene, then wipe completely dry.

Also check the distributor cap for cracks or tracking between the high tension terminals on both the inside and outside of the cap. Renew the cap if cracks or tracking is evident.

Check the carbon brush in the centre of the distributor cap for evidence of arcing and renew as necessary.

9. FLUID AND HANDBRAKE WARNING LIGHT

DESCRIPTION AND OPERATION

The purpose of this unit which is positioned in the facia panel is two fold.

(1) To indicate that the handbrake is in operation either fully or partly.

(2) To indicate when the fluid in the master cylinders has reached a low level.

There are three switches involved, one mounted on the propeller shaft tunnel below the handbrake assembly and operated by an extension on the handbrake lever which depresses the switch when the lever is in the full off position. The other two switches are located in the caps of the master cylinder reservoirs and operated by means of small floats which ride on top of the fluid activating the switch when the fluid falls below the correct level.

The switches are wired through the ignition switch. When the ignition is on and the handbrake is applied the warning light in the facia panel will glow but will become extinguished when the handbrake has been fully released, providing the brake fluid in the reservoir is at the correct level.

Should the warning light continue to glow after the handbrake has been fully released, it indicates that the brake fluid in the reservoir is at a low level. If the fluid level is found to be correct the cause of the handbrake warning light remaining on must be investigated.

Should the warning light fail to extinguish when the

handbrake is fully off and the brake fluid levels are correct, check that the spring steel lever is contacting the interrupter switch correctly before examining the wires for short circuits.

Examine the handbrake for full travel and the spring steel bracket for misalignment. Apply the handbrake and switch on the ignition, when the warning light should glow. If the warning light fails to glow when the handbrake is applied and the ignition is switched on, before checking the warning light bulb ensure that the spring steel lever is clearing the interrupter switch plunger. If it is not doing so, bend the lever away from the plunger or renew as necessary.

NOTE: It is necessary to remove the tail shaft tunnel cover as described in the BRAKE SECTION to gain access to the interrupter switch.

10. TRAFFIC HAZARD WARNING DEVICE

DESCRIPTION

This unit is fitted to vehicles exported to the U.S.A. in order to comply with the traffic regulations for the State of New York.

The system operates in conjunction with the four flashing turn indicator lights.

A separate toggle switch controls the system, operation of which causes the four indicator lights to flash simultaneously. A red warning light incorporated in the circuit and situated in the dash facia indicates when the hazard warning system is in operation.

The flasher can unit which is situated behind the sub panel is similar in appearance to the one used for the turn indicators but it is different regarding internal circuits, and care must be taken to ensure that only the correct unit is fitted.

11. WINDSCREEN WIPER

DESCRIPTION

The wiper unit is of a two speed type incorporating a limit switch which automatically controls the parking of the wiper arms. The drive is by link type transmission and the unit is controlled by a three position switch.

TO TEST

(1) Using a moving coil voltmeter check the voltage at the motor. This reading should be 11.5 volts with the wipers operating normally. Readings below this figure indicates faulty connection and this should be located and corrected before proceeding further with the tests.

(2) With the linkage mechanism disconnected the speed of the unit should be as follows:

Normal 44 – 48 RPM
High   58 – 68 RPM

Operating current draw under no load (motor only) should not exceed 2.5 amperes at low speed and 1.7 – 2.4 at high speed.

Adjustment of limiting switch (parking)

This can be adjusted by turning the knurled nut located on the bulkhead. Turn the nut only one or two serrations at a time and test the effect of each setting before proceeding.

REMOVE AND INSTALL

(1) Disconnect the battery.

(2) Disconnect the ball joint from the throttle shaft at the pivot bracket, remove the two screws holding the bracket.

(3) Remove the snap clip from the bulkhead and disconnect the cables.

(4) Remove the two retaining screws holding the instrument panel and located at the top right hand and left hand corners, and disconnect the ball joint from the central wiper spindle housing.

(5) Remove the four screws retaining the wiper motor to the bulkhead and withdraw the motor complete with the attached link rod.

(6) Installation is the reverse of the foregoing procedure.

NOTE: Care must be taken not to alter the length of the link rod because any alteration in length will place the wiper arms out of phase with each other.

12. LIGHTS

DESCRIPTION

The head lamps comprise two 12 volt round units with pre-focused double filament bulbs, (vehicles for export to the United States are provided with adapters to enable sealed beam units to be fitted), front rims and dust seal rubber rings.

Because the light spread and its position on the kerbside in the dipped position is a function of the lensing and bulb design, care must always be taken when renewing any of the parts to ensure only correct items are fitted.

The rear lights consist of two combination units incorporating the turn signal lamp and the tail/stop lamps mounted above the bumper bar on either side of the rear end of the body. Illumination of the rear number plate is by means of two lamps one on either side of the number plate compartment located between the two bumper bar overriders.

The front parking and turn signals are also combination units and are mounted just above bumper bar level in the panel, with the flasher section in the outer position.

A reversing light is provided and mounted in the centre of the tail panel. There is also an interior luggage compartment light mounted inside the compartment which operates when the lid is raised. The interior cabin light is operated both manually and by opening the doors.

REMOVE AND INSTALL HEADLAMP

(1) Remove the six screws holding the outer glass retaining ring to fender and remove glass.

(2) Release the three screws holding the head lamp ring and remove rim from unit and withdraw reflector unit.

(3) Remove plug with attached wires from rear of the unit.

(4) Release bulb retaining spring clips and withdraw bulb.

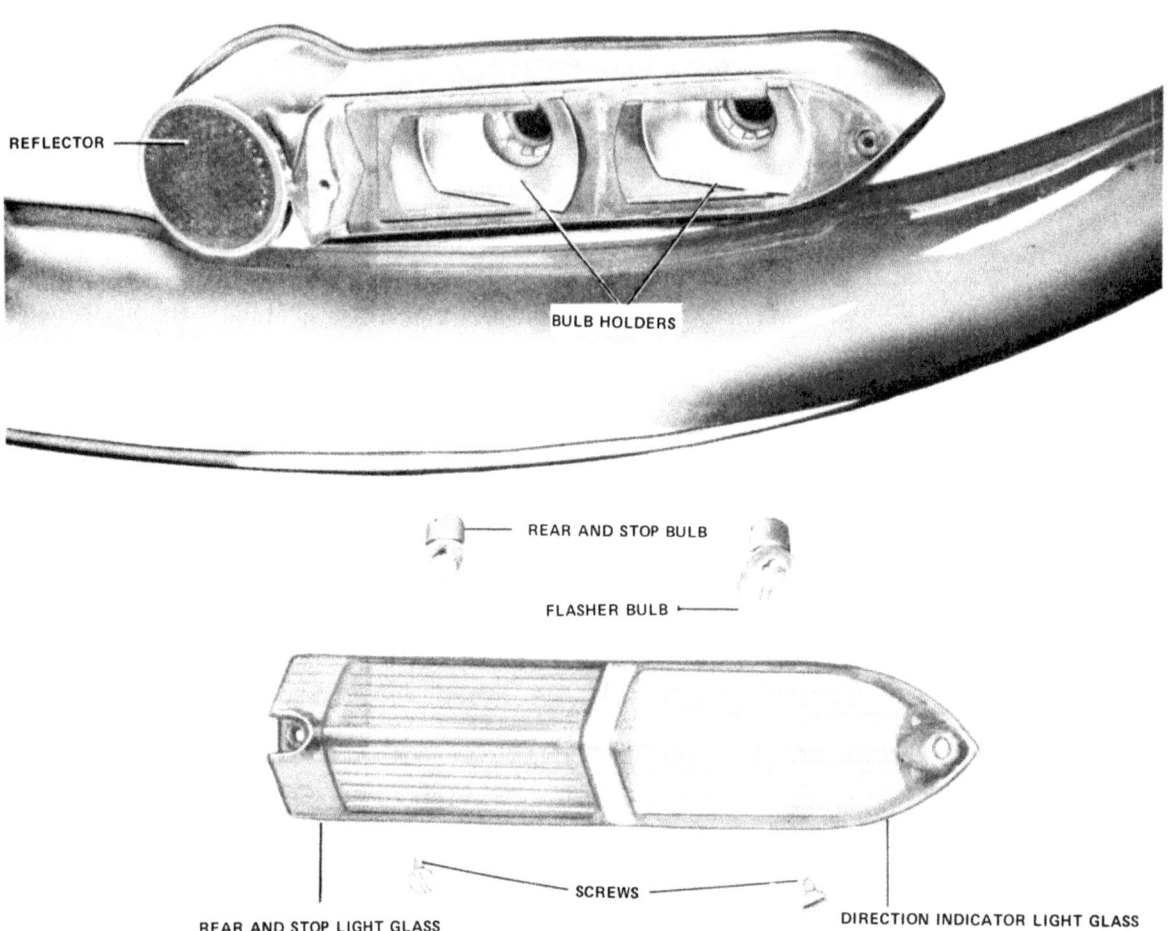

Dismantled View of Rear Lights (4.2 Shown).

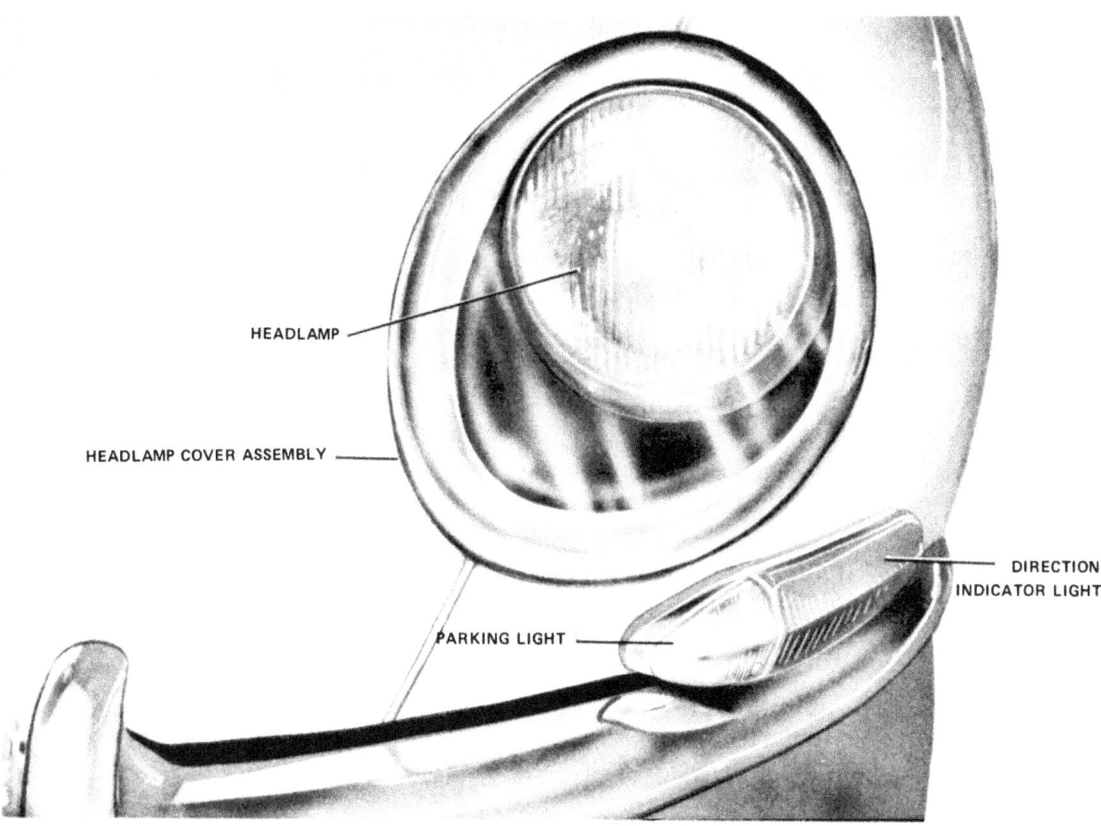

View of Front Lights (4.2 Model Shown).

(5) Installation is the reverse procedure.

NOTE: When assembling ensure that the groove in the bulb plate mates up with the raised portion in the bulb retainer.

ADJUSTMENT OF HEADLIGHTS

(1) Remove the outer rims and glass, refer to Remove and Install.

(2) Adjustment of the beam is by means of two slotted screws, one at the bottom of the unit and the other approximately 45% up the side.

(3) The screw at the bottom of the unit provides vertical adjustment of the beam and the screw at the side horizontal adjustment.

If a headlight aimer machine is not available, the adjustment can be obtained as follows:

(a) Place the vehicle on a level surface 25 feet from a suitable wall or panel.

(b) Measure the distance from the headlamp centres to the floor or ground. Scribe a horizontal line at the height on the wall or board.

(c) Adjust the beams so that the bright centre spots are on the line indicated in (b) above. The distance between centres of the beam at the point of contact should be 43 inches and diametrically equidistant from the centre of the vehicle.

13. INSTRUMENTS AND MISCELLANEOUS UNITS

REMOVAL OF INSTRUMENT PANEL

The instrument panel is hinged and access to the instruments can be obtained by removing the two thumb screws in each top corner and allowing the panel to hinge downwards. The panel can be removed completely and to do this the following procedure should be adopted.

(1) Disconnect the battery.

(2) Remove the two screws located in each top corner and allow the panel to hinge down as described above.

(3) Remove wires from instruments etc. after identifying and marking each connection in some suitable way to ensure correct re-installation.

(4) Remove the harness and clips from the panel and withdraw the two hinge pivot bolts from the support brackets.

(5) Removal and installation of the instruments from the panel is simply a matter of removing or replacing the holding screws and withdrawing or re-positioning each unit.

FUSE UNIT

Four model 4 F.J. fuse units, each carrying two fuses and two spares, are incorporated in the electrical system and are located behind the instrument panel.

Access to the fuses is obtained by removing the two instrument panel screws located in the top left and right hand corners. The instrument panel will then hinge downwards exposing the fuses and fuse indicator panel, which indicates the circuits concerned with the fuses. It is most essential that only the correct value fuses be used otherwise damage can occur to the units which the fuses are intended to protect.

FLASHER UNIT

The flasher unit is housed in a sealed cylindrical container plugged into a base block which is a part of the main wiring system and attached to the bulkhead behind the facia panel on the right hand side.

Connections to the unit are so designed that incorrect attachment of the wires is practically impossible.

The operation of the flasher lamps is obtained by means of a switch contained in the unit, which is operated by the alternative heating and cooling of an actuating wire. There is also incorporated a small relay to operate the warning lights in the dash panel to indicate to the driver that the signals are operating correctly.

NOTE: Do not confuse this unit with the hazard warning flasher unit fitted to vehicles exported to the United States.

KEY TO WIRING DIAGRAM (3.8 MODELS).

1. Generator.
2. Regulator RB310.
3. Regulator RB340.
4. Ignition warning light.
5. Distributor.
6. Ignition coil.
7. Fuel pump.
8. High beam warning light.
9, 10, 11, 52 Fuses.
12. Brake fluid indicator.
13. Engine temperature relay.
14. Engine (Otter) fan switch.
15. Handbrake switch.
16. Engine blower motor.
17. Brake fluid switch.
18. RH stop light.
19. Brake fluid switch.
20. LH stop light.
21. Heater motor.
22. Heater switch.
23. Stop light switch.
24. Oil pressure gauge.
25. Voltage regulator.
26. Temperature gauge.
27. Temperature sending unit.
28. Oil pressure sending unit.
29, 30, 31 Panel edge lights.
32. Panel light switch.
33, 34, 35, 36 Panel lights.
37. RH Tail light.
38, 40 Number plate lights.
39. LH Tail light.
41. Fuel gauge tank unit.
42. Fuel level warning light.
43. Fuel gauge.
44. Reversing light.
45. Reversing light switch.
46. Choke switch.
47. Choke warning light.
48. Interior light.
49. Dipper switch.
50. Clock.
51. Cigar lighter.
53. 8-way plug and socket.
54. 4-position light switch.
55. 3-position light switch.
56. Battery.
57. Starter solenoid.
58. Windscreen washer.
59. Windscreen washer switch.
60. Horn push.
61. Horn relay.
62. Ignition switch.
63. Starter push.
64. Ammeter.
65. Starter motor.
66, 67 Horns.
68. RH headlight.
69. LH headlight.
70. RH parking light.
71. LH parking light.
72. RH direction indicator light.
73. LH direction indicator light.
74, 75 Fog lights (optional).
76. Map light.
77, 79 Door switches.
78. Map light switch.
80. Direction indicator and headlight flasher switch.
81. RH flasher warning light.
82. LH flasher warning light.
83. Flasher unit.
84. Windscreen wiper switch.
85. Windscreen wiper.
86, 87, 88, 89, Panel lights.
90. RH direction indicator light.
91. LH direction indicator light.
92. Windscreen wiper park switch.
93. Interior light switch.

COLOR CODE —

W	— White	PW	— Purple/white tracer	RBK	— Red/black tracer
R	— Red	GW	— Green/white tracer	WLG	— White/light green tracer
P	— Purple	GR	— Green/red tracer	GBR	— Green/brown tracer
G	— Green	WR	— White/red tracer	BKW	— Black/white tracer
BR	— Brown	LG	— Light green	BKR	— Black/red tracer
BK	— Black	RW	— Red/white tracer	BLG	— Blue/green tracer
BL	— Blue	WP	— White/purple tracer	BLY	— Blue/yellow tracer
RG	— Red/green tracer	GBK	— Green/black tracer	BRY	— Brown/yellow tracer
PG	— Purple/green tracer	WBR	— White/brown tracer	BKG	— Black/green tracer
GY	— Green/yellow tracer	GBL	— Green/blue tracer	RLG	— Red/light green tracer
WG	— White/green tracer	BRP	— Brown/purple tracer	YLG	— Yellow/light green tracer
PY	— Purple/yellow tracer	BRW	— Brown/white tracer	LGBK	— Light green/black tracer
GP	— Green/purple tracer	BRG	— Brown/green tracer	BRLG	— Brown/light green tracer
PB	— Purple/black tracer	BLW	— Blue/white tracer	LGBR	— Light green/brown tracer
RY	— Red/yellow tracer	BLR	— Blue/red tracer	LGBL	— Light green/blue tracer

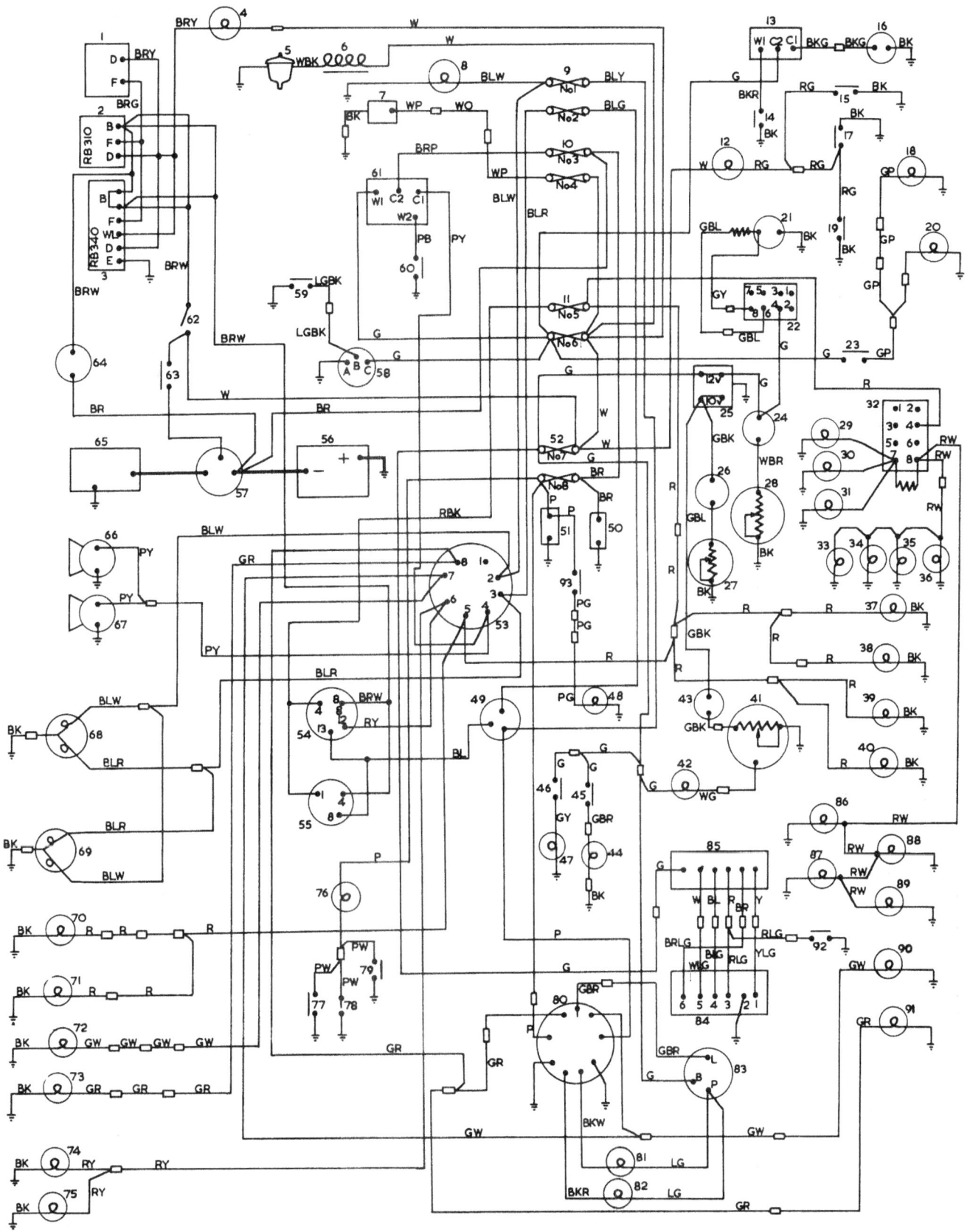

Wiring Diagram (3.8 Models).

KEY TO WIRING DIAGRAM (4.2 MODELS).

1. Alternator.
2. Regulator.
3. Ignition switch.
4. 3AW Ignition warning light unit/later cars.
5, 6 Horns.
7. Ignition warning light.
8. Ignition warning light pressure switch.
9. Horn relay.
10. Horn push.
11, 12 Fuse unit.
13. Distributor.
14. Ignition coil.
15. Line fuse.
16. 6RA relay.
17. Control switch.
18. Warning light.
19. Rear window heater.
20. Stop light switch.
21. RH stop light.
22. LH stop light.
23. Engine blower motor.
24. Engine (Otter) fan switch.
25. Fuel pump.
26. Water temperature gauge.
27. Water temperature sending unit.
28, 29 Brake fluid switches.
30. Hand brake switch.
31. Windscreen washer (later models).
32. Brake indicator light.
33. Windscreen washer switch.
34. Windscreen washer.
35. Auto transmission dial light.
36, 37 Fuse units.
38, 39 Fuse units.
40. Clock.
41. Auto transmission inhibitor switch.
42. Auto transmission inhibitor switch relay.
43. Battery.
44. Starter push.
45. Ammeter.
46. Starter motor and solenoid.
47. Hazard flasher unit (US).
48. Hazard warning light (US).
49. Hazard switch (US).
50. 8-way plug and socket.
51, 52 Fuse units.
53. High beam warning light.
54. Instrument voltage regulator.
55. Oil pressure gauge.
56, 57, 58 Panel edge lights.
59. Panel light switch.
60. Oil gauge sending unit.
61, 62, 63, 64 Panel lights.
65. RH tail light.
66. Number plate light.
67. LH tail light.
68. Number plate light.
69. Fuel gauge.
70, 71, 72, 73 Panel lights.
74. Fuel level warning light.
75. Fuel gauge tank unit.
76. Choke warning light.
77. Choke warning light switch.
78. Reversing light.
79. Reversing light switch.
80. Reversing light switch (2+2).
81. Dipper switch.
82. 4-position light switch.
83. 3-position light switch.
84. Heater switch.
85. Cigar lighter switch.
86. Cigar lighter.
87. RH headlight.
88. LH headlight.
89. RH parking light.
90. LH parking light.
91. RH front direction indicator light.
92. LH front direction indicator light.
93. Heater resistance.
94. Heater motor.
95. Interior light switch.
96. Direction indicator and headlight flasher switch.
97. Flasher unit.
98. RH rear direction indicator.
99. LH rear direction indicator.
100. Windscreen wiper park switch.
101. Windscreen wiper motor.
102. Windscreen wiper switch.
103. RH flasher warning light.
104. LH flasher warning light.
105. Interior light.
106. Map light switch.
107, 108 Door courtesy switches.
109. Map light.
110, 111 Fog lights.
112. Line fuse.

COLOR CODE

W	— White	GBK	— Green/black tracer
R	— Red	WBR	— White/brown tracer
P	— Purple	GBL	— Green/blue tracer
G	— Green	BRP	— Brown/purple tracer
BR	— Brown	BRW	— Brown/white tracer
BK	— Black	BRG	— Brown/green tracer
BL	— Blue	BLW	— Blue/white tracer
RG	— Red/green tracer	BLR	— Blue/red tracer
PG	— Purple/green tracer	RBK	— Red/black tracer
GY	— Green/yellow tracer	WLG	— White/light green tracer
WG	— White/green tracer	GBR	— Green/brown tracer
PY	— Purple/yellow tracer	BKW	— Black/white tracer
GP	— Green/purple tracer	BKR	— Black/red tracer
PB	— Purple/black tracer	BLG	— Blue/green tracer
RY	— Red/yellow tracer	BLY	— Blue/yellow tracer
PW	— Purple/white tracer	BRY	— Brown/yellow tracer
GW	— Green/white tracer	BKG	— Black/green tracer
GR	— Green/red tracer	RLG	— Red/light green tracer
WR	— White/red tracer	YLG	— Yellow/light green tracer
LG	— Light green	LGBK	— Light green/black tracer
RW	— Red/white tracer	BRLG	— Brown/light green tracer
WP	— White/purple tracer	LGBR	— Light green/brown tracer
		LGBL	— Light green/blue tracer

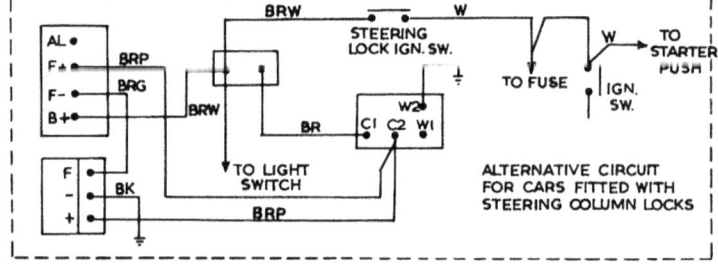

Wiring Diagram (4.2 Models).

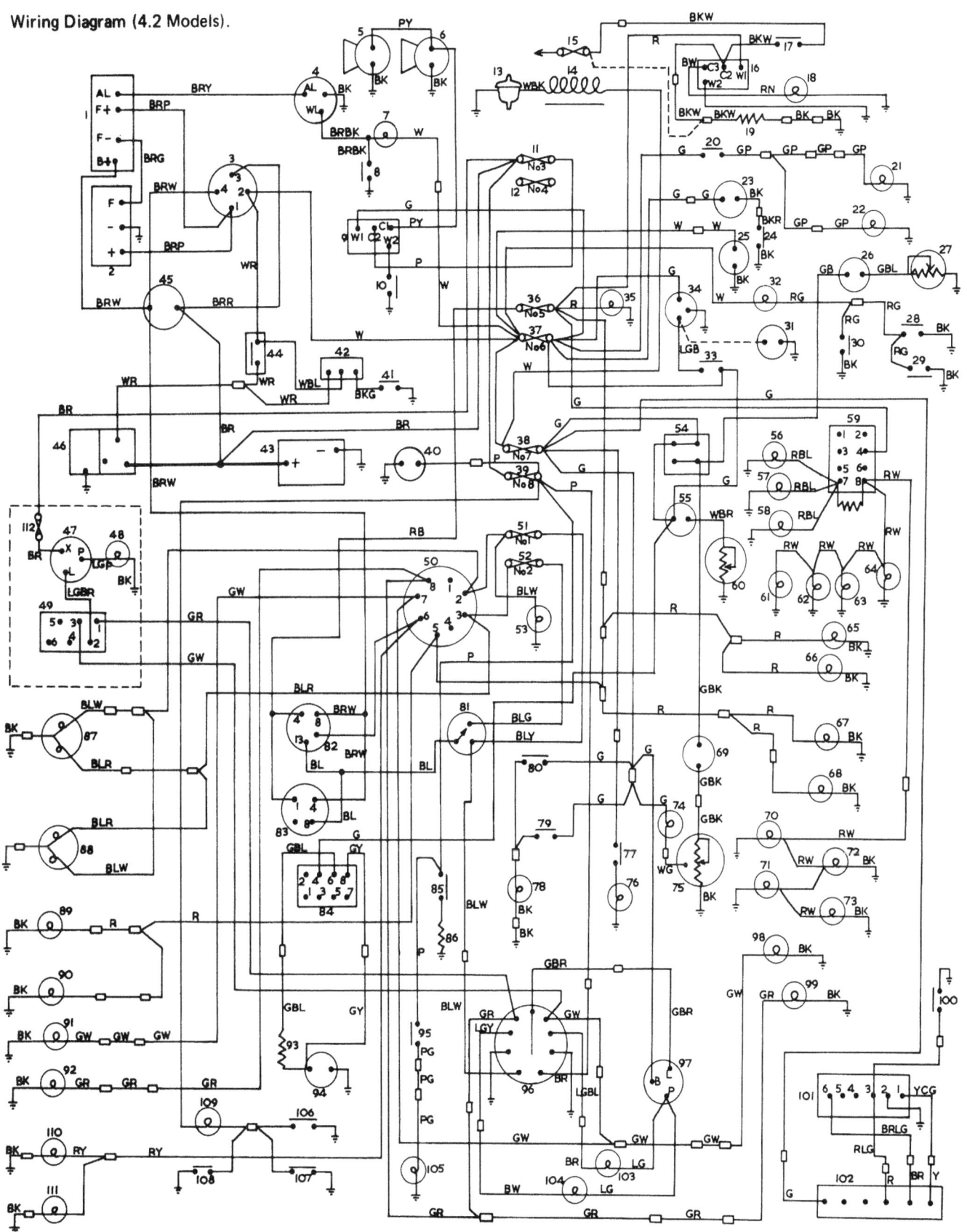

HORNS – TO REMOVE, ADJUST AND INSTALL

(1) Remove the outer headlamp rim and glass.

(2) Remove the three screws from the headlight duct to the panel and withdraw the duct through headlight glass aperture. The horn can now be seen through the aperture.

(3) Remove the securing bolts, disconnect the wires and withdraw the horn.

(4) To adjust remove the cover, connect an 0-20 moving coil ammeter in series with the horn. Release the contact nut and adjust the contact until the draw is 13-15 amperes at 12 volts.

(5) Re-lock adjuster and re-check.

(6) Reassembly and installation is the reversal of the above procedure.

CARBURETTOR MIXTURE CONTROL WARNING LIGHT

To Set Switch:

(1) Set the carburettor mixture control .250" from the bottom limit of its travel, when a click will be heard. Using the two nuts on the threaded shank of the switch, position the switch so that the warning light ceases to glow when the ignition is switched on.

(2) Actuate the lever up and down several times and make any final adjustments necessary.

TACHOMETER AND CLOCK

The tachometer which also includes the clock is electrically operated and both units are provided for in the wiring harness. The clock is wired to the general 12 volt current supply and the tachometer is connected to an AC generator mounted to the rear of the right hand camshaft.

To Test Operation:

(1) Attach an AC voltmeter across the terminals of the generator as a rough guide for this test, it can be assumed that 100 rpm = 1 volt output. If current is evident, check the leads by attaching the voltmeter across the other end of the leads at the point where they connect to the tachometer. If there is continuity at this point and no reading on the tachometer it is evident that a fault exists in the instrument unit and it must be removed for repair.

(2) If no reading is recorded at the generator terminals, that unit should be removed and tested for internal fault.

TO ADJUST CLOCK

(1) Adjustment is provided by means of a small screw surrounded by a circular seal and located at the rear of the instrument.

(2) If the clock is gaining turn the screw towards the minus sign, or to the positive sign if losing.

NOTE: Commencing at the following chassis numbers:
  'E' Type Open Seater 850702 RHD and 879324 LHD
  'E' Type Fixed Head Coupe 861169 RHD and 888543 LHD

The electric clock fitted to the tachometer dial incorporates a rectifier to prevent fouling of the contact points in the clock.

If the clock is removed for servicing and subsequent bench testing, it is most important that the terminal of the clock be attached to the negative side of any test current and the outer casing positively earthed. Failure to observe this procedure will destroy the rectifier.

INSTRUMENT VOLTAGE REGULATOR

This unit is located at the top right hand side of the rear of the instrument panel. The purpose of the unit is to ensure a constant power supply at a determined voltage to the Fuel and Water temperature gauges to avoid errors due to low battery voltage.

It is of utmost importance that no power be applied to these instruments other than through the voltage control unit or a suitable substitute. Failure to observe this procedure will result in serious damage to the instrument units.

14. ELECTRICAL FAULT DIAGNOSIS

BATTERY AND GENERATOR SYSTEM

(1) **Battery undercharged.**

Possible cause	Remedy
(a) Loose or broken generator drive belt.	– Adjust or renew belt.
(b) Faulty or incorrectly adjusted generator regulator.	– Renew or adjust regulator unit.
(c) Faulty battery.	– Renew or repair battery.
(d) Faulty generator.	– Overhaul or renew generator.
(e) Fault in charging circuit wiring.	– Check and repair or renew wiring harness.
(f) Faulty connections in charging circuit.	– Check and renew or repair component/s.

(2) **Battery overcharged.**

	Possible cause	Remedy
(a)	Faulty or incorrectly adjusted generator regulator unit.	– Renew or adjust regulator.
(b)	Faulty battery.	– Renew or repair battery.
(c)	Faulty generator.	– Overhaul or renew generator.
(d)	Faulty charging circuit wiring or connections.	– Check and renew or repair faulty components.
(e)	Shorted field wire.	– Renew field.
(f)	Grounded field wire.	– Repair field.
(g)	Shorted cell in battery.	– Renew battery.

(3) **Charge indicator light remains on.**

	Possible cause	Remedy
(a)	Loose or broken generator drive belt.	– Adjust or renew drive belt.
(b)	Faulty or incorrectly adjusted generator regulator unit.	– Check and renew or adjust regulator unit.
(c)	Faulty generator.	– Check and overhaul generator.
(d)	Low regulator voltage setting.	– Check and adjust voltage setting on regulator unit.
(e)	Sticking brushes in generator.	– Free up or renew.
(f)	Grounded field coil.	– Overhaul generator.
(g)	Open circuit in field.	– Overhaul generator.

(4) **Charge indicator light does not operate.**

	Possible cause	Remedy
(a)	Light bulb blown.	– Check and renew faulty bulb.
(b)	Open circuit in wiring or bulb socket.	– Check and rectify open circuit.

(5) **Noise in drive belt or generator.**

	Possible cause	Remedy
(a)	Drive belt frayed or out of alignment with pulleys.	– Renew drive belt and/or align pulleys.
(b)	Loose generator mounting bolts or worn bearings.	– Tighten mounting bolts and/or renew bearings.
(c)	Loose generator pulley.	– Tighten pulley retaining nut.
(d)	Faulty generator.	– Overhaul or renew generator.
(e)	Fan belt too tight.	– Adjust correctly.
(f)	Incorrectly seated brushes.	– Dress brushes.
(g)	High mica between commutator bars.	– Undercut.

(6) **Arcing at generator brushes.**

	Possible cause	Remedy
(a)	Out of round commutator.	– Machine.
(b)	Dirty or glazed commutator.	– Clean.
(c)	Weak brush springs.	– Renew springs.
(d)	Excessive voltage output.	– Adjust voltage control.

BATTERY AND STARTING SYSTEM

(1) Starter lacks power to crank engine.

	Possible cause	*Remedy*
(a)	Battery undercharged.	– Check charging system and rectify as necessary.
(b)	Battery faulty, will not hold charge.	– Check and repair or renew battery.
(c)	Battery terminals loose or corroded.	– Clean and tighten terminals.
(d)	Faulty starter motor.	– Check and overhaul starter motor.
(e)	Faulty starter solenoid switch or contacts.	– Check and renew solenoid as necessary.
(f)	Worn or dirty starter brushes.	– Renew or clean.
(g)	Sticking brushes.	– Free, clean, renew.

(2) Starter will not attempt to crank engine.

	Possible cause	*Remedy*
(a)	Open circuit in starting system.	– Check for: dirty or loose terminals, dirty commutator, faulty solenoid, faulty switch.
(b)	Discharged battery.	– Check for fault or short circuit in system.
(c)	Battery fully charged but will not crank engine.	– Check for: locked drive and ring gears, internal starter fault or seized engine.
(d)	Weak cell in battery.	– Renew battery.

HEADLAMP SYSTEM

(1) Lamps fail to light.

	Possible cause	*Remedy*
(a)	Burnt out sealed beam unit/s.	– Check and renew faulty unit/s.
(b)	Open circuit in wiring or connections.	– Check and rectify.
(c)	Faulty light switch.	– Check and renew switch.
(d)	Burnt out fuse, if fitted.	– Eliminate cause and renew fuse.

(2) Lamps flare with engine speed increase.

	Possible cause	*Remedy*
(a)	Faulty battery.	– Check and renew or repair battery.
(b)	Battery in low state of charge.	– Recharge battery and check charging system.
(c)	High resistance or faulty connections between generator and battery.	– Check circuit and rectify condition.
(d)	Poor earth connection between battery and engine or generator.	– Check battery earth lead and strap between engine and body.
(e)	Voltage regulator setting too high or unit inoperative.	– Check and adjust voltage regulator setting.

DIRECTION INDICATOR LIGHT SYSTEM

(1) Indicator warning light does not burn and no audible clicking from flasher unit, when turn is selected on switch lever.

	Possible cause	*Remedy*
(a)	Fuse blown.	– Rectify fault and renew fuse.
(b)	Bulb blown on one or both sides.	– Check system and renew bulb/s.
(c)	Faulty flasher unit.	– Renew flasher unit. Do not attempt repair.
(d)	Faulty direction indicator switch.	– Renew or repair switch.
(e)	Fault in wiring circuit.	– Check and repair fault.

(2) Indicator light operates at a very slow rate.

	Possible cause	Remedy
(a)	Faulty or incorrect flasher unit.	– Renew.
(b)	One bulb blown or break in circuit.	– Renew, repair.
(c)	High resistance in circuit.	– Check earth connections.
(d)	Incorrect bulbs fitted.	– Renew with correct wattage bulbs.

(3) Indicator warning light does not flash but audible clicking from flasher unit, when turn is selected on switch lever.

	Possible cause	Remedy
(a)	Warning light bulb blown.	– Check and renew bulb.
(b)	Front bulb blown on opposite side to turn selected.	– Check and renew bulb.

(4) Both warning lights flash weakly and at greater than normal speed when turn is selected on switch lever.

	Possible cause	Remedy
(a)	Front bulb blown on turn side.	– Check and renew bulb.
(b)	Rear bulb blown on turn side.	– Check and renew bulb.
(c)	Faulty flasher unit.	– Check and renew flasher unit.

(5) Both indicator warning lights burn constantly when turn is selected on switch lever.

	Possible cause	Remedy
(a)	Front and rear bulbs blown on turn side.	– Check and renew bulbs.
(b)	Faulty flasher unit.	– Check and renew flasher unit.

IGNITION SYSTEM

(1) Engine will not start.

	Possible cause	Remedy
(a)	Fault in ignition primary wiring.	– Check circuit and repair as necessary.
(b)	Faulty ignition switch.	– Renew ignition switch.
(c)	Fault in coil primary winding.	– Renew coil.
(d)	Burnt or dirty contact breaker points.	– Clean or renew and adjust points.
(e)	Faulty capacitor or capacitor lead.	– Check and renew capacitor.
(f)	Fused or broken low tension wire from breaker arm to low tension terminal.	– Renew low tension terminal block and wire.
(g)	Fault in coil high tension circuit.	– Test and renew coil as necessary.
(h)	Cracks in distributor cap.	– Renew distributor cap.
(i)	Crack in distributor rotor.	– Renew distributor rotor.
(j)	Faulty high tension leads.	– Check and renew leads.
(k)	Faulty or incorrectly adjusted spark plugs.	– Renew or clean and adjust spark plugs.

(2) Engine starts but misfires under load.

	Possible cause	Remedy
(a)	Faulty, dirty or incorrectly adjusted spark plugs.	– Renew and/or clean and adjust spark plugs.
(b)	Dirty or incorrectly adjusted contact points.	– Clean, adjust or renew points.
(c)	Uneven wear on distributor cam.	– Check and overhaul distributor.
(d)	Condensation moisture in distributor cap.	– Check and dry out and examine cap for cracks.
(e)	Cracked spark plug insulator/s.	– Renew faulty spark plug/s.
(f)	Faulty ignition coil.	– Check and renew coil.

(3) Engine runs but lacks power.

Possible cause — *Remedy*

(a) Ignition timing incorrectly set or contact points require adjusting. — Check and readjust timing and/or contact points.

(b) Centrifugal advance mechanism seized or excessively worn. — Overhaul distributor.

(c) Vacuum advance unit inoperative. — Check for broken vacuum pipe or faulty unit.

(d) Vacuum advance unit operates but ineffective. — Advance unit link disconnected or broken.

HEATING AND WINDSCREEN WASHING EQUIPMENT

1. HEATER AND VENTILATION

DESCRIPTION

The heater and ventilating equipment consists of a heater unit which is connected to the engine cooling system and incorporates a two speed electrically driven fan mounted on the engine side of the bulkhead. Air from the heater is conducted through ducts fitted with two doors and situated behind the instrument panel, and two vents at the bottom of the windscreen to provide demisting and defrosting. Control of the system is by means of a lever on the dash panel and the fan switch.

The heater units fitted to the 2+2 cars are identical to that fitted to other 'E' Type cars except for the air distribution controls. The outlets, situated under the duct behind the instrument panel, are fitted with finger operated direction controls on the facia board. Fully rotating the right hand knob anti-clockwise will cut off the supply of air to the interior or direct the air flow to the windscreen ducts. Reverse rotation of the knobs will progressively redirect air from the windscreen to the car interior.

TEMPERATURE CONTROL

The heating and ventilating control panel on the dash is equipped with two levers which have locations as follows:

The heat control lever which controls the amount of water flowing through the heater element has two main positions, cold and hot. With the lever position at 'cold' the water from the engine cooling system is completely cut off. Placed in the 'hot' position a maximum flow of water is obtained. By placing the control in intermediate positions varying degrees of heat may be obtained.

The air control lever is arranged the same as the other lever but controls the amount of air passing through the system.

AIR DISTRIBUTION

The proportion of air directed to the windscreen or the interior of the car can be controlled by the position of the two doors situated under the duct behind the instrument panel.

With the doors fully closed the maximum amount of air will be directed to the windscreen for rapid defrosting or demisting.

The air flow through the system can be considerably increased by the use of the electrically driven fan, which has two speeds.

TO REMOVE AND INSTALL

(1) Drain the engine cooling system.
(2) Disconnect the battery.
(3) Slacken the two hose clips securing the hoses to the heater.
(4) Remove the heater air control flap cable.
(5) Disconnect wires from fan motor at snap connector.
(6) Remove the four bolts holding heater body to scuttle.
(7) Remove the two screws securing the heater bracket to the sub-frame and remove heater unit.
(8) Installation is the reversal of the foregoing procedure.

NOTE: There is the possibility that fumes may be drawn into the interior of the car when travelling in dense traffic and in these circumstances it is advisable to close the heater air vent and switch off the motor.

2. WINDSCREEN WASHING EQUIPMENT

DESCRIPTION

The windscreen washer equipment comprises a glass water container incorporating an electrically driven pump mounted in the engine compartment and connected by hoses to two jet attachments positioned at the exterior base of the windscreen. Water under slight pressure (4.5 sq.in) is delivered to the directional jets by the pump which is controlled by a switch on the dash panel.

OPERATION

The washer equipment is intended to be used in conjunction with the windscreen wipers to remove foreign matter from the windscreen. The correct method of operation is to lift the switch lever and release immediately when the washer should operate at once and coninue to function for approximately six seconds. Always allow a lapse of time before operating the switch for a second time.

If the washer does not function immediately check the water level. The washer should not be used in under freezing conditions because the fine jets of water spread over the screen will tend to freeze up. Operation of the unit for more than a few seconds when the container is empty or the the water frozen will damage the unit.

REPLENISHMENT OF CONTAINER

Only clean water should be used and over filling must be avoided. Fill only up to the bottom of the container neck.

Replenishment is necessary when the water level has fallen to a point where the top of the auxiliary reservoir is uncovered. If the water level is allowed to fall below the above level, the automatic operation will cease and water will only be delivered while the switch is held on.

To avoid damage from frost add denatured alcohol (methylated spirits) as follows:-

The underside of the rubber filler cover will be found to form a measure. Two of these measures of denatured alcohol should be added per container of water. No other additives should be used.

ADJUSTMENT OF JETS

This can be achieved by turning the jet unit with a screwdriver. It is necessary to adjust the direction of the water jets in conjunction with a road test because of the deflection caused by the air stream.

LUBRICATION

If the motor is found to be running slowly, remove the cover from the container and apply one or two drops of light machine oil to the felt pad situated in the gap between the cover and the motor unit. Do not over-lubricate because if the oil finds its way into the water, smearing of the windscreen will result.

TEST IN POSITION

(1) Connect a suitable ammeter in series with the operating switch. Switch on motor. If the motor does not operate and/or the current reading exceeds 2 amps, remove the motor and check that the impeller spindle turns freely.

(2) If the spindle is not free, the motor will have to be dismantled for further inspection and repair.

DISMANTLE

(1) Disconnect external attachments and remove the cover from the container unit.

(2) Remove the screws securing the motor to the cover, taking care not to lose the intermediate loose coupling which connects the armature to the pump spindle coupling.

(3) Remove the coupling attached to the armature shaft by holding firmly with a pair of suitable pliers, and with a second pair of pliers withdraw the coupling from the shaft.

(4) Remove the two screws from the bearing plate and remove the bearing plate and rubber gasket.

(5) Remove the two terminal screws, remove the terminal nuts and brushes and withdraw the armature. Take care not to lose the bearing washer which fits loosely on the armature shaft.

(6) Reassembly is the reversal of the foregoing procedure, with the inclusion of the filling of the bearing recess in the motor with Rocol Molypad Molybdenised grease.

BENCH CHECK

(1) If the armature is damaged or shows signs of overheating, the unit should be replaced.

(2) The resistance of the armature windings should not exceed 2.8 - 3.1 ohms.

(3) If the brushes are less than .0625" in length they must be renewed.

(4) The commutator should be in a smooth and clean condition. If not, clean with a soft cloth soaked in petrol. Where necessary it may be polished with very fine glass paper.

BODY

1. WINDSCREEN AND REAR WINDOW

TO REMOVE – OPEN CARS

(1) Remove the two Philips screws securing the windscreen stay to the centre top of the windscreen frame.

(2) Remove the two pillar caps from the windscreen frame pillars.

NOTE: The two Philips screws holding each cap have different size heads and must be refitted to the same position when installing the screen.

(3) Remove the screen pillar trim welts by withdrawing away from the flange on the pillars.

(4) Using a suitable drill, remove the two pop rivets (exposed by the removal of the welt – operation 3) which retains the chrome finisher to each pillar and prise the finishers from the screen rubber.

(5) Remove the chrome finisher from the bottom of the windscreen rubber.

(6) Lift one end of the rubber insert and withdraw completely.

(7) Using a suitable blunt thin bladed tool, break the seal between the rubber and the windscreen aperture flange.

(8) Using the flat of the hand, strike the windscreen from the inside starting at the top corner and working down to the bottom.

(9) Withdraw the screen and remove the top frame by inserting a flat blunt bladed tool between the sealer and the glass and gently prise away the frame.

TO INSTALL

(1) Clean all old sealer from screen and flange and examine the rubber for damage.

If the screen was broken and not by an external object or force, the body aperture should be carefully checked for damage or distortion which could exert pressure on the screen.

(2) Attach the rubber to the windscreen aperture with the flat side of the rubber towards the rear.

(3) Fit the windscreen to the rubber by inserting the bottom edge first and then working in both directions, lift the rubber over the edge of the remaining section of the screen.

(4) Insert the rubber sealing strip with the rounded edge to the outside.

NOTE: A special inserting tool is available and required for this operation (Churchill Tool JD.23).

(5) Pass the sealing rubber through the handle and the wire formed diamond shaped aperture of the tool. Allow only approximately .250" of the rubber to protrude through the wire formed diamond shaped section and commencing in the middle of the bottom section of the screen rubber, press the wire section of the tool and the rubber into the groove of the windscreen rubber, press down on the end of the insertion rubber to hold it in position and draw the tool along the groove allowing the insertion rubber to feed through the tool.

(6) Using a suitable pressure gun, apply sealer to the areas between the rubber and the body flange and repeat the process between the glass and the rubber. Remove any excess sealer from the screen using petrol or other suitable material. Do not use thinners as this can damage the paint work.

(7) Fit the chrome strip on top of the windscreen rubber and bend to suit contour if necessary.

(8) Place the chrome strip on the rubber over the sealing strip and lift the rubber over the chrome finisher.

(9) Refit the windscreen top frame. It is advisable to always use a new length of sealing strip and care must be taken not to use undue pressure. If difficulty is experienced in fitting the frame apply a small amount of soapy water to the strip and the glass.

(10) Coat the inside of the pillar refinisher with a suitable adhesive, place the finisher on the rubber over the sealer strip and lift the rubber lip over the edge of the refinisher.

(11) Secure the finisher to the screen pillar with two pop rivets inserted in the original holes.

(12) Refit the chrome screen pillar caps. It is essential that the flat countersunk screw is fitted to the inside face of the pillar capping and the raised screw to the top face. Failure to ensure this will prevent the hood from fitting correctly to the screen frame.

TO REMOVE – FIXED HEAD COUPE

(1) Remove the two pillar chrome finishers from the windscreen rubber and repeat with the upper and lower finishers.

(2) Proceed as indicated in operations 6, 7 and 8 of *TO REMOVE – OPEN CARS*, and withdraw the windscreen.

TO INSTALL

Installation procedure is the same as outlined in *TO INSTALL – OPEN CARS*, with the exception of items 9, 11 and 12 of that section.

REMOVE REAR WINDOW – FIXED HEAD COUPE

(1) The procedure for removal of the rear window is the same as that outlined in items 5, 6, 7 and 8 of *REMOVE WINDSCREEN – OPEN CARS*.

(2) Withdraw the glass.

REFIT REAR WINDOW

The procedure for installing and sealing the rear window is similar to that of the windscreen. Refer to items 1 to 6 of *INSTALL WINDSCREEN – OPEN CARS*.

2. DOOR GLASS

REMOVE AND INSTALL DOOR GLASS

(1) Remove inner control handles and trim as described in the appropriate section.

(2) Remove clear plastic sheet which is stuck to the door frame with contact cement.

(3) Remove the six screws holding the closing strip to the door frame.

(4) Wind the window down until the roller on the regulator is accessible through the aperture in the bottom section of the door frame.

(5) Unscrew regulator stop pin which is situated in the end of the channel attached to the glass.

(6) Raise the window until the regulator channel is above the door panel.

(7) Ease the regulator slide from the channel and withdraw the glass.

Installation is the reversal of the removal procedure with the exception that the runner should be suitably greased.

3. DOOR GLASS REGULATOR

TO REMOVE AND INSTALL

(1) Remove interior handles, trim, glass and frame as described in the appropriate sections.

(2) Remove the nuts securing the regulator to the door frame, and the four regulator spring securing screws.

(3) Lower the regulator mechanism within the door frame and withdraw through the aperture at the bottom of the panel.

Installation is the reversal of the foregoing procedure with the exception that the mechanism should be suitably greased.

4. DOOR LOCKS AND HANDLES

REMOVE AND INSTALL INTERIOR HANDLES

(1) Note the relative positions of the handles.

(2) Insert the blade of a suitable screw driver between the handle and the spring cap and press the cap inwards. This will expose the retaining pin.

(3) Using a suitable fine punch, remove the pin from the handle and shaft.

(4) Remove the handle from the squared shaft and withdraw the escutcheon and spring.

(5) The same procedure applies to the window winder handle.

Installation is the reversal of the removal procedure with the exception that care must be taken to position the handles in their respective original positions.

EXTERIOR DOOR HANDLES

(1) This handle is held by two small studs and nuts, one at the extreme end of the small section and the other at the base of the handle near the push button assembly.

(2) Access to the holding studs is through the aperture in the door frame.

(3) Raise the door glass to fully closed position.

(4) Remove the two nuts described in item (1) above.

(5) Installation is the reversal of the removal procedure.

DOOR LOCK MECHANISM

(1) Remove the remote control link circlip from the lock lever.

(2) Release the spring holding the bottom of the outside handle link to the dowel on the lock intermediate lever.

(3) Remove the four screws holding the lock to the end section of the door.

(4) Press the assembly inwards and slightly downwards and pass around the window channel which is immediately behind it.

Installation is the reversal of the removal procedure with the exception that the assembly should be suitably greased prior to fitting.

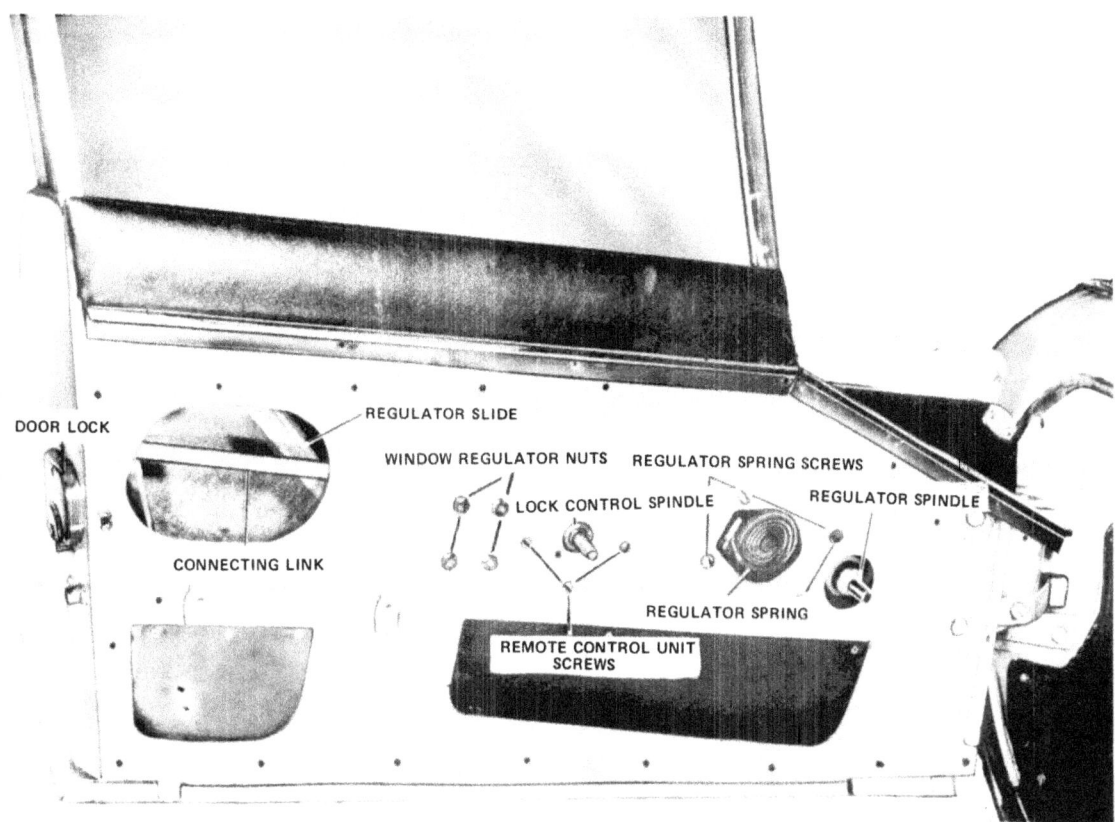

Door Assembly with Trim Panel Removed.

STRIKER PLATE ASSEMBLY

(1) The striker plate may be removed by extracting the three Philips head counter sunk screws. However this assembly should not be disturbed if avoidable.

(2) Positioning of the striker plate is by a process of trial and error until the door can be easily opened and closed without rattling, lifting or dropping.

(3) The striker plate must always be in a position where it is in the horizontal plane relative to the door axis.

5. DOOR TRIM

REMOVE AND INSTALL

(1) Remove the interior door and window winder handles as described in Section 4.

(2) Remove the top chrome strip from the door casing by inserting a screwdriver under the strip at the door hinge end and levering the strip away from its retaining spring clip.

(3) Repeat for the remaining four spring clips.

(4) Detach the spring clips by removing the five drive screws.

(5) Insert a thin bladed screwdriver between the trim and the door frame and prise off the trim which is secured by twenty-one clips.

(6) Refitting is the reversal of the removal procedure.

6. BONNET AND LUGGAGE COMPARTMENT

REMOVE, ADJUST AND INSTALL BONNET

(1) Disconnect the electrical multi pin socket from the left side of the bonnet.

(2) Suitably mark the hinge positions to facilitate installation.

(3) Remove the two nuts and washers securing the bonnet hinges to the front sub-frame mounting pin.

(4) Remove the two pivot pins and nuts securing the helper spring mechanism to the sub-frames.

(5) Support the bonnet and remove the four screws securing the left hand hinge to the bonnet.

(6) Remove the hinge noting the amount and location of the packing pieces between the hinges and the bonnet.

(7) Slide the right hand hinge off the mounting pin and remove the bonnet from the vehicle.

Installation is the reversal of the removal procedure.

NOTE: The multi pin electrical socket will only fit into the plug one way. It is therefore essential to align the socket correctly with the pins.

ADJUST (EARLY CARS)

(1) To ensure locking of the bonnet, adjustment is provided by packing pieces inserted under the bonnet lock plate and attached by two screws to the bonnet.

(2) Add or remove packing pieces as required until bonnet locks firmly.

ADJUST (LATER CARS)

(1) Adjustment is provided by means of rubber buffers attached to the adjustable spigot pins.

(2) Release the spigot pin locknut, turn the pin until the lock pawl retains the bonnet firmly when locked.

(3) Re-tighten the locknut.

REMOVE AND INSTALL LUGGAGE COMPARTMENT LID

(1) Lift the lid, and on fixed head coupe lower the stay to hold the lid in position. On open 2 seater the lid is held in the open position by the action of two helper springs.

(2) Suitably mark the original positions of the hinges on the lid.

(3) Remove the four screws and remove the lid.

(4) Suitably mark the positions of the hinges on the body and remove the four screws securing the hinges to the body.

(5) Installation is the reversal of the removal procedure.

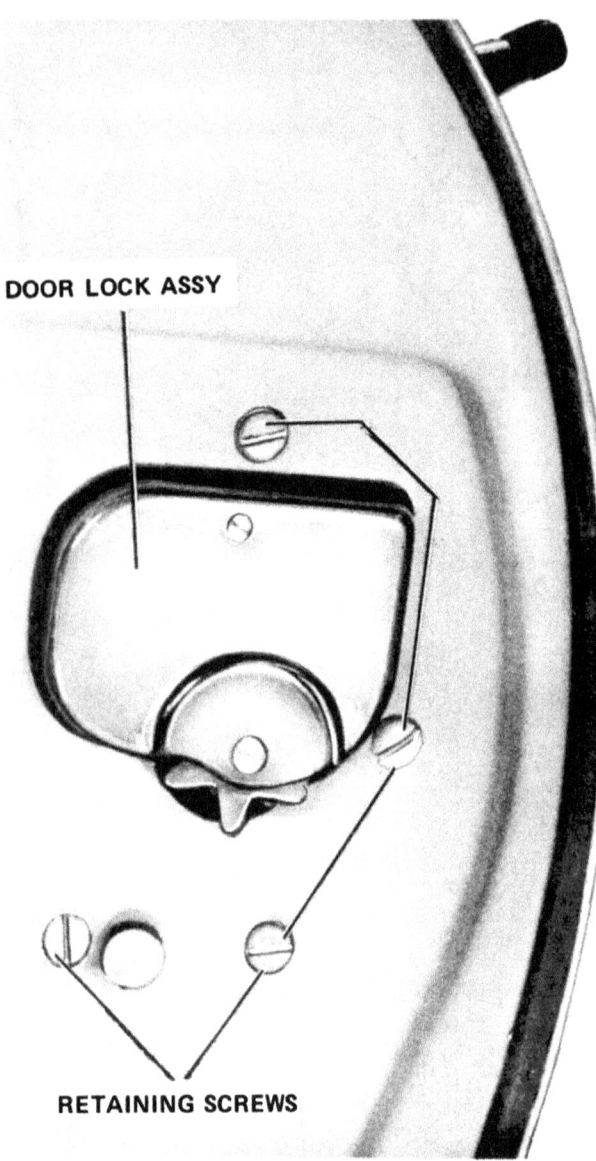

End View of Doors Showing Lock in Position

7. SEATS AND RUNNERS

REMOVAL

(1) Remove cushions from front seats.

(2) Remove the four screws securing each seat assembly to the runners and lift off the seat.

(3) Slide the runners rearwards and remove the two screws securing the front of the runners to the floor.

(4) Slide the runners forward and remove the two screws retaining the rear of the runners to the floor.

(5) Installation is the reversal of the removal procedure.

Location of the Screws for Adjustment of the Luggage Boot Lid Striker (Fixed Head Coupe).

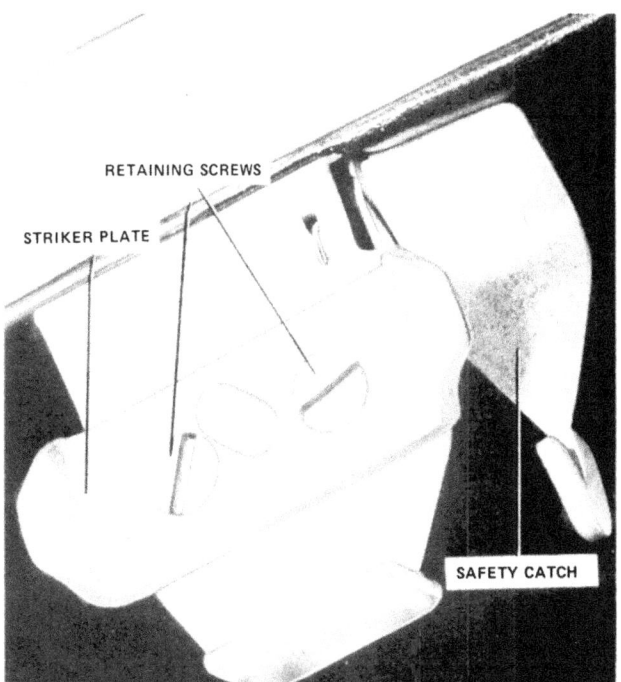

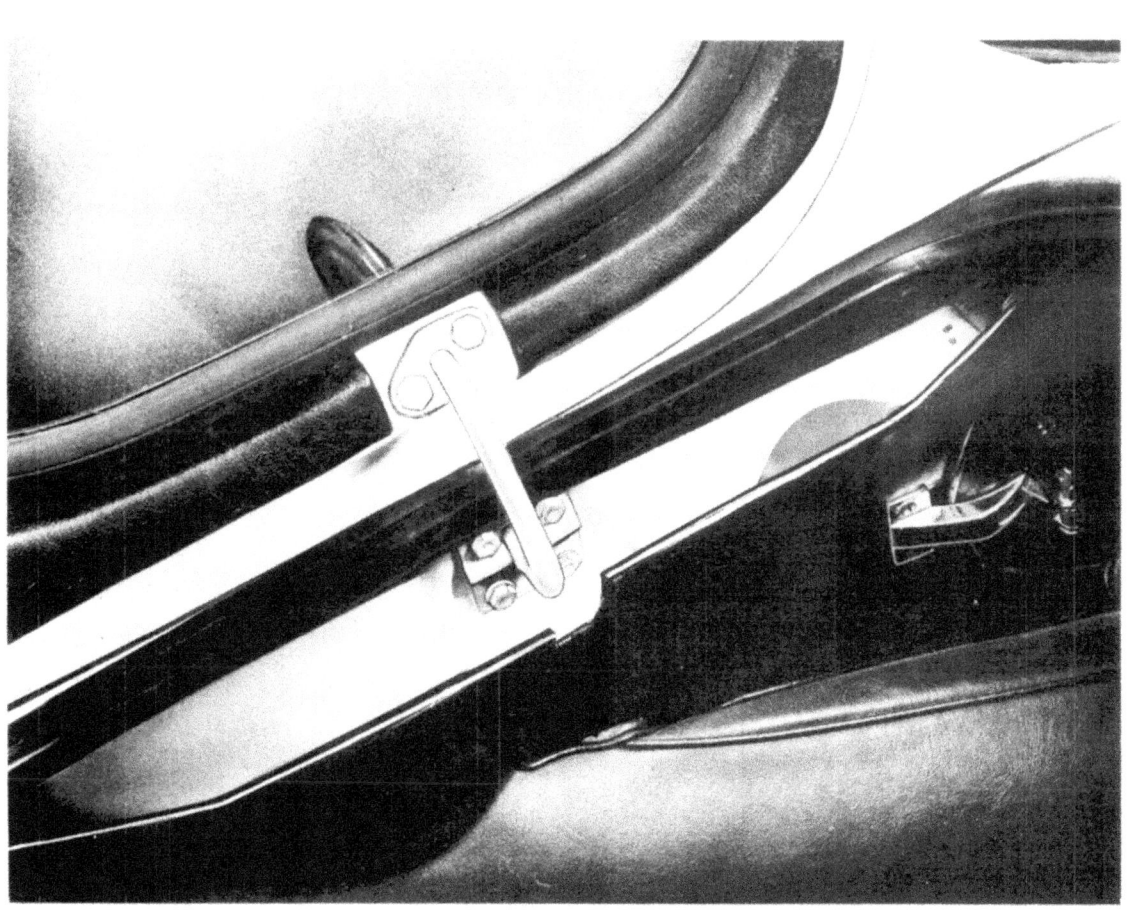

Luggage Boot Lid Hinge.

NOTES

WHEELS AND TYRES

SPECIFICATIONS

Road Wheels:
    Type .... Cross wire spoke with centre lock, knock-on hub cap.
    Number of spokes 72
    Rim diameter .... 15"
    Rim section 5K
Tyre type and size:
    Type .... Conventional tyre and tube. (RS.5)
    Size .... 6.40 x 15

Tyre pressures:
    Front – normal use up to 130 mph   23 psi.
    Rear – normal use up to 130 mph .   25 psi.
    Front – sustained high speeds ....   30 psi.
    Rear – sustained high speeds .....   35 psi.

Optional tyre type .... Dunlop SP41.HR
    Size .... 185 x 15
Tyre Pressures:
    Front and rear – up to 125 mph ..   32 psi.
    Front and rear – sustained 125 mph   40 psi.

1. DESCRIPTION

Conventional tyres and tubes are standard equipment fitted to wire spoke wheels on "E" type vehicles.

The wheels are attached to the hubs by a centre lock and knock-on hub cap.

Chrome-plated wheels are not fitted to cars used for racing.

For racing, a special tyre as well as a rim is serviced by the manufacturers for fitting on the rear but must not be used on the front.

2. WHEEL AND TYRE ASSEMBLY

TO REMOVE – WHEEL

(1) Apply the handbrake.
(2) Tap the threaded hub cap loose.
(3) Raise the vehicle on a jack.
(4) Unscrew the hub cap fully and withdraw the wheel. Installation is a reversal of the removal procedure.

TO MAINTAIN

Proper tyre and wheel maintenance is essential for economical and safe operation.
(1) Maintain correct tyre pressures.
(2) Properly tighten wheel hub cap
(3) Periodically inspect tyres for damage or abnormal wear.
(4) Periodically inspect rims for damage, especially to the flange and shoulders.
(5) Periodically rotate tyres (approximately every 3,000 miles).
(6) Maintain proper wheel balance.

NOTE: Tyre pressures should always be checked when tyres are cold, preferably after the car has been parked overnight.

Incorrect tyre pressures can adversely affect tyre wear and steering.

TO REMOVE – TYRE AND TUBE

(1) Remove the wheel from the vehicle as described under *TO REMOVE – WHEEL.*
(2) Remove the valve cap and valve core.
(3) Separate both the inside and outside beads from the wheel flanges so that both beads are in the base of the rim.
(4) Using tyre irons with rounded edges, lever the bead of the tyre over the wheel flange while keeping the tyre beads at the opposite end to the lever pushed into the rim base.

NOTE: Exercise care during operation (4) to ensure that the tyre irons do not damage the inner tube against the edge of the wheel flange.

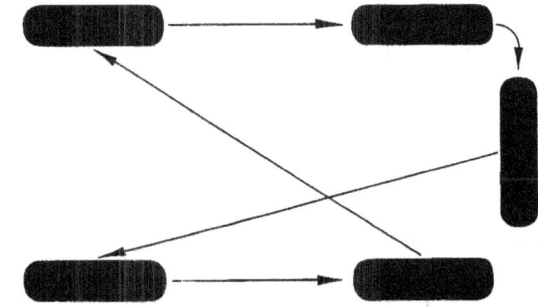

Diagram for Correct Wheel Rotation to Prolong Tyre Life and Minimise Wear.

(5) Push the valve of the inner tube into the interior of the tyre and withdraw the inner tube out between the bead of the tyre and the wheel flange.

(6) Using the tyre irons lever the remaining bead over the wheel flange while keeping the opposite end pressed into the rim base.

TO INSTALL

(1) Ensure that the inner faces of the wheel flanges are clean and smooth.

(2) Engage one bead of the tyre on the wheel flange and taking small bites, lever the remainder of the bead over the flange while keeping the opposite end pushed into the rim well base.

(3) Position the inner tube inside the tyre and insert the valve through the hole in the wheel, screw a valve core removing tool on the end of the valve to prevent the valve from slipping into the interior of the tyre when the other tyre bead is being positioned on the wheel.

(4) Fit the second bead of the tyre over the wheel inner flange, using the tyre irons or a rubber mallet, ensure that the tyre section nearest the tube valve goes over the wheel flange last.

NOTE: Position any dots on the side of the tyre adjacent to the tyre valve to maintain correct tyre balance.

(5) Stand the wheel and tyre upright, fit the valve core, and inflate the tube until the tyre beads just commence to position themselves on the wheel flanges.

(6) Bounce the tyre on the floor several times to position the tyre beads evenly on the wheel, then inflate the tyre and tube to the recommended pressure.

(7) Check the valve core for leakage and instal the valve cap.

(8) It may be necessary to have the static and dynamic balance adjusted which can only be effected by special balancing equipment.

Wear in Centre of Tread Due to Over Inflation.

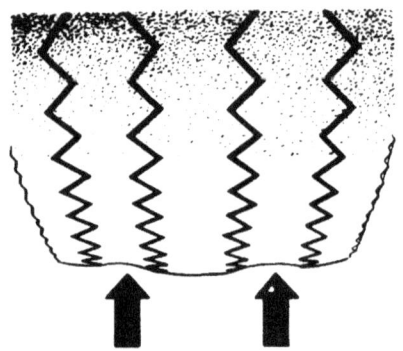

Wear Due to Under Inflation.

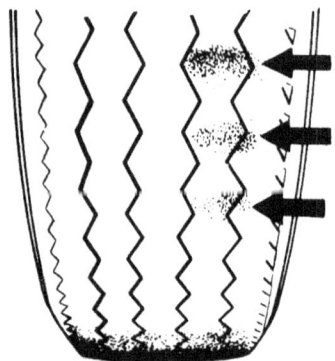

Spotty or Irregular Wear.

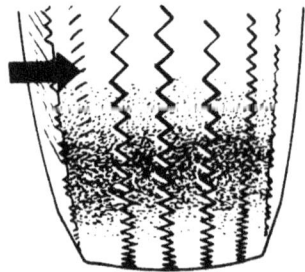

Wear Due to Incorrect Camber Angle.

3. TYRE WEAR DIAGNOSIS

1. **Abnormal wear on both sides of tread.**

    Possible cause
    - (a) Under inflated tyres.
    - (b) Overloading.

    Remedy
    - Inflate to recommended pressure.
    - Reduce maximum loading.

2. **Abnormal wear in centre of tread.**

    Possible cause
    - (a) Over-inflation of tyres.

    Remedy
    - Reduce to recommended pressure.

3. **Abnormal wear on inside of tread.**

    Possible cause
    - (a) Insufficient camber angle.
    - (b) Sagging front suspension.
    - (c) Loose or worn front hub bearings.
    - (d) Bent stub axle or carrier.
    - (e) Loose or worn suspension components.

    Remedy
    - Check front end alignment, and rectify.
    - Check and rectify.
    - Check and adjust or renew hub bearings.
    - Check and renew faulty components.
    - Check and renew faulty components. Align front end.

4. **Abnormal wear on outside of tread.**

    Possible cause
    - (a) Excessive camber angle.

    Remedy
    - Check front end alignment and adjust as necessary.

5. **Spotty or irregular wear**

    Possible cause
    - (a) Static or dynamic unbalance of wheel and tyre assembly.
    - (b) Lateral run-out of wheel.
    - (c) Excessive play in wheel hub.
    - (d) Excessive play in steering knuckle ball joints.

    Remedy
    - Check and balance wheel and tyre assembly.
    - Check and true-up wheel.
    - Check and adjust or renew hub bearing.
    - Check and renew ball joints.

6. **Lightly worn spots at centre of tread.**

    Possible cause
    - (a) Static unbalance of wheel and tyre assembly.

    Remedy
    - Check and balance wheel and tyre assembly.

7. **Flat spots at centre of tread.**

    Possible cause
    - (a) Repeated severe brake application.
    - (b) Lack of tyre rotation.

    Remedy
    - Revise driving habits.
    - Periodically change tyres by rotation of wheel and tyre assembly.

8. **Heel and toe wear (saw tooth effect).**

    Possible cause
    - (a) Over-loading.
    - (b) High speed driving.
    - (c) Excessive braking.

    Remedy
    - Revise maximum loading.
    - Avoid as far as possible.
    - Revise driving habits.

9. **Feathered edge on one side of tread pattern.**

   Possible cause
   (a) Sharp inside edge – excessive toe in.
   (b) Sharp outside edge – excessive toe out.
   (c) One tyre sharp inside edge, other tyre sharp outside edge.

   Remedy
   – Check and adjust wheel alignment.
   – Check and adjust wheel alignment.
   – Check for bent steering arm and renew.

LUBRICATION AND MAINTENANCE

ENGINE

(1) Check engine oil level daily and top up as necessary with engine oil as recommended.

(2) Drain and refill every 3,000 miles or even sooner if vehicle is operating under very dusty or extreme conditions.

(3) Replace oil filter and seal every 3,000 miles at the time of the engine oil change (Paper Element).

(4) Remove the sparking plugs, clean, adjust and test every 3,000 miles and renew every 12,000 miles.

(5) Check and adjust if necessary the upper timing chain at 6,000 miles.

COOLING SYSTEM

(1) Check the water level in the radiator header tank daily.

NOTE: If the vehicle is at normal operating temperature, use care when removing the radiator pressurised cap to avoid scalding.

(2) Drain, flush and refill the cooling system every 12,000 miles.

FUEL SYSTEM

(1) Top up carburettor hydraulic piston dampers every 3,000 miles.

(2) Check and adjust if necessary the carburettor slow running.

(3) Clean fuel line filter and tune carburettors every 6,000 miles.

(4) Renew air cleaner paper element every 12,000 miles.

(5) Remove and clean the fuel tank filter every 12,000 miles.

(6) Lubricate with engine oil all moving parts of throttle linkage.

GEARBOX

(1) Check oil level every 3,000 miles and top up as necessary with gearbox oil as recommended.

NOTE: On 2 + 2 cars with automatic transmission follow the procedure described under AUTOMATIC TRANSMISSION section.

(2) On manual transmissions drain and refill the gearbox every 12,000 miles.

REAR AXLE

(1) Check oil level every 3,000 miles and top up as necessary with rear axle oil as recommended.

(2) Drain and refill rear axle every 12,000 miles.

(3) On early models lubricate universal joints on rear half shafts every 3,000 miles with recommended grease.

PROPELLER SHAFT

On early models lubricate universal joints and sliding joint with recommended grease every 3,000 miles.

STEERING GEAR

(1) Lubricate the steering housing assembly, tie rod ends, upper and lower stub axle swivel joints with recommended grease every 3,000 miles.

(2) Check and adjust if necessary the front wheel alignment.

REAR SUSPENSION

(1) Lubricate the lower suspension arm inner and outer fulcrum bearings with recommended grease every 6,000 miles.

FRONT WHEEL BEARINGS

Check and adjust if necessary wheel bearing end float and lubricate with recommended grease every 12,000 miles.

REAR WHEEL BEARINGS

Lubricate hub bearings with recommended grease every 12,000 miles.

TYRES

Test when cold and inflate to specified pressure weekly.

BATTERY

Check and top up electrolyte with distilled water as required or at least monthly. Ensure that connections are clean.

BODY

(1) Check and lubricate the following components with a few drops of engine oil: Door hinges and locks, luggage compartment hinges and lock, bonnet hinges and catches, cover hinge on fuel filler, seat runners and adjusters, windscreen wiper arms.

(2) Check that the drain holes at the base of the doors are free of obstruction.

(3) Every 12,000 miles check and tighten if necessary all body and chassis securing nuts, bolts and screws.

BRAKE AND CLUTCH RESERVOIRS

(1) Check reservoirs and top up with recommended hydraulic fluid, if necessary, every 1,000 miles.

(2) Flush and refill system with new fluid every 12 months or at master cylinder overhaul.

CLUTCH

(1) Check clutch free travel at the slave cylinder and adjust if required.

(2) Apply a drop of oil to the slave cylinder push rod clevis pin.

BRAKES

(1) On early models check and adjust handbrake if required.

(2) Every 6,000 miles examine the brake friction pads for wear.

(3) Lubricate with a few drops of engine oil the brake pedal bearing and hand brake compensator linkage and clevis pins.

GENERATOR OR ALTERNATOR

(1) Check belt condition and tension every 6,000 miles and adjust if necessary.

(2) Every 6,000 miles insert a few drops of engine oil into the generator end bush.

STARTER MOTOR

Re-oil bushes with light engine oil at overhaul.

DISTRIBUTOR

(1) Every 3,000 miles check the condition and gap of the contact points. Clean and adjust, or replace, as necessary.

(2) Lubricate the cam bearing through the rotor arm spindle with a few drops of engine oil, and the centrifugal timing control through the base plate aperture.

(3) Lightly smear the faces of the cam with grease but avoid contaminating the contact points.

AUTOBOOKS WORKSHOP MANUALS

ALFA ROMEO GIULIA 1300, 1600, 1750, 2000 1962-1978 WSM
BMW 1600 1966-1973 WSM
BMW 2000 & 2002 1966-1976 WSM
BMW 2500, 2800, 3.0 & 3.3 1968-1977 WSM
BMW 316, 320, 320i 1975-1977 WSM
BMW 518, 520, 520i 1973-1981 WSM
FIAT 1100, 1100D, 1100R & 1200 1957-1969 WSM
FIAT 124 1966-1974 WSM
FIAT 124 SPORT 1966-1975 WSM
FIAT 125 & 125 SPECIAL 1967-1973 WSM
FIAT 126, 126L, 126 DV, 126/650 & 126/650 DV 1972-1982 WSM
FIAT 127 SALOON, SPECIAL & SPORT, 900, 1050 1971-1981 WSM
FIAT 128 1969-1982 WSM
FIAT 1300, 1500 1961-1967 WSM
FIAT 131 MIRAFIORI 1975-1982 WSM
FIAT 132 1972-1982 WSM
FIAT 500 1957-1973 WSM
FIAT 600, 600D & MULTIPLA 1955-1969 WSM
FIAT 850 1964-1972 WSM
JAGUAR MK 1, 2 1955-1969 WSM
JAGUAR S TYPE, 420 1963-1968 WSM
JAGUAR XK 120, 140, 150 MK 7, 8, 9 1948-1961 WSM
LAND ROVER 1, 2 1948-1961 WSM
MERCEDES-BENZ 190 1959-1968 WSM
MERCEDES-BENZ 220/8 1968-1972 WSM
MERCEDES-BENZ 220B 1959-1965 WSM
MERCEDES-BENZ 230 1963-1968 WSM
MERCEDES-BENZ 250 1968-1972 WSM
MERCEDES-BENZ 280 1968-1972 WSM
MINI 1959-1980 WSM
MORRIS MINOR 1952-1971 WSM
PEUGEOT 404 1960-1975 WSM
PORSCHE 911 1964-1973 WSM
PORSCHE 911 1970-1977 WSM
RENAULT 16 1965-1979 WSM
RENAULT 8, 10, 1100 1962-1971 WSM
ROVER 3500, 3500S 1968-1976 WSM
SUNBEAM RAPIER, ALPINE 1955-1965 WSM
TRIUMPH SPITFIRE, GT6, VITESSE 1962-1968 WSM
TRIUMPH TR4, TR4A 1961-1967 WSM
VOLKSWAGEN BEETLE 1968-1977 WSM

VELOCEPRESS AUTOMOBILE BOOKS & MANUALS

ABARTH BUYERS GUIDE
AUSTIN-HEALEY 6-CYLINDER WSM
AUSTIN-HEALEY SPRITE & MG MIDGET 1958-1971 WSM
BMW 600 LIMOUSINE FACTORY WSM
BMW 600 LIMOUSINE OWNERS HAND BOOK & SERVICE MANUAL
BMW ISETTA FACTORY WSM
BOOK OF THE CARRERA PANAMERICANA - MEXICAN ROAD RACE
COMPLETE CATALOG OF JAPANESE MOTOR VEHICLES
CORVAIR 1960-1969 OWNERS WORKSHOP MANUAL
CORVETTE V8 1955-1962 OWNERS WORKSHOP MANUAL
DIALED IN - THE JAN OPPERMAN STORY
FERRARI 250/GT SERVICE AND MAINTENANCE
FERRARI 308 SERIES BUYER'S AND OWNER'S GUIDE
FERRARI BERLINETTA LUSSO
FERRARI BROCHURES AND SALES LITERATURE 1946-1967
FERRARI BROCHURES AND SALES LITERATURE 1968-1989
FERRARI GUIDE TO PERFORMANCE
FERRARI OPP, MAINTENANCE & SERVICE H/BOOKS 1948-1963
FERRARI OWNER'S HANDBOOK
FERRARI SERIAL NUMBERS PART I - ODD NUMBERS TO 21399
FERRARI SERIAL NUMBERS PART II - EVEN NUMBERS TO 1050
FERRARI SPYDER CALIFORNIA
FERRARI TUNING TIPS & MAINTENANCE TECHNIQUES
HENRY'S FABULOUS MODEL "A" FORD
HOW TO BUILD A FIBERGLASS CAR
HOW TO BUILD A RACING CAR
HOW TO RESTORE THE MODEL 'A' FORD
IF HEMINGWAY HAD WRITTEN A RACING NOVEL
JAGUAR E-TYPE 3.8 & 4.2 WSM
LE MANS 24 (THE BOOK THAT THE FILM WAS BASED ON)
MASERATI BROCHURES AND SALES LITERATURE
MASERATI OWNER'S HANDBOOK
METROPOLITAN FACTORY WSM
MGA & MGB OWNERS HANDBOOK & WSM
MG MIDGET TC, TD, TF & TF1500 WORKSHOP MANUAL
OBERT'S FIAT GUIDE
PERFORMANCE TUNING THE SUNBEAM TIGER
PORSCHE 356 1948-1965 WSM
PORSCHE 912 WSM
SOUPING THE VOLKSWAGEN
SOLEX CARBURETORS (EMPHASIS ON UK & EU AUTOMOBILES)
SU CARBURETORS (EMPHASIS ON UK AUTOMOBILES)
TRIUMPH TR2, TR3, TR4 1953-1965 WSM
TUNING FOR SPEED (P.E. IRVING)
VEDA ORR'S NEW REVISED HOT ROD PICTORIAL
VOLKSWAGEN TRANSPORTER, TRUCKS, STATION WAGONS WSM
VOLVO 1944-1968 ALL MODELS WSM
WEBER CARBURETORS (EMPHASIS ON ALFA & FIAT)

BROOKLANDS BOOKS & ROAD TEST PORTFOLIOS (RTP)

AC CARS 1904-2009
ALFA ROMEO 1920-1933 ROAD TEST PORTFOLIO
ALFA ROMEO 1934-1940 ROAD TEST PORTFOLIO
BRABHAM RALT HONDA THE RON TAURANAC STORY
BUGATTI TYPE 10 TO TYPE 40 ROAD TEST PORTFOLIO
BUGATTI TYPE 10 TO TYPE 251 ROAD TEST PORTFOLIO
BUGATTI TYPE 41 TO TYPE 55 ROAD TEST PORTFOLIO
BUGATTI TYPE 57 TO TYPE 251 ROAD TEST PORTFOLIO
DELAHAYE ROAD TEST PORTFOLIO
FERRARI ROAD CARS 1946-1956 ROAD TEST PORTFOLIO
FIAT 500 1936-1972 ROAD TEST PORTFOLIO
FIAT DINO ROAD TEST PORTFOLIO
HISPANO SUIZA ROAD TEST PORTFOLIO
HONDA ST1100/ST1300 PAN EUROPEAN 1990-2002 RTP
JAGUAR MK1 & MK2 ROAD TEST PORTFOLIO
LOTUS CORTINA ROAD TEST PORTFOLIO
MV AGUSTA F4 750 & 1000 1997-2007 ROAD TEST PORTFOLIO
TATRA CARS ROAD TEST PORTFOLIO

VELOCEPRESS MOTORCYCLE BOOKS & MANUALS

AJS SINGLES & TWINS 250cc THRU 1000cc 1932-1948 (BOOK OF)
AJS SINGLES 1955-65 350cc & 500cc (BOOK OF)
AJS SINGLES 1945-60 350cc & 500cc MODELS 16 & 18 (BOOK OF)
ARIEL 1939-1960 4 STROKE SINGLES (BOOK OF)
ARIEL LEADER & ARROW 1958-1964 (BOOK OF)
ARIEL MOTORCYCLES 1933-1951 WSM
ARIEL PREWAR MODELS 1932-1939 (BOOK OF)
BMW M/CYCLES R26 R27 (1956-1967) FACTORY WSM
BMW M/CYCLES R50 R50S R60 R69S (1955-1969) FACTORY WSM
BSA BANTAM (BOOK OF)
BSA ALL FOUR-STROKE SINGLES & V-TWINS 1936-1952 (BOOK OF)
BSA OHV & SV SINGLES - 250cc 1954-1970 (BOOK OF)
BSA OHV & SV SINGLES 1945-54 250-600cc (BOOK OF)
BSA OHV SINGLES 350 & 500cc 1955-1967 (BOOK OF)
BSA PRE-WAR MODELS TO 1939 (BOOK OF)
BSA TWINS 1948-1962 (BOOK OF)
BSA TWINS 1962-1969 (SECOND BOOK OF)
CATALOG OF BRITISH MOTORCYCLES (1951 MODELS)
DOUGLAS PRE-WAR ALL MODELS 1929-1939 (BOOK OF)
DOUGLAS POST-WAR ALL MODELS 1948-1957 FACTORY WSM
DUCATI 160cc, 250cc & 350cc OHC MODELS FACTORY WSM
HONDA 50 ALL MODELS UP TO 1970 INC MONKEY & TRAIL (BOOK OF)
HONDA 90 ALL MODELS UP TO 1966 (BOOK OF)
HONDA MOTORCYCLES 125-150 TWINS C/CS/CB/CA WSM
HONDA MOTORCYCLES 250-305 TWINS C/CS/CB WSM
HONDA MOTORCYCLES C100 SUPER CUB WSM
HONDA MOTORCYCLES C110 SPORT CUB 1962-1969 WSM
HONDA TWINS & SINGLES 50cc THRU 305cc 1960-1966 (BOOK OF)
HONDA TWINS ALL MODELS 125cc THRU 450cc UP TO 1968 (BOOK OF)
INDIAN PONYBIKE, BOY RACER & PAPOOSE ILL PARTS LIST & SALES LIT
J.A.P. ENGINES 1927-1952 & MOTORCYCLES 1934-1952 (BOOK OF)
LAMBRETTA ALL 125 & 150cc MODELS 1947-1957 (BOOK OF)
LAMBRETTA LI & TV MODELS 1957-1970 (SECOND BOOK OF)
MATCHLESS 350 & 500cc SINGLES 1945-1956 (BOOK OF)
MATCHLESS 350 & 500cc SINGLES 1955-1966 (BOOK OF)
MOTORCYCLE ENGINEERING (P. E. Irving)
NORTON 1932-1947 (BOOK OF)
NORTON 1938-1956 (BOOK OF)
NORTON DOMINATOR TWINS 1955-1965 (BOOK OF)
NORTON MODELS 19, 50 & ES2 1955-1963 (BOOK OF)
NORTON MOTORCYCLES 1957-1970 FACTORY WSM
NORTON PREWAR MODELS 1932-1939 (BOOK OF)
NSU PRIMA ALL MODELS 1956-1964 (BOOK OF)
NSU QUICKLY ALL MODELS 1953-1963 (BOOK OF)
RALEIGH MOPEDS 1960-1969 (BOOK OF)
ROYAL ENFIELD SINGLES & V TWINS 1934-1946 (BOOK OF)
ROYAL ENFIELD SINGLES & V TWINS 1937-1953 (BOOK OF)
ROYAL ENFIELD SINGLES 1946-1962 (BOOK OF)
ROYAL ENFIELD 736cc INTERCEPTOR FACTORY WSM
ROYAL ENFIELD 250cc & 350cc SINGLES 1958-1966 (SECOND BOOK OF)
SPEED AND HOW TO OBTAIN IT
SUNBEAM MOTORCYCLES 1928-1939 (BOOK OF)
SUNBEAM S7 & S8 1946-1957 (BOOK OF)
SUZUKI 50cc & 80cc UP TO 1966 (BOOK OF)
SUZUKI T10 1963-1967 FACTORY WSM
SUZUKI T20 & T200 1965-1969 FACTORY WSM
TRIUMPH PRE-WAR MOTORCYCLE 1935-1939 (BOOK OF)
TRIUMPH MOTORCYCLES 1935-1949 (BOOK OF)
TRIUMPH MOTORCYCLES 1937-1951 WSM
TRIUMPH MOTORCYCLES 1945-1955 FACTORY WSM
TRIUMPH TWINS 1945-1958 (BOOK OF)
TRIUMPH TWINS 1956-1969 (BOOK OF)
VELOCETTE ALL SINGLES & TWINS 1925-1970 (BOOK OF)
VESPA 1951-1961 (BOOK OF)
VESPA 125 & 150cc & GS MODELS 1955-1963 (SECOND BOOK OF)
VESPA 90, 125 & 150cc 1963-1972 (THIRD BOOK OF)
VESPA GS & SS 1955-1968 (BOOK OF)
VILLIERS ENGINE (BOOK OF)
VINCENT MOTORCYCLES 1935-1955 WSM

PLEASE VISIT OUR WEBSITE
www.VelocePress.com
FOR A DETAILED DESCRIPTION
OF ANY OF THESE TITLES

Please check our website:

www.VelocePress.com

for a complete
up-to-date list of
available titles